Linguistic Fieldwork

This book is a collection of original essays on the practice of linguistic fieldwork and language documentation. Twelve of the leading field linguists in the world have written personal essays about the study of languages in a natural setting. Drawing on extensive research experience, they pass on the lessons they have learnt, review the techniques that worked best in practice, and discuss a variety of relevant topics, including the attitude of the linguist, the structure and content of the work session, the varied roles of native speakers, and the practical and personal challenges of doing research in an unfamiliar environment. Covering a wide range of field areas, and written in an accessible manner, the book will be indispensable to fieldworkers in linguistics, anthropology, folklore, and oral history.

PAUL NEWMAN is Professor in the Department of Linguistics and Director of the West African Languages Institute at Indiana University. His recent books include *Nominal and Verbal Plurality in Chadic* (1990) and *The Hausa Language: An Encyclopedic Reference Grammar* (2000).

MARTHA RATLIFF is Associate Professor of Linguistics in the Department of English at Wayne State University. Her book *Meaningful Tone* was published in 1992.

D1111751

Linguistic Fieldwork

edited by

Paul Newman
Indiana University

and

Martha Ratliff
Wayne State University

CAMBRIDGE
UNIVERSITY PRESS

PUBLISHED BY THE PRESS SYNDICATE OF THE UNIVERSITY OF CAMBRIDGE
The Pitt Building, Trumpington Street, Cambridge, United Kingdom

CAMBRIDGE UNIVERSITY PRESS
The Edinburgh Building, Cambridge CB2 2RU, UK
40 West 20th Street, New York, NY 10011–4211, USA
10 Stamford Road, Oakleigh, VIC 3166, Australia
Ruiz de Alarcón 13, 28014 Madrid, Spain
Dock House, The Waterfront, Cape Town 8001, South Africa

http://www.cambridge.org

First published 2001

Printed in the United Kingdom at the University Press, Cambridge

Typeface Times New Roman 10/12 pt   *System* QuarkXPress™ [SE]

A catalogue record for this book is available from the British Library

Library of Congress Cataloguing in Publication data

ISBN 0 521 66049 1 hardback
ISBN 0 521 66937 5 paperback

Contents

Figures

Tables

Notes on contributors

SHOBHANA L. CHELLIAH is Assistant Professor of Linguistics in the Department of English, University of North Texas. She has written on all aspects of Meithei, a Tibeto-Burman language of Northeast India, from phonetics to language ideology. A comprehensive treatment of this language is found in her book *A Grammar of Meithei*, Mouton, 1997. She is currently engaged in the textual analysis of pre-twentieth century Meithei narratives.

GERRIT J. DIMMENDAAL is currently Professor of African studies at the University of Cologne (Germany). He previously was in the Department of African Languages at the University of Leiden, where he served for a period as editor of the *Journal of African Languages and Linguistics*. His research has focused on the documentation of little-known and endangered Nilo-Saharan languages, with special attention to social setting and contact phenomena. His most important books include *The Turkana Language*, Foris, 1983, and *Surmic Languages and Cultures* (with Marco Last), Köppe, 1998.

NANCY C. DORIAN is Professor of Linguistics in the departments of German and Anthropology at Bryn Mawr College. She has conducted long-term fieldwork on Scottish Gaelic in former fishing villages in Scotland, with shorter fieldwork stints among other Gaelic speakers and among the secular (non-Anabaptist) Pennsylvania German speakers of Berks County, Pennsylvania. Her best-known books are *Language Death: The Life Cycle of a Scottish Gaelic Dialect*, University of Pennsylvania Press, 1981, and the edited volume *Investigating Obsolescence: Studies in Language Contraction and Death*, Cambridge University Press, 1989.

NICHOLAS EVANS is Reader in Linguistics at the University of Melbourne. He is the author of some fifty articles on Australian languages as well as a grammar and dictionary of Kayardild, Mouton de Gruyter, 1995, and a forthcoming grammar of Bininj Gun-wok. He is co-editor of

Archaeology and Linguistics: Aboriginal Australia in Global Perspective (with Patrick McConvell), Oxford University Press, Australia, 1997. Among his current research interests are the effects of culture on polysemy, intonation, and prosody in Australian languages, and the use of linguistic evidence in the process of getting legal recognition for Aboriginal land and sea tenure.

DANIEL L. EVERETT is Research Professor of Linguistics at the University of Manchester (England). He was Chair of the Department of Linguistics and Professor of Linguistics and Anthropology at the University of Pittsburgh from 1988–99. His most recent books are *Why There are no Clitics*, SIL, 1996, and *Wari': The Pacaas Novos Language of Western Brazil* (with Barbara Kern), Routledge, 1997. Currently he is working on grammars of Piraha and Banawa, Indian languages of the Amazon.

DAVID GIL is Scientific Researcher in the Department of Linguistics, Max Planck Institute for Evolutionary Anthropology, Leipzig, Germany, and Associate Professor, Department of Audiology and Speech Sciences, Universiti Kebangsaan Malaysia, Malaysia. He has conducted basic research on a large number of languages including Maricopa, Georgian, Turkish, Hebrew, Tagalog, and Japanese. In addition to his more than seventy-five articles, he is the author of the forthcoming book *Malay/Indonesian Linguistics*, Curzon Press.

KEN HALE is Professor in the Department of Linguistics and Philosophy at the Massachusetts Institute of Technology. His primary research has been on the syntax, morphology, and lexical structures of the Pama-Nyungan languages of Australia, the Uto-Aztecan and Athabaskan languages of the US Southwest, and the Misumalpan languages of Nicaragua and Honduras. He is a prolific author with over a hundred publications to his credit, including *An Elementary Warlpiri Dictionary*, IAD Press, 1995. He has long championed the view that the scientific study of less common/non-Western language will make the most strides when native speakers of these languages are drawn actively and seriously into the process. He is an elected member of the American Academy of Arts and Sciences and the National Academy of Sciences, and is a former President of the Linguistic Society of America.

LARRY M. HYMAN is Professor and Chair of the Department of Linguistics at the University of California, Berkeley. He has made several field trips to Nigeria and Cameroon with the goal of understanding languages on both sides of the Bantu/non-Bantu divide. His many publications include *Phonology: Theory and Analysis*, Holt, Rinehart and Winston, 1975, *A*

Theory of Phonological Weight, Foris, 1985, and two recently co-edited collections: *Theoretical Aspects of Bantu Tone* (with Charles W. Kisseberth), CSLI, 1998, and *Bantu Historical Linguistics: Theoretical and Empirical Perspectives* (with Jean-Marie Hombert), CSLI, 1999. He was one of the early editors of *Studies in African Linguistics*.

IAN MADDIESON is Research Professor in the Department of Linguistics at the University of California, Berkeley. He is a founding member of the Committee for the World Congresses of African Linguistics. For many years he held a position in linguistics at UCLA where, in conjunction with Peter Ladefoged, he carried out large-scale projects whose goal was documentation of the phonetics of endangered languages. His extensive fieldwork has taken him to Papua New Guinea, Micronesia, Melanesia, Australia, Taiwan, Dagestan, and a number of countries in east and west Africa. His best-known books are *Patterns of Sound*, Cambridge University Press, 1984, and *The Sounds of the World's Languages* (with Peter Ladefoged), Blackwell, 1996.

FIONA MC LAUGHLIN is Assistant Professor of Linguistics and African Studies at the University of Kansas. She has taught linguistics at the Université Abdoulaye Moumouni Dioffo in Niamey, Niger and the Université Gaston Berger in Saint-Louis, Senegal, and has served as Director of the West African Research Center in Dakar, Senegal. Her research has focused primarily on the morphology, phonology, and sociolinguistics of languages in the northern Atlantic group. Recent publications include "Noun classification in Wolof: When affixes are not renewed," *Studies in African Linguistics* (1997) and "Consonant mutation and variation in Seereer-Siin reduplication," *Phonology* (2000).

MARIANNE MITHUN is Professor of Linguistics at the University of California, Santa Barbara. She has done extensive fieldwork with speakers of Mohaw, Cayuga, Tuscarora, Central Pomo, and Central Alaskan Yup'ik, and has worked with a number of communities in their projects to document and revitalize their traditional languages. Her most recent book is the comprehensive and authoritative volume *The Languages of Native North America*, Cambridge University Press, 1999.

PAUL NEWMAN is Professor and former Chair of Linguistics at Indiana University, where he is also Adjunct Professor of Anthropology and Director of the West African Languages Institute. He was the founding editor of the *Journal of African Languages and Linguistics*. His research has consisted of both descriptive and historical/comparative work on Chadic languages of northern Nigeria. His most recent books are *Nominal and Verbal Plurality in Chadic*, Foris, 1990, *On Being Right:*

Greenberg's African Linguistic Classification and the Methodological Principles which Underlie It, African Studies Program and Institute for the Study of Nigerian Languages and Cultures, Indiana University, 1995, and *The Hausa Language: An Encyclopedic Reference Grammar*, Yale University Press, 2000.

MARTHA RATLIFF is Associate Professor and former Director of the Linguistics Program in the Department of English, Wayne State University. She is one of the founders of the Southeast Asian Linguistics Society, for which she has organized meetings and edited conference proceedings. She has also served as chair of the LSA Committee on Endangered Languages and their Preservation. Her primary research has been on Hmong and related languages, but she has also investigated general questions on the nature of tone from broader historical and typological perspectives. Her book *Meaningful Tone* was published by the Southeast Asian Studies Program, Northern Illinois University, 1992.

KEREN RICE is a Professor of Linguistics at the University of Toronto. She has conducted extensive fieldwork on Slave, an Athapaskan language of northern Canada. Her publications include *A Grammar of Slave*, Mouton de Gruyter, 1989, which was awarded the Leonard Bloomfield Book Prize by the Linguistic Society of America, and *Morpheme Order and Semantic Scope: Word Formation in the Athapaskan Verb*, Cambridge University Press, 2000.

THIERNO SEYDOU SALL received a traditional Koranic education in Senegal and taught Arabic in rural schools before winning a scholarship to study at the African Islamic Institute in Khartoum. Upon his return to Senegal, he began teaching Arabic in the public school system. After passing the baccalauréat as an independent candidate, he enrolled in Cheikh Anta Diop University, where he obtained the licence and maîtrise degrees. He is currently an Arabic teacher at Amadou Trawaré College in Dakar.

Introduction

Paul Newman and Martha Ratliff

After a long period of neglect, fieldwork in linguistics is beginning to attract real attention and interest again in the United States. This interest has been sparked by a concern in the discipline about endangered languages but now transcends that specific issue. The trend is evident in the involvement of national and international organizations in the effort to publicize the need for language documentation; the growing number of conferences and workshops on endangered languages, linguistic fieldwork, and the role of data in the formulation of linguistic theory; the growth in training programs in linguistic fieldwork; and the greater success fieldworkers have experienced in winning government as well as private grants to support language documentation projects. The Linguistic Society of America (LSA) has provided leadership with the first three of these efforts: its interest in endangered languages and fieldwork was made formal in 1992 when the Committee on Endangered Languages and their Preservation was established. In 1994, the LSA issued a policy statement on "The Need for the Documentation of Linguistic Diversity." Symposia on fieldwork are now a regular part of the program of the LSA annual meetings and courses on fieldwork practice have routinely been offered in recent years at the LSA summer linguistics institutes.

This book is intended to serve two main purposes: (a) to convey the intellectual excitement of linguistic fieldwork; and (b) to give a realistic picture of the complex and involved business of describing language as it is used by actual speakers in natural settings. While acknowledging the difficulties in collecting reliable and comprehensive basic field data, we want to stress the vital importance of doing so, not just as an end in itself, but for the advancement of the linguist's various goals, including the elucidation of Universal Grammar, the discovery of principled variation across different types of languages, and the reconstruction of earlier forms of languages. We hope the book will be of interest to all linguists, as well as to fieldworkers in allied disciplines such as anthropology, sociology, and folklore; but we especially want to inspire students and younger scholars to undertake this important primary work upon which the rest of the discipline depends.

1

To this end, we have invited twelve experienced fieldworkers, plus one fieldworker's teacher/assistant, to share their scientific and personal perspectives on the challenges of linguistic fieldwork. The authors were each given the freedom to choose specific issues or experiences that were important in their own development and practice as fieldworkers. The resulting chapters run the gamut in content from morphemes to money, and in tone from scholarly to confessional. The book does not pretend to be a manual on field methods *per se*, covering the essential elements of elicitation and analysis in a systematic, step-by-step way (see, for example, Nida 1947, Harris and Voegelin 1953, Lounsbury 1953, Longacre 1964, Samarin 1967, Labov 1972, Bouquiaux and Thomas 1976, Comrie and Smith 1977, Vaux and Cooper 1999). Nonetheless, we trust that the book will be useful – both to those teaching field methods courses and to those themselves preparing to go into the field – as a handbook encompassing methodologies and insights that have been particularly helpful to some of the best fieldworkers in our profession.

In the remarks that follow, we briefly take up certain basic "frame-setting" issues which come up repeatedly in the chapters to follow and which we therefore take as thematically important to any discussion of the human aspect of linguistic fieldwork. These issues, which relate to work styles and relationships, and to the rewards, difficulties, and responsibilities of fieldwork, are:
- the roles of native speakers in linguistic fieldwork (and the relation of these roles to the variety of terms used to refer to them),
- the advisability of learning to speak the language under study,
- the inherent tension between the need for a well-developed plan and the exigencies of the field situation which often make modification or abandonment of plans necessary,
- the balance between the real-life difficulties of living in the field and the intellectual and personal pleasures of fieldwork, and
- a consideration of the ethical responsibilities of linguistic fieldwork.

We will close with an enumeration of important topics that are not addressed in this book but which we hope will be taken up in subsequent works by us or by others.

"Informants"

It is immediately obvious upon reading introductions to grammars and descriptions of fieldwork practice that different linguists use different terms to refer to the native speakers with whom they work. In this book alone, we have "consultant" (Chelliah, Everett, Hale, Rice), "speaker" (Evans,

Mithun, and others), "teacher" (Evans, Mc Laughlin and Sall), "interlocutor" (Gil), "source" (Dorian), "subject" (Maddieson), "assistant" (Mc Laughlin and Sall), and "informant" (Dimmendaal, Hyman) – this latter term being the traditional designation of long-standing in linguistics as well as in anthropology. The lack of unanimity in the terms used reflects different types of native speaker involvement in linguistic research; differences in customary usage by linguists who work in different parts of the world; and modern-day sensibilities as to the rights of speakers, especially in disadvantaged communities, and a desire to choose terminology that conveys what is felt to be the proper respect, often as an antidote to perceptions and, unfortunately, realities of insensitivity in the past. Of these three reasons for the use of different terms, it is most instructive to dwell for a moment on the first: the fact that native speakers may play quite different roles in the conduct of linguistic research (see, for example, Bouquiaux and Thomas 1976, esp. pp. 62–75; Cameron *et al.* 1992; Hale 1964/65, 1972; Meeussen 1962). For brief, focused, and technical studies such as the laboratory-in-the-field work described by Maddieson, the term "subject" appropriately captures the nature of the relationship between linguist and native speaker. (It is when the native speakers are really "subjects" that the complex issue of human subjects review comes most clearly into play. See the LSA statement on the Web at http://www.lsadc.org/humsubjs.html, and King, Henderson, and Stein 1999.) At the opposite end of the scale, some speakers are employed as language teachers while others, who have had prior training in linguistics themselves or who have managed to learn a good deal about linguistics by working with the field linguist, are employed as research assistants or even as true consultants in the normal, non-technical use of the term. As a number of the authors have noted (Dimmendaal, Evans, Mithun, Rice), some speakers have special talents which the alert fieldworker will recognize and utilize – for example, one may tell wonderful stories, another may do transcription well, some may be remarkable wordsmiths, others may be adept at transforming simple sentences into corresponding negatives or passives or topicalizations, and others may have the patience of Job when it comes to providing one full paradigm after another. I (Ratliff) worked initially with three speakers of Hmong in my fieldwork. One had perfectly clear articulation, and was an ideal model for the impressively complex sound system of the language, although he appeared to have no interest in his own language or in the research itself. Another was no more a native linguist than the first (and he had a lisp), but was a fine native anthropologist, and could hold forth at length about cultural components of the language. The third was a natural linguist: he could understand the purpose of the research and produce exactly what I requested and, moreover, he could find patterns in the data independently. The three people could have been called "vocal coach," "cultural advisor," and "assistant" (or "co-investigator"), respectively.

Whether the linguist does or does not choose to refer to native speakers with distinct terms that reflect the type of contribution made is probably not of essential importance, nor is the choice of the default term, except as it relates to the sociology and ethos of our profession and the wishes of the native speakers themselves. Although some scholars consider "informant" to be a pejorative term, thought to denigrate the contribution of the native speaker, not to mention being unhappily evocative of "informer," in Africanist circles this association is not necessarily made, as can be seen from the following passage from Dimmendaal's chapter, which reveals that, for this author, "informant" is the neutral term, to be interpreted differently (and in this passage, quite positively) in light of each individual's contribution:

> What makes a good informant, and how do we select the person? The role I advocate is that of a co-investigator or colleague with intellectual curiosity, who not only speaks the language one intends to investigate, but also has intuitions about its structure and enjoys talking about it. (Dimmendal, chapter 3, this volume, p. 61)

Yet many linguists trained in the United States over the past twenty years have tended to avoid this term and replace it by "consultant" (Aissen 1992: 10), regardless of his or her geographical area of specialization. What remains important to all our authors, and to all good fieldworkers, we contend, is that the relationship between fieldworker and the speakers of the language under study be an open and respectful one, and that the talents of the speakers be developed and put to use in a productive and creative way. The positive effects of that basic stance far outweigh the facile issue of terminology.

In the past, almost all discussions of "informants" (for example, Nida 1947, Healey 1964, Hale 1972) have been from the perspective of the field linguist. A refreshing and enlightening view from the other side is provided by Sall's contribution in the Mc Laughlin and Sall chapter.

Learning to speak the language

The matter of whether or not it is worthwhile to learn to speak the language under study is raised by six authors, and is the primary subject of Everett's chapter on the monolingual method. It is perhaps not surprising to note that all six (Dimmendaal, Dorian, Evans, Everett, Gil, and Mc Laughlin) report that speaking ability contributed greatly to their fieldwork success (and that lack of speaking ability hindered their progress). It no doubt would seem odd to an anthropologist that this is even worth mentioning, since the anthropological tradition – or at least ideal (Burling 1984) – holds that fieldwork should be carried out in the native language (but see the classic exchange between Mead 1939 and Lowie 1940). That this is not so in our field, where our subject is language, is worth a moment's reflection. Unlike anthropologists, we do not regard language as a key that allows us to unlock the secrets of culture as the object of study; for us language *is* the object and therefore, perhaps, something to hold at arm's length for the sake of scientific objectivity. (This certainly was the view of positivist neo-Bloomfieldian linguists.) Another problem is that field methods courses, where students get their first idea of how basic field research is to be conducted, typically focus on structured elicitation techniques, using a speaker of a language unknown to the students as the bearer of the object of study, but seldom requiring or even suggesting that the students actually aim for conversational fluency or try to interact with the speaker – who invariably has full command of English – in his or her own language. This is undoubtedly because useful information can in fact be obtained without proficiency in speaking or understanding much of the language, and because in some types of fieldwork, such as the phonetic work described by Maddieson, or other short-term projects or survey work, language proficiency does not seem necessary nor is it feasible.

A common obstacle to learning the language under study is that the linguist may already be struggling with the acquisition of a field language/lingua franca that is essential for practical and administrative purposes. This could be Russian for someone planning on doing research on a minority language in the former Soviet Union, Arabic for research on Berber languages in Morocco, Tagalog for research in the Philippines, or Swahili in Tanzania. The dissertation research that I (Newman) did on Tera, a Chadic language spoken in northern Nigeria, was carried out through the medium of Hausa, the large language that serves as the lingua franca throughout the area. This was the language that I also needed for the daily requirements of food and lodging and for administrative interactions with local officials. Since my initial level of competence in Hausa was rudimentary, a major objective during the first three months was improving my fluency in Hausa, although elicitation work on Tera was simultaneously being carried out. Trying to learn to speak Tera at the same time would have been an insurmountable challenge, or so it seemed back then. The reality is that it never occurred to me that I *ought* to learn to speak Tera, although I gradually acquired a passive knowledge of the language. With hindsight, it seems obvious that I naturally would have picked up fluency in Hausa along the way, and that the linguistic research *per se* would have been much more effective and insightful if I had put serious effort into learning Tera from the very beginning.

When linguists work with some language for a year, more or less, the benefits of being able to interact directly in the language of study rapidly become clear. Proceeding as though one's primary aim were to learn to speak a language, even if it is not so, is an effective strategy if one's real goal is to document the language (Hale). If the linguist knows the language, he or she can learn a tremendous amount by merely listening (Dimmendaal, Dorian, Mc Laughlin and Sall). Social integration and acceptance of the linguist by the community – which in turn leads to a more successful working and living situation – is often dependent on how well linguists learn to speak (Everett). Linguists who speak the languages they study develop instincts for structure that can lead to deeper inquiries (Gil). And if the linguist can converse, speakers of moribund languages may be stimulated into regaining memories of a language long unused (Evans). Although there may be occasions when it is socially inappropriate to try to speak the language of study (see Mufwene 1993 for a special case involving the creole Gullah), we nonetheless endorse the views expressed throughout this book on the importance of gaining language proficiency as a necessary part of most linguistic fieldwork, and we encourage students and scholars contemplating fieldwork to take on the extra demands of this task with good grace.

Flexibility and open-mindedness in fieldwork

Another theme that is evident throughout these chapters is the importance of flexibility and openness in fieldwork. This can be manifested by the willingness to abandon one's original plan and do what makes most sense in the field, given on-site discovery of what is possible and what is most compelling (Hyman). Flexibility may take the form of giving up on a specific day's work when one finds that the speaker with whom one is working is uninterested or unable to give information on that day's topic (Rice). It often underlies the decision to balance linguist-controlled elicitation techniques with the collection and analysis of texts (Chelliah, Mithun). More generally, it involves a particular stance with regard to the speaker: if one regards the speaker as a collaborator rather than a passive and unreflecting source of answers to preset questions, one is likely to spot new features and patterns in supposedly familiar systems of the language and even discover entirely new systems or principles of linguistic organization (Chelliah, Gil, Mithun). But the creative overthrow of one's plans is dependent on having clear plans to begin with. This may seem an obvious point; however, since in field methods courses students are expected to work on a language *ex nihilo*, the unspoken message may be that knowing something about the language under study ahead of time is a kind of "cheating." As a number of authors have advised (Chelliah, Dimmendaal, Everett, Gil, Hale, Mithun, Rice), prior study of everything conceivable that may be relevant to the study of the language at hand – earlier descriptions of the language as well as linguistic theories of every stripe – is important; it is never better to approach a language in ignorance. Fieldwork is part of a bigger enterprise: questions of interest to the linguistic community and concerns about the final product cannot help but guide and frame the work we do. Thus, each work session needs to be carefully planned with explicit or implicit goals in mind. As Hale puts it:

> Whether or not one has access to earlier scholarship on the language one studies, I consider it absolutely essential to have a "script" (or "protocol") when one goes to a working session with a speaker of the language. It is not always necessary to follow the script, but it is a necessary item, if only to fall back on when, as often happens, one's head simply ceases to work, particularly in the investigation of difficult syntactic problems . . . (Hale, chapter 4, this volume, p. 84)

Yet the most rewarding fieldwork experiences may come from discovering either the presence of new linguistic structures – or the absence of expected ones – that one's "script" would never have predicted. This is the main thrust of Gil's chapter. It is the creative tension between these two equally important imperatives – training, preparation, and planning on the one hand, and flexibility to improvise and intellectual openness and venturesomeness to see things with "new eyes" on the other – which defines the fieldwork experience.

Personal/psychological aspects of fieldwork

Two seemingly contradictory themes permeate the chapters in this book: (a) fieldwork is personally and intellectually challenging and exciting (Gil, Hyman); and (b) fieldwork is difficult and/or stressful (Dorian, Mc Laughlin). The answer is that both are correct; how much one or the other dominates depends on the accident of circumstances and the personality and disposition of the investigator. That is, if they were honest, most linguists would admit that they have a love/hate relationship with fieldwork. Whereas there are a few fieldworkers for whom being in the field is next to Nirvana, and a few who claim that they can't stand it – although it doesn't always prevent them from going back time and again – most fieldworkers enjoy what they do, while at the same time tempering their enthusiasm with realistic caveats about the difficulties of carrying out research in the field. They like fieldwork – they even love fieldwork – but they acknowledge that it has its tough moments and its unpleasant aspects. "In the final analysis, fieldwork is yet another addition to our repertoire of ways to make ourselves uncomfortable" (Kleinman and Copp 1993: viii). The contributors to this book, like the editors, all hold very positive attitudes about fieldwork – that, of course, is why they agreed to contribute to this volume – but even the most upbeat, Hyman, for example, describe frustrations along the way.

The attractions of fieldwork, discussed either explicitly or implicitly by the authors in this book, are probably too obvious to warrant discussion. There is the joy of discovery – one can become a world's authority on a language in twenty minutes – and the excitement of overcoming intellectual obstacles. There is the enriching experience of getting to know and learning to live in a culture and society different from one's own. There is the sense of satisfaction when some person in the community you don't even know comes up to you and says, "It makes us proud to have you learn to speak our language and show the world that it is valuable enough to be studied and written down." And there is the professional pride in knowing that you have provided basic documentation on a language (perhaps endangered, perhaps not) that future scholars, whether theoreticians or typologists or historical linguists, will continue to draw on for years to come.

The negatives tend to be somewhat less well known since most brief introductions to descriptive grammars or passing acknowledgments in articles generally ignore them. But they are equally real (see Newman 1992). Negatives may relate to (a) inadequacy in linguistic preparation and/or language-learning talents; (b) equipment breakdowns (Hale); (c) disease, accidents, and other health risks (see Howell 1990; Lee 1995); (d) food and housing problems; (e) money issues – a seldom discussed but common source of frustration, conflict, and uncertainty (Mc Laughlin, also see Newman 1992; Ottenberg 1990: 144); (f) "bad" (whether incompetent or dishonest) informants; (g) personal discomfort or incompatibility with local culture, practices, values, and world view (see Kleinman and Copp 1993: 10–13; Malinowski 1967); (h) practical and emotional problems in working on endangered languages with aging last speakers (Evans, also see Craig 1997); (i) strained relations with government officials or with resident missionaries (Dimmendaal); (j) worries about loved ones back home; (k) worries about children (whether babies or teenagers) *not* back home, i.e., there in the field (see Cassell 1987); (l) boredom and loneliness; and the list goes on. (We have purposely not included *bad luck* since what is often described as bad luck usually relates to a person's inability to respond imaginatively and appropriately to misfortunes and difficulties rather than to external events totally outside the individual's control. See Hale's discussion of the positive aspects of his failure to return to Karawala as planned.)

It is a testimony to the resourcefulness and dedication of scholars such as the authors in this book and to the seductive appeal of fieldwork that individuals choose to do linguistic fieldwork and, having done so, look forward to the opportunity to do it again and again.

Ethical concerns

Linguistics is a discipline whose leading practitioner, Noam Chomsky, has written and spoken extensively on the political and ethical responsibilities of intellectuals (e.g., Chomsky 1969, 1992). It is thus ironic that, as compared with such sister disciplines as anthropology and sociology (Cassell 1980, Ellen 1984, Fluehr-Lobban 1991, Geertz 1968, Koepping 1994, Mitchell 1993, Rynkiewich and Spradley 1976), linguistics has paid so little attention to ethical concerns. (Interestingly, the LSA is not among the more than thirty professional societies and organizations that contribute to the *Professional Ethics Report,* a publication of the Committee on Scientific Freedom and Responsibility, Professional Society Ethics Group, of the American Association for the Advancement of Science.) The panel held at the 1998 annual meeting of the LSA on "Practical Fieldwork: Conflicting Constraints on the Ethical Researcher," organized by Colleen Cotter and Sara Trechter, was marked both by the size and liveliness of its audience – and by its rarity.

Concerns about ethically appropriate behavior in the field are implicit in all the contributions to this volume, but on the whole receive only passing mention (Mc Laughlin and Sall being an exception). And to the extent that professional ethics is touched on, the focus is almost exclusively on responsibilities and obligations towards one's informant(s) and sometimes the related question of covert tape recording. There are, however, a myriad of other tough issues and questions that cannot be explored here but which we would like to raise for consideration by fieldworkers in the future. How forthright should fieldworkers be in explaining their scholarly objectives to officials approving research permits or to members of the language group to be studied, people who very often understand little if anything about linguistics? Is secrecy in and of itself necessarily inappropriate (see Mitchell 1993)? What responsibilities does one have to adhere in a meaningful way to university regulations regarding human subjects research (see King, Henderson, and Stein 1999, Penslar 1995)? What should one do to protect the anonymity of one's sources? Conversely, what constitutes proper acknowledgment of the contribution of the people who provided data or assisted in other ways? With regard to texts, stories, and songs, what are the intellectual property rights of their creators and/or narrators (see Greaves 1994)? What recompense if any does a fieldworker owe the community as a whole for allowing him or her to be an uninvited guest? That is, apart from avoiding bad behavior, does the fieldworker have a positive duty to devote time and energy to community projects, and if so how much (see Newman 1999)? Conversely, if a linguist has been contracted to do practical work in the field – for example, prepare literacy materials (perhaps in a majority language for use by minority-language speakers), is it ethical for the linguist to steal time away to do pure research that he or she feels is of critical importance, such as documenting an endangered language? As residents, albeit temporary, in a community, should fieldworkers remain silent and uninvolved if they happen to be witnesses to extortion, violence, robbery, or sexual exploitation? Should fieldworkers take the side of the minority communities whose languages they are studying in conflicts with (repressive) central governments? In considering the two previous questions, to what extent should fieldworkers be guided by their own ethical/political principles, and to what extent should they keep in mind the impact of their political activism on other fieldworkers, present or future, who have research interests in the country or region? What are the ethics of using grant monies for tangential scientific projects or for well-meaning community activities not specified in the original proposal? What obligations does the fieldworker have to include host country scholars or advanced students in research projects? And when one gets back from the field, how long may one monopolize one's field materials before making them freely available to others?

In general, the ethical issues facing field linguists are not very different from those that anthropologists have long dealt with. It is thus important that linguists planning fieldwork should familiarize themselves with the relevant anthropological literature. It is also essential, however, that field linguists carefully review their field experiences in order to identify those ethical problems that are unique to our discipline.

Questions and challenges for the future

In closing, we need to mention a few topics, in addition to professional ethics, which have not received detailed coverage in this book, but which are important to a complete account of fieldwork practices today.

First, most of the fieldwork described in this book is of intermediate to fairly long, but limited, duration: work done originally over a period of some months to perhaps a year and a half, usually conducted in the first instance with the focused goal of a dissertation in mind. This can be a one-time experience, after which the linguist turns to other concerns. Alternatively, it can represent the start of a lifetime dedication to fieldwork as one's primary research activity, as exemplified by Evans' and Mithun's chapters, and by the practice of some European field linguists who have appointments in research institutes rather than in universities. A different model, implicit in the methodological approach advocated in Everett's chapter, is that of North American or European scholars who have chosen to settle permanently in Africa or South America or Southeast Asia, where they are in a sense always in or close to the field. The aim here is to study all aspects of the local language, often with the goal of producing practical literacy or other materials. Another model, illustrated in Hale's chapter, is the short-term engagement of the linguist to serve a community in a professional capacity. Finally, an important model, not represented in this volume, is survey fieldwork: the rapid collection of word lists, sample phrases and sentences, texts, and other materials from a number of languages and dialects in a particular area. The goal of this type of fieldwork is to identify what is spoken where, and by whom, in a poorly-researched area, and to collect short wordlists and other data of limited scope for purposes such as genetic classification, historical reconstruction, language contact study, or language/dialect geography. Survey work requires different kinds of skills from in-depth long-term linguistic research: one has to have a good ear and be able to work fast, switch gears quickly, and adjust to different people. One is also presented with different challenges, both physical and intellectual, and different rewards. Not all linguists, even highly experienced field linguists, are cut out for this kind of work, but when done well (and sometimes even when not done well!) survey work can make an invaluable contribution to our knowledge base.

A second area that we have not addressed is the increasing importance of computers for information storage and analysis in fieldwork. The necessity of computers in fieldwork, where the object of study is language in all its tiny particulars and myriad forms, is now unquestioned – but since it is a body of knowledge that is rapidly expanding, we felt that any chapter devoted to this issue would become hopelessly dated after only a few years. We refer the reader to Maddieson's chapter on the use of technology in phonetic fieldwork, and to the articles by Johnston (1995) and Antworth and Valentine (1998), which describe computer software for the field. Because of the ever-changing nature of computerization, one can expect that articles on this subject in the future will more appropriately be published in electronic form rather than on paper.

Finally, we are well aware that fieldwork is being conducted by linguists in other countries and that this book reflects methodology as developed and practiced primarily by North American, Australian, and Western European linguists. This restriction is due not only to limits on the size of the book at hand but also to a decision to adhere to a coherent, if consequently constrained, focus. We acknowledge that important linguistic fieldwork traditions exist in, for example, India, Russia, and China: a welcome contribution to this discussion would involve learning what our counterparts in other parts of the world are doing, and what aspects of their methods and training programs have met with greatest success.

Conclusion

Field linguists typically conduct research in isolation from one another, often for long periods of time. Several of our authors describe how they had to figure things out on their own, and managed, with difficulty and triumph, to do so – usually by trial and error. Yet it is interesting to see how a "virtual community" emerges from the experiences of the isolated individuals in these pages as certain themes are repeated: the importance of adequate preparation, of studying language in context, of paying attention to speaker's cues and concerns, of remaining flexible and open, and, if possible, of becoming a speaker. The heartening message seems to be that the more fieldworkers talk and write about their experiences, the more they *can* learn from one another, and thus they need not go into the field totally unprepared. We offer this book as a contribution to the ongoing conversation.

REFERENCES

Aissen, Judith L. 1992. Fieldwork and linguistic theory. In *International Encyclopedia of Linguistics*, vol. 2, ed. William Bright, pp. 9–10. New York: Oxford University Press.

Antworth, Evan L., and J. Randolph Valentine. 1998. Software for doing field linguistics. In *Using Computers in Linguistics: A Practical Guide*, ed. John Lawler and Helen Aristar Dry, pp. 170–96. London: Routledge.

Bouquiaux, Luc, and Jacqueline M. C. Thomas. 1976. *Enquête et description des langues à tradition orale*. 3 vols., 2nd edn. Paris: SELAF. (Translated by James Roberts as *Studying and Describing Unwritten Languages,* Dallas: SIL (1992).)

Burling, Robbins. 1984. *Learning a Field Language*. Ann Arbor: University of Michigan Press.

Cameron, Deborah, *et al.* 1992. *Researching Language: Issues of Power and Method*. London: Routledge.

Cassell, Joan. 1980. Ethical principles for conducting fieldwork. *American Anthropologist* 82:28–41.

Cassell, Joan (ed.). 1987. *Children in the Field: Anthropological Experiences*. Philadelphia: Temple University Press.

Chomsky, Noam. 1969. *American Power and the New Mandarins*. New York: Pantheon Books.

  1992. *Chronicles of Dissent: Interviews with David Barsamian*. Monroe, Maine: Common Courage Press.

Comrie, Bernard, and Norval Smith. 1977. Lingua descriptive studies. *Lingua* 42:1–72.

Craig, Colette. 1997. Language contact and language degeneration. In *Handbook of Sociolinguistics*, ed. Forian Coulmas, pp. 257–70. Oxford: Blackwell.

Ellen, R. F. (ed.). 1984. *Ethnographic Research. A Guide to General Conduct*. (ASA Research Methods in Social Anthropology) New York: Academic Press.

Fluehr-Lobban, Carolyn (ed.). 1991. *Ethics and the Profession of Anthropology*. Philadelphia: University of Pennsylvania Press.

Geertz, Clifford. 1968. Thinking as a moral act: ethical dimensions of anthropological fieldwork in new states. *Antioch Review* 28:139–58.

Greaves, Tom (ed.). 1994. *Intellectual Property Rights for Indigenous Peoples: A Sourcebook*. Oklahoma City: Society for Applied Anthropology.

Hale, Kenneth. 1964/65. On the use of informants in field-work. *Canadian Journal of Linguistics* 10:108–19.

 1972. Some questions about anthropological linguistics: the role of native knowledge. In *Reinventing Anthropology*, ed. Dell Hymes, pp. 382–97. New York: Vantage Books.

Harris, Z. S., and C. F. Voegelin. 1953. Eliciting in linguistics. *Southwestern Journal of Anthropology* 9:59–75.

Healey, Alan. 1964. *Handling Unsophisticated Linguistic Informants*. Canberra: Linguistic Circle of Canberra Publications (Series A – Occasional Papers, 2).

Howell, Nancy. 1990. *Surviving Fieldwork: A Report of the Advisory Panel on Health and Safety in Fieldwork, American Anthropological Association*. (Special publication of the American Anthropological Association, 26) Washington, DC: American Anthropological Association.

Johnston, E. Clay. 1995. Computer software to assist linguistic field work. *Cahiers de Sciences Humaines* 31(1):103–29.

King, Nancy M. P., Gail E. Henderson, and Jane Stein (eds.). 1999. *Beyond Regulations: Ethics in Human Subjects Research*. Chapel Hill: University of North Carolina Press.

Kleinman, Sherryl, and Martha A. Copp. 1993. *Emotions and Fieldwork*. (Qualitative Research Methods, 28) Newbury Park, CA: Sage.

Koepping, Klaus-Peter (ed.). 1994. *Anthropology and Ethics*. Fribourg: Séminaire d'Ethnologie.

Labov, William. 1972. Some principles of linguistic methodology. *Language in Society* 1:97–120.

Lee, Raymond M. 1995. *Dangerous Fieldwork*. (Qualitative Research Methods, 34) Newbury Park, CA: Sage.

Longacre, Robert. 1964. *Grammar Discovery Procedures: A Field Manual*. The Hague: Mouton.

Lounsbury, Floyd. 1953. Field methods and techniques in linguistics. In *Anthropology Today*, ed. A. L. Kroeber *et al.*, pp. 401–16. Chicago: University of Chicago Press.

Lowie, Robert H. 1940. Native languages as ethnographic tools. *American Anthropologist* 42:81–9.

Malinowski, Bronislaw. 1967. *A Diary in the Strict Sense of the Term*. New York: Harcourt, Brace and World.

Mead, Margaret. 1939. Native languages as field work tools. *American Anthropologist* 41:189–206.

Meeussen, A. E. 1962. L'informateur en linguistique africaine. *Aequatoria* 25(3):92–94.

Mitchell, Richard G., Jr. 1993. *Secrecy and Fieldwork*. (Qualitative Research Methods, 29) Newberry Park, CA: Sage.

Mufwene, Salikoko. 1993. Investigating Gullah: difficulties in ensuring "authenticity." In *Language Variation in North American English: Research and Teaching*, ed. A. Wayne Glowka and Donald M. Lance, pp. 178–90. New York: Modern Language Association.

Newman, Paul. 1992. Fieldwork and field methods in linguistics. *California Linguistic Notes* 23(2):2–8.

      1999. "We has seen the enemy and it is us": the endangered languages issue as a hopeless cause. *Studies in the Linguistic Sciences* 28(2):11–20.

Nida, Eugene. 1947. Field techniques in descriptive linguistics. *International Journal of American Linguistics* 13:138–46.

Ottenberg, Simon. 1990. Thirty years of fieldnotes: changing relationships to the text. In *Fieldnotes: The Makings of Anthropology*, ed. Roger Sanjek, pp. 139–60. Ithaca: Cornell University Press.

Penslar, Robin Levin (ed.). 1995. *Research Ethics: Cases and Materials*. Bloomington: Indiana University Press.

Rynkiewich, Michael A., and James P. Spradley (eds.). 1976. *Ethics and Anthropology: Dilemmas in Fieldwork*. New York: John Wiley.

Samarin, William J. 1967. *Field Linguistics: A Guide to Linguistic Field Work*. New York: Holt, Rinehart, and Winston.

Vaux, Bert and Justin Cooper. 1999. *Introduction to Linguistic Field Methods*. Munich: Lincom Europa.

1   Fieldwork as a state of mind

Larry M. Hyman

Fieldwork has been so much a part of linguistic research – a linguistic given, so to speak – that we have rarely bothered to define it. The most immediate image is that of a linguist packing up materials, equipment, and non-linguistic paraphernalia to embark on a journey to a remote field site where the planned linguistic investigation will be executed. In the ideal case, the researcher develops a relationship with the language, culture, and people that cannot be duplicated in any other setting. The experience often includes acquiring some proficiency in the language, or at least knowledge of how it is used in actual practice. One will attempt to assemble a lexicon, establish the phonetic and phonological properties, and analyze the grammar and discourse functions by means of elicitation, observation, and, possibly, participation. The field notes and tapes which result from these activities will guide future write-ups, perhaps a monograph and/or articles which describe what has been learned in the field.[1] Originally identified with anthropology, such an array of activities has, until recently, served as the prototypical definition of linguistic fieldwork.

It is therefore quite striking that the term "fieldwork" has recently come to mean something quite different, at least in the United States. It is now not uncommon for graduate students and younger scholars, whose linguistic interests may be quite un-fieldlike (see section 2), to include mentions such as "fieldwork on Kikuyu, Toba Batak, and Kannada" in their job application letters and curricula vitae when they have, in fact, done all of their research at their home institution. What is meant by such "fieldwork" is that the linguist has worked with an *informant*, either individually or as part of a field methods course. In either case the person might have worked with only one speaker and looked at only one aspect of the language, e.g., the phonetics of stop consonants or the semantics of stative adjectives. I doubt whether linguists conflated "fieldwork" and "informant work" in this way twenty to thirty years ago. I at first thought that use of the former term to refer to the latter simply represented some kind of careless confusion. Upon deeper reflection, however, I find that it is difficult to define what exactly is meant by linguistic fieldwork – and why eliciting data from a Kikuyu, Toba Batak, or Kannada speaker in California does not qualify.

In this paper, I have two goals. First, I am interested in defining what is (or might be) meant by "fieldwork" in the general linguistic context. Second, after providing something of an answer to this question, I present a personal view of how linguistic fieldwork has guided my own development as an Africanist and general linguist.

1.   What is fieldwork?

As indicated above, there is some lack of clarity as to what constitutes "fieldwork" within the discipline of linguistics. Thus, what may be regarded as fieldwork to one linguist may not qualify as the same for another. I propose that there is a prototypical notion of "linguistic fieldwork," but that this term is applied differently by individual linguists according to the ways in which the targeted enterprise diverges from the prototype. My purpose here is to clarify these notions and try to provide some reason why a distinction between field versus non-fieldwork is a useful one in linguistics.

What is fieldwork? To answer this question, we might first adopt the strategy of addressing its opposite: What kind of linguistic research would *not* constitute fieldwork? Among the most obvious candidates would be any type of research that does not involve human participation beyond the investigator. In other words, fieldwork must not only be conducted in the first person, but also involve either a second person (elicitation) or a third person (observation). For something to be considered fieldwork, the researcher must acquire linguistic material *directly* from other speakers. Working either by introspection or by means of linguistic data collected by others should, thus, automatically disqualify the enterprise from the category of fieldwork. But does it?

I think everyone would agree that introspecting on language – even if done in "the field" – is not fieldwork. The same conclusion would probably be reached by most linguists with respect to a situation where a researcher goes to the field and works exclusively on written materials or tapes provided by other researchers there. Even if the same language is spoken all around the locus of this research, if the researcher (or a co-worker) does not directly gather data from speakers, one is unlikely to report the activity as fieldwork. I will, therefore, assume this aspect of the research as a given in all that follows.

The next attempt would be to exclude any type of interpersonal linguistic research that does not involve "going to the field." It is clear that two years of dissertation research on Kikuyu in Kenya will meet three prototypical features of fieldwork: distance, exoticism, and duration. One typically thinks of fieldwork as research done at a distance from the local reference point (e.g., one's university or home), involving a language (and culture) that is not familiar, and taking some amount of time to accomplish. All three of these features are gradient, and thus measurable on a scale going from zero to greatest geographical and cultural distance and time. The effect of each is seen in holding each feature constant at zero. Thus, consider first the case where distance = zero. Participation in a year-long field methods course on Kikuyu at one's university (e.g., in California) would represent a reasonable time commitment, and the targeted Bantu language would be sufficiently exotic to English speakers from either a genetic or typological perspective. However, it is hard to think of the field methods classroom, located where it is, as a field site – i.e., unless the goal was to study the classroom activity itself. The same could be said about individual research in the same university, e.g., informant work with a Kikuyu speaking graduate student, which may even extend over several years. Transport either activity to Kenya and it will seem more appropriate to list the experience as joint or individual fieldwork. That is, "fieldwork on Kikuyu" on one's vita becomes synonymous with "I've worked on Kikuyu in Kenya."[2]

Now consider the issue of exoticism. Since at least the late-nineteenth century, linguistic field research has been identified with cultural anthropology, whose practice has been to study "exotic" cultures and their languages (Geertz 1984). At the opposite extreme would be the study of one's own language. Imagine the same field methods course at an American institution, but substituting a dialect of American English for the language. Interestingly, I am unaware of any such course ever having been contemplated, even though there might be advantages to replacing introspection with the rigorous study of informant judgments in this way. Of course, linguists do use each other to test judgments about their own language. It is not uncommon for a linguist to walk down the hall and elicit some English sentences from a colleague ("Can you say X?"). Even if done on a regular basis, one wouldn't think of this as fieldwork. (One might even overlook this as informant work, except after reflection, since the latter, like fieldwork, prototypically involves not only a language other than one's own, but also the act of setting up an "informant session.") The same would probably be true if an English-speaking linguist ventured over to a language department to ask about sentences in French, Spanish, or German, languages whose closeness to English guarantees that they will rarely be used in field methods courses. Change this, however, to a dialect of Thai or Burmese, and all of a sudden we have a field language! Thus, I could imagine extensive class or individual informant work being listed on one's vita as "fieldwork on Burmese," but hardly "fieldwork on French."

The third issue, duration, is weaker than the other two, but also enters into the equation. It is harder to consider linguistic research fieldwork when the time factor is very limited. Someone who passes briefly through Nairobi and arranges a couple of informant sessions, makes recordings, or runs experiments with Kikuyu speakers would usually not refer to these activities as fieldwork. What is lacking is the time commitment. Fieldwork is not something that one thinks of popping in to and out of for a few days. However, the accident of being in Kenya, this being an "exotic" faraway country, does seem to add to the likelihood that this research, even if brief, will be listed as fieldwork.

By taking a low value on any one of the above three scales, a research effort may seem more versus less field-like. There are three additional issues that now need to be factored in: methodology, subject matter, and goals. Concerning methodology, I have up to now grouped together two different ways of working: elicitation and observation. The essential difference between the two derives from the role of the investigator: in elicitation, the researcher necessarily plays an active role in generating the data. Whether working with informants or in a laboratory setting, the methodology is essentially experimental. In both cases there is a response to the stimulus (e.g., "How do you say X?") and this response is matched and analyzed. In both cases the data are necessarily taken out of normal linguistic context – unless the intended study is of the informant or laboratory setting. Observation, on the other hand, need not (and, in some cases, must not) involve the active participation of the researcher. The ideal situation is where the fieldworker unobtrusively records the linguistic event: a spontaneous interaction between speakers, a narrative, a political speech, etc. While both methodologies may be used by the same researcher, the two are not equal in the equation; observation better fits the prototype of fieldwork. While it is hard to view informant work with other speakers of one's own language as fieldwork, the term seems quite appropriate where what is involved is the observation, recording, and analysis of the use of one's own language in the classroom, courtroom, department store, etc.

This naturally leads us to ask what is the role of the subject matter in defining linguistic fieldwork. In principle, almost anything can be studied in the field. However, in building the prototype, we note that certain issues seem more to be "field topics" than others. The reason for going to the field is, of course, to find speakers of languages chosen for linguistic investigation. Beyond this, however, one can distinguish two situations. The first is where the research question(s) could have been studied at home, if only native speakers were available. Most informant work falls in this category. The second situation is where the research could only have been done *sur place*. Virtually all sociolinguistic and ethnolinguistic work falls in this category. The model is provided by linguistic anthropology, whose goal is to study language in its natural cultural setting. Duranti (1994) differentiates between "field linguistics" (pp. 15–17), which could, in principle, have been done without going to the field, versus "ethnographic linguistics" (pp. 17–18), which requires going to the field. The distinction might be clearer for anthropologists than for linguists, given that the threshold for acceptable "ethnography" is lower in linguistics than it is in anthropology. Thus, if one had a number of informants in the United States, one could interrogate them on cultural as well as linguistic matters – and their interaction. Now, if the cultural setting does not exist in the country to which the native speakers are displaced, an ethnographic study of it will only be possible in the field. To the extent that anthropologists become interested in language, it is typically for the purpose of using it as a window into culture. On the other hand, when linguists become interested in cultural anthropology, it is typically for the purpose of contextualizing language. In other words, while both groups are potentially interested in the interface between language and culture, the arrows are going in opposite directions: language $\rightarrow$ culture (for anthropologists) versus culture $\rightarrow$ language (for linguists). Thus, most of the issues on which even field linguists conduct their research are not ethnographic in nature. Consequently, there are few cases where a linguist will go to the field out of a "logical" necessity. Instead, the motivation will be a practical one: to find speakers of languages that are not available close to home.

This brings me to the final issue: goals. In deciding to go to the field, linguists can be motivated by rather different goals: descriptive, historical, theoretical. They may wish to describe a language, or study historical and comparative issues (e.g., internal dialect grouping, external genetic relations, contact phenomena, etc.). Or the goal may be to study (typically predetermined) phenomena which bear on theoretical issues in phonology, syntax, semantics, etc. The linguist may have in mind to write a full grammar of a language, possibly informed by a specific theoretical framework, possibly not. The reason can also be practical, e.g., translation, as in the field research of many members of the Summer Institute of Linguistics. The relevant distinction, another scalar property, that I would like to suggest is between linguists who are theory-driven versus languages-driven. On the one extreme is the descriptive linguist who goes to the field to discover (and ultimately describe) heretofore undocumented languages. On the other extreme is a theoretical linguist who goes to the field to study a specific language which has been predetermined to bear on a crucial issue of linguistic theory. Few linguists at this end of the scale would go on a "fishing expedition," not knowing what, if anything, will pay off from the point of view of advancing (typically universalist) linguistic theory. A languages-oriented field researcher, on the other hand, typically welcomes the unknown and is excited to find never-before-seen phenomena, whether in the field or from the written record. Even if limited to informant work, the field is likely to become a major component of this research. Most theoretical linguists decide to study aspects of a language because they have some reason to think that they will bear on specific issues of theory. They don't need to see – let alone revel in – new and wild phenomena. In fact, the view has occasionally been expressed that "we have enough data" (see p. 28). Can one imagine a field linguist, however theoretically knowledgeable, ever making such a statement? Of course, some theoretical linguists share the love of languages with their non-theoretical counterparts, and the same linguist can participate in both theoretical and non-theoretical enterprises, but the two logical extremes exist in real people.

It is safe to say that field linguists are a motley group, some theoretical, some not, some historically or comparatively oriented, some not. Some go to the field motivated by an interest in a particular part of the world and its people, while others focus on the data and miss much of what is around them (music, art, etc.). Despite this complexity, it is, in fact, not hard to recognize a field linguist. I have been struck by the similarity in "spirit" when different area specialists convene. Whether the focus is on Africa, the Americas, or Southeast Asia, what seems to be constant is the excitement of doing field research on languages. An audience at this kind of meeting can react excitedly to the discovery of a new language or dialect, the demonstration of a genetic relationship between two languages, the existence of a case system marked by tone, the use of ideophones, and the effect of urbanization on a specific language community. Even though some of those present, myself included, have serious theoretical interests, we are temporarily freed of that concern to marvel in the particulars of the languages in which we have chosen to specialize. At these meetings you can get on the program without having to relate to general or theoretical linguistics, because what unites the majority of those present is the love of discovery in "the field," admittedly a squishy category.

In table 1.1, I summarize the notion of "prototypical linguistic fieldwork" as developed in the preceding paragraphs. Most of the features indicated are scalar (e.g., distance, duration), so one should consider the logical endpoints of each scale in determining their appropriateness. In only one case, introspection, does it seem clear that the negative extreme from the prototype automatically disqualifies the activity as fieldwork. If the other countertypes are bundled, however, the result can be something that seems quite un-fieldlike. One's individual intuitions of what constitutes linguistic fieldwork can be tested by varying the combinations of the above features, perhaps slightly redefining them or adding more.

Table 1.1 *The features of prototypical linguistic fieldwork*

	Fieldwork prototype	Fieldwork countertype	Least field-work-like
Elicitee	Other	Self	Introspection
Elicitor/observer	Self	Other	Secondary data
Distance	Far	Near	One's domicile
Setting	Small	Large	City, university
Duration	Long	Short	Brief stopover
Language	Exotic	Well-known	One's own
Subject matter	A language in its natural/ cultural context	Language in general as a formal system	Abstract syntax
Data	Naturalistic	Controlled	Synthetic speech
Motivation	Languages-driven	Theory-driven	

The last opposition between theory-driven and languages-driven research might be the most controversial. Many linguists combine elements of both, and have been known to change hats. Despite such metamorphoses and the subtlety of the distinction in the first place, those I refer to as theory- versus languages-driven researchers typically recognize each other and, in extreme cases, have epithets for those with whom they see themselves being diametrically opposed. This has shown up in two ways. First, there have been theoreticians throughout the generative era who have been disdainful of "descriptivists" ("empiricists," "butterfly collectors," etc.), who, of course, were already present in the field before linguistic theory gained its current preeminence. On the other hand, there has been a negative reaction by fieldworkers against ivory tower theoreticians, who acquire most of their data via introspection. To the extent that these theorists address exotic data, descriptivists of the languages regard this work as deforming the data beyond recognition.[3] Some of this tension is by now legendary. In discussions in the 1960s and 1970s both theory- and languages-driven linguists used virtually the same terms in describing their perceived opposites, who, allegedly, did not understand "how Language works" versus "how languages work." In reality, it is hard to see how the two can exist without each other – at least this has been my view and practice.

Given all of the above complexities, I contend that linguistic fieldwork is not so much a discrete, definable activity as it is a state of mind. We have surveyed some of the difficulties involved in specifying what constitutes fieldwork in linguistics – and hence why there is a confusion between informant work in a classroom, home, or office versus work "in the field." Some linguists will surely not agree with either my characterization of the problem, or in my conclusion, but here it is. The true fieldworker is a *languages-driven* person who may devote his or her activities to any number of goals: linguistic theory, description of languages, comparison of languages, reconstruction of languages, development of language materials for the community, etc. All of these are potential applications of fieldwork. At the same time, these same goals can be (and often are) undertaken without fieldwork. Since I have engaged in all of these activities, I should now like to illustrate by means of my own personal experience how one's linguistic work can be enriched by the fieldwork experience and "mentality."

2.   Fieldwork as a state of mind

When invited to contribute to this book, my initial reaction was "no, I don't do fieldwork – I do informant work." However, when I translate the question to ask whether I am a "fieldworker," all of a sudden I feel I should answer in the positive. My background includes two years of field research in Nigeria and Cameroon, where the questions I was interested in required me to go directly to the villages where the languages and dialects were spoken. Although this took place over twenty years ago, I have not lost the field experience: its effects continue in virtually all of the work I do. Specifically, I suggest that fieldwork is a *state of mind*: it is possible to be a fieldworker without constantly going to the field, and it is possible to go to the field without becoming a fieldworker. Thus, in some sense, I still do field research with informants in my office.

As an overview, throughout my career my research has centered around three interests. First, I have been concerned with the documentation of the languages of the Niger-Congo family in Africa. Second, I have been involved in comparative and historical work within this family. And third, my work has attempted to illuminate the contributions these languages make to our understanding of language in general, particularly in the area of phonology. Thus, my research activities and resulting publications have fallen within two fields: African linguistics and general linguistics. My contributions to these two fields have been both synchronic and diachronic. Indeed I find it hard to do descriptive work on a language without simultaneously considering what is or can be known about its history, especially as concerns resemblances and differences with closely related languages. Similarly, I find it difficult to investigate a language's historical development without concern for the general or theoretical motivation for changes that affect its grammar, phonology and lexicon.

Guiding my approach to linguistics is the idea that languages have a "story" to tell: it is our job to find these stories and figure them out. When I was a graduate student planning my dissertation-year field trip to Nigeria and Cameroon, I was struck by the differences between the agglutinative

Bantu languages in the east and the related, more isolating "Kwa-like" languages to the west. I felt confident that if I could just find the "missing link(s)" between east and west (which I thought would be in northern Nigeria), I could solve a number of diachronic problems within Niger-Congo: the origin of nasalized vowels, the origin of high vowel reduplication, the origin of tone, the origin of nasal consonants in Bantu noun prefixes, the origin of serial verbs. Every language of the area would potentially have something to say about these (and other such) diachronic problems. It was my job to study these languages and determine the *stories* they each had to tell.[4]

The motto I developed to describe my way of working was: if languages could only speak, they would tell you what they have to offer in them and what it all means. Since they can't tell us, we have to figure it out. While this may seem obvious today, it contrasts with the perception I had of what was supposed to be important in linguistics thirty years ago. When I entered graduate school in 1968, the most prestigious research was in the area of English transformational grammar. Theory was at the center of linguistics, and English was at the center of theory. One professor told me at the time that we did not know enough about other languages, except maybe French, to use them for universal theory. Another was famous for his statement, "If it's a universal, show it to me in English."[5] In those days, it was hard to be an old-fashioned linguist of any sort, let alone an old-fashioned fieldworker. The only excuse for going to the field would be to advance our theoretical knowledge of language.

This "excuse" was foremost on my mind when I left for northern Nigeria in July 1970 to conduct research for a planned dissertation in phonological theory. As a student I had published two articles (Hyman 1970a, 1970b) in support of abstractness in phonological theory. Drawing on data collected in a field methods course at University of California, Los Angeles (UCLA), I had shown that Nupe, which lacks [ɛ] and [ɔ], borrows Yoruba [Cɛ] and [Cɔ] as [Cʲa] and [Cʷa], rather than [Ce] and [Co]. I argued that the nativization process did not proceed by substituting the most "phonetically similar" sounds, but rather operated with reference to the (abstract) phonological structure of Nupe. In Hyman (1970b) I developed a set of principles to account for the nativization of borrowings into Nupe from Hausa. I had reason to believe that Gwari, another language in the Nupe group that had also borrowed heavily from Hausa, might therefore provide further theoretical insights into these issues.

I thus departed for Nigeria with the immediate goal of studying the perception of foreign sounds and the nativization of Hausa borrowings in Nupe and Gwari. Based on the speed at which I worked, I remember thinking that I would conduct the research in a couple of months, write up the dissertation in a couple more months, and then devote myself to the comparative and historical questions that also interested me. Being so sure of this time-table, I modified my original plan and got permission to spend the second six months of my year in Cameroon, where my goal was to work on distantly related Bamileke (see below), which I thought could also be involved in my "missing link" theory.

For several reasons, the theoretical dissertation never materialized, although I did go to Gwari country. I had been instructed by a Nigerian professor to go to St. Malachy's College, a Catholic secondary school outside Minna, where I could seek help to find lodging. I don't know how it happened, but in introducing myself, I surprised myself by announcing to the Irish Father that I had come to work on a grammar of Gwari. (Had I been holding this intention from myself?) I then asked if he could help me find a place to stay. Being alone for the summer, he was delighted to have company and offered to put me up in one of the spare bedrooms. Father Mullally put me in touch with two Gwari teachers who lived nearby and were on summer break. It was an ideal situation: I met two hours in the morning with the first teacher, and two hours in the afternoon with the second. In between I prepared my informant sessions, and at night I went through all my notes over and over, keeping a log of my questions and thoughts. I found Gwari to be an excellent language in which to study grammaticalization processes, e.g., the historical origins of particular verbal constructions. I remember obsessing about this with such excitement that I spent countless nights without sleeping. At some point, I wrote a letter to Russell Schuh, who was conducting fieldwork then in Potiskum, some distance away in northern Nigeria. I told him that I was deeply worried about my insomnia, which I feared might continue until I would collapse. Russ responded as a true fellow fieldworker, telling me about his similar excitement about tone in Ngizim, in which, he said, "It's amazing what you can do with two tones." (We continued our exchange in Los Angeles, which ultimately developed into Hyman and Schuh 1974.)

In the context of the Nigerian field, it was hard to think about the distant theories I had left back home. I did make a feeble attempt to get some subjects for a perception test, and to look at some borrowings, but I was hooked on the Gwari grammar. After seven weeks in Minna, I returned to the University of Ibadan where I finished and published *Essentials of Gwari Grammar* (Hyman and Magaji 1970).

In the process, I discovered that I wasn't just hooked on Gwari. I was hooked on Africa. I wrote my dissertation advisor the good news about my accomplishments and indicated to her that I now planned to visit Benin [then Dahomey], Togo, Ghana, and Ivory Coast, and then go to Cameroon for the next six months, where my goal would be to write a similar grammar of the Fe'fe' dialect of Bamileke (Eastern Grassfields Bantu), which I had found to be a much harder language than anything I knew in Nigeria. But what about my dissertation? I asked if I could please submit the Gwari grammar for this purpose? Or, if not, could I staple together a collection of my published, theoretical papers? *Anything* to be freed from the doctoral burden that was weighing over me and threatened to get in the way of my intensified Africanist calling – and my Bamileke grammar.

The answer came back "no" on both questions. So I arrived in Cameroon without a dissertation topic in sight. I even contemplated abandoning my degree and never going back. There was so much work that had to be done, so many languages that had to be described, so much to learn and to contribute. The Monsignor in Minna was so delighted with my Gwari grammar that he begged me to do another stay, at his expense, so I could write a similar grammar of the other large language in his diocese, Dakarkari, a member of a different Niger-Congo group, the Plateau sub-branch of Benue-Congo; but I was now set on working in Cameroon.

In January 1971, I settled into the Mission de Banka in Cameroon, where an informant was provided to meet me every afternoon. Within days of my arrival, I found myself in the middle of a political struggle between "my" dialect (which I had innocently chosen, because it was the first in which there was an indigenous literacy program, Nufi) and another dialect that had just replaced it on the radio. There was concern about my presence. I was summoned by the *sous-préfet* and forced to leave the department and go to Yaoundé, the capital, to seek permission to conduct my research. (I had told the Cameroonian consulate in Lagos that I was going to Cameroon to conduct research, but they had said nothing about a research permit – which hadn't been necessary in Nigeria because I was enrolled as an "occasional student" at the University of Ibadan). With all of these problems, I remember wishing that I had never left Nigeria.

After two weeks of waiting in Yaoundé, my research permit finally came through. However, my grammar of Bamileke never materialized. One reason was that, at about the same time, a Benedictine Father returned to the same mission where I was after a sojourn of nineteen years in France. He had just published *Le Bamileke des Fe'fe'* (Ngangoum 1970), which seemed to fit the need. Another was that I was starting to get feelers and job offers from America and felt ultimately that it would be in my best interest to pursue a position back home. However, I had no dissertation. I tried desperately to find a topic, based on Bamileke. The Fe'fe' dialect that I had set out to investigate had lost almost all affixes and left me with the kind of "isolating" language of little interest to a phonologist or morphologist. Even the tone system did not seem to offer much complexity or theoretical interest – despite what we were later to find out about the Dschang dialect.

My salvation came from my friendship with a Breton priest, Père LePage, who was stationed in Company (Banja). One day in Banka, he told me that he would be borrowing the Land Rover to spend two weekends in a row in the two most isolated villages in the area, Fondanti and Fondjomekwet. I asked my Bamileke host and head of the mission, l'Abbé Tchamda, what they spoke there, and he replied, "Ah, c'est un fe'fe' très nuancé!" So I went. On each weekend, while Père LePage said mass and met with people, I stayed outside getting wordlists and a few grammatical items from the villagers who had been attracted by the rare visit of an outsider.

I quickly discovered what had happened to Fe'fe'. Where Fe'fe' had final long vowels, Fondanti and Fondjomekwet had final consonants, i.e., *CVC > Fe'fe' CVV; and these final C's "came back" as liaison consonants when a following vowel-initial possessive or object pronoun followed the noun or verb, e.g., *cii* 'feed', *ciim-a* 'feed me'; *yii* 'see', *yiin-a* 'see me'. I was on my way to fleshing out a full dissertation dealing with both synchronic and diachronic phonological issues. Based on this experience, I then sought out speakers of other dialects and got comparative wordlists that allowed me to start reconstructing Proto-Bamileke forms.

When I returned to the United States, I worked on my dissertation at UCLA, while I taught my first year at the University of Southern California (USC). One day in the Linguistics reading room, newly appointed faculty member Benji Wald came in and started talking to me about the Swahili dialects and related languages on the East African coast he had just studied in the field. In light of my own experience with the largely monosyllabic Fe'fe', I was especially envious about what he told me regarding variations in the morphology. In a break during his enthusiasm, I interjected, "I envy you! Your languages are *so* interesting," clearly implying that mine weren't. Benji replied, "*All* languages are interesting. You just have to figure out what the issues are."

Since that time I have mentioned my Fe'fe' experience to others, sometimes as advice to graduate students as they leave for the field: If at any time there is a lull in your work, or you can't seem to find what the interesting issues are, get the next dialect, then the next, then the next, etc. In this way the languages (dialects) themselves will *tell* you what's interesting. It's harder for a group of dialects to hide their "stories" (cf. Elimelech 1977, who covered seven dialects of Etsako in Nigeria to verify his tonal hypotheses).

It was this way – in the field – that a strategy was born that has since guided my work: get related languages. They will tell related stories. While this strategy is most easily carried out in the field, where there is greatest access to languages and dialect variation, it can often be adopted outside the primary language communities. This is what working on Bantu (with its approximately 500 languages) represents for me today. As I like to say,

"Once you have seen one Bantu language, you've seen them all – but they're all different!" The so-called Narrow Bantu languages are all cut from the same mold, a kind of theme and variations; consequently, they are easily compared. Thus, one can see how related languages manipulate parameters in their treatment of tone, direct object properties, anaphors, etc. What I particularly like is to focus on an area where different languages resolve "conflicts" in different ways. For example, Bantu languages are widely known for their derivational verbal suffixes: causative *-ic-, applicative *-id-, reciprocal *-an-, causative *-į-, passive *-u-. In many languages we see clear evidence that this is the preferred order of these suffixes, at least as far as the morphotactics of the language are concerned. However, as noted by many scholars, e.g., Guthrie (1962), there also is a tendency for such suffixes to occur in a compositional order where an outer suffix has scope over an inner suffix. Baker (1985) cites Bantu data in support of his "mirror principle" (see also Alsina 1999). However, as a number of us at Berkeley have shown, the mirror principle will often be at odds with the morphotactics, e.g., an applicativized reciprocal, which, by the mirror principle, should produce the morphotactically dispreferred sequence -an-id-. Similarly, the applicative-causative sequence -id-į- is frequently at odds with the morpho-syntactic structure [[[root] causative] applicative] that underlies it. Based on the phonological effects of causative -į- in many such cases, Polak-Bynon (1975) suggests that an input sequence CVC-į-id- undergoes a metathesis of the suffixes to produce CVC-id-į-, which I have reanalyzed as a cyclic effect (Hyman 1994). In short, since scope (or the mirror principle) and morpho-tactics are often at odds in Bantu languages, the latter provide a fruitful field in which to explore the parameters by which suffix ordering is deter-mined in natural language.

While my comparative approach has, to my mind, been successful in yielding results, I have perceived occasional puzzlement from non-fieldworkers on this strategy. At the conference on "The Syntax–Phonology Connection" held at Stanford (Inkelas and Zec 1990), there were several papers dealing with the interaction between tone and syntax in different Bantu languages. During one coffee break I remarked to two non-Bantuist formal phonologists that, if we could systematically map out what happens in the syntax–phonology interface throughout the Bantu zone, we would really learn a great deal about what is possible. One of them – not a field-worker – replied, "Why only Bantu?" It is of course true that one must ulti-mately consider a wide range of geographically and genetically diverse languages. I am simply speaking of the advantage of exploiting what different language families have to offer – and, where possible, doing rigor-ous comparative work on isolable phenomena that have theoretical and typological significance.

I recall another incident back in 1974 where my interlocutor expressed more than puzzlement. I was about to return to Cameroon for six months with a variety of projects in mind. The first was to collect tonal alternations in thirty dialects of Bamileke. As mentioned above, Fe'fe', the dialect of my dissertation, has lost almost all of its affixes. It also has lost second root syllables and undergone numerous sound changes. The result is a distinctly monosyllabic word structure, e.g., **li-sɔ̀ŋá > sē̃ʔ* 'tooth'. However, as Voorhoeve (1971) had shown from a similar dialect, Bangangte, the historical tones of the lost vowels are still there, "floating," as it were. One such example involves the two nouns *yú* 'thing' and *mə́n* 'child'. Although both are pronounced with H(igh) tone in isolation, when combined to form a genitive noun+noun construction, the result is *yú ⁿmə́n*. As indicated by the downstep markers ⁿ, the second noun *mə́n* now is "doubly downstepped" from the level of the previous H of *yú*. To account for the full range of such alternations, Voorhoeve discovered that such noun+noun combinations would have had an underlying sequence of seven tones, five of which are "floating": /`yú` + ´ + `mə́n`/. This is shown in the following autosegmental representation:

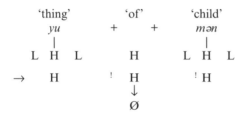

The floating L(ow) tones that precede each linked H belong to the historical noun class prefix, while those that follow it originally belonged to the lost second root syllable. The one floating H is the genitive ("associative" or "connective") marker, a tonal morpheme which is H tone following most noun classes.[6] The reason why *yú* and *mə́n* do not combine as H-H (as would be the case with H nouns lacking these floating tones) is now evident. As indicated in the last line, each floating L that is wedged between H's causes the following H to downstep. This hypothetically yields the H-ꞌH-ꞌH sequence, where each !H is one step lower than the preceding H. Note, however, that the second H is floating and hence will not be realized. Although needed to produce the second downstep, it is deleted. The result is H-ⁿH: a H followed by a "double downstepped" H.

My proposal, then, was to see how these historical tones, which we had reconstructed for Proto-Bamileke, were realized in different dialects. At this time one of my former teachers asked: "Where's the theory? Why go and collect tones? We have lots of data!" Although my interest was in finding out how tone works, i.e., what is possible, I could not say that I was pushing or testing any particular theory. And yet I was convinced that the effort would be worth it. If the trip had been planned after the appearance of Goldsmith (1976), I could, of course, have answered that I was testing the claims of autosegmental tonology. I don't think this would have significantly changed the project, since my hope would be for the insights reported in the resulting study (Hyman and Tadadjeu 1976) to be of use beyond the life of any one theory.

As a fieldworker with an eye open to theory, I am myself often puzzled by those theoreticians who cannot relate to what I consider an interesting finding or observation unless one couches it within a theory. It is as if they cannot appreciate the "puzzle" without translating the discussion into formal theoretical terms. If these data do not obviously bear on some aspect of theory, why are they interesting? I don't think that this state of mind is compatible with that of the fieldworker.

3.   Conclusion

The above part of my personal history has been designed to show how fieldwork has guided my own work as an African and general linguist. The group-specific comparative strategy I developed in Nigeria and Cameroon is of course followed particularly by historical linguists interested in a particular language family or subgroup. It is more rarely adopted for synchronic purposes, where the goals of cross-linguistic typology and formal theory require consideration of all languages and language families. It is thus for this reason that the colleague cited earlier asked "Why only Bantu?" For him it doesn't matter what the language is. For me it does. If I achieve some result in one Bantu language, I cannot help asking what happens in the next (and the next and so on). In my experience this line of pursuit has always led to discoveries and understanding beyond that achieved in studying the original language. I kind of look at this in pragmatic terms: If Bantu language X has given us these fruit, why not take advantage and build on this foundation?

I believe that this approach to general linguistics correlates with my having had field experience. But does it make sense to refer to fieldwork as a state of mind? I think so. If not clear from the preceding, then let me add two further qualities of fieldworkers. The first is the love of discovery, of going out into the unknown in search of uniqueness. Whether documenting rare speech sounds or the unique details of out-of-focus marking in Aghem, language particulars usually excite fieldworkers, who take visible "pride" in their language(s). Much of the rhetoric of generative grammar has been to reduce surface differences to underlying sameness, hence, in principle, denying privileged status to any individual language. The field-worker, on the other hand, establishes a special relationship with his or her language (and its speakers), which, in its extreme manifestation, can be translated as "the world turns around my language." In some cases, field linguists might in fact be on location primarily because of their *attraction* to this or that language, country, or geographical area. Here we have a sub-jectivity that draws the scholar to think of his language(s) as special. I have to say that I myself have had this reaction in studying a number of lan-guages from Gwari and Bamileke in Africa to Gokana and Luganda in the United States, among others.

The second quality of the fieldwork mental state I would like to discuss is what I would call a dedication to "whole language," if that term had not been adopted for other purposes. There are linguists who only work in pho-netics, or only in phonology, or only in syntax. This is a luxury of the com-partmentalization of academia – not only into departments, but into subdisciplinary specialties. In the field, however, one cannot say, "Oh, that's the syntax, I only do phonology." Typically one does not want to. As a field-worker one's objective is to study whatever is out there. One can arrive in the field with the intention of working on tone, but to study tone, one has to study utterances; but, when one studies utterances, other issues come up. While this happens in non-field situations as well, the pull to *act* on things outside one's original purpose is a typical feature of the fieldworker state of mind. In Berkeley in 1973, two students and I met with a Shona informant to study his tone system. Instead, we became distracted by the conflict between person/animacy, semantic role, and grammatical relation hier-archies in interpreting sentences like the English pair "a package was sent the child" versus "the package was sent a child." This so engrossed us that the tone project never got off the ground – but see Hawkinson and Hyman (1974) for what did. When you are a fieldworker (= state of mind), you don't cast such things aside. It is thus interesting to me that most Africanists I know, whether theoretically inclined or not, have published on phonologi-cal, morphological, syntactic and semantic issues arising from the study of their languages.

The preceding example is one where we could have done the tone system, but found something else that intrigued us even more. In the non-field situ-ation, it is also common – because it is possible – to shift gears to another area when the first area runs up a brick wall. In the field, however, there are some brick walls that simply *have* to come down before progress can be made on anything else. Because one is typically not free to move and change languages, one therefore has to stick it out. One hears about the excitement and thrills of fieldwork; but there is nothing worse than being stymied by (what seems to be) an intractable problem: one can't solve it, but one can't go ahead without it. I am reminded of a letter written many years ago to a member of our research team in Cameroon who was struggling with the notoriously complex tonal contrasts and morphotonemics of a Grassfields Bantu language. The letter was written by the late Jan Voorhoeve, a major Africanist and tonologist.

Last remark. You started tonal analysis, and you hint at a personal instability. Be sure to meet the biggest crisis of your career if you are not prepared to fail constantly in the tonal analysis. I regard myself as a stable person and the tonal analysis still pushes me to the fringes of self-control. It is clear agony. All of the old feelings of inferiority will heap up in you. You will think that any other linguist would have solved the problems, but you are unable to do so. You will go in circles, coming back to refuted hypotheses, refuting them once more, and so on. . . . I cannot understand how Larry manages to keep happy without really knowing the system. Larry is way off the truth in the verbal system, he knows it, and he is still happy. I am not. I am suffering. I have worked at it with a good informant for the last 8 months and it has not been solved . . . [but] . . . Please let it not ruin your pleasure in Linguistics.

For fieldworkers with the requisite state of mind, it wouldn't. Part of the pleasure of fieldwork lies in the daily challenges: the tougher the challenge, the greater the personal and intellectual rewards. Just think of working on the world's most complex, most marked language, with every consonantal and vocalic complexity known to man, morphophonemics of the most opaque variety, and tonal distinctions and alternations that must be mastered in order to progress in even the simplest aspects of the language's complex grammar. A worst linguistic nightmare to some, this is the fieldworker's joy. Speaking for myself, I'd go "there" in a minute.

NOTES

1 In pre-generative America, a common sequence procedure was to submit a grammar of the field language as one's dissertation, followed later by a published dictionary, and, ultimately, a collection of texts.
2 Of course, the *field* can be geographically near, e.g., an American Indian reservation may be a short drive away from one's university. I have also referred to the possibility that the classroom (or one's home, etc.) might be used for the purpose of sociolinguistic fieldwork. This shows that lack of distance can be counteracted by the nature of research. Thus, if one's goal is the study of language use in context, the field can be anywhere – and the field language can be one's own (see below).
3 "They don't care about the language" is something I have heard from fieldworkers in describing what they consider to be formal theoretical excesses. This, too, is scalar. Although never verified, it was rumored that one missionary allegedly reacted badly to me and other members of the Grassfields Bantu Working Group because we came to spend only a few months doing research in the area versus his many years of commitment. If true, then we were seen as the theoretical usurpers.

4 In the early 1980s I was struck by the new vocabulary of GB syntacticians, who talked in terms of having a "story" about some *data* from a language. This contrasted with my own use of the word "story": for me, the *data* tell a story about Language, *not the linguist.* This correlates with the distinction I drew in section 1 between being theory- versus languages-driven.

5 Since I am equally narrow-minded today, I would rather say, "If it's a universal, show me in Bantu!" At least my favorite family has 500 languages!

6 Note that the corresponding sequence would reconstruct in Proto-Bantu as **kì-júmà + kí-á + mù-jánà*, which we would take to be extremely close to the Proto-Grassfields Bantu form as well.

REFERENCES

Alsina, Alex. 1999. Where's the mirror principle? *The Linguistic Review* 16:1–42.

Baker, Mark. 1985. The mirror principle and morphosyntactic explanation. *Linguistic Inquiry* 16:373–416.

Duranti, Alessandro. 1994. *From Grammar to Politics: Linguistic Anthropology in a Western Samoan Village.* Berkeley and Los Angeles: University of California Press.

Elimelech, Baruch. 1978. *A Tonal Grammar of Etsakǫ.* (University of California Publications in Linguistics, 87) Berkeley and Los Angeles: University of California Press.

Geertz, Clifford. 1984. Distinguished lecture: anti anti-relativism. *American Anthropologist* 86:263–78.

Goldsmith, John. 1976. Autosegmental Phonology. Ph.D. dissertation, MIT.

Guthrie, Malcolm. 1962. On the status of radical extensions in Bantu languages. *Journal of African Languages* 1:202–20.

Hawkinson, Anne K., and Larry M. Hyman. 1974. Hierarchies of natural topic in Shona. *Studies in African Linguistics* 5:147–70.

Hyman, Larry M. 1994. Cyclic phonology and morphology in Cibemba. In *Perspectives in Phonology*, ed. Jennifer Cole and Charles Kisseberth, pp. 81–112. Stanford: CSLI.

1970a. How concrete is phonology? *Language* 46:58–76.

1970b. The role of borrowing in the justification of phonological grammars. *Studies in African Linguistics* 1:1–48.

Hyman, Larry M., and Daniel J. Magaji. 1970. *Essentials of Gwari Grammar.* (Occasional Publications of the Institute of African Studies, 27) Ibadan: University of Ibadan Press.

Hyman, Larry M., and Russell G. Schuh. 1974. Universals of tone rules: evidence from West Africa. *Linguistic Inquiry* 5:81–115.

Hyman, Larry M. and Maurice Tadadjeu. 1976. Floating tones in Mbam-Nkam. In *Studies in Bantu Tonology*, ed. Larry M. Hyman, pp. 57–111. (Southern California Occasional Papers in Linguistics, 3) Los Angeles: University of Southern California.

Inkelas, Sharon, and Draga Zec (eds.). 1990. *The Phonology-Syntax Connection.* Stanford: CSLI.

Ngangoum, Bernard. 1970. *Le bamiléké des fe'fe'. Grammaire descriptive usuelle.* [place of publication not indicated]

Polak-Bynon, Louise. 1975. *A Shi Grammar: Surface Structures and Generative Phonology of a Bantu language*. Tervuren: Musée Royal de l'Afrique Centrale.

Voorhoeve, Jan. 1971. Tonology of the Bamileke noun. *Journal of African Languages* 10(2):44–53.

2 Who shapes the record: the speaker and the linguist

Marianne Mithun

With the accelerating loss of linguistic diversity in our world, it is a time for serious thought about how to record as much as possible of the richness still around us. In many cases what we choose to document may be the principal record of an entire linguistic tradition, both for the descendants of the speakers and for others seeking to understand the possibilities of the human mind. It is a time to consider not only how to fill recognizable gaps in current knowledge, but also how to provide the basis for answers to questions we do not yet know enough to ask. In most cases, these goals can best be met by a mix of styles of collaboration between speakers and linguists. The product of fieldwork will ultimately be shaped not only by the nature of the language, but also by the methodologies chosen, by the roles assumed by the speakers, and by the preparation and sensitivity of the linguist.

1.   Methodology

The record that results from linguistic fieldwork depends of course on the goal of the particular project, which in turn determines the kinds of methodologies that will be effective. The goal may be quite specific, such as understanding patterns of vowel harmony. It may be as ambitious as the documentation of an entire language in as much depth as possible. In the current situation, it is useful to consider not only the match between the project and the language, but also the appropriateness of the project to the community in which the language is used. Where language use is widespread and vigorous, it is natural to follow the interests of both the speakers and the fieldworker. Where the speech community is fragile, however, time with skilled speakers is a finite resource. A decision to pursue one line of research will necessarily leave other aspects of the language undocumented. Under such circumstances, it is also good to remember that any record made is likely to be used for other purposes later on. This means that the data should be as accurate and explicit as possible on all counts, not just with regard to the point under discussion. Even in a paper on relative clause formation, for example, it is worthwhile to take pains to insure that

34

transcription be reliable, that morphological analysis be explicit and precise, and that illustrative examples represent utterances that are syntactically, semantically, and pragmatically valid.

Research methodologies are usually chosen for their potential to produce the material desired. At the same time, the choice of methodology can also shape the resulting product in ways researchers may not always be aware of. Finding the optimal mix of methodologies can be facilitated by an awareness of the potential rewards and limitations of the options.

The primary methodology used in most courses in linguistic fieldwork is direct elicitation. Students are taught to ask speakers for translations of words or sentences from a contact language such as English. They are instructed in the kinds of material to collect, such as vocabulary ('house', 'my maternal aunt'), number contrasts ('rock', 'rocks'), verbal paradigms ('I run', 'he runs'), tense contrasts ('I run', 'I ran'), basic word order ('John loves Mary', 'the two large dogs'), conjoined structures ('I ran and John walked', 'I ate spinach and John peas'), relative clauses ('I saw the man you met', 'the man who met you liked you'), sentential complements ('I know that you were not seen by the man'), reference across clauses ('John saw the dog who bit him', 'John kissed Mary and left'), and other specific structures.

A second kind of methodology, the recording of connected speech, has formed the core of much linguistic fieldwork over the past century, particularly in North America. The tradition of text collection arose in part from a desire to document the rich cultures of the speakers, but it was also seen as a tool for understanding languages in their own terms, rather than through European models (Darnell 1996, Goddard 1996, Mithun 1996). The texts served as the basis for grammatical description. In his introduction to the inaugural issue of the *International Journal of American Linguistics*, Franz Boas noted that, "While until about 1880 investigators confined themselves to the collection of vocabularies and brief grammatical notes, it has become more and more evident that large masses of texts are needed in order to elucidate the structure of the languages" (Boas 1917: 1). The texts transcribed by these researchers are impressive, though Boas himself was keenly aware of the difficulties of capturing spontaneous speech with pen and ink: "The slowness of dictation that is necessary for recording texts makes it difficult for the narrator to employ that freedom of diction that belongs to the well-told tale, and consequently an unnatural simplicity of syntax prevails in most of the dictated texts" (Boas 1917: 1). He was also conscious of the limitations of dictation for capturing the most prevalent use of speech in daily life, conversation: "On the whole, however, the available material gives a one-sided presentation of linguistic data, because we have hardly any records of daily occurrences, every-day conversation, descriptions of industries, customs, and the like" (Boas 1917: 2). With the modern accessibility of audio and video recording devices, these limitations have been lifted, and speech can now be recorded from a variety of genres, including conversation.

Both direct elicitation and the recording of spontaneous speech are important tools, each with a variety of uses. But neither is sufficient for all purposes, and much can be missed if one of them is overlooked.

1.1   *Phonology*

Languages vary tremendously in their accessibility at the outset of fieldwork. Some have small inventories of sounds, while others have large ones. In some languages distinctions are generally easy to hear, while in others they may be more subtle. For example Mohawk, an Iroquoian language of Quebec, Ontario, and New York State, distinguishes just two oral stops *t* and *k*, while Central Pomo, a Pomoan language of Northern California, distinguishes seventeen oral stops *p, pʰ, p̓, b, t̪, t̪ʰ, t̪̓, d, t, tʰ, t̓, k, kʰ, k̓, q, qʰ,* and *q̓* as well as various affricates. There may be unusual distinctions in tone, voicing, length, or voice quality. The complexity of syllable structure can also present challenges at the outset. While some languages generally show simple (C)V(C) syllables, others exhibit pervasive complex consonant clusters. Thus in Yup'ik, an Eskimoan language of southwestern Alaska, we typically find words of simple syllable structure, such as *qalarteqatartua* 'I am going to speak' (Elizabeth Ali, speaker), while in Spokane, a Salishan language of Washington State, we find words like *ntk̓ʷk̓ʷátɬqʷɬt* 'it accidentally fell in the mouth, someone accidentally said something that was long forgotten' (Carlson and Flett 1989: 181). Some languages and dialects are customarily spoken more slowly and deliberately than others, and some speakers simply speak more clearly than others.

Becoming attuned to the sounds of an unfamiliar language can take time and concentration, particularly if the language contains subtle phonetic distinctions, a sizable inventory of consonants or vowels, and complex phonological patterns. Direct elicitation of individual words is an obvious way to begin the process. Before one is familiar with the sound patterns and grammatical markers of a new language, it can be difficult to hold even a brief stretch of speech in the mind long enough to transcribe it. There is too much to think about all at once. In the early stages of work, elicitation can also help to put speakers at ease. A request for the word for 'tree' can be less daunting than a request for an eloquent speech to a microphone.

Of course certain aspects of phonology cannot be observed in the careful pronunciation of single words, but emerge only in spontaneous connected speech. Even vowel harmony may cross word boundaries in fluent speech in some languages. Probably the most dramatic example of phonological structure that appears only in connected speech is that of intonation or prosody, an area of language structure with important implications well beyond the domain of phonology.

1.2   The lexicon

Elicitation is obviously a useful tool for collecting vocabulary. If one is working with bilingual speakers of Yup'ik and wants to know the term for 'walrus', the easiest way to find out is to ask "How do you say 'walrus'?." Vocabulary is an essential part of the record, both for the community and for future scholarship. Direct elicitation is especially effective for collecting lists of certain kinds of words, such as numerals and terms for body parts, plants, animals, and relatives. It can be useful for recording culturally significant vocabulary, such as names of foods, medicines, songs, dances, ceremonies, tools, items of clothing, and kinsmen. It can also yield the kinds of words most useful in determining genetic relationships. Terms for numerals, body parts, and elements of nature such as 'sun', 'fire', and 'water' tend to be relatively stable over time and are likely to have been recorded for other languages as well. They are also the kinds of words that tend to come to mind easily for speakers. At the beginning of the collaborative work, as rapport is being established, it can be easier for a speaker to come up with a word for 'three' or 'stone' than for 'idiosyncrasy' or 'parallelism'.

If the goal of the undertaking is to document what is special about the language, however, direct elicitation alone cannot suffice, even within the realm of vocabulary. The lexicon can provide a powerful resource for understanding how speakers have organized the kaleidoscope of their experience into concepts. The vocabulary of Yup'ik, like that of most languages, bears clear witness to the natural and social contexts in which the language has evolved, as can be seen in such verbs as *payu-* 'to have one's legs so cramped by cold that one cannot move', *pukug-* 'to eat bits of meat clinging to a bone after most of the meat has been removed, to pick berries carefully from scattered sites because they are few in number', and *tunrir-* 'to feel embarrassed because one is imposing on someone; to feel beholden because of an inability to reciprocate for things someone has done for one; to feel embarrassed by the actions of someone (such as a child) for whom one feels responsible' (Jacobson 1984).[1] Vocabulary can show both special distinctions and surprising generalizations that speakers have found useful.

Elicited vocabulary tends to be heavily weighted toward nouns, especially terms for concrete, tangible objects, and terms with counterparts in the contact language. Words such as 'man', 'woman', 'house', 'fire', 'water', and 'sky' usually predominate in elicited lists. Verbs and other parts of speech are rarer, as are more abstract and culturally-specific terms. There are many words one might simply not think to ask about, such as the Yup'ik *pavani* 'up there away from the river', *iryagte-* 'to be smoky from a distant fire', *kassug-* 'to encompass', *kau-* 'to reach into a container or hollow place', *nacete-* 'to look around or survey one's surroundings from a high vantage point', *nalluyur-* 'to feel uncomfortable with or unwelcome by someone', *narurte-* 'to act against accepted standards of behavior', *pellertar-* 'to tend to feel squeamish around wet, messy things', *qakete-* 'to resubmerge after coming to the surface (of fish, seal)', *qaliqar-* 'to get sick and die from eating foods said to be incompatible, such as aged fish and salmonberries', and *yit'e-* 'to have a stranger come upon one, to come upon as a stranger'. A bias toward nouns is particularly unfortunate for languages in which verbs predominate strongly in natural speech.

Ultimately elicitation provides an effective tool for collecting long lists of basic lexical items, but a substantial proportion of the most interesting vocabulary emerges only in spontaneous speech, in what speakers themselves choose to say in different contexts.

1.3   Grammatical structure

Direct elicitation can be a valuable tool for the documentation of grammar as well. At the beginning of work with a bilingual consultant, it can allow us to check for possible grammatical distinctions. We might, for example, elicit forms like those in (1).

(1) Yup'ik: George Charles, speaker

qayaq	kayak	*atsaq*	berry
qayak	two kayaks	*atsak*	two berries
qayat	three or more kayaks	*atsat*	three or more berries

From these words we might hypothesize that Yup'ik distinguishes singular, dual, and plural number on nouns. The exercise can also prepare us to recognize morphological markers and syntactic constructions when they appear another time. If, sometime later, we come across the Yup'ik word *teriak* 'weasels', we might hypothesize that it is a dual noun, which it is, and that the final *-k* is not part of the root, which is correct. If we come across the word *kipusvigtellinilria* 'he went to the store', and we have learned from previous elicitation that the root *kipute-* is 'buy', and the suffix *-vik* a locative nominalizer, we can untangle this construction more quickly: *kipute-vik-te-llini-lria* 'buy-place.where-go.to-apparently-3.SG.PARTICIPIAL' = 'it seems he went to where one buys'.

Elicitation can be crucial for filling in paradigms, for securing forms we can predict to exist. In Mohawk, all verbs contain pronominal prefixes identifying the core arguments of the clause. Prefixes in intransitive verbs refer to one party, and those in transitive verbs refer to two. The prefixes distinguish first, second, and third persons; inclusive and exclusive first persons; masculine, feminine, and neuter third persons; singular, dual, and plural numbers; and two cases. A sample intransitive paradigm can be seen in (2). (Examples are given here in the practical orthography currently in use in all six Mohawk communities. A key to the phonetic values is given in note 1 at the end of the chapter.)

(2) Mohawk intransitive agent paradigm: Rokwaho Dan Thompson, speaker

k-ó'kwats	I'm digging	(1.SINGULAR.AGENT)
ten-ó'kwats	you and I are digging	(1.INCLUSIVE.DUAL.AGENT)
ki-ó'kwats	you all and I are digging	(1.INCLUSIVE.PLURAL.AGENT)
iaken-ó'kwats	s/he and I are digging	(1.EXCLUSIVE.DUAL.AGENT)
iaki-ó'kwats	they and I are digging	(1.EXCLUSIVE.PLURAL.AGENT)
s-ó'kwats	you're digging	(2.SINGULAR.AGENT)
sen-ó'kwats	you two are digging	(2.DUAL.AGENT)
tsi-ó'kwats	you all are digging	(2.PLURAL.AGENT)
r-ó'kwats	he is digging	(MASCULINE.SINGULAR.AGENT)
n-ó'kwats	they two (males) are digging	(MASCULINE.DUAL.AGENT)
ronn-ó'kwats	they all (males) are digging	(MASCULINE.PLURAL.AGENT)
iak-ó'kwats	she is digging	(FEMININE.SINGULAR.AGENT)
ken-ó'kwats	they two are digging	(FEMININE/NEUTER.DUAL.AGENT)
konn-ó'kwats	they all are digging	(FEMININE/NEUTER.PL.AGENT)
i-ó'kwats	it (an animal) is digging	(NEUTER.SINGULAR.AGENT)

All of the participants represented by the pronominal prefixes in (2) are grammatical agents, individuals who actively instigate and control an action. An entirely different paradigm is used for grammatical patients, those affected but not in control: *wak-i:ta's* 'I'm sleeping', *ionkeni:-ta's* 'we two are sleeping', *ionkwén:-ta's* 'we all are sleeping'.

The transitive paradigms are much larger, because the transitive pronominal prefixes represent a combination of two parties: a grammatical agent and a grammatical patient. Not all features are distinguished in every combination, but there are nearly sixty different pronominal prefixes for most transitive verbs. A small sample of a transitive paradigm is in (3).

(3) Mohawk partial transitive paradigm: Rokwaho Dan Thompson, speaker

kón-hsere'	I'm following you
kení-hsere'	I'm following you two
kwá-hsere'	I'm following you all
ták-hsere'	you're following me
takení-hsere'	you're following us two
takwá-hsere'	you're following us all

The shape of each pronominal prefix is affected by the shapes of surrounding morphemes. The neuter agent, for example, appears variously as *ka-*, *ken-*, *w-*, and *i-* at the beginning of a word, *ka-* before consonants, *ken-* with stems beginning with *i* (*ka-i* > *ken*), *w-* before the vowels *a, e,* and *en,* and *i-* before the vowels *o* and *on.*

(4) Mohawk neuter agent 'it': Rokwaho Dan Thompson, speaker

<u>ka</u>-hnekíhrha'	<u>it</u> drinks
<u>kén</u>-tskote'	<u>it</u> is sitting, perched, at home
<u>w</u>-è:iahre'	<u>it</u> remembers
<u>i</u>-ó'kwats	<u>it</u> is digging

Elicitation is obviously an important tool for amassing a comprehensive record of the pronominal prefix system, a central part of the verbal morphology and the grammar as a whole. It is a quick way of determining whether number is distinguished in the prefixes, which it is: <u>s</u>-ó'kwats 'you (one) are digging', <u>sen</u>-ó'kwats 'you two are digging', <u>tsi</u>-ó'kwats 'you (three or more) are digging'; whether gender is distinguished, which it is: <u>r</u>-ó'kwats 'he is digging', <u>iak</u>-ó'kwats 'she is digging', <u>i</u>-ó'kwats 'it is digging'; and whether inclusive and exclusive are distinguished in first person, which they are: <u>ten</u>-ó'kwats 'you and I are digging', <u>iaken</u>-ó'kwats 'she and I are digging'. Obviously one could spend a long time recording spontaneous Mohawk speech waiting to hear a specific set of contrasting forms like these, or even a particular form such as 'we (he and I) remembered them (two women)'.

Yet in the realm of grammar, even more than in vocabulary, elicitation alone can lead to misinterpretation and, perhaps more often, keep us from discovering some of the most exciting features of a language, those we would not know enough to request.

As noted, the elicitation of paradigms like the Yup'ik sets in (1) can alert us to the fact that Yup'ik distinguishes singular, dual, and plural number in nouns. If the stimulus for forms in the target language always originates in the contact language, however, it can be easy to misinterpret the true functions of the elicited forms and the systems of which they are a part. Elicitation of singular and plural nouns from good Mohawk speakers can produce paradigms like those in (5).

(5) Mohawk nominal paradigms

áhta	shoe	otsikhè:ta'	sugar, candy
ahtahshòn:'a	shoes	otsikhe'ta'shòn:'a	candies
áhsire'	blanket	ono'ónsera	squash
ahsire'shòn:'a	blankets	ono'onserahshòn:'a	squashes

The analysis seems straightforward: the ending *=shòn:'a* appears to be a plural marker. But spontaneous speech in Mohawk contains surprisingly few occurrences of this ending, even when multiple objects are under discussion. In (6a) neither the term *raotitshé:nen* 'their domestic animal' nor the term *è:rhar* 'dog' is plural. The plural sense comes only from the pronominal prefix *konti-* 'they' in the verb. In (6b) the speaker had several apples, but there is no marker of plurality in the utterance at all.

(6) Mohawk nominals without plurals: Warisose Kaierithon, speaker
  a. *Ne raotitshé:nen*   *è:rhar*   *wa'kontiia'táhton*
     ne   raoti-tshenen   *è:rhar*   *wa'-konti-ia't-ahton*
     the 3.PL.POSS-domestic.animal dog FACTUAL-NEUTER.PL-body-disappear

     the their animal   dog they disappeared bodily
     Their dogs got lost.

  b. *sewahió:wane'*   *wátien.*   *Kóh, íisewak*
     se-w-ahi-owan-e'   *wak-i-en*   *koh i-sewa-k*
     one-NEUTER-fruit-be.large-ST 1.PATIENT-have-ST here EP-2.PL.AGENT-eat
     apple   I have   here eat, everyone
     I have some apples. Here, eat, everyone.

A closer look at the use of the clitic *=shòn:'a* in spontaneous speech shows that it is not actually a plural, but a distributive. It distributes entities over various situations, particularly over possessors or types. The speaker cited in (7) was describing a good homemaker. No number marking appears on the nouns 'hide' and 'fur': *kanéhon* could mean 'a hide' or 'hides', and *ówhare'* 'fur' or 'furs'. The distributive enclitic *=shòn:'a* appears on 'belongings' and 'blankets', however, because the homemaker made clothes for *each* member of her family, and individual blankets for *each one*.

(7) Mohawk distributives on nominals: Warisose Kaierithon, speaker
  Tiótkon   ionhkwennión:ni   *raonawenhshòn:'a*
  tiotkon   ie-ahkwenni-onni   *raon-awen=hshòn:'a*
  always   FEMININE.AGENT-clothing-make.IMPRF   3.PL.POSS-belonging=
                                                  DISTRIBUTIVE
  always   she clothing-makes   their various belonging(s)

  kanéhon   tánon'   ó'whare'   ióntstha',
  ka-nehon   tanon'   o-'whare'   ie-at-sth-ha'
  NEUTER-hide   and   NEUTER-fur   FEMININE.AGENT-MIDDLE-use-IMPRF
  skin(s)   and   fur(s)   she uses

  ne   ò:ni'   iakonnià:tha'   *ne   raonahsire'shòn:'a.*
  ne   ohni'   iak-onni-a't-ha'   *ne   raon-ahsire'=shòn:'a*
  the also   FEMININE.AGENT-make-INST-PRF the 3.PL.POSS-blanket=
                                                  DISTRIBUTIVE
  the also   she makes with (them)   the their various blanket(s)
  She was always making clothes and blankets from the animal skins.

Though the word *ahtahshòn:'a* was given as a translation of 'shoes' in (5), speakers do not use it for a pair of shoes; the simple noun *ahta* is more appropriate. The distributive form *ahtahshòn:'a* is used for a variety of different kinds of shoes, as in a shoe store. The basic noun *otsikhè:ta'* is used for sugar, a piece of candy, or even a whole basketful of candy canes; the distributive *otsikhe'ta'shòn:'a* is used for an array of different kinds of candy, perhaps candy canes, lollipops, fudge, etc. The noun *ono'ónsera* is used for a squash, melon, cucumber, or, for example, a bag of butternut squashes, a box of melons, or a basket of cucumbers; the distributive *ono'onserahshòn:'a* is used to cover the whole category of squashes, pumpkins, melons, and cucumbers, or to refer to a collection of different kinds of objects from the category. When devising labels for the aisles in a local grocery store, speakers came up with the term *ierakewahtha'shòn:'a* for the section displaying paper products: tissues, paper napkins, paper towels. (The term is based on *ie-rakew-aht-ha'* indefinite.agent-wipe-instrumental-imperfective 'one wipes with it'.) The distributive form would not be appropriate for an aisle displaying only paper towels.

Skilled Mohawk speakers often provide distributive forms ending in =*shòn:'a* as translations of English plural nouns, particularly when a contrast is set up in elicitation sessions, because they are straining to satisfy a request for a distinction that has no exact Mohawk equivalent. They themselves sometimes come up with paradigms like those in (5) when constructing curricula for Mohawk language classes, under pressure to produce materials acceptable to outside educational boards. Yet these same speakers do not use the distributive forms as simple plurals in their own speech, a fact that might not come to light under elicitation alone.

Another grammatical construction that has excited considerable theoretical interest is one termed 'switch reference'. Haiman and Munro (1983:ix) define the construction as follows: "Canonical switch-reference is an inflectional category of the verb, which indicates whether or not its subject is identical with the subject of some other verb." Among their examples are those in (8) from the Papuan language Usan.

(8) Usan switch reference: Reesink, cited in Haiman and Munro (1983: ix)

    a. *Ye   nam   su-<u>ab</u>*   *isomei.*
       I   tree   cut-SAME.SUBJECT   I.went.down
       I cut the tree and went down.

    b. *Ye   nam   su-<u>ine</u>*   *isorei.*
       I   tree   cut-DIFFERENT.SUBJECT   it.went.down
       I cut the tree and it went down. = I cut the tree down.

Switch reference would seem to be an easy construction to elicit. One simply asks a speaker for translations of English conjoined sentences: 'How do you say "John danced and sang"?,' and 'How do you say "John danced and Sam sang"?.' If different inflectional markers appear on the verbs in the two sentences, they are identified as markers of switch reference.

Central Pomo appears to offer just such a system. The sentences in (9) were elicited as translations of 'He sang and danced' and 'I sang and he danced'.

(9) Central Pomo switch reference: Frances Jack, speaker

a. $k^h\acute{e}$ $\check{c}e\cdot n\acute{o}\underline{n}$ $k^h\acute{e}$ $me\cdot n\acute{e}w.$
   $k^h\acute{e}$ $\check{c}an\acute{o}\text{-}\underline{in}$ $k^h\acute{e}$ $ma\text{-}n\acute{e}\text{-}w$
   song   sing-SAME   song   by.kicking-set-PERFECTIVE
   He sang and (<u>he</u>) danced.

b. $\Omega a\cdot$ $k^h\acute{e}$ $\check{c}e\cdot n\acute{o}w\underline{da}$ $mu\cdot l$ $k^h\acute{e}$ $me\cdot n\acute{e}w.$
   $\Omega a\cdot$ $k^h\acute{e}$ $can\acute{o}\text{-}w\text{=}\underline{da}$ $mu\cdot l$ $k^h\acute{e}$ $ma\text{-}n\acute{e}\text{-}w$
   1.AGT   song   sing-PERFECTIVE=DIFFERENT   3.AGT   song   by.kicking-set-PRF

<u>I</u> sang and <u>he</u> danced.

In (9a), where the subjects are the same, the ending -$(i)n$ appears on the first verb. In (9b), where the subjects are different, the ending =da appears on the first verb. Further elicitation seems to confirm the pattern.

Similar patterns also appear in spontaneous speech. In (10), where both clauses share the same subject, the first verb shows the ending -in.

(10) Central Pomo spontaneous speech: Frances Jack, speaker

   $Q^h\acute{a}$ $da\cdot l\acute{u}t\underline{in}$ $\underline{t}a\cdot$ $mu\cdot l$ $d\acute{o}\check{c}$
   $q^h\acute{a}$ $da\text{-}lu\text{-}\underline{t}\text{-}\underline{in}$ $\underline{t}a\cdot$ $mu\cdot l$ $d\acute{o}\text{-}\check{c}\text{-}\Omega$
   water   pushing-add-MULTIPLE.EVENT-SAME   guess   3.AGT   do-SML-PRF
   After adding water (to the leached acorns), she made it (bread).

In (11), where the subjects are different, the first verb shows the ending =da.

(11) Central Pomo spontaneous speech: Florence Paoli, speaker

   $Me\cdot nda$ ya $hl\acute{a}\cdot\Omega wac\underline{da},$
   $me\cdot nda$ ya $hla\text{-}\cdot\Omega w\text{-}ac\text{=}\underline{da}$
   while   1.PL.AGT   go.PL-around-IMPERFECTIVE.PL=DIFFERENT
   While <u>we</u> were walking around,

   $\hat{c}\acute{a}\cdot\Omega yem$ Ωel yal $p^hw\acute{\imath}w.$
   $\hat{c}\acute{a}\cdot\check{c}\text{-}yem\text{=}\Omega el$ yal $p^h\text{-}wi\text{-}w$
   man-old=the   1.PL.PAT   visually-perceive-PERFECTIVE
   <u>this old man</u> was looking at us.

But a closer look at natural speech reveals seeming exceptions to the pattern. The two clauses in (12) share the same subject 'he' (a particular man), but the marker =da DIFFERENT appears on the verb 'live'.

(12) Central Pomo spontaneous speech: Frances Jack, speaker

   $Q^h\acute{\imath}s\acute{a}\check{c}awda$ yal $\varsigma a\cdot l$ $\Omega\check{c}^h\acute{a}w\underline{da},$
   $q^h\acute{\imath}s\acute{a}\check{c}aw\text{=}da$ yal $\varsigma a\cdot l$ $\Omega\check{c}^h\acute{a}\text{-}w\text{=}\underline{da}$
   winter=at   1.PL.PAT   with   sit.SG-PERFECTIVE=<u>DIFFERENT</u>
   In the wintertime when <u>he</u> was living with us,

ʔma		mú·ṭu	síkčiw		ʔe.
ʔ=ma		mú·ṭu	sick-či-w		ʔe
COPULA=FACTUAL		3.PAT	sick-INCHOATIVE-PERFECTIVE		COPULA
<u>he</u> got sick.					

The clauses in (13) have different subjects, but the marker *-in* SAME appears.

(13) Central Pomo spontaneous speech: Eileen Oropeza, speaker

ʔá· kiy	kʰe	k̓úči· ʔel ṭayal
ʔá·=kiy	kʰe	k̓úči·=ʔel=ṭayal
1.AGT=too	1.POSS	children=the=PLURAL.PATIENT

Me too, my grandchildren,

béda	yáʔkʰe	híntil	kʰé ʔel	ba·néhdu<u>n</u>,
bé=da	yá=ʔkʰe	híntil	kʰé=ʔel	ba-né-h-du-<u>n</u>
this=at	1.PL.POSS	Indian	song=the	stepping-set-PRF-IMPRF-SAME

when <u>I</u> dance an Indian dance,

ʔúda·w	šwáyli	q̓lúṭa·ĉaĉ.
ʔúda·w	šwáy=li	qalú-ṭ-aĉ-aĉ
really	laughter=with	die.PLURAL-MULTIPLE.EVENT-IMPRF.PL-IMPRF.PL

<u>they</u> just die laughing.

Most fieldworkers would probably agree that speakers rarely make mistakes; when their speech fails to conform to the analysis, it is usually the analysis that is faulty. This construction is no exception. The markers *-in* and *=da* are not actually indicators of switch reference, but rather part of a paradigm of clause linkers, used to join related ideas into single sentences. There are three pair of such markers. One pair is used in irrealis constructions such as conditionals, imperatives, and most futures, and is translated variously 'if', 'when', and 'and'. The other two pair are used in realis constructions. One of these links consecutive events and is typically translated 'and then'. The other links simultaneous events or states and is translated 'while', 'when', 'whenever', or occasionally 'and'.

(14) Central Pomo clause linkers (Mithun 1993):

	SAME	DIFFERENT	
Irrealis	*-hi*	*=hla*	if, when, and
Realis			
Consecutive	*-ba*	*=li*	and then
Simultaneous	*-in*	*=da*	while, when, whenever, and

The SAME and DIFFERENT markers indicate whether speakers are packaging the events described together as elements of a single main event (SAME) or separately as distinct events (DIFFERENT). Actions packaged together are typically performed by the same agent, within the same time frame, at the same location, etc. It is thus not surprising that the SAME linkers *-hi*, *-ba*, and *-in* appear most often to link clauses sharing the same subject in their English translations. Actions performed by different people are most often packaged as distinct events, so the DIFFERENT linkers =*hla*, =*li*, and =*da* most often link clauses with different subjects. But the actual function of the linkers is not to mark reference. In (12) 'When he was living with us, he got sick', living with the speaker's family and getting sick were packaged as distinct situations even though the same man was involved in both. In (13), the dancing and laughing were packaged together as parts of a single event, though the first was done by the speaker and the second by her grandchildren.

The functional distinction between the markers is neatly mirrored in their forms. The morphemes linking components of the SAME event are verbal suffixes, tightly attached to the verb. Those linking DIFFERENT events are clausal enclitics, loosely attached to the clause as a whole (which is usually verb-final). The system provides speakers with choices for packaging information. If the analysis of the markers were based entirely on sentences elicited as translations from English, their true functions might never be apparent; the way they fit structurally into the rest of the grammar would remain obscure; and the powerful ways in which they are exploited by speakers might never be appreciated.

An obvious value of the documentation of natural connected speech is that it permits us to notice distinctions and patterns that we might not know enough to elicit, and that might not even be sufficiently accessible to the consciousness of speakers to be volunteered or retrievable under direct questioning. This material is in many ways the most important and exciting of all. Linguistic theory will never be moved ahead as far by answers to questions we already know enough to ask as it will by discoveries of the unexpected. A simple example can be seen in Central Pomo. In response to a request for a sentence meaning 'I almost fell down', Frances Jack, a highly skilled speaker, gave the Central Pomo translation in (15).

(15) Central Pomo elicited translation: Frances Jack, speaker
ṭoˑ   *čʰnáˑwsiw*
ṭoˑ   *čʰnáˑ-w=si-w*
1.SG.PATIENT   fall-PERFECTIVE-almost-PERFECTIVE
I almost fell.

In spontaneous conversation, however, a slightly different form appears.

(16) Central Pomo spontaneous phrasing: Frances Jack, speaker
čʰnáˑwsiwwiya
čʰnáˑw=siw=wiya
FALL-PERFECTIVE=ALMOST=PERSONAL.AFFECT
I almost fell.

The ending =*wiya* on the verb is part of an evidential system used by speakers to specify the source and reliability of information they are communicating. Another evidential marker can be seen in the passage in (17), again from spontaneous conversation. The enclitic =*ka* indicates that the source of the information is inference on the part of the speaker.

(17) Central Pomo inferential evidential: Florence Paoli, speaker

Shirleywet̓   *našóyya*   *ʔdúčka...*
Shirley=wet̓   *našóy=ya*   *ʔdú-č-ʔ=ka*
Shirley=POSSESSIVE   young.lady=NEW.TOPIC   marry-SEMELFACTIVE-
                                                      PRF=INFERENTIAL

He must have married Shirley's daughter.
[That's why I didn't understand at first.]

Mu·lʔkaman   *Shirleywet̓*   *našóy*   *ʔdúč*
mu·l=ʔ=ka=man   *Shirley=wet̓*   *našóy*   *ʔdú-č-ʔ*
that=COPULA=INFERENTIAL=that   Shirley=POSS   young.lady   marry-
                                                                                  SML-PRF

It must have been Shirley's daughter he married.

The evidential enclitic =*ma* in (18) below is a factual, indicating that the information expressed is established general knowledge.

(18) Central Pomo factual evidential: Florence Paoli, speaker

mi·   *q̓dí*   *čó·čkaw*   *mu·lʔma*
mi·   *q̓dí*   *čó·-č-ka-w*   *mu·l=ʔ=ma*
there   good   become-SEMELFACTIVE-CAUSATIVE-PRF   that=COPULA=
                                                                              FACTUAL

It turned out to be a pretty good thing.

Two more evidential enclitics can be seen in (19). Three Central Pomo speakers had been sitting around a table conversing for hours, enjoying the company and intent on creating a record of natural speech. The use of evidentials specifying the source of information can be seen in Mrs. Paoli's suggestion that they take a breather. The clitic =*ya* in the first line indicates that she personally witnessed the event she is relaying ('my tape wore out'), and the clitic =*la* in the clitic second line that she actively performed and controlled the action herself ('I said ...').

(19) Central Pomo experiential evidentials: Florence Paoli, Frances Jack, speakers

FP   *Kʰe*   *tapeʔel*   *čʰóčya*
      kʰe   *tape=ʔel*   *čʰó-č=ya*
      my   tape=the   not.exist-INCHOATIVE-EXPERIENTIAL.EVIDENTIAL

      My tape wore out.

[FJ to MM: Did we run out of tape (on the tape recorder)?]

FP   *ṭo·*   *ʔe*   *čʰóčay*
      ṭo·   *ʔe*   *čʰó-č-ay*
      1.SG.PATIENT   COPULA   not.exist-INCHOATIVE-DISTRIBUTIVE

híihduwla
hii-h-du-w=*la*
say-SEMELFACTIVE-IMPERFECTIVE-PERFECTIVE=PERFORMATIVE.EVIDENTIAL
I said I'm the one who ran out.

FJ *čanú   čʰóčay*
    čanú   čʰó-č-ay
    word   not.exist-INCHOATIVE-DISTRIBUTIVE
    No more words.   [laughter]

The evidential markers are so well integrated into the grammar that their use is largely unconscious. If one tries to elicit them with English prompts such as 'I heard that . . .' or 'It is a known fact that . . .' or 'Apparently . . .', speakers provide translations with full verbs, adverbials, or clauses.

The Central Pomo evidential markers often do more than specify the source and reliability of information. As in many languages, they can also function to structure discourse. If the only function of hearsay evidentials in narrative, for example, were to specify the fact that the narrator had heard the story from someone else rather than witnessing it at first hand, a hearsay evidential should appear just once at the beginning of a story. But these evidentials typically appear throughout narratives, at specific points. The hearsay evidential *ʔdo·* is underlined in the passage in (20). Here, each line represents an intonation unit; indentation represents a continuation in the fall of pitch; periods represent a final pitch fall; and lines flush left begin with a pitch reset.

(20) Central Pomo hearsay evidentials: Frances Jack, speaker

Bal maṭú· ʔel ʔdoma,	This story, they say
ƙúči· yačó·kʰeṭ maṭú·maṭu·maw,	has been told for children
ʔiʔwíya·=kay,	about Coyote and
šá·ǫawo·lo.	the Waterdogs.
ʔiʔwí čá·č ʔel ʔdoma, . . .	Coyote Man, they say,
wáymin . . .	is always
ma· baʔnáwan hé· ma·	fooling people or
dú·du· ma· yhé·n.	playing pranks on people.
Bal ʔdoma,	Now, they say, a certain
mačí há·n.	day was coming.
Mu·l ʔdoma. . .	And here they say . . .
bal napʰóʔli ʔdoma,	at this village, they say
šṭú· šbúma·ʦe·n;	there will be basketweaving;
ʔel ʔelya	whichever one
báʔanhaw ǫdí šbúw ʔel	weaves the best
mú·ṭu ʔdoma ʔúda·w loǫ maná·ʔyawʔkʰe.	will be paid a lot of things.
Bal ʔdoma ʔul . . . ʔiʔyúʔčawʔkʰe.	Now, they say they're going to start.

The quotative evidential serves to structure the text, appearing with new scenes and topics of discussion, and often in summary or evaluative statements at the ends of passages. Such a discourse function would of course not be seen in elicitation.

A third type of methodology is sometimes used in linguistic work with speakers: the elicitation of judgments. The researcher constructs a sentence and asks speakers whether the sentence is grammatical or not, or whether one referring expression is coreferent with another. The method can provide quick answers to specific queries, but, particularly in the documentation of endangered languages, it should be used with caution. Speakers typically find it easy to voice judgments about such matters as appropriate allomorphy (*indecided* versus *undecided*), and, in languages with relatively rigid constituent orders, alternative orders (*under the table* versus *table the under*, or *John apples likes* versus *John likes apples*). But particularly at higher levels of structure, intuitions are not always as accessible or as easily articulated. Sentences invented by a non-speaker may be deemed incorrect for a wide variety of reasons, from mispronunciation to inappropriate lexical choice to the pragmatic incompatibility of co-occurring syntactic structures. Conversely, ungrammatical sentences may be accepted because they represent a laudatory effort by a non-native speaker. Grammaticality judgments often do not actually pertain to the issue at hand, and the introduction of invented data into the literature can distort the record of the language.

2.   The role of the speaker

An important ingredient in productive fieldwork is an appreciation of the central role and unique contributions of speakers. This point might seem so obvious as to not merit mention, but consciousness of it can have a substantial effect on the quality of both the experience and the record produced.

Communities and speakers can differ considerably in their awareness of and attitudes to their language. For some, language provides a strong, conscious symbol of identity, a cultural resource to be cultivated and enjoyed; for others, it is simply a utilitarian tool, given little attention. Sometimes skilled speakers fear that they know nothing about their mother tongue, because they did not learn it formally in school and their knowledge is largely unconscious. During the early stages of collaboration, it is important that the speaker realize that he or she is the expert, that the way a skilled speaker speaks *is* the essence of the language. This realization can be facilitated in several ways. One is by beginning with questions that require little concentration under stress and that elicit material the speaker is certain to know, such as counting from one to ten. It is important at this point and beyond to be aware of what speakers can be expected to be conscious of. It would be a mistake to initiate fieldwork by asking how many consonants there are in the language, whether tone is distinctive, whether the language is ergative, or whether there is switch-reference. Responses to such questions come from linguistic analysis, not from native-speaker intuition. Demanding answers to such questions, even with less technical terminology, can make speakers highly uncomfortable, and can result in responses that lead the researcher down the wrong track. It can also create an unfortunate social situation in which the researcher openly rejects opinions that have been offered, on demand, by the speaker.

Particularly in the early stages of collaboration, the contribution of the speaker can be shaped in powerful ways by small actions on the part of the linguist. Speakers are often working hard to understand just what is desired, since the responsibilities of a linguistic consultant are not everyday knowledge in most societies. If I ask for names of trees, my goal is fairly clear. But when the speaker volunteers further information, such as other words that sound like 'oak', the literal meaning of the term for 'black oak', where black oak trees grow, what the wood is used for, how acorn mush is made, or what happened the year there were no acorns, I can react in various ways. I can steer the speaker back onto my track, either by interrupting gently or by waiting politely until he or she comes to a stopping place. Or I can listen attentively, and I can write down what is said. My response can convey more forcefully than words the value I place on each kind of information offered, and, in turn, determine what will be volunteered in future work. (Like all people, of course, speakers differ in their sensitivity to the attitudes of those around them.) In my own experience I have found it worthwhile to write down almost everything offered by speaker-consultants. I may not be sufficiently knowledgable at the time to appreciate the implications of what is being said, but, over and over, comments volunteered by speakers have later provided the key to analyses, confirmed budding hypotheses, or unveiled aspects of the language I might never have discovered on my own. Speakers also have background knowledge of context that an outsider may lack, particularly in small communities where much common knowledge is assumed. Speakers know about local history, geography, customary and expected behavior, and relationships among people living and dead. For the fieldworker, a command of basic vocabulary and grammar may not be enough to make sense out of what people are saying as they talk, a necessary prerequisite to insightful grammatical analysis.

One subtle attitude on the part of the researcher can have a particularly important effect in shaping the record. It has been my experience that good speakers have a sense of the difference between not only what is grammatical and what is ungrammatical, but also of what is said and what could be said but is not. Such intuition is easy to stifle if the wrong signals are given. Central Pomo, like many languages of western North America, contains verbal prefixes indicating the means or manner of action. Thus in addition to the verb *yá·q̓* 'know', there are derived verbs *ba-yá·q̓* 'obey' (recognize by sound), *da-yá·q̓* 'recognize by feeling with the hands', *ʔ-yá·q̓* 'recognize by touch (with fingers)', *pʰ-yá·q̓* 'recognize by sight', *qa-yá·q̓* 'recognize food by tasting', and *s-yá·q̓* 'recognize drink by tasting'. These prefixes occur in large numbers of verbs. Built on the verb *ṭáw* 'feel, sense', there are derived verbs *ba-ṭáw* 'hear' ('sense by sound'), *da-ṭáw* 'feel with the hand', *ʔ-ṭáw* 'touch with the fingers', *pʰ-ṭáw* 'see, appear', *qa-ṭáw* 'taste food', *s-ṭáw* 'taste a drink'. There are other prefixes in the set as well, as in *ča-ṭáw* 'feel by sitting or lying, as a hard chair or lumpy bed', *h-ṭáw* 'feel with a stick, as testing the depth of water', *m-ṭáw* 'feel warmth, be cooked', *š-ṭáw* 'heft, lift an object to see how heavy it is', and *čʰ-ṭáw* 'feel, as the hard shell of walnuts when cracking them'. But not all possible combinations of prefixes and roots occur. There are, for example, no verbs **ča-yá·q̓* 'recognize by sitting' or **š-yá·q̓* 'recognize by dangling'. When asked about such possibilities Mrs. Jack would answer something like 'that would mean to recognize by sitting, but it's not a word in our language'. All aspects of her answer are interesting. The first part shows that, on some level, the structure of the system is accessible to her. She did not read or write the language or do technical linguistic analysis, so this was part of her knowledge as a speaker. The second part demonstrates the distinction between possible and actual words. It is not surprising that speakers have felt little need to coin words meaning 'recognize by sitting' and 'recognize by dangling'. The prefixes are used to create labels for nameworthy concepts, lexical items that are created for the purpose at hand. The meanings of the formations are not necessarily equivalent to the sum of their parts. A combination of the prefix *h-* 'by poking, jabbing' with the root *yól* 'mix' yields *h-yól* 'add salt or pepper' (from the motion used with a salt shaker); the combination *s-* 'by sucking' with *yól* 'mix' yields *s-yól* 'eat bread, cookies, doughnuts, etc., and wash them down with tea or coffee'. Good consultants can become quickly attuned to the interests of researchers with whom they collaborate. It is all too easy to get caught up in the systematicity of structural patterns and squelch fine intuitions about the actual status of constructions. Often structures formed by analogy in the heat of passionate elicitation do not actually exist in the language, for important reasons.

Speakers vary in their interests and talents, and a sensitivity to this variation can be helpful in making the best use of their contributions. Some speakers have astounding vocabularies and are highly articulate in discussing lexical differences, skillfully describing fine shades of meaning and pinpointing the contexts in which particular lexical items are used. Other speakers are intrigued by grammatical structure and are thrilled to discover the vast systematicity underlying their skills. As speaker-linguists, they can bring relevant material to discussions that a linguist alone might never unearth; they can mull over questions that would hold little interest for non-linguists; and they can contribute valuable judgments about the meanings and functions of particular constructions. Some speakers are especially sensitive to nuances of style and register, able to point out the effects of lexical and grammatical choices. Some are talented storytellers. For many speakers, the collaborative endeavor opens up an exciting world of intellectual discovery; for others, its value lies more in the social relationship that evolves between collaborators. In all cases, being attuned to the special skills and tastes of speaker-collaborators can make a substantial difference in the success of the enterprise.

In many ways, the more the speaker is invited to shape the record, the richer the documentation of the language, and the more we will learn about the extent to which languages can vary. In communities with large numbers of speakers, in which the language is used in a variety of contexts, certain kinds of documentation are feasible that are impossible elsewhere, such as comparisons of language use across different ages, genders, social groups, geographical areas, and contexts. But even where speakers are few, the more we can document speech in its natural function, in spontaneous interaction among speakers, with the give and take of true communication, the more we can learn about the language in its own terms. Speakers often shape the record most effectively when they are given the opportunity to choose what to say and how to say it.

3.   The role of the linguist

Of course linguists do more than hold the microphone. They shape the record in obvious ways, such as selecting certain lines of research and methodology. They can also shape it in more subtle ways. Some ways come from individual styles of interaction. Others are rooted in preparation before the work begins, both practical and intellectual. It is certainly useful to learn as much as possible beforehand about the history, culture, and physical environment of the community in which the language is spoken, and what equipment should be taken along for living and working in the community. It also crucial, particularly now as numbers of speakers are shrinking and time is of the essence, that the fieldworker bring as much technical skill and theoretical awareness to the project as possible.

Especially in work with an endangered language, experience in phonetic transcription and basic linguistic analysis is a must. The time and patience of speakers are too precious to waste. Distinctions missed the first time around will certainly slow down the work and may never be caught at all.

Good training should also result in an ability to identify gaps in the record, forms and constructions that can be predicted to exist but which are unattested. If early in work with Mohawk speakers I discover that there is a verb *ró'kwats* 'he is digging' (as in example (2)), I can predict that there should be a verb 'they are digging'. The answer is likely to be reliable: *ronnó'kwats* 'they are digging'. I can then check the shape of this prefix with other verb stems, as in *rati-hnekíhrha'* 'they drink'. I could have predicted that a masculine plural form of the verb 'drink' should exist, but I could not have predicted that its shape would be *rati-*.

At the same time, it is important to develop a sensitivity to the difference between filling gaps and creating structure. Particularly for disappearing languages, the record should provide a true representation of the language; otherwise some of the inherent logic of the grammar may be obscured, and future theoreticians may forever be trying to integrate non-occurring structures into their models of language. One day an excellent speaker of an interesting language came to see me, nearly in tears. He had been hired by another scholar to help out in a field methods class, and had been enjoying the early work. He had no trouble coming up with words in his language as they were requested, and he repeated every word over and over with infinite patience and brilliant clarity. At this point, however, he confessed that he realized he was not a good speaker at all and should not be the one entrusted with the work. He was being asked for translations of sentences like 'The ball was hit by the man', and 'The cat was chased by the dog'. Try as he might, he simply did not know the answers. In fact his language does not contain a passive construction. Other grammatical devices are used for foregrounding and backgrounding participants, and for focusing on resultant states. He had tried producing word-for-word equivalents of the English passives, but was sensitive enough to recognize that they were not part of the language. His sensitivity was actually one of the reasons he was such a fine consultant. Another speaker might have capitulated, allowing the word-for-word calques to remain in the record. The forms would have been the product of competence in English, not the resources of the language under study.

Preparation for fieldwork must also include a solid background in linguistic theory. The interplay between theory and data is especially dynamic in the context of field research. The more we know about the grammatical categories and patterns that have already been recognized in languages, and about how they are predicted to interact, the more effective we will be at identifying them in the language under study and at noticing exceptions to expected patterns. Someone naively expecting all languages to follow the nominative/accusative pattern of English, for example, could experience considerable anguish when confronted with a language exhibiting ergative/absolutive case marking. If ergative systems were already familiar, however, the pattern could be recognized early on the basis of relatively little data, and the researcher could move on to investigate the special properties of the system at hand. This might involve, for example, watching for the distribution of the pattern and noting whether it appears in all tenses, aspects, and moods; with all persons; with both nouns and pronouns; and whether it governs clause-combining constructions. At the same time, insights gained through sensitive fieldwork come back to shape theory, enriching the theoretical tools that future researchers can bring to their own fieldwork.

4.   Conclusion

The impending disappearance of so many languages calls for special attention to the goals of current fieldwork and the best methods for achieving them. In this context, it is not appropriate to limit the record to data pertinent to issues of current theoretical interest. What we choose to document now may be all the information available to future descendants of speakers curious about their linguistic heritage. It may also be the only material available to future researchers seeking answers to questions we do not yet know enough to ask. We cannot hope to anticipate all future needs, but we can consider the kinds of decisions that will shape the record produced. Among such decisions are choice of methodologies, the roles assumed by speaker-collaborators, and the training and preparation of researchers. Much current fieldwork consists of direct elicitation of individual words and sentences in the target language. This procedure can be effective when one is first becoming acquainted with the phonology and morphology of an unfamiliar language, and for compiling substantial lists of basic vocabulary. But if the research is limited to eliciting translations of English vocabulary and syntactic constructions, collecting grammaticality judgments, and checking off known typological diagnostics, we may miss what is unexpected about the language under study. In so doing, we risk depriving the speakers' descendants of what is special about their heritage, and we lose opportunities to expand our own theoretical horizons. If speakers are allowed to speak for themselves, creating a record of spontaneous speech in natural communicative settings, we have a better chance of providing the kind of record that will be useful to future generations. The search for what is special in a language does not necessarily entail a rejection of the quest for language universals. It can provide the opportunity to arrive at finer and deeper generalizations that are grounded in real language, rather than conjecture.

NOTE ON TRANSCRIPTION

1. The Central Alaskan Yup'ik and Mohawk examples cited here are given in the practical orthographies currently in use in the communities in which the languages are spoken. The symbols used for Yup'ik, along with their approximate phonetic values, are: p [p], t [t], c [ts] or [tʃ], k [k], q [q]; voiced fricatives v [v], l [l], s [z], y [y], g [ɣ], r [ʁ], ug [ɣʷ], ur [ʁʷ]; voiceless fricatives vv [f], ll [ɬ], ss [s], gg [x], rr [χ], urr [χʷ]; nasals m [m], n [n], ng [ŋ]; and vowels i [i] or [e], a [a], u [u] or [o], e [ə]. The apostrophe, seen in the name Yup'ik, indicates that the preceding syllable is stressed in contexts where regular phonological rules would predict it to be unstressed.

In the Mohawk practical orthography, oral obstruents are t [t, d], k [k, g], and s [s]; resonants are n [n], r [r] or [l], w [w], and i [y before a vowel]; laryngeals h [h], and ' [ʔ]; oral vowels i [i], e [e], a [a], o [o]; and nasal vowels en [ʌ̃] and on [ũ]. An acute accent (´) indicates stress with high or rising tone, and a grave accent (`) indicates stress with falling tone. The colon (:) indicates vowel length.

The Central Pomo examples are cited in standard Americanist phonetic symbols. In the second line of block examples, hyphens (−) set off affixes, and the equals sign (=) sets off clitics.

REFERENCES

Boas, Franz. 1917. Introductory. *International Journal of American Linguistics* 1:1–8.
Carlson, Barry, and Pauline Flett. 1989. *Spokane Dictionary*. (University of Montana Occasional Papers in Linguistics, 6) Missoula, Montana.
Darnell, Regna. 1996. What are texts for these days? In *Studies in Honour of H. C. Wolfart*, ed. John D. Nichols and Arden C. Ogg, pp. 163–70. Winnipeg: Algonquian and Iroquoian Linguistics.
Goddard, Ives. 1996. The description of the native languages of North America before Boas. *Handbook of North American Indians* 17:17–42.
Haiman, John, and Pamela Munro (eds.). 1983. *Switch Reference and Universal Grammar*. Amsterdam: John Benjamins.
Jacobson, Stephen. 1984. *Yup'ik Eskimo Dictionary*. Fairbanks: Alaska Native Language Center.
Mithun, Marianne. 1993. "Switch-reference": clause combining in Central Pomo. *International Journal of American Linguistics* 59:119–36.
     1996. The description of the native languages of North America: Boas and after. *Handbook of North American Indians* 17:43–63.

3   Places and people: field sites and informants

Gerrit J. Dimmendaal

When linguistic research takes place in the natural setting where the language under investigation is spoken rather than at a desk in an air-conditioned office at one's home university, this has consequences for the endeavor. In the field, one becomes part of a social network in the speech community under investigation, and thus this type of research necessarily involves as much personal and social effort as it does linguistic "brain work."

Descriptive linguistics appears to have more standard ways of working with informants than, say, ethnography does. In current anthropology, skepticism about the ethnographer's ability to understand and convey (what are assumed to be) subjective experiences encountered in the field seems to dominate the discussion. In empirical linguistic research, one may also run into epistemological problems, some of which the linguistic field-worker – and the theoretical linguist consulting descriptive sources – can ill afford to ignore. The interpretation of most linguistic signs requires a context in time and space. Researchers have to try and find out whether variation in speech between informants they consult are the result of elicitation techniques or whether they truly reflect linguistically interesting variables in the data. Formalizing linguistic field methods is possible only to a certain extent. The rest depends on the serendipity of the individual linguist and elusive insights that no clearly defined eliciting procedure seems to be able to insure. Below, I present some practical guidelines for the basic investigation of (relatively) undescribed languages that is to be carried out in conjunction with native-speaker informants. Although my own fieldwork experience has been mostly in remote areas of Kenya and Ethiopia, I believe that what I am presenting are widely accepted and approved methods that have proved to be useful as analytical tools by a variety of linguists working around the globe.

1.   Preparing oneself for the field

There is usually a scientific and a practical side to preparing oneself for a field trip. At the risk of stating the obvious, let us go step-by-step through some of these aspects.

For most parts of the world, genetic relationships between languages are fairly well understood, at least at the lower levels. Studying all available literature on the language itself is of course essential, but looking at material on related languages is also an important way of preparing for the field. In some parts of the world, however, genetic relationships are remote, or one is dealing with what appear to be linguistic isolates – at least given our current understanding. When planning to investigate such a language, for example in South America or Papua New Guinea, gaining knowledge about unrelated languages in the area is the best alternative way of preparing oneself for the field since they will probably manifest significant areal features, such as tone or ergativity.

It is also important to familiarize oneself with what is known about the culture of the speakers of the language for a number of reasons. In the first place, cultural factors – using this term in the broadest possible sense – may have a direct impact on the language, as in the case of kinship systems or color terminology. But equally important, the more one knows in advance about the culture, the more one can avoid personal and cultural transgressions that could jeopardize one's ability to work in a particular community.

Having done all the background reading, one has to face the necessary practical arrangements to be made for a field trip with respect to transportation, permissions, health, and finances (see Newman 1992). Getting into contact with researchers or other individuals who know the area in question is undoubtedly the best way of obtaining information on logistic matters. Most people are more than willing to share their hard-earned knowledge, and thus one should not feel shy about asking for information from people even though they may be total strangers. The prevalence of e-mail nowadays makes communication easy and inexpensive.

Empirical linguists inevitably have to face practical and political realities of fieldwork situations. Many countries where little-documented languages are spoken require the investigator to submit a research proposal in order to obtain research clearance and a long-term visa. Although administrative efficiency, or the lack thereof, varies tremendously from country to country, one needs to be prepared for the worst, that is, one cannot overestimate how long the process may take. Some researchers try to bypass the normal requirements by entering the country where the research is to be carried out on a short-term tourist visa with the idea of regularizing their status later. Whether this is advisable – or ethical – will vary from circumstance to circumstance, but it is always a risky proposition.

Once in the country, contacting and visiting officials at the ministerial level, as well as at the regional and local level, tends to be part and parcel of the procedure for obtaining research clearance. Sometimes such officials go beyond the call of duty in that they "suggest" names of individuals who, according to them, would make excellent informants for the researcher in question. It is important, however, that the researcher remain in control when selecting informants. In this respect, I strongly subscribe to the view expressed by Wax (1971: 368) that "[whereas] getting the assistance or protection of powerful officials is generally a good idea, too close an association with leaders or 'important people' can greatly limit the scope of fieldwork."[1]

For researchers going out into the field, in particular those doing so as part of their "rite of passage" for a Ph.D. (or, less commonly, an MA) degree, time is money; the sooner one can start the actual research, the better. But one may not always meet with interest in one's project at all official levels of the host country. The fieldworker may be keen on getting to the field as quickly as possible, but he or she needs to build in a margin for delays in obtaining proper research clearance before actually starting in on the work. Apart from personal interests, it is wrong to jeopardize opportunities for future researchers by failing to play by the official rules of the host country when it comes to scientific research and research clearance.

In this connection, it is crucial to affiliate oneself with universities or other teaching and/or research institutions in the host country. By so doing, one can find out about ongoing research by fellow scholars who share common interests. Also, the future of the field is best guaranteed when those with training in linguistics in the host country are involved in active projects. One might even want to consider making use of undergraduates or graduate students from an Arts faculty or linguistics program as research assistants at some point during the fieldwork. Relations with the host institution can be strengthened by offering to give lectures on work in progress from time to time during the fieldwork year.

2.   The field site

Assuming that one has successfully arrived in Kenya or Brazil or Thailand armed with the appropriate permissions and research clearances, there is still the important question of where one actually wants to settle in order to carry out the research (not to mention how to get there). For some remote areas it is sometimes preferable, or even necessary, to settle in a town outside the actual area where the language to be investigated is spoken. I myself have been in situations in the field where my presence, though officially licensed by authorities at the ministerial level, was not appreciated by local authorities. The latter were afraid that an outsider might interfere with some of their illegal practices and therefore tried every way they could to force me out of the area. Sometimes it is inadvisable to stay right where the language is spoken for reasons of personal safety, whether having to do with political unrest, civil war, rampant lawlessness, endemic health problems, or virulent epidemics. In some parts of the world, food supplies are insufficient to host a guest, even if he or she is willing to pay handsomely. In such cases, researchers may be able to stay only if they bring their own supplies, which for long stays is not a simple matter.[2] At times it is simply easier and more efficient (and more comfortable) to work with informants outside their home area.[3] In general, one has to decide for oneself whether one can cope, both physically and emotionally, with local circumstances, recognizing that one is often talking about a long period of isolation and possible hardship, not just a weekend safari.

At any rate, one needs time to get adjusted to the field situation and to establish rapport with the people whose language one intends to study. When settling down with the intention of spending several months or more in an area, acceptance by the speech community is crucial. (My experience is that the actual reception accorded to the field linguist differs widely across societies and even between neighboring groups.) As Wax (1971: 50) has argued, one will probably always remain an outsider; but one can at least try and become an integral, participating, and hopefully respected member of the local community. One should not be disappointed, however, if acceptance seems terribly slow: it often takes a considerable amount of time before bonds of mutual trust are established in the social limbo between two distinct cultures. In choosing to work in a community, the investigator has to be prepared for personal and social frustration along with the intellectual excitement. Good personal relationships with individual members of the community are of great importance, because they can serve as guides through the cultural complexities of the community.

The community whose language one intends to analyze often does not understand what the foreign investigator is after, and thus interest in their speech may be met with surprise. It is not uncommon to be confronted with a negative attitude by speakers toward their own language "because it has no writing tradition." Realizing that their language can be written, just like the more prestigious languages in the area that already have writing systems, may help to boost the self-esteem of the speech community in question and stimulate their interest in the linguist's work.

3.   Selecting and working with informants

Once one is settled in a suitable area, one may start looking for informants. Whether informants require payment for their service or not depends on local cultural norms. In some areas, payment would be taken as an insult; in others, non-payment would be unthinkable. If there is to be payment, one needs to find out what wages are appropriate by talking to people who know the area. The researcher – who from a local perspective is inevitably deemed to be rich – doesn't want to be thought of as a cheapskate; at the same time, paying wages far above the local scale can cause dissension and disruption. Where direct payment is inappropriate, there are usually alternative ways of providing remuneration, e.g., contributing to the education of relatives or to the acquisition of practical household materials. Anyone who has suffered through the ordeal of buying Christmas presents or gifts to be taken home to friends after a long trip realizes how time consuming such activities are. Linguists who work in an area where cash payments can be made are the lucky ones! Linguists who don't work in such areas, however, cannot shirk the responsibility of finding out what needs to be done and devoting the time necessary to doing it properly.

Situations may also change rapidly. Over the past few decades professional photographers, for example, have traveled around the world in order to produce picturesque documents of societies in remote areas, usually with well-furnished working budgets because the commercial success of their final products is guaranteed beforehand. Because such commercial photographers sometimes pay hundreds of dollars for a few snapshots of "the wild and exotic," they cause difficulties for low-budget researchers – a category to which many linguistic and anthropological fieldworkers belong, especially graduate students – since the financial expectations of the informants have been raised too high. I had such an experience during a field trip to the Surmic area in southwestern Ethiopia with an Ethiopian colleague. Rather than give in to the inflated rate, we decided to try and bring remuneration for informants' services back in line with the more regular wages in the area. Real diplomatic skills were needed in order to explain our position, and although it discouraged a number of speakers from acting as informants, we eventually did find willing and competent speakers to work with us.

It should be kept in mind that there is a widely held view by informants that researchers will get rich by doing what they are doing. Surely, the fieldworker is financially far better off back home than the average informant – although the relatively low priority accorded to empirical linguistic research at many universities nowadays makes the ultimate "pay off" for the research endeavor somewhat hazardous. And as a presumably wealthy linguistic investigator, one may have to assume willy-nilly the role of (temporary) employer, something that most Ph.D. students are not prepared for. Because of the extra cash being pumped into the system, the potential impact of a researcher's presence, albeit temporary, should not be underestimated.

Given the financial incentives, there are usually a number of individuals offering their help as informants. Not just anyone, however, is a reliable data supplier, for practical as well as scientific reasons. An informant must be available for reasonable periods of time, ideally several hours a day. Even when informants turn out to be particularly good, one often has to give them time off or release them from their linguistic work so that they can carry out their actual job or handle other ongoing responsibilities. Getting used to regular schedules, Western ideas of punctuality, and fixed working hours is another factor of adaptation that may take time. Good informants are not necessarily born as such; many have to be molded and nurtured.

The gender issue often plays a role in informant selection as well. One comes across stories where female investigators working with male informants or male investigators working with female informants cause the spouses of the informants to become jealous because of the daily contact with the researcher. In many societies, it would be totally out of the question for a male researcher to work with a woman (unless, perhaps, she were quite old). There is usually less prohibition against women researchers working with men, although they may be subjected to sexual harassment, especially if they are single (and more especially if they disregard local dress codes and standards of propriety).

It is common for linguists to work with only two or three principal informants (if not just one!). By consulting only one informant, there is a risk of unnecessarily attaching relevance to idiosyncratic usages of that particular speaker. This relates to the representativeness problem. Of course, one wants a corpus that is representative of the speech community at large. In order to make valid inferences about a particular language, consultation with several informants is to be preferred. It also provides better protection against error. Where there is a choice, i.e., where several good informants are available, this opportunity should be taken.

The desirability of having multiple informants also follows from the fact that different informants may have different talents. One intelligent informant who is well trained may be adequate during the initial stages of the research; but as the research develops, more specific talents may be required from different informants. That is, their required roles may vary with the particular goals one has in mind, as well as with the domains of grammar on which one intends to concentrate.

In looking for specific details, for example concerning specialized vocabulary, one usually requires several additional informants who may be consulted on a more *ad hoc* basis. In my work on Turkana, for example, I noticed that elderly women had an excellent knowledge of names for local medicinal plants. The same speakers would not have qualified as useful informants, for example, in eliciting complex paradigms. Specialized vocabulary, such as biological nomenclature, can be of considerable morphological or lexical interest (e.g., for compositional semantics). Using picture books on mammals and birds in the area where the language is spoken is the best way of identifying the referential meaning of terms. Through this, one may also be able to avoid translations in publications such as 'kind of bird' or 'kind of antelope'. And, as I experienced during my research on the Turkana language, picture books on mammals in the area can trigger enthusiasm among informants and serve as a cultural catalogue or cook book on the kind of animal that tastes better than some other animal, or the one that tastes absolutely the best.

I personally have no experience with group participatory research, which some fieldworkers employ. Kutsch Lojenga (1996) describes an interesting experiment with between ten and fifteen speakers of Ngiti (a Nilo-Saharan language of the Democratic Republic of Congo), in which she tried to raise the awareness of the group for the sound and tone system of their language. But, as pointed out by the author, the general principles of participatory research can be applied to other domains as well, including syntax, semantics, and discourse analysis.

It is useful to note down the basic life stories of informants before starting to work with them. Information about speakers' knowledge of other languages (or dialects of a language) is important for the assessment of the data collected, in particular when one is confronted with variation between speakers. In many parts of the world, monolingualism is the exception. Speakers in multilingual settings usually have a second, perhaps dominant, language which they have spoken ever since childhood or for a considerable part of their lives. A person's first language may have been superseded by another, or the person may have more than one first language. Potential informants with such linguistic backgrounds should not necessarily be excluded on a priori grounds. The linguist's common insistence on "mother tongue" speakers as informants may be misplaced.

What makes a good informant, and how do we select the person? The role I advocate is that of a co-investigator or colleague with intellectual curiosity, who not only speaks the language one intends to investigate, but also has intuitions about its structure and enjoys talking about it. I strongly subscribe to Pike's perception of the native speaker as a person who is an observer of items and a talker-about items (Pike 1981: 86). Interestingly, members of a speech community often are able to identify "good speakers" and they can direct the investigator towards such people. Preferably, one looks for someone of good social standing in a community, but of course one can't always know in advance; sometimes one only finds out by trial and error.

When I first started conducting fieldwork on Turkana (Nilotic, Kenya) for my Ph.D., I was keen on getting extensive data sets as quickly as possible in order to get my research underway. A credo that I did not consider at the time, but something I would strongly recommend now, is, as Wax (1971: 108) puts it, "slow is beautiful" and "fast is bad." In passionately trying to get a lot of data in a short period, I began hiring several informants at the same time until I discovered that some of them were truly excellent while others, although wonderfully nice people, were hopeless as informants. Mindful diplomacy was needed in order to "dismiss" those informants who turned out not to be fit for the job. The crucial point, therefore, is not to commit oneself too firmly at an early point, and to use discretion before selecting key informants. One certainly should avoid making long-term financial commitments to anyone lest one finds that one is stuck with a permanent fixture on the payroll.

There are numerous reasons why informants may turn out not to be the best candidates for the job. An ability to whistle the tonal melody of words in tone languages is of tremendous help to the researcher; but not all informants are capable of this. Also, their knowledge of the contact language may be insufficient to be able to go beyond the elementary level of collecting wordlists. Furthermore, the actual tolerance of speakers towards foreign speech – e.g., mispronounced or more or less ungrammatical sentences – also seems to vary considerably. Some informants are too easily satisfied (or else are too polite) to criticize the investigator when the latter tries to reproduce transcribed data by reading them out loud to the informant. It is thus essential that informants be instructed to correct the investigator whenever he or she makes mistakes.

Sometimes informants fail to understand what the researcher is after, or they do not have enough patience for the job, i.e., they get irritated when asked to repeat a word or sentence. They may turn out to be – or sometimes they already have been – excellent informants for anthropologists studying their culture; but if they get bored stiff when asked to produce plural forms for nouns and repeat them three times, they are not the most suitable candidates as informants. (I owe this observation to Alex de Voogt, who bases this example on his experience with fieldwork among the Hadza of Tanzania.) Moreover, some informants complain about the monetary arrangements all the time, making the working relationship tense and unpleasant. In general, one wants to avoid ending up in a cul-de-sac where both the informant and the researcher are frustrated and confused about each other's intentions and expectations. Watchful consideration and judgment are therefore in order, before arriving at a more definitive selection of one's primary assistants.

Informants can be trained in their job, and so some improvement along the line is possible. Moreover, an initial mistake in judgment by the researcher is not necessarily fatal because informants can sometimes be assigned alternative duties. For example, those who turned out to be less suitable for elementary data collection in my investigation of Turkana phonology and morphology did a good job at a later stage in collecting stories on tape. It is a truism but worth repeating that different informants have different talents. Some are truly excellent at explaining semantic subtleties, while others have deep intuitions about the sound structure of their language. Such specialized talents should be exploited during the investigation process.

The best informants normally enjoy their work and often put in great efforts to ensure that they provide solid data; they are language teachers in the truest sense. They sometimes go home in order to double-check data with other speakers of the language or to do some further introspection on the structure of their language. One of my best informants during my Turkana fieldwork, SE, took up on such duties on various occasions. He was a colorful person, who had trained as a nurse in Nairobi. After the training, he was employed by missionaries in his home area amongst his fellow Turkanas. He was assigned the duty of running the small dispensary in the settlement where I was based. SE was not only a smooth talker and womanizer, he was also an extremely sharp character. Being fully aware of the intricacies of his language, he did not mind going through long lists of paradigms, because he knew that was the only way to come to grips with the underlying structure. One day, when we were going through absolutive and nominative case paradigms, which are distinguished by way of tone in Turkana, SE remarked at one point: "There is something funny here!" All of a sudden he realized that a group of nouns with identical tones in the absolutive case fell into two distinct conjugational classes in the nominative. As it turned out, the same two classes emerged when these nouns were put in the plural. Obviously, we were dealing with the neutralization of tonal distinctions in certain environments, but underlyingly we had to assume two distinct tonal patterns for these two groups (see Dimmendaal 1983, esp. pp. 242–43 and 256–58). But SE wanted to make sure he was right, and so he went home in order to think of other examples, and also to double-check his pronunciation with other Turkana speakers. As he told me the next day when we continued our fieldwork, his friends agreed fully with his pronunciation; but when he had reported on his field session earlier that day, his friends had started laughing about the things this foreign researcher had asked him, such as to translate sentences like: 'the house is good', 'the cup is good', 'the cow is good', and 'I see the house', 'I see the cup', 'I see the cow'. His friends had wondered about all this useless talk the researcher was apparently interested in. But with his inquisitive mind, SE knew there was a deeper purpose to this exercise (triggering nominative versus absolutive case).

Then, one day early in the morning, SE appeared on my doorstep. He came to inform me that he had been expelled by the missionaries from his job as a nurse and that he was forced to leave since he had been dropped from their payroll. I was shocked and asked him about their reasons. Apparently, he had been accused of a promiscuous life style, and the missionaries, being afraid of their image, had decided he should be dismissed. As a result, I lost one of my best informants, and somebody who had been absolutely wonderful to me as a person. SE had protected me on various occasions as an inexperienced fieldworker and stranger to the culture of the Turkana. He constantly warned me to be less naive and credulous, and to be more alert if something was about to happen. He really felt responsible for me, as was especially demonstrated on one occasion during the initial stages of my research in the Turkana area. One morning, when I woke up in the settlement where I did my fieldwork, I realized the camp was completely empty; I was the only person left. So where had everybody gone? Apparently, the night before the neighboring Päkoot people, with whom the Turkana people had been on hostile terms as long as they could remember, had raided the area where I lived. They had taken cattle, camels, and goats along with them, and those who could not defend themselves had fled into the bush. I apparently had spent the night fast asleep, dreaming of fruit cocktails and cold beers in remote places like Nairobi. From then on, SE decided he should protect this crazy foreigner against potential danger. We became close, and during his spare time from his nursing job SE did excellent work as an informant.

It should be kept in mind that it does not require formal education to be a good informant, nor is age or occupation necessarily important. Sometimes one comes across good informants by sheer coincidence, as happened with me a few years back when looking for speakers of Baale, a little-known Surmic (Nilo-Saharan) language spoken in the Ethiopia–Sudan borderland. As the home area of the Baale people was not accessible at that time, speakers had to be found elsewhere. When checking for the presence of Baale speakers in the neighboring (multilingual) settlement of Dimma, local inhabitants introduced me to a young man who they claimed was a smart person and a Baale speaker. As it turned out, he was a "natural linguist." Although he had never been to school and was illiterate, he knew within weeks after having started work as an informant what verb paradigms were about. ("Would you like the negative forms too?") This young man also manifested a rare ability to point out structural and functional similarities between his language and Amharic, the contact language.

Some speakers apparently have an active sense of form-to-meaning relationships in different languages they have mastered, or can be so trained. The lucky ones of us have met with such brilliant informants. Back in the

1970s, when I was an undergraduate student at Leiden University, the late
A. E. Meeussen reported on his investigation of Lega, a Bantu language of
the Democratic Republic of Congo. He too had met with an ideal informant just by coincidence. While Meeussen was sitting outside under a
shady tree consulting his Lega informant, there were the usual spectators
observing the linguist as he asked questions of the type "How do you say
such-and-such in your language?" In Bantu languages of the region, there
is usually a distinction between high and low tone. At some point while
observing the field researcher, who was trying to transcribe tonal patterns
of words, one of the spectators spoke up. While looking over the investigator's shoulder, this observant and curious spectator remarked: "Ce n'est pas
comme ça, monsieur" [pointing his index finger downwards in order to
indicate a grave accent , i.e., low tone], "c'est comme ça" [pointing his index
in the air in order to indicate an acute accent, i.e., high tone]. As Meeussen
found out on checking, his tonal transcription had been wrong and the
observer had been right – the man became Meeussen's best informant for
the language.

There are probably many native speakers who could make a really important contribution to our understanding of language structure if only they
had the opportunity for training. Such latent capacities can be developed
through informal training by collaborating linguists, e.g., with respect to
technical vocabulary and basic concepts, but usually the indigenous knowledge goes untapped. One sometimes feels sorry for such talented informants – and for the field of linguistics – because with proper training they
presumably could do a better job of cracking the structure of their language than could the linguist, who is simply using them as native-speaker
assistants.

It is not desirable to constrain the participation of informants, given the
potential depth of knowledge they may have as co-workers. After all, doing
fieldwork is not a controlled experiment where the subjects have to be kept
in the dark about what is going on. The capacity of informants for introspection is an advantage rather than a liability. Speaker's intuitions, sharpened by the research encounter, help guide the direction of research.[4]

Whether informants are literate or illiterate is usually not important in
the early stages of the research, although research becomes easier at later
stages if speakers have some knowledge of reading and writing. But here,
too, essentially illiterate informants exposed to writing systems may manifest rare talents when they have an inquisitive mind. During a follow-up
field trip to Ethiopia to work on Baale again, I continued my research with
the bright informant encountered during the first trip. While trying to transcribe Baale words, I was corrected at one point by this informant. By then
he had only begun to learn how to read and write in Amharic and English.

But by simply observing my transcription of words using IPA symbols, he had found out what they referred to. And so at one point he remarked: "I don't think it is that sound [drawing *o* with his index finger], I think it is that one" [drawing the IPA symbol ɔ]. Of course he was right! I think it is important to convince informants that they should correct or criticize the one who is paying them a salary, but who at the same time is trying to understand their language. And fortunately this informant did not hesitate to do so.

4.   Elicitation techniques and the role of informants

When initiating the investigation, it is useful to start eliciting nouns from a basic vocabulary list (of which there are many floating around). With respect to the collection of body-part terminology, it is useful to have pictures or drawings available (as found, for example, in Bouquiaux and Thomas 1992). Although there are clear-cut cognitive constraints on body partonymy (as shown, for example, by Andersen 1978), it is important to be able to have the informant point out what the referential domain is for a particular body-part term. Through this, one may also become aware, incidentally, of linguistic taboos.

Once a few hundred words have been collected, one may get down to the serious business of analyzing the sound structure of the language. Phonologies tend to be symmetrical (up to a point). By plotting phonemic segments onto a chart using manner and place of articulation as basic distinctive features, one quickly becomes aware of what will turn out to be either accidental or systematic gaps. A basic understanding of language typology in this respect not only creates an awareness of common and less common sound patterns, but it also helps in working out what might be expected given the segmental inventory collected at different stages. If, for example, a bilabial ejective /p'/ occurs in some word(s) collected up to that point, other ejective sounds can be expected to be found.

Once a basic understanding of the segmental and suprasegmental inventory has been reached, one may move from scheduled elicitation (following some wordlist) to analytical elicitation techniques. For example, in order to check whether words with a particular canonical shape or segmental structure occur, there is no reason why one can't ask an informant, "Can you think of a word beginning with *t'a*, or *k'a*?"

It takes a while to get under the skin of a particular language. One's ears have to get tuned in to the sounds of the language under investigation. Improving the quality of the transcription of a little-known language needs to be given high priority in the early stages of research, but it is an ongoing process. Coming to grips with the sound system can be accomplished in several ways. The investigator may try to read the transcribed words out loud to the informant in order to have him or her judge the validity of the transcription and pronunciation. The investigator may also use discrimination tests, by contrastively pronouncing words that, so it seems, sound similar but are not identical. Alternatively, the investigator may produce two variant pronunciations for a particular word and ask the informant to point out which one is correct or which one sounds better. Oftentimes the answer may be that neither of the two pronunciations is acceptable, and so more work is needed in order to find out what is wrong. By using the "rhyming method", one may systematically generate possible root shapes in the language under scrutiny. To this end one needs to have a basic understanding of the segmental inventory of the language as well as of the canonical shape of words. By verifying all logically possible combinations of segments, one may systematically generate (near-) minimal pairs as well as systematic distributional gaps (e.g., of consonants before specific vowels, or vice versa). The investigator may want to repeat such exercises with several informants; this is both to avoid boredom and because their talents in doing these exercises may vary. Whether informants will actually come up with minimal pairs or near-minimal pairs often depends more on the language than on the speaker's talents: obviously, this discovery procedure is easier to apply in languages with essentially monosyllabic structures than in agglutinative languages with trisyllabic and quadrisyllabic words.

Although one normally has to operate as if the native speaker is always right, the fact is that informants are not infallible and do not always provide natural, reliable data. During a field methods class with a speaker of Samo (a Mande language spoken in Burkina Faso), I noticed that in normal speech the informant would palatalize alveolar stops before front vowels; but when the students in the class tried to imitate the pronunciation by using slight palatalization with alveolar consonants before front vowels, the informant corrected them by repeating the pronunciation without any palatalization. It is possible that those trying to imitate him had exaggerated the degree of palatalization. Alternatively, the phonetic palatalization may have been there, but since the informant was himself being trained in linguistics, his reaction might have been due to an awareness of the non-distinctive nature of the palatalization process. It is also possible that he only became aware of this palatalization once it had been pointed out to him, and so he preferred to leave it out in order to approach a formal pronunciation that was closer to the presumed underlying form. Astute speakers are not necessarily unaware of subphonemic details. Thus, individuals may avoid low-level phonetic realization rules in careful pronunciation, or they may exaggerate differences in order to help the investigator who is having a hard time hearing some distinction.

The key rule throughout the fieldwork is to analyze collected data after each session. One should spend at least half of the working day not only analyzing data in order to extract the essential structure, but also rechecking and preparing new questions for the next session. However much one probes one's material while in the field, it is impossible to anticipate all analytical problems, and so most investigators need a second opportunity to recheck data collected during the first period, to fill in annoying gaps in paradigms, and to generally extend the corpus. Research projects aiming at general descriptions of languages should ideally be set up accordingly, i.e., with two periods of fieldwork, one of up to nine months and a second one of around six months. Still, we all make mistakes even after long and (sometimes) multiple periods of fieldwork, and theoreticians and typologists using such first-author sources for their cross-linguistic work should realize that.

Recording wordlists on tape, with the assumption that one can transcribe and analyze them after one has returned from the field, is a fatal error. Recordings may be used for all kinds of analytical purposes, e.g., measuring vowel length, the first and second formant for vowels, consonant length, or pauses between clauses and sentences. However, systematic recording presupposes considerable familiarity with the language, i.e., the basic system has to be understood first in order for such recordings to be useful. Naive tape recordings may be potentially biased in several respects. There is the danger of list or elicitation intonation, whereby inherent stress, pitch, or some other prominent prosodic feature such as tone may get lost or at least affected. Also, although words reproduced in isolation may be grammatically "neutral," most of the time they are not. Instead, the informant usually tries to translate with a certain discourse context in mind, thereby offering a noun in some case or other (e.g., nominative or absolutive) and a verb in some particular inflexion (e.g., verbal noun or imperative).

The issue of recording raises an ethical question. Whereas natural speech is more likely to occur when speakers are not aware they are being observed, there is a problem here of acceptable professional conduct. To me, taping speech (whether dialogues or some other form of simple conversation) without permission simply is not to be done. Even when permission is granted, linguists must safeguard the confidentiality and well-being of the individual(s) with whom they work. With this proviso in mind, I think modern audiovisual equipment provides a wonderful means of recording discourse in all its variety, an opportunity which should be exploited in future research, in particular when studying the ethnography of speaking. Exemplary case studies are the documentaries by Ivo Strecker and Jean Lydall on the Hamar group living in southern Ethiopia. The documentaries contain perfect accompanying illustration material for the fascinating monograph by Strecker (1988) on Hamar politeness strategies and cultural notions of "face," i.e., of social identity in the sense of Brown and Levinson (1987). In order to be able to do this kind of anthropological linguistic research, however, one needs not only an in-depth knowledge of the language, but also the consent and trust of the community.

In my experience, the investigation of tense and aspect belongs to the most complex domains of language study. In addition to the *Lingua* questionnaire and suggestions in Bouquiaux and Thomas (1992), there are interesting proposals in Dahl (1985) on how to go about investigating tense and aspect in a little-known language. Also, the referential meaning of nouns (in terms of definiteness or specificity) is an intricate topic that is extremely hard to investigate on the basis of elicitation. In the end, it is texts or connected discourse in general in the language under investigation which provide the most important clues for analysis of these grammatical domains.

Eliciting verb paradigms can at times be a tedious, albeit necessary, job, although it may be more exhausting for the researcher than for the informant. Once the Baale speaker I worked with had developed a concept of verbal paradigms ('I went, you went, (s)he went . . .' etc.), he was hard to stop in his elicitation. After several weeks of fieldwork, with over a hundred pages of verb paradigms, and with new morphophonemic complications cropping up every time, the informant still enjoyed teaching me about the complexities of his language and laughing over the desperation of the researcher who developed a feeling that he was nowhere near an exhaustive listing of morphophonemic alternations or verb categories in this language. Whenever boredom or lack of concentration is observed with the informant (or researcher – we all have our good days and bad days), one may want to intersperse the structured elicitation with "small talk" about completely different topics.

Sometimes informants wonder why the investigator is unnecessarily repetitious (from their perspective). When asking someone to repeat words or paradigms elicited several weeks earlier (in order to double-check pronunciation or conjugations and declensions), one should not be surprised when the informant rebukes: "This is what I told you two weeks ago; don't you trust me, do you think I am lying?" And so some explaining is in order, e.g., that one is not too sure whether one has heard a word correctly.

5.   Indigenous knowledge and cultural problems in interpretation

It is important to keep in mind that our field techniques are often culturally biased, especially when the goal is to capture the subjective experiences of informants. This is almost certainly the case, for example, with respect to the investigation of basic color terminology. A standard way of investigating this lexical field is by using a Munsell color chart, as I did at the time of my research on Turkana. Although the methodological validity of the research plan (showing color chips to informants) appears to be widely accepted by linguists, I now have serious doubts whether this is a valid way to arrive at an understanding of the meaning of color terms cross-linguistically. For example, the choice of material – whether one is dealing with the color of clay or the fur of animals or textiles, etc. – appears to play an important role in color naming; accordingly, just using color chips to investigate color terminology is a rather limited and at times totally artificial exercise which informants themselves may object to. (See Dimmendaal 1995 for some further methodological observations on this type of anthropological linguistic research.) An alternative, and probably more appropriate, method of collecting color terminology would be to try and have the informant describe the color of items in the natural environment.

Linguists in general work with certain notions that one assumes to be universal, because this is what human beings want to talk about, or so we think! As Lys Ford (personal communication) has pointed out, based on her extensive experience with Australian languages, grammatical constructions involving comparison ('bigger', 'better', 'younger', 'smarter') are unnatural in some speech communities, because there is no cultural reason to compare one person or thing with another.

When investigating deictic systems in languages, many of us have started out from what again has turned out to be a culturally constructed tool. When I began my research on Turkana, I assumed that cardinal directions were basic to all speech communities. Later I learned that only the terms for 'east' and 'west' represented truly cardinal directionals in the Turkana speech community; the other two terms that I thought corresponded to 'north' and 'south' in actual fact basically referred to 'up (in the air), elevated' and 'down, on the ground', something that became clear once native speakers started using these terms in describing the environment (Dimmendaal 1995).

The various issues raised above also relate to what Quine (1960) has referred to as the "problem of the Radical Translator." Informants may be satisfied when the researcher has learned an approximate meaning, but this may still be different from a correct definition of what a term actually refers to in the language investigated. Understanding the meaning of a word or sentence in the language under investigation probably is the most challenging task for the investigator. Apart from asking for a translation into the contact language, asking informants to describe a situation or context where the use of a particular word or construction would be considered appropriate is another fruitful way of getting at the meaning. A further controlling device would be to ask informants to translate items back from the contact language into the language under investigation at a later point.

Since grammaticality judgments are often contingent upon proper contexts, initial assessments by informants should be treated with great care. The problem is, how can one be sure an informant is rejecting a decontextualized utterance for formal syntactic reasons ("You cannot put the subject after the verb") or because the utterance makes no sense ("In the real world it is not common for inanimate entities to act as agents")? Informants' judgments on the grammaticality of sentences, and related to that, the semantic interpretation of utterances, are usually geared toward the question of whether such an utterance would make sense in the real world. A pertinent illustration of this is found in a study by Barshi and Payne (1996) on Maasai. The authors tested the role of context and constituent order in determining the extra-participating mapping selection in this language. For their experiment, Barshi and Payne probed speakers of Maasai for the interpretation of sentences with an affected pronominal object expressed on the verb, e.g., 'me' in a sentence such as 'The man will open-me the box'. Since, in Maasai, the word for 'man' can also mean 'husband', there are two readings for this example: (1) 'My husband will open the box'; (2) 'The man will open my box'. Although the second interpretation is possible, it is not as likely an interpretation for speakers of Maasai as the first. The results of this experiment suggest that language users did not resolve the mapping choice strictly in terms of sentence-internal clues such as linear order of elements or notions such as subject and object, but crucially relied on what was already in their attention, as established in the discourse and cultural context.

Looking for natural discourse is at the heart of the matter. Any serious investigation into the syntax and pragmatics of a language should involve the collection of a corpus of oral or written texts. Collecting and transcribing texts on the basis of spoken language is a time-consuming, though necessary and, ultimately, rewarding enterprise. Alternatively, or in addition, one can teach informants to write stories in their own language. If there is no orthography for the language, as is often the case for little-studied languages, informants who are literate in some language may try to write stories by using an improvised orthography based on another language whose writing systems they know.

Analyzing texts together with informants sometimes leads to surprising findings. Azeb Amha (personal communication) has provided a neat example of this. The language she investigated, Maale (southern Ethiopia), belongs to the Omotic branch of Afroasiatic, a language group that is widely assumed to be rather strictly verb-final, with all its concomitant typological features regarding the position of adpositions, auxiliaries, etc.

The SOV order is indeed prominent in Maale, although OSV order also occurs when eliciting transitive sentences in isolation. An examination of texts, however, revealed that subjects or objects may follow the verb given proper discourse contexts. And it is exactly the fact that these sentences are now part of a paragraph (as a discourse unit) that makes it possible to detect the proper discourse context in which such alternative orders are allowed or preferred.

I now strongly believe that it is important for authors discussing syntactic issues in a particular language or from a cross-linguistic perspective to indicate in their publications how the data were elicited. I have not always practiced this wisdom myself; but it seems methodologically sound to me to explain whether data were obtained through translation of sentences, through other elicitation techniques, or through text analysis, since this may affect the reliability of the data, including speakers' grammaticality judgments.

6.   Learning to speak the language under investigation

An alternative, important source which helps to enhance one's understanding of a language is the observation of speakers' behavior. Dixon (1984: 199) refers to such a case: "It was a useful reminder of the limitations of asking questions over a desk – it is no substitute at all for living with a language, observing it being used, and using it oneself." Dixon was referring back to a conversation he had been listening to between two elderly speakers of Dyirbal (North Queensland, Australia), the language Dixon had been studying for some time. The chat involved what Aussies commonly refer to as "chin wagging." But the conversation had more than gossip value, as it made the investigator aware of a particular grammatical phenomenon (in this case a referential expression, 'that thing remembered from the past').

By listening to people' s conversations, and by trying to speak the language oneself, one arrives at a deeper understanding of the language under investigation. This strategy is comparable to the anthropologist's technique of participant-observation versus structured interviews. Many of us are poor at accurately reporting our own speech habits, and so indirectly, one may learn about the potential gap between the informant's norms and actual practice. Also, languages have formulas as standard ways of saying things. Knowledge of a body of institutionalized or "lexicalized" utterances and of conventions for reporting events enriches the description of a language. By trying to practice these, one gets to know about differences between what is grammatically correct and what is idiomatic.

Gaining metacommunicative competence requires knowledge of cultural norms, as anyone who has tried to learn a foreign language will acknowledge. When I did my fieldwork on Turkana and tried to use the language, I was corrected on various occasions, not necessarily because of my pronunciation or the ungrammaticality of the utterance I produced, but because what I was trying to say did not make sense from a pragmatic point of view. For example, a simple phrase such as "Let's go!," which I at one point used in addressing a ten-year-old boy who was going to help me carry some goods, met with laughter from the bystanders. When I questioned whether there was something wrong with my pronunciation, the answer was "No, but as an adult you don't say 'let's go' to a ten-year-old. You just go, and he follows!"

These days it is not uncommon to report on languages based on the speech of one person who happens to be in the country of the researcher, often as a student or as the spouse of a student or a visiting scholar. Given the large number of undocumented languages, and the rapidity with which many of them are disappearing, this is understandable. But if one aims at a full and meaningful description of a language, this is far from adequate. Moreover, speaking for myself, such work can never replace the enriching human experience of living in another culture and trying to come to grips with the language through interaction with key informants and other members of that community.

ACKNOWLEDGMENTS

A first draft of this article was written while I was a Visiting Scholar at the Research Centre for Linguistic Typology, the Australian National University (ANU), Canberra. I would like to express my sincere gratitude to the directors of the Centre, Sasha Aikhenvald and Bob Dixon, for their invitation to join the research team for six months. They provided an important impetus not only because of their intellectual stance as experienced and enthusiastic fieldworkers, but also because of their long-term commitment to empirical linguistics. I would also like to thank the members of the Research Centre, the Department of Linguistics, and the Research School for Asian and Pacific Studies of ANU for being such wonderful colleagues. I am also deeply indebted to Azeb Amha and Paul Newman for their unreserved encouragement as well as their extensive comments on an earlier draft.

NOTES

1 While numerous books have appeared over the years on anthropological fieldwork, I would rank Wax (1971) among the most informative and balanced monographs of its kind for linguistic fieldworkers, because it manifests a professional mantra I strongly subscribe to.

2 The practical problem of keeping oneself fed is a pervasive theme in the classic and beautifully written book *Winter*, by the anthropologist Cornelius Osgood (1953).

3 As pointed out by Paul Newman (personal communication), the linguist who lives with the people and truly learns the local languages is probably the exception rather than the rule, although linguists are more than willing to let the lay person think that that's what they do. It is more common for a linguist working in Central America, for example, to live in a Spanish-speaking town (where some speakers of a small Indian language can be found to do research with, e.g., at a secondary school) rather than live out in the bush. Similarly, scholars working on small Chadic languages in Northern Nigeria are more likely to set up shop, so to speak, in a reasonable-sized town where Hausa is the lingua franca than they are to face the practical difficulties of living in a small isolated village far from the main road.

4 In his classic manual of linguistic fieldwork, Samarin (1967: 41) talks about the need to provide training for informants, with the goal of getting them to think about their language "in terms of broad generalizations based on what is actually said or could be said."

REFERENCES

Andersen, Elaine S. 1978. Lexical universals of body-part terminology. In *Universals of Human Language*. vol. 3: *Word Structure*, ed. Joseph H. Greenberg, pp. 335–68. Stanford: Stanford University Press.

Barshi, Immanuel, and Doris Payne. 1996. The interpretation of "possessor raising" in a Maasai dialect. In *Proceedings of the Sixth International Nilo-Saharan Linguistics Conference*, ed. M. Lionel Bender and Thomas J. Hinnebusch, pp. 207–26. (Special issue of *Afrikanistische Arbeitspapiere*, 45)

Bouquiaux, Luc, and Jacqueline Thomas, trans. by James Roberts. 1992. *Studying and Describing Unwritten Languages*. Dallas: Summer Institute of Linguistics.

Brown, Penelope, and Stephen C. Levinson. 1987. *Politeness: Some Universals in Language Usage*. Cambridge: Cambridge University Press.

Dahl, Östen. 1985. *Tense and Aspect Systems*. Oxford: Blackwell.

Dimmendaal, Gerrit J. 1983. *The Turkana Language*. (Publications in African Languages and Linguistics, 2) Dordrecht: Foris.

    1995. Studying lexical-semantic fields in languages: nature versus nurture, or where does culture come in these days? *Frankfurter Afrikanistische Blätter* 7:1–29.

Dixon, R. M. W. 1984. *Searching for Aboriginal Languages: Memoirs of a Field Worker*. St. Lucia: University of Queensland Press.

Kutsch Lojenga, Constance. 1996. Participatory research in linguistics. *Notes on Linguistics* 73:13–27.

Newman, Paul. 1992. Fieldwork and field methods in linguistics. *California Linguistic Notes* 23(2):2–8.

Osgood, Cornelius. 1953. *Winter*. New York: W. W. Norton.

Pike, Kenneth L. 1981. Wherein lies "talked-about" reality? In *A Festschrift for Native Speaker*, ed. Florian Coulmas, pp. 85–91. The Hague: Mouton.

Quine, Willard Van Orman. 1960. *Word and Object*. Cambridge, MA: MIT Press.

Samarin, William J. 1967. *Field Linguistics: A Guide to Linguistic Field Work*. New York: Holt, Rinehart and Winston.

Strecker, Ivo. 1988. *The Social Practice of Symbolization: An Anthropological Analysis*. London: Athlone Press.

Wax, Rosalie H. 1971. *Doing Fieldwork: Warnings and Advice*. Chicago: University of Chicago Press.

4   Ulwa (Southern Sumu): the beginnings of a language research project

Ken Hale

The story which will be told in this chapter is not the story of a mature and fully established language project. Rather, it is a report on the very beginnings of a program of research on an indigenous language of the Nicaraguan Atlantic Coast. It is a before-and-after study, so to speak, reporting on the events preceding the researcher's first field trip and contact with members of the language community, the research done on the trip itself, and the outcome in relation to future stages of the project. The language involved – called Ulwa, or more loosely Sumu – is the southern variety of the Sumu group. The northern variety, now called Mayangna, is documented in Norwood (1997). It is to this latter variety that the term Sumu was generally applied until recently.

Ulwa is spoken primarily by inhabitants of Karawala, a town of 935 near the mouth of the Rio Grande, the large waterway that separates the Northern and Southern Autonomous Atlantic Regions. Some 30 residents of the nearby town of Kara also speak Ulwa. At Karawala itself, there are Ulwa speakers, according to a recent survey, but most young members of the Ulwa community itself no longer use Ulwa, as Miskitu is the primary language of the town (for details, see Green and Hale, in press). Though the exact number of speakers is not known, it is clear that Ulwa is a distinct minority within the overall Sumu population of approximately 8,000, just as Sumu itself is a minority in relation to the much larger and linguistically dominant Miskitu population of the Atlantic Coast, which numbers 70,000.

1.   The origins of the Ulwa language project

The scientific investigation of a given language cannot be understood in isolation. In carrying out field research, linguists are inevitably responsible to the larger human community which its results could affect. This truth has special significance in contemporary Nicaragua, where current linguistic work began, in a real sense, as a consequence of important historical and sociopolitical developments within a country that was working to build a successful revolution for all its people. Linguistic research on the Atlantic Coast must be understood, above all, within the context of the Autonomy Project, an important part of which is the formal recognition, safeguarding, and strengthening of the intellectual wealth of the peoples of the region. (The "Autonomy Project" is a program that began during the Sandinista government. Among other things, it gave official recognition to the indigenous languages of the Atlantic Coast and, where feasible, established educational programs for them in the form of bilingual and intercultural programs.) A central means for the expression of this wealth is language, and the Autonomy Project has formally recognized this both by forming and supporting linguistic research projects and by bringing the products of linguistic research to bear in education, through bilingual/bicultural education programs and through the publication of materials in the indigenous languages.

The origins of the Ulwa language project lie fundamentally in the Autonomy Project. The research was not initiated in the first instance by the investigator, as is more typically the case in field research. Rather, it was commissioned by members of the Ulwa community, partly in response to the success of a Rama language project and partly because of a very real fear that the status of the Ulwa people as a minority, in relation both to the other Sumu communities and to the Miskitu, would result in the degradation and eventual loss of their own recognizably distinct linguistic tradition. Addressing this sort of concern on the part of Atlantic Coast communities is one of the most important functions of the Autonomy Project.

In the summer of 1987, a request was made by a representative of the Ulwa community that the Regional Committee of the FSLN (Frente Sandinista de Liberacion Nacional) in Bluefields begin research on the Ulwa language. Colette Craig of the Rama Language Project was asked to undertake this work. Because of her responsibilities to the Rama study, however, she would have had to postpone working on Ulwa, and so she suggested that I undertake at least the initial phase of fieldwork. This would mean that the Ulwa project could possibly start as soon as January, 1988, when I planned to be in Bluefields teaching in a bilingual education workshop with teachers from the Rio Grande area.

Through Craig, I was given a letter from Carlos Castro of the Regional Committee inviting me to consider initiating an Ulwa language project. I accepted the invitation eagerly and began to write a research proposal to be sent to CIDCA, which would be my institutional sponsor in Nicaragua, and to the Regional Committee. CIDCA (Centro de Investigaciones y Documentacion de la Costa Atlantica (Center for Research and Documentation of the Atlantic Coast)) is a research organization, associated with the Central American University, which was established to do economic, ecological, cultural, anthropological, and linguistic work on the Atlantic Coast. The proposal was for an initial phase consisting of only two brief trips. It was designed to accomplish three modest ends: (1) to obtain enough basic data to prepare brief but informative introductions to the vocabulary and grammar of Ulwa; (2) to determine, on the basis of these materials, the principal differences between Ulwa and Northern Sumu; and (3) to get an initial idea of the manner in which an Ulwa language project, in the true sense, could develop, i.e., grow into an autonomous language project whose character and direction were in the hands of the community.

In October 1987, I was able to discuss my proposal in detail with Charlie Hale, an anthropologist who works in the Rio Grande region and who is well known to the people of Karawala. In December, he presented aspects of the proposal to the community and, together, they formulated a plan of action according to which an Ulwa speaker, chosen by the community, would meet me in Bluefields the following January at the conclusion of the bilingual education workshop. This person would work with me in the CIDCA offices for a week, accompany me on a brief trip to Karawala, and return with me for a final week of work in Bluefields.

The community elected Abanel Lacayo Blanco, a man of 53, to work with me on Ulwa. This action had an extremely beneficial effect on the research. While it meant that I was not free to choose my own linguistic consultant, it greatly streamlined the process of getting started on the language. Moreover, it is not very likely that I could have chosen a consultant more perfectly equipped to work at the speed required by the brief period (two and a half weeks) remaining before I would have to return to my university. Lacayo speaks excellent Miskitu, as well as Ulwa, and he also commands English, Spanish, and the Twahka variant of Northern Sumu. The entire range of his linguistic abilities proved useful in my research. Moreover, he took the task of documenting Ulwa very seriously.

Accordingly, fieldwork on Ulwa began in January 1988, as scheduled. Aspects of the linguistic research itself will be discussed in the sections to follow; but before proceeding, I will mention a short trip to Karawala that occurred midway in the research period.

The Karawala visit represented the first step in the important process of creating an awareness on the part of the Ulwa speakers that work on their language was under way, as they had requested; that a member of their community, chosen by them, was directly involved in the research; and, most importantly, that the character of the project was something they would have a say in. Arrangements for travel to Karawala were made by the Regional Committee, taking advantage of a trip planned by Tomas Kelly, the FSLN representative responsible for the Rio Grande region. Colette Craig, whose work in the Rama language project inspired the original Ulwa request, was also able to take part in the trip. This was fortunate, not only because of the valuable advice and help she gave, but also because this association with the Rama language program enhanced the credibility of the embryonic Ulwa project. Furthermore, the trip enabled Craig to be introduced to the Ulwa community in anticipation of her own eventual research on the language, tentatively projected to focus on the speech of the Ulwa people at Kara, recent refugees from the west, whose history has involved Spanish, not Miskitu, as the primary language of external contact.

Our stay in Karawala was brief – only a day and a half. The purpose of the visit was to give the people of Karawala information about the language project. This was accomplished in part by talking to individuals and small groups, and in part by means of a brief presentation at a town meeting. Lacayo took it upon himself to escort us around the town, to orient us spatially within it, and to introduce us to people he felt we should meet. We made an effort to meet individuals who we had been told might be expected to take a special interest in the project and, eventually, form a committee to oversee its work.

At the town meeting, a number of concrete materials were shown to illustrate the kinds of materials that would be developed in the Ulwa project. These included several pages of an unfinished brochure on the Ulwa alphabet and the elementary dictionaries of Miskitu and Rama published under the auspices of CIDCA. The alphabet brochure was presented as a project that might be completed in the Karawala school, on the model of current work in the Rama program. The dictionaries exemplified a more long-term project, which would require the involvement of Ulwa speakers for a number of years. As an initial step, I proposed to prepare as quickly as possible a preliminary vocabulary of Ulwa on the basis of the material obtained in January. This would be set out in a format approximating that of a full-fledged dictionary of the language and would therefore serve as an example of the work that would need to be done to produce such a document. I would bring this preliminary vocabulary back to Karawala in March, during a break in my teaching schedule. At that time I would meet with Lacayo and other interested people to discuss how to proceed in the business of correcting and augmenting the preliminary vocabulary, with a view to producing an Ulwa dictionary. The proposed March visit to Karawala was to be the second of the two field trips projected in my original proposal to the Regional Committee and to CIDCA.

Due perhaps to nervousness, I erred in my presentation to the Karawala town meeting by failing to emphasize the importance of forming a group of knowledgable Ulwa speakers to serve as consultants and overseers to the project. Such a group would be crucial in making this effort a true community project and, therefore, a meaningful part of the Autonomy process. It was not enough that it had been commissioned by the community. Speakers of Ulwa must also be directly involved in the research, in the practical application of its results, and in decisions concerning its conduct. I attempted to correct this error by letter, by talking to individuals, and by introducing Lacayo to dictionary-making activities in which he could involve others. I also planned to make this the first priority in my proposed March trip to Karawala, bearing in mind, of course, that realization of the ideal situation here faced certain practical problems, the most urgent of which was financial support for individual Ulwa speakers whose involvement in linguistic research might remove them from their regular sources of income.

Following the town meeting, we left Karawala and returned to Bluefields, where a final week of research on Ulwa was undertaken.

2.   Ulwa as a Sumu language: implications for research

Ulwa belongs to the Sumu subfamily of Misumalpan, a small language family whose name was constructed from syllables contained in the names of the languages which are believed to belong to the group. These are Miskitu and Sumu, of eastern Nicaragua and Honduras, and (the now extinct) Matagalpa-Cacaopera, of western Nicaragua and El Salvador. Misumalpan, in turn, is believed to be related to Chibchan, the family to which Rama belongs.

The Sumu subfamily consists of two closely related languages, Ulwa (or Southern Sumu) and Mayangna, a dialect complex found in Nicaragua and Honduras. At the time this project began, the precise nature of the relationship between Ulwa and Mayangna was not known, in part because of the fact that Ulwa was not extensively documented. One of the purposes of my research on the language was to arrive at a better understanding of the relationships within the Sumu group and, ultimately, of the relationships between Sumu and Miskitu, within Misumalpan, and between Misumalpan and its putative Chibchan relatives (for some comments and references, see Hale 1991, Craig and Hale 1992). The immediate comparative concern, however, was that of determining the relations internal to the Sumu group.

The literature on Mayangna includes both a grammar (Norwood 1997) and two dictionaries (von Houwald 1980; McLean Cornelio 1996). In addition, there is an active bilingual education program serving the Mayangna community, and a substantial body of written literature exists in that language. By contrast, when I began to plan for my fieldwork on Ulwa, the material I had at my disposal was limited to the vocabularies and grammatical notes published in the 1920s by Lehmann (1920) and Conzemius (1929). Although these materials are excellent, they left many questions concerning Sumu relationships unanswered.

Within the Ulwa language project, the concern with such comparative issues was motivated by historical, scientific, and educational considerations. Each of these concerns related, in one way or another, to the fact that the project was responsible to the speakers of Ulwa and, therefore, to their aspirations in the context of important developments under way in present-day Nicaragua. So some care was taken in the preparatory and initial stages of the investigation to place Ulwa within the Sumu group, partly because this issue was seen as important in determining the character of the research project.

One question was whether Ulwa "deserved" a full study. Or was it so close to Mayangna as to warrant nothing more than, say, a listing of its lexical and grammatical divergences from the latter? As a linguist, my attitude is that *every* language deserves a full study, resources permitting. In the Ulwa case, there was a compelling reason to undertake the research, apart from strictly linguistic motivations – the speakers of the language wanted it to be documented. Linguistic research which seeks to be responsible to the people whose language is the object of investigation must take seriously certain practical questions. One such practical consideration was the very real need to know the position of Ulwa in relation to Mayangna in order to plan for the integration of Ulwa into the educational programs of the Ulwa community. Briefly, the results of the comparative study of the Sumu languages determined that the lexical and morphological differences were too great to permit Ulwa to be accommodated easily within the Mayangna-based bilingual education program, so educational projects involving Ulwa would have to develop their own materials.

3.   Fieldwork on Ulwa

In order to address the comparative issue properly, research on all aspects of Ulwa grammar and lexicon had to be undertaken. In this section and in the remainder of this chapter, I will discuss aspects of the actual research and the planning for it.

3.1   *Planning and methodology for research on Ulwa*

My attitude to the notion "linguistic field methods" or the notion "what one should do in linguistic field research" is this: Do whatever you need to do in order to learn the language. That is to say, take the position that you are there to *learn* the language and do whatever you have to in order to achieve that end. (This is assuming that your purpose is to *document* the grammar and lexicon, as opposed, say, to a project whose purpose is ethno-linguistic or sociolinguistic in nature, in which case documentation of the grammar will be presupposed.) The methodological strategy of setting oneself the goal of learning the language – whether this is a *real* purpose in the research, or merely a convenient fiction – has the effect, assuming it is applied successfully, of virtually guaranteeing adequate coverage. Another benefit of the strategy is that it automatically adapts to virtually all conceivable situations ranging from one extreme, in which the language under investigation has never been recorded at all before, to the opposite extreme, in which the language (say English) has been the object of linguistic research for centuries, has a vast literature, and the researcher's goal is to investigate a particular, as yet only partially understood, grammatical sub-system (e.g., the grammar of transitive/intransitive verb pairs, such as that seen in *I broke the pot* versus *the pot broke*).

If one accepts as valid the strategy just mentioned, this will determine, to a large extent, the planning one does in preparing oneself linguistically for the actual fieldwork. In principle, one has the choice of either utilizing or ignoring previous work done on the language. Assuming the work is good, our strategy decides the issue, since it demands that we make whatever use of the existing literature we can in order to get into the language to learn it. In my case, I had available the works of Lehmann (1920) and Conzemius (1929), consisting of comparative vocabularies, with grammatical notes, in Sumu and Miskitu. I also had the CIDCA grammar of Miskitu, the dictionary of Miskitu by Marx and Heath (1961), and some knowledge of Miskitu through study and through work in bilingual education workshops on the Atlantic Coast. This access to Miskitu was important to me in my work on Ulwa. Moreover, I was able to use what I knew of Miskitu to assess the general quality of the work of Lehmann and Conzemius and, thereby, to determine whether their materials on Ulwa and the Mayangna varieties could be relied on. My conclusion, on the basis of their control of Miskitu data, was that their work was of excellent quality (though not totally devoid of mistakes). I can also say, with my first contact with Ulwa speakers now behind me, that my admiration for these early investigators continues undiminished.

At a later point in my research, though not soon enough to help in the planning stage, I had available to me a pre-publication draft of the excellent new grammar of Mayangna by Norwood (1997). During my last week in the field, I was able to use this work in checking to see if certain elements that Norwood had documented for Mayangna also existed in Ulwa. Following the field trip, I was able to obtain a copy of the Mayangna dictionary by von Houwald (1980). While these two newer works will be of great value in planning future research on Ulwa, the works that played the greatest role in planning for the initial phase were those of Lehmann and Conzemius. They permitted me to gain a basic understanding of Sumu verbal and nominal morphology, to begin acquiring a basic vocabulary of Ulwa, and to form an initial conception of internal relationships within the Sumu subfamily, as well as relationships between Sumu and other Misumalpan languages.

Lehmann's work includes a list of twelve hundred concepts, identified by a German, Spanish, or English gloss, and rendered, where possible, into Miskitu, Mayangna, and Ulwa. Although the Ulwa column is sparse in some lexical categories, particularly verbs, the work as a whole proved to be extraordinarily useful to me in planning for my first sessions with an Ulwa speaker. In particular, the word lists enabled me to prepare, quickly and efficiently, a protocol for use in eliciting material for an elementary vocabulary of Ulwa, which was to be the first concrete product of the research project. In fact, the principal research guide that I assembled for myself was a copy of Lehmann's comparative vocabularies arranged in a bound folder in such a way that each page of the list had opposite it a blank page on which I could write Ulwa forms. As a part of my advance preparation, I placed a check mark beside each concept that I wanted to elicit in my first "pass" in acquiring an Ulwa vocabulary. Since Lehmann had done the very difficult work of assembling a list of concepts appropriate to Central America, I was spared an enormous amount of labor in the preparatory stage; and the initial work of Conzemius in documenting the nominal and verbal morphology of the Misumalpan languages was also instrumental in getting me to a position – in advance of my first trip – at which I could easily understand "what was happening" in the very first sentences I elicited for Ulwa. It would have been a serious mistake not to utilize the early work of these excellent scholars – the speed with which actual fieldwork on Ulwa was able to proceed owes much to their contributions to the linguistics of the Atlantic Coast.

I should point out here that there is always a tendency to distrust the work of early scholars since one often does not have a solid basis on which to judge their work fully. This tendency to distrust is encouraged, in part, I imagine, by disconcerting fluctuations and inconsistencies in the orthography – often overly detailed phonetically and, consequently, highly variable from one point to the next. Only with hindsight, after actual contact with speakers of the language, can the full value of such early work be appreciated. While this skepticism and doubt is, in a manner of speaking, an injustice to the early scholars, it is healthy and absolutely necessary in the context of field research on a little documented language. No matter how good one feels about the abilities of earlier researchers, the material must be checked again and again. In the case of Ulwa, every item had to be rechecked, not only for accuracy in the transcription of consonants and vowels, including an initially difficult-to-hear length contrast in the latter, but also for certain basic morphological properties, for example, the formation of the construct state (for nouns), and the formation of the "theme," or base for inflection (for verbs), not to mention all that must be determined eventually concerning the relationships between lexical items and the syntactic structures in which they appear. These latter bits of information, with rare and idiosyncratic exceptions, were completely absent from the early vocabularies, of course.

Whether or not one has access to earlier scholarship on the language one studies, I consider it absolutely essential to have a "script" (or "protocol") when one goes to a working session with a speaker of the language. It is not always necessary to follow the script, but it is a necessary item, if only to fall back on when, as often happens, one's head simply ceases to work, particularly in the investigation of difficult syntactic problems. In the beginning stages of fieldwork it is especially important to have a script, because – assuming you have the *right* script – this is the best way to get into the language quickly without, at the same time, having to use your mind to make plans on the spot. If one plans ahead of time, it should be possible in the eliciting sessions themselves to concentrate just on the forms of the language. Don't mix jobs, in the initial phase, at least – it is too exhausting. This methodology, of course, carries a risk with it – namely, the risk of rigidity. Thus one always must be willing to abandon the prepared script at any time in order to follow an interesting lead. This does not violate the principle of minimizing exhaustion; in fact, it helps to relieve it. This mixture of procedures leads to chaotic looking field notes – ones you will probably be ashamed to show to your colleagues – but, in the end, the work will be better and richer. A cardinal rule, in this regard, is the following: If your language consultant volunteers something not in the planned script, write it down immediately, and follow it up if something comes to mind in relation to it. If you can't see the relevance, never mind; write it down anyway. Its importance will become clear eventually – in fact, your best clues about the language will probably come from such notes.

Returning to the Ulwa project, although there existed seemingly reliable material on the language, that material would have to be checked and rechecked. This I knew, because I was aware of certain facts about the Misumalpan languages which told me in advance that certain forms would have to be collected for each lexical item in order to document it properly. Since my purpose in the initial phase was to prepare an elementary vocabulary, containing entries approximating those of a complete and adequate dictionary, I resolved to document adequately each lexical item I obtained, in relation to its phonology, its morphology, and its syntactic properties. Despite the leg up that the earlier work on the language had given me, this meant that, for the field context itself, it made sense to operate as if Ulwa were completely unknown linguistically and to proceed as if I were documenting it for the first time – a fiction, to be sure, but one that seemed to me to be methodologically sound in this instance.

In starting work on Ulwa, I decided to follow the procedure I have used elsewhere – North America, Mexico, Australia – in working on a "new" language. The first session, for example, would involve eliciting basic vocabulary – I usually start with body-part terms – with a view, at this early point, of getting used to the sounds of the language and to developing a way of writing it. And I would proceed in this manner through the basic vocabulary (of some 500 items) I had originally isolated from Lehmann's list until I reached a point when I felt enough at ease with the Ulwa sound system to begin getting the vocabulary items in sentences rather than in isolation. This would be an important juncture in the research, since the study of the grammar could begin at that point, and the morphological and syntactic properties of each lexical item could be obtained, in conformity with my principal goal in this phase of fieldwork. Moreover, certain lexical categories, verbs in particular, can be elicited efficiently only in sentences.

In working on a new language, it is often wise to refrain from obtaining sentences, or other long stretches of speech, until the sound system of the language is mastered to some extent. It is good, therefore, to start by eliciting nouns, which can be obtained in isolation. It is important, when sentences are obtained, to have phonological control over the material contained in them. The point at which it makes sense to begin eliciting sentences is actually quite early, but it differs from language to language. Ulwa has a sound system that is exceedingly forthcoming in this regard and, while details of the system (e.g., aspects of vowel length, sonorant devoicing, and the accent system) will probably take a considerable amount of time to understand fully, it is possible to feel quite comfortable writing Ulwa words almost immediately. In fact, after just a couple of words, it seemed rather pointless in this instance to refrain further from getting lexical items in sentential contexts.

Ulwa is easy to write down partly because it has a straightforward three-vowel system (/a, i, u/). The vowels are pronounced in a manner which approximates that of the cardinal positions associated with these three vowel symbols – close to, but slightly more lax than, the Spanish values associated with them. The only difficulty in hearing the Ulwa vowels is length – each vowel has a short and a long counterpart, giving a total of six vowel phonemes in the language. (Long vowels are indicated by a circumflex diacritic, following the established, but seldom actually observed,

Miskitu orthographic practice.) The length feature accounts for the existence in Ulwa of such minimal pairs as *bas* 'hair' versus *bâs* 'three'.

The syllable structure of Ulwa also contributes to the ease with which the language can be written. Each syllable begins with at most one consonant (except for some borrowings from English and Miskitu, which begin with two), the nucleus of each syllable is always a vowel, and a given syllable may be closed with at most one consonant. Diphthongs include four short and four long: /*ai, au, ui, iu; âi, âu, ûi, îu*/.

Finally, the consonant inventory of Ulwa represents, for the most part, a highly "unmarked" type, consisting of a series of three unaspirated stops /*p, t, k*/, two voiced stops /*b, d*/, the fricative /*s*/, the glides (or semivowels) /*w, y*/, and the laryngeal /*h*/. A mildly complex feature of the Ulwa consonant system is found in the inventory of sonorants. The nasals, (flap) rhotics, and laterals occur in pairs of voiced and voiceless, the latter written with an *h* following the appropriate alphabetic symbol. Like their voiceless stop counterparts, the nasals are in three positions of articulation, bilabial, apico-alveolar, and dorso-velar: /*m, mh; n, nh; ng* (= [ŋ]), *ngh* (= [ŋh])/. The flaps and laterals are all apico-alveolar: /*r, rh; l, lh*/.

The symbols just introduced comprise the "alphabet" with which I wrote Ulwa when I gathered data on it and when I wrote up my results. It is identical to the alphabet that has been in use for Miskitu for many years; the same has also been adopted for Northern Sumu. The fact that it is perfectly adequate for Ulwa, and the fact that it is already in use in other Misumalpan languages, make the choice of this alphabet extremely convenient, though the choice cannot be considered final until it is approved by members of the Ulwa community.

3.2   *The language of elicitation*

Prior to meeting Abanel Lacayo, with whom I was to work on Ulwa, I had met several members of the Ulwa community of Karawala in the context of the Miskitu bilingual education workshop in Bluefields. From these people, I had formed a good picture of the general linguistic situation at Karawala, and I had determined that I would have a choice of three languages to use in eliciting Ulwa – Spanish, English, and Miskitu. I decided to use Miskitu, the language best known to Karawala residents and the one which would enable me to obtain Ulwa data with the greatest speed. I would, of course, have recourse to English or Spanish where necessary. Although there were drawbacks associated with the choice of Miskitu, I reasoned that, since I would be returning to work on Ulwa again, the biases introduced in the data through the use of Miskitu would eventually be recognized and avoided when more "monolingual" eliciting procedures could be employed.

The danger involved in using Miskitu is one familiar to me from other areas of multilingualism – parts of contemporary Aboriginal Australia, for example. It is often the case that the grammars of languages under such conditions of intensive contact have "converged," becoming typologically similar, if not virtually identical. As a result, it is very possible for a speaker to "imitate" exactly the structure of a second language when translating it. This creates a methodological problem in that one is occasionally uncertain whether or not a form obtained in elicitation truly represents the structure of the language being studied. So, for example, when I ask for the Ulwa corresponding to the Miskitu sentence below, is the response in some sense "true" Ulwa? Or is it merely an Ulwa "copy" of the Miskitu?

(1) Miskitu:

Yang	sula	kum	kaik-ri	plap-an.
I	deer	one	see-NFOBV1	run-PAST3

I saw a deer and it ran away.

Ulwa:

Yang	sana	as	tal-ing	îr-ida.
I	deer	one	see-OBV1	run-PAST3

I saw a deer and it ran away.

These sentences correspond exactly, morpheme for morpheme, with one very slight exception. In Miskitu, the obviative ending on the first verb ('see') reflects a tense distinction which is neutralized in Ulwa. In both languages, this ending represents the category "first person obviative" (glossed OBV1 above) – i.e., the subject of the verb in the initial clause is first person, and the reference of the subject changes in the second clause (from 'I' to 'deer'). This switch in subject reference is known as subject obviation (glossed OBV), or switch reference. In Miskitu, in addition to these categories, the tense distinction future/nonfuture is marked – the marking is nonfuture (glossed NF) in the sentence cited above. In Ulwa, the tense categories are neutralized completely in the obviative endings. Thus, *total* imitation is impossible, for morphological reasons. But the syntactic correspondence is perfect.

It is reasonable to be suspicious of such a close match between the stimulus and the response. In this case, we happen to know that the surviving Misumalpan languages share, as an integral part of their grammars, the system of "verb sequencing" which is exemplified by this Miskitu–Ulwa comparison. Thus, we can be sure, in this instance, that the Ulwa is as natural as the Miskitu.

The situation is different, however, in the case of certain other constructions. I cannot be sure, for example, that I have a proper understanding of the Ulwa relative clause. Compare the following Miskitu and Ulwa forms:

(2) Miskitu:
[*Yang sula   kaik-rî*]   *ba   plap-an.*
I   deer   see-PAST 1   the   run-PAST 3
The deer I saw ran away.

Ulwa:
[*Yang sana   tal-ikda*]   *ya   îr-ida.*
I   deer   see-PAST 1   the   run-PAST 3
The deer I saw ran away.

Here again, the two languages share an identical structure, the so-called "internally headed" relative clause, known to be a favored type in Miskitu. The dependent clause (bracketed above) is simply nominalized, by means of the immediately following definite article (*ba* in Miskitu), and the semantic "head" of the relative clause (*sula* 'deer', in the Miskitu version) simply appears in its logical position within the dependent clause – i.e., object position preceding the verb, as expected in this verb-final language. Thus, in this type of relative construction, the semantic head does not appear external to the dependent clause, as it does in the English translation, for example. The Ulwa version corresponds precisely to the Miskitu. In the short time available to me, I was not able to determine whether this is in fact the favored form for the relative clause in Ulwa; I have reason to be cautious in this instance, since it is known that it is the *externally* headed relative clause which is favored in Northern Sumu (cf. Norwood 1997) – though even there, as a translation of the Miskitu, the internally headed form was readily given by a speaker of the Twahka dialect:

(3) Twahka (Northern Sumu):
[*Yang   sana   tal-na-yang*]   *kidi   k-îra-na.*
I   deer   see-PAST-1   the   3-run-PAST
The deer I saw ran away.

It is clear from this example that it would be a mistake to rely exclusively on Miskitu in eliciting Ulwa, but this was not the plan in any event. The use of a separate language of elicitation is solely an expedient in the initial phase, during which an elementary understanding of the structure of the language is being acquired. As soon as possible, monolingual methods must be employed in obtaining Ulwa data, methods which do not rely on a language other than Ulwa itself. The data collected monolingually can be used to "correct for" any Miskitu influences in the data of the initial phase. The harm associated with the use of Miskitu in the first phase is minimal, in my judgment. And, in fact, the two bodies of data – that elicited through Miskitu and that elicited monolingually – will constitute a source of information on an important aspect of the Ulwa linguistic situation, namely, the extent to which Ulwa imitates Miskitu in the course of translation. A potential hazard will become a virtue.

Interestingly, while Ulwa morphosyntactic structures are close and often identical to their Miskitu counterparts, and no conscious attempt is made to keep the two languages distinct in this regard, there is a conscious effort on the part of Ulwa speakers to avoid using lexical items which are identical to Miskitu ones. This was especially true in the context of eliciting sessions, where it was perceived that only "pure" Ulwa should be given. There is a perception among Sumu people generally that Miskitu occupies a position of greater power in relation to Sumu, which actually is so. The Sumu people also perceive that the purity and continued existence of their languages are threatened by the sociopolitically more powerful Miskitu language. A concern for purity in Ulwa usage is therefore understandable, and it was a factor which had to be dealt with in the context of field research on Ulwa.

Although not universal among Ulwa speakers, there is a feeling among some that any Ulwa word which is identical to its Miskitu counterpart is a borrowing and, given the perceived language-status asymmetry in the community, it is generally felt that the borrowing must be from Miskitu into Ulwa. Such speakers attempt, where possible, to avoid giving words of this sort in eliciting sessions, though they use them freely in conversation. Such words are avoided even where it can be shown that the borrowing was in the other direction, i.e., in cases where the word in question is in fact "pure Ulwa," to the extent that this notion makes sense.

In the first days of work on Ulwa, the avoidance practice described above extended even to the first person pronoun, which has the form *yang* in both Miskitu and Sumu. This was somewhat problematic, since there is no convenient replacement for it. In many cases, one can take advantage of the fact that Ulwa is a so-called "pro-drop" language – i.e., one can omit the subject of a sentence, because the inflection on the verb is rich enough to permit identification of the person and number categories of that argument. Thus, one can omit the first person pronoun in (4a) below, giving (4b):

(4) (a) *Yang*   *sana*   *as*   *tal-ikda.*   I saw a deer.
         I   deer   one   see-PAST 1

    (b) *Sana*   *as*   *tal-ikda.*   I saw a deer.
         deer   one   see-PAST 1

This is one way to avoid using the pronoun *yang*, but it is not really practical or realistic, since, in normal Ulwa speech, the pronoun is frequently kept. Another avoidance technique which was tried was that of using the expression *muihki* (*kat*) 'my (very) person/body' in place of the pronoun. But since this is grammatically a third person form, its use as a first person pronoun, which would otherwise require first person agreement (on the verb, for example), created uncertainty in forming phrases and sentences requiring such agreement.

Having noticed that *yang* appeared often and without hesitation in Ulwa conversations which I overheard, I suggested that it was not necessary to avoid using that pronoun in our eliciting sessions. I pointed out that *yang* is more thoroughly integrated into the grammar of Ulwa than its Miskitu look-alike is into the grammar of that language. In Ulwa, the independent pronoun is cognate with elements appearing in the system of verbal inflections – these cognate elements are, specifically, the first person object prefix *yâ-*, and the first person subject suffixes *-yang*, *-ng*. In Miskitu, no obvious relationship exists between the independent pronoun *yang* and the verbal inflections. Thus, if borrowing is involved at all, it is as likely as not that it was in the opposite direction, from Sumu into Miskitu. Be this as it may, the avoidance of *yang* was discontinued after the first week of work and, in general, considerations of linguistic purity ceased to play a significant role in the research, except that I was requested to place a mark beside each Ulwa item that was identical to the Miskitu, so that it could be checked later with older speakers.

3.3   Some notes on Ulwa: data from the first page

If there is any mystery associated with fieldwork, it is quickly dispelled by a glance at some actual field notes. By way of introducing some of the Ulwa data obtained on my first trip, I will reproduce here the material appearing on the very first page of my field notes. My field notes are always chaotic, since I dash from topic to topic, and I regularly abandon my own rules of conduct. This is not true of all linguists, I hasten to say. Many linguists have beautifully organized and easily legible notes. So the notes the reader is about to see are those of a linguist who works in the "messy" tradition. They will require some comment.

(5) First page of field notes, January, 1988

   1. *tuki, tu:ki da-láka (twisi latwan), muihki tuki da-lá:pai.*
      man tú:ma dala:pai pi. (man twisam latwan ki?)
      alas tu:ka itukwana. (witin twisa tara)
   2. *tinipas; muihki tikipas, man támapas,*
      alas takapas.
   3. *kungkimap/k; muihki kungkimap/k*   k?
      kungmamap/k, alas kungkamap/k.
   4. *ánà:ni; muihki ana:ki (?);*
      mán anà:ma, álas anà:ka.
   7. *nangkitak (kaikma), nangmatak, nangkatak,*
      mining nangnitak, manna balna nangmanatak,
      mining balna nangnitak.
 10. *makdaka (nakra), mikdiki (naikra), mamàkdaka,*
      alas makdaka, minìkdinika (wan nakra). |needs work

15. *tapa (kiama), muihki kat tapà:ki (kiaima), man tapama,*
   alas tapà:ka, tapa:ni.

---

sana as talikda	| *manna balna palka sana taldamna pi?*
(sula kum kaikri)	| *(man nani pali sula kaikram ki?)*
sana taldam pi?	| *alas balna sana taldidi* (sic!).
(sula kum kaikram ki?)	| *(witin nani swalya ba kaikan)*
alas sana talda.	| *yakau tala sana:kaya.*
(witin sula kum kaikan)	| *(bukra kaiks swalya ba)*
mining balna sana as talwida.	|
(yawan sula kum kaikan)	|
(also *yang nani,* no dist?*)*	|

The numbers (1–4, 7, 10, 15) correspond to the numbering in Lehmann's list. Forms given in parentheses are the Miskitu used in eliciting or, occasionally, the Miskitu given by Lacayo to translate an Ulwa form volunteered by him. My commentary will take each item on the page in turn.

The first item, glossed in German as *Zunge* 'tongue', appears in Lehmann's list as *tuisa* or *twisa* (with a macron and an accent on the [*i*]) for Miskitu and *tu-ke* (with an accent and a macron on the [*u*]) for Ulwa. I used the Miskitu form *twisi* 'my tongue' to elicit an Ulwa form, getting *tuki*, which I first wrote with a short [u], then with a long vowel (notated by means of a colon at this stage, [*u:*]). I immediately broke my own rule and obtained a sentence, which I was not really prepared to handle. I asked for the Ulwa equivalent of *twisi latwan (sa)* 'my tongue is sore', and I got a form which I wrote as *tu:ki daláka*. I would now write this as *tûki dalâka*. For the same meaning, I also got *muihki tuki da-lá:pai*, which I would now write *muihki tûki dalâpai*.[1] Note that *muihki*, rather than the more usual *yang*, was given as the first person pronoun here. I now know that *dalâka* is a noun or an adjective, meaning 'pain' or 'painful', and that *dalâpai* is the third person present form of the verb *dalânaka* 'to hurt, ache'. At the time, I knew none of this, of course, and was not really prepared to write the words down. I was perplexed by the accentuation of the forms, and thought that the first syllable must be some sort of partially detached proclitic, since it did not bear the main stress (hence the hyphenation). For some reason – Miskitu influence, undoubtedly – I expected all words to bear initial stress. I later determined that, in Ulwa, the second syllable is stressed if it is heavy (i.e., is closed or has a long vowel) and the first is light. The other sentences were elicited to obtain the second and third person possessive forms: *man tu:ma dala:pai pi* 'does your tongue hurt?'; *alas tu:ka itukwana* 'his/her tongue is big'. These would be written the same now, but with the circumflex notation for vowel length, in place of the colon. In addition to filling out the singular possessive paradigm, I learned that polar (or 'yes–no') questions are formed by means of the particle *pi* (later corrected to *pih*) placed at the end of the sentence.

In eliciting the second item, glossed *Mund* 'mouth' in Lehmann, I followed the common Miskitu practice of using the first person inclusive *wan bíla* 'our (incl.) mouth' as a citation form. This yielded something I was not then expecting, namely the form *tinipas*. I knew that this involved an infix, but I was not expecting *-ni-*, which I assumed was exclusively a Mayangna element. I had not yet figured out that Mayangna third person regularly corresponds to Ulwa first inclusive (cf. Hale 1991).

The first and second items illustrate nicely the general characteristic of Misumalpan nominal possessive paradigms that the affixes marking person of possessor are sometimes suffixed to the noun, sometimes infixed in it:

(6)   *tû* 'tongue'   *tapas* 'mouth'
1   *tû-ki*   *ti-ki-pas*
2   *tû-ma*   *ta-ma-pas*
3   *tû-ka*   *ta-ka-pas*

The third item on Lehmann's list, glossed *Lippe* 'lip', is remarkable only because I had difficulty initially hearing the position of articulation of final stop consonants, which are unreleased and, therefore, do not present to the listener the tell-tale burst so useful for identification. At first I heard the final stop of this form, which I know in fact to be *kungmak*, as a bilabial – hence the fluctuating notation *p/k*.

The fourth item, glossed *Zahn* 'tooth', gave me my first inkling of how the stress system worked. My notes here are confusing, but I was beginning to see that the second syllable, where strong, receives stress. Lehmann's seventh item, glossed *Nase* 'nose', is straightforward, but it exemplifies for the first time (in my notes, at least) that the plural suffix *-na*, which appears on the first and second person pronouns (as in *yang-na* 'we (excl.)' and *man-na* 'you (plural)'), also appears on the corresponding possessive, as in *nang-ma-na-tak* 'your nose' (you plural), beside *nang-ma-tak* 'your nose' (you singular).

The item numbered 10 in Lehmann's list, *Auge* 'eye', is accompanied by the notation "needs work." I did not understand what was going on in this form. For one thing, it would seem that the first and third person forms are represented only by the expected vowel harmony – the actual person markers are not separately discernible. Moreover, there is an apparent repetition of the infix *-ni-* in the first inclusive form. I was not yet ready to understand these features. On the other hand, this item helped to confirm the account of Ulwa stress which began to develop. The second person form, and the first inclusive form as well, showed stress on the second syllable, as expected. Lehmann's item 15, *Ohr* 'ear', shows the same stress pattern, but it illustrates a problem of hearing which continues to be a real one for me – that of hearing a final long vowel. My transcriptions of words like *tapâ* 'ear', when these are unaccompanied by suffixes, fluctuate in regard to the length of the final vowel. The final syllable in such cases is also the second syllable, and it should therefore receive the main stress, making its length easy to hear. But this does not appear to be the case, to my hearing, at least.[2] I continue to have difficulty with this. I also failed to record length on the second vowel of *tapâma* 'your ear', though I did record that vowel as bearing stress (as expected of a long vowel in that position). The use of a grave accent (`) in marking some main stresses reflects my perception, at the time, that the pitch on the associated vowel was level, or even somewhat depressed, rather than raised, as might be expected of a stressed vowel.

My notes were taken on a blank page facing the page from Lehmann's work which I was using to help cue my eliciting. I made use of only seven items from the first page of Lehmann's list, so the facing page on which I was working had some space left over. I decided that, whenever this happened, I would fill it up with other Ulwa material, material that would get me further into the grammar and make me more able to elicit, with understanding, longer stretches of Ulwa speech. The material appearing at the bottom of the first page, below the line, represents this sort of "page filler." In this instance, various past tense forms of the Ulwa verb *talnaka* 'to see' are obtained in response to Miskitu sentences involving the corresponding verb (*kaikaia*) in that language. The sentences depict various events of seeing a deer: *sana as talikda* 'I saw a deer'; *sana taldam pi(h)?* 'did you see the/a deer?'; *alas sana talda* 'he/she saw the/a deer'; *mining balna sana as talwida* 'we (plural incl.) saw a deer; *manna balna palka sana taldamna pi(h)?* 'did you (plural) really see a deer?'; *alas balna sana taldida* 'they saw the deer'; *yakau tala sanaka ya* 'see that deer (yonder)!' From this a partial past tense paradigm of the verb *talnaka* is obtained:

(7)		singular		plural
	1	*talikda*	excl.:	- - - - - -
			incl.:	*talwida*
	2	*taldam*		*taldamna*
	3	*talda*		*taldida*

The missing form (*talikdana*) was obtained at a later time. In the original notes, the third person plural form was recorded incorrectly as **taldidi*, and a question was raised concerning the first person inclusive. Specifically, the issue was whether there was in fact a distinction in Ulwa between inclusive and exclusive first person. In addition to the past tense forms, the singular imperative was also obtained (the plural was obtained later). The sentence containing the imperative also illustrates other points of Ulwa grammar, e.g., the fact that a noun must appear in the construct state following a demonstrative determiner, and the noun may itself be followed by a definite article. The sequence *sana:kaya* in the above transcription corresponds to what I would now write as *sanaka ya* 'the deer', consisting of the construct state of the noun *sana* 'deer' and the definite article *ya*. Interestingly, in the notes, this noun phrase is extraposed to the right of the verb, leaving the demonstrative stranded in the original pre-verbal position appropriate to the object. I can be certain that this sentence, and its Miskitu equivalent, were volunteered, since I myself would not have had enough confidence to elicit the sentence using the marked (extraposed) order in Miskitu *bukra kaik-s swalya ba* (yonder see-IMP deer:CONSTR the). This is an example, therefore, of the sort of side benefit one gets by writing down everything one's consultant offers. The interest of this example consists, in part, in the fact that it shows that the construct state induced by a preceding demonstrative remains on the noun when it is extraposed. A small detail, perhaps, but one I would not have thought to look for at the time – the information came "for free."

With hindsight, I can see that this page contains a lot of information which I could not possibly have appreciated when the data were collected. This is the typical condition, for me at least. I must let the material rest for a time, and move on to other items in my prepared elicitation plan. I return to the beginning, to correct and fill in gaps, only after gaining some experience with the language. Each fieldworker has a personal style, I imagine, and, in my case, I find it exhausting to try to fill in gaps, to complete paradigms, and the like, when I first encounter them. I get impatient and irritable when I try to do it. Thus, for example, I did not, on the first day, press for the inclusive–exclusive distinction, which did not come out as straightforwardly as I had expected it would. In the interests of forward motion and of concession to my own style of work, I momentarily postponed eliciting this sector of the verbal paradigm. But in this particular case, even after a wait, little headway was made. The inclusive–exclusive distinction exists in Miskitu and in Mayangna, and it was recorded for Ulwa by Conzemius. It turns out, however, that the situation in this regard is not altogether clear in contemporary Ulwa. The expected forms exist, but their use has changed somewhat. In any event, time constraints simply did not permit me to get to the bottom of the matter. The picture I have now is that *yangna* (*balna*), the historic first exclusive, remains in that use, while *mining*, the historic inclusive, is now used for both inclusive and exclusive. Future work will tell whether this is correct.

In general, the fieldwork proceeded in this manner until, at a point in the final week, I began to introduce a "monolingual" technique, in parallel with continuing elicitation in the pattern exemplified above. The new routine was introduced with a view to devising a program of research which Lacayo could carry on after I left the field. In the following paragraphs, I will reproduce and comment on a later section of my notes, one which represents this second technique.

3.4 More notes on Ulwa: an Ulwa dictionary project

In conformity with my assumptions concerning the relationship between the Ulwa language project and the community of Ulwa speakers, in particular, that the project was the property of that community, I hoped to make it possible for work on the language to continue during my absence. Accordingly, Lacayo and I developed a project which he could carry on in Karawala, one which would furnish data for the study of Ulwa grammar and, at the same time, supply material for entries in an eventual dictionary of Ulwa.

The project made use of the *Diccionario Elementar del Miskitu* that had recently been published by CIDCA. This served as the "script" for the project. The project itself was to proceed as follows: the Ulwa equivalent of each entry in the Miskitu dictionary was to be determined and exemplified by means of an Ulwa sentence, hopefully one which would reveal as much as possible about its meaning and its grammatical properties. This is a method which I often use to obtain sentences in a manner which reduces to a minimum any possible contamination from a language other than the one being studied. To this extent, it is a "monolingual" method; the illustrative sentences are volunteered and, therefore, are independent of any language of elicitation.

The following items are the first entries obtained as this dictionary project was being discussed and developed by Lacayo and myself. The entries are reproduced as they were first written down, except that an English translation has been added in brackets, following the parenthetic Miskitu. The entries appear in the alphabetic order determined by the Miskitu, as in the CIDCA dictionary.

(8) Some Ulwa dictionary entries (notes pp. 119–20)

> *Dî auhka (ail)* [oil]
> *Dî auhka karak yâmanh kisnaka. (Ail wal plas kiskaia.)*
> [Oil is for frying bananas.]
> *Mahka (ailal)* [much, many]
> *Kasnaka dîka mahka lauka. (Piaia dûkia ailal bâra sa.)*
> [There is much food.]
> *Pâpangh (aisa)* [father]
> *Yang pâpanghki kau dalâka talyang. (Yang papiki ra*
> *latwan kaikisna.)* [I love my father.]
> *Yulnaka (aisaia)* [to speak, say]
> *Mâmahki kau yul as yultuting. (Mamiki ra sturi kum*
> *aisaisna.)* [I'm going to say a word to my mother.]

Sapitka (albanghkia) [abyss]
 Sûlu as sapitka kau wauhdi âwi yawada. (Yul kum
 albanghkia ra kauhwi dimi wan.)
 [A dog fell into the abyss.]

In these entries, the Ulwa sentences represent data of a primary character, essentially uninfluenced by any other language – each is simply invented, to illustrate a lexical item, and is not given as a translation. By contrast, the Miskitu sentences are given as translations of the Ulwa, and if any linguistic mimicry is involved here, it is the Miskitu which imitates the Ulwa. In fact, in the second entry, the Miskitu imitates the Ulwa expression for 'food' – i.e., *kasnaka dîka* 'thing to eat' – using the literal translation *piaia dûkia* instead of the more common Miskitu word *plun* 'food'.

Data obtained in this way are somewhat less tractable than the data obtained by translation, and there is a certain amount of chance involved in relation to coverage. Structures which exist in the language may, by chance, never show up in material of this sort, no matter how extensive. However, the data are more trustworthy. And the coverage problem just mentioned is balanced by the fact that structures often emerge which one could never obtain through elicitation, since one can never know a priori what structures a new language will have – thus, the coverage problem itself demands use of methods which enable a speaker to use his or her linguistic knowledge freely, without undue influence from a distinct language of elicitation. The sensible thing to do, therefore, is to use all techniques which succeed in obtaining data, while making allowances for the risks involved in each.

In these five entries, a number of features of Ulwa grammar are illustrated. The first entry, for example, illustrates the use of an infinitival as the main predicate in a clause. I must confess at this point, however, that I do not fully understand what is happening in this sentence. My English translation does not properly reflect the Ulwa (or the Miskitu) which, more literally, would be something like 'To fry bananas with oil'. It is not clear what the subject of the infinitive should be taken to be. Further work is still required here, in fact.

In the third entry, the idiomatic expression *dalâka talnaka* 'to love' (lit. 'to see pain') appears. This is identical to the Miskitu expression *lâtwan kaikaia*, which I had known beforehand, and if I had used the Miskitu to elicit the Ulwa, I would have wondered about the authenticity of the latter. Since the Ulwa was primary here, however, it seems to me reasonable to accept the Ulwa and Miskitu expressions as a genuine equivalents – i.e., an idiomatic expression shared by the two languages.

The fourth entry illustrates an Ulwa cognate object construction. The verb *yulnaka* 'to speak, say' appears there in the expression *yul yulnaka* 'to say a word', literally 'to speak speech'. The noun *yul* 'speech, word, language' functions as the direct object, and the argument corresponding to the individual to whom the speech is addressed is marked for case by means of the postposition *kau*, which has both accusative and dative case functions.

The final entry here illustrates the so-called serial verb construction, an important feature of Misumalpan grammar generally (see Norwood 1997 for examples in Mayangna). The final three words in the Ulwa sentence constitute a series of verbs denoting the idea 'fall into'. The first verb, in the proximate participial form *wauhdi*, expresses the principal action, that of falling (cf., *wauhdanaka* 'to fall'); the second, also in the proximate participial form *âwi* from the verb *âwanaka* 'to enter', expresses the notion of movement into an area (the abyss, in this case); and the final verb, in the fully inflected past tense form *yawada* 'went', expresses the direction of the action, as is often required in Ulwa sentences depicting motion. (In this instance, we have direction "away from speaker's point of reference" (expressed by *yawanaka* 'to go'), as opposed to direction "toward speaker's point of reference" (normally expressed by *wânaka* 'to come').)

Volunteered sentences obtained in the course of dictionary work of this sort are a rich source of grammatical information. To be sure, longer texts – traditional stories, oral ethnographic essays, conversations, and autobiographies – are also extremely valuable and must be obtained. However, I find the volunteered sentences of the dictionary to be especially valuable. They are, in effect, texts themselves, albeit short ones, and they are much more manageable than long texts. For the initial phases of language work, they have the advantage of being transcribed easily. Each sentence, or textlet, by virtue of its brevity, presents a minimum of new problems or mysteries, permitting the linguist to arrive quickly at some understanding of what is going on.

This lexicon-based strategy was to play a role in the next phase of the Ulwa project. The plan was that Lacayo would, as his time permitted, continue to work on the dictionary in the manner illustrated above until mid-March, when I hoped to return. I arranged with CIDCA to continue paying a salary to Lacayo during my absence, in order to compensate him for the time spent on the project. In addition, I left with him a set of 3 x 5 cards on which to make entries, a box of ball-point pens, a cassette tape recorder, batteries, and tape. Although he did not feel comfortable doing so, Lacayo could write Ulwa forms, using the Miskitu orthography. The tape recorder would make the work proceed more quickly and more enjoyably, as it could all be done orally. Moreover, it would ensure that the Ulwa length distinctions would be recorded – these are normally ignored in Miskitu writing practice. But since I could not be sure how long the tape recorder would keep working, I made sure Lacayo had materials to write with – these would not otherwise be available in Karawala, and the opportunity to repair a broken recorder would be nil anywhere on the Atlantic Coast.

I have not heretofore mentioned the use of tape recorders. Normally, I tape everything I obtain. But since this trip was short, and I needed to work quickly, I recorded very little. I wanted to make sure that I had a reasonably good written record of everything, partly because I was never fully confident of the recording equipment I had with me or in my ability to hear everything accurately on the recording. I felt that if I recorded, I would have to write as well – almost doubling the demands on the little time I had. Accordingly, I decided to minimize recording. Although I feel that I had no real choice in the matter, I would not consider this to be the right decision under more relaxed conditions. Rather, I would advise taping everything, if at all possible.

This concludes my account of the actual collection of Ulwa data during the January trip to Bluefields and Karawala. I will turn now to some concluding remarks, following a brief description of my unsuccessful attempt to return to Karawala in March, 1988, and a brief account of subsequent developments.

4.   Epilogue

After returning to my university at the beginning of February, I began to do the work required to produce the preliminary Ulwa vocabulary which I had promised to bring back to Karawala in March. I got help the of David Nash, a colleague of mine in the Warlpiri Dictionary Project of the Center for Cognitive Science, MIT, and we put together a small book of some 500 Ulwa entries, with glosses in Spanish, Miskitu, and English. To the extent possible, each entry was made as complete as possible. Not all entries were successful, by any means, but in the best ones, the necessary grammatical and semantic information was included, and at least one informative example sentence was given, with Spanish translation. An introduction on the writing system was included (written in Spanish) together with sample nominal and verbal paradigms and a short comparative vocabulary of Ulwa and Northern Sumu. The book was to serve both to provide an example of what a printed dictionary entry would look like and to provide a base upon which to build, by correcting and expanding the many deficient entries, and by integrating into it the work being done by Lacayo. In addition to the pocket-sized book, a large format double-spaced version of the vocabulary was made for the purpose of incorporating corrections and additions.

My plan was to go to Karawala with copies of the vocabulary and, together with Lacayo, discuss with interested Ulwa speakers the possibility of continued documentation of the language, preferably to be carried out largely by members of the community. However, due in part to a delay brought about by President Reagan's introduction of troops into Honduras, the time available for the March trip was compressed to less than two weeks. It is not wise to attempt to get from Massachusetts to Karawala, and back, in a period so short as that. As it turned out, I got within fifty kilometers of Karawala when the outboard motor of the *panga* which was transporting me failed definitively. It had taken me a week and a half to get that far, and it was clear that, with Easter week beginning, it was not going to be possible for me to resume my journey.

I got close, but not close enough. Setbacks of this sort are common in fieldwork. My experience in this instance was a picnic compared to some I have heard about. Moreover, the trip was not a complete failure. I met lot of fine Nicaraguans I had not known before, and it was even possible to recheck and extend some of my Ulwa data with Karawala people in Bluefields and with fellow passengers on the ill-fated *panga*. I also heard, by rumor, that Lacayo was involving others in his work on Ulwa. This was superb news, and while I longed to get to Karawala and to talk to him, it is possible that my failure to manage it was a good thing, better in the long run for the development of an autonomous community-based Ulwa language project.

I had prepared a sort of "language kit" for Lacayo and others at Karawala – a small suitcase containing copies of the Ulwa vocabulary, a copy of the Marx and Heath Miskitu dictionary, a copy of Lehmann's comparative list, a copy of von Houwald's dictionary of Mayangna, a new tape recorder with batteries and tape, many pens, markers, pads of paper, and a variety of other items that would be useful in carrying out the work of documenting Ulwa. In addition, Basilio – a member of the Rama Language Project – prepared for me a set of pages for an Ulwa alphabet book, to be illustrated by Karawala school children; this was also included. Since I was not able to reach Karawala myself, I left this kit (together with instructions for its use) at CIDCA in Bluefields, to be delivered when possible.

I have taken some time here to discuss my failed attempt to return to Karawala because I believe that the best sort of conclusion I can write to this chapter is one which is forthright about the realities of fieldwork in an isolated area. Mishaps of the type described above often discourage people against the whole business of fieldwork; but it must be remembered that having an unsuccessful trip on one particular occasion says nothing at all about what will happen the next time. Moreover, no such trip is a complete failure; the trick is to turn each trip into some sort of success. The most important thing to remember is that this type of fieldwork is a long-term affair: it proceeds in small steps over many years. Efficiency, in the usual modern-day sense of the term, is not the point. What matters is eventual success, and that will be measured by the extent to which work on the language is integrated in a meaningful way into the life of the community of people who speak it.

This represents the story up to March, 1988. I made a trip in July of that year, with the intention of going to Karawala, but I hurt my back and had to stay in Managua and Bluefields, where I worked with Lacayo as before. When I was finally able to return to Karawala, in January, 1989, a six-member Ulwa Language Committee had been formed, composed of three elders and three school teachers. This team, called Ulwah Yulka Tunak Muihka Balna (UYUTMUBAL) and Comité del Idioma Ulwa (CODIUL), had by then prepared enough entries to produce a second edition of the vocabulary. This was subsequently printed up as a book and distributed, together with a number of children's books written down by the Language Committee. The committee also built a house in which to work and house visiting linguists. Thomas Green, a graduate student from MIT, worked with the team for two years, with funding from the National Science Foundation. A third version of the vocabulary, now worthy of the name "dictionary," should appear soon – a provisional version is on the web at <http://members.tripod.com/~ulwa/index.html>. The Ulwa Language Committee is concerned presently with the question of teaching the language in the school.

Like most other language projects on the Atlantic Coast, the Ulwa project must contend with extraordinary economic difficulties and imperatives of priority. In all honesty, it must be said that its fate is uncertain.

NOTES

1 These revisions in the transcription reflect some gradual progress in hearing stress and length in Ulwa. The analysis, which finally emerged well into the 1990s, would be better reflected by omitting the length diacritic on *dalâpai, dalâka*, and *dalânaka*. The vowel in question is stressed, according to an exceptionless rule of Ulwa – unknown to me in 1988 – and stressed open syllables are regularly lengthened.

2 To this day, I hear alternation in these CVCV forms. Where the final vowel is stressed, in conformity with the general rule, that vowel is lengthened, as expected. Where the initial syllable is stressed, its vowel is not especially long.

REFERENCES

Conzemius, Edward. 1929. Notes on the Miskito and Sumu languages of Eastern Nicaragua and Honduras. *International Journal of American Linguistics* 5:57–115.

Craig, Colette, and Ken Hale. 1992. A possible Macro-Chibchan etymon. *Anthropological Linguistics* 34:173–201.

Green, Thomas, and Ken Hale. In press. Ulwa, the language of Karawala, Eastern Nicaragua: Its position and prospects in Modern Nicaragua. *International Journal of the Sociology of Language* 132:185–201.

Hale, Ken. 1991. El Ulwa, sumo meridional: un idioma distinto? *WANI*, 11, Managua, Nicaragua.

Houwald, Gotz Dieter von. 1980. *Diccionario Español-Sumu Sumu-Español.* Managua: Ministerio de Educación.

Lehmann, Walter. 1920. *Zentral-Amerika, Teil I, Die Sprachen Zentral-Amerikas in ihren Beziehungen zueinander so wie zu Süd-Amerika und Mexiko*, 2 vols. Berlin: Dietrich Reimer.

Marx, W. G., and G. R. Heath. 1961. *Diccionario Miskito-Español/EspañolMiskito.* Bethlehem, PA: The Moravian Church in America. (4th printing 1992).

McLean Cornelio, Melba E. 1996. *Diccionario Panamahka.* Managua: CIDCA.

Norwood, Susan. 1997. *Gramática de la Lengua Sumu.* Managua: CIDCA.

5 Escaping Eurocentrism: fieldwork as a process of unlearning

David Gil

1. Learning and unlearning

In her adventures in wonderland, Alice fell into a deep pool of her own tears, and then met a mouse:

"O Mouse, do you know the way out of this pool? I am very tired of swimming about here, O Mouse!" (Alice thought this must be the right way of speaking to a mouse: she had never done such a thing before, but she remembered having seen, in her brother's Latin Grammar, "A mouse – of a mouse – to a mouse – a mouse – O mouse!") (Lewis Carroll, *Alice in Wonderland*)

Like other children of her time, Alice had been brought up to believe that not only Latin but also English has six cases: nominative, genitive, dative, accusative, ablative, and vocative.

How this came about is quite obvious. In those days, grammarians worked within traditions that were based on the classical languages of antiquity. So when they first began to examine English, they encountered a language without nominal case marking. Accordingly, they concluded that the Latin cases were there – only invisible.

Today, the discipline of linguistics is more enlightened: we think we know better. But do we really? It is a conspicuous fact about contemporary linguistics that it was developed primarily by speakers of European languages, is practiced mostly in European languages, and even today exhibits a disproportionate concern with the study of European languages. Inevitably, the European history and sociology of the field results in a Eurocentric bias with regard to its content. If in previous centuries it was Latin that was imposed on English and other European languages, today it is English, or Standard Average European, which, via Eurocentric linguistic traditions, is being imposed, often inappropriately, on languages spoken in other parts of the world.

However, in recent years, there is an emerging consensus that this bias must be overcome, through increased efforts directed towards the investigation of languages spoken in other parts of the world. And indeed, as suggested by the various chapters in this volume, one of the best ways to escape

Eurocentrism is to engage in fieldwork, and to immerse oneself in a non-European language.

Among the well-known joys of linguistic fieldwork is the discovery of exotic new linguistic objects, patterns, categories, and structures. As a graduate student in a field methods class at UCLA in the late 70s, I remember trying to investigate the syntax and semantics of quantifier scope in Maricopa, a Yuman language of the southwestern USA. (A comprehensive description of Maricopa grammar can be found in Gordon 1986.) Having painstakingly prepared a set of drawings showing so many men carrying so many suitcases in a variety of complex and confusing combinations, I presented these drawings to the speaker, Polly Heath, and asked her how she might describe the various states of affairs depicted. To my surprise and disappointment, she found the task extremely difficult, and after several attempts at getting reliable data, I gave up in despair. Fortunately, however, this was a classroom situation, and our instructor, Pam Munro, was there to come to the rescue. The problem, she explained, had nothing to do with the intricacies of quantifier scope that I was interested in, but rather with something much more mundane: the verb "carry," and the suitcases, or, more specifically, the shape in which I had, rather arbitrarily, drawn them. In Maricopa, it appears, there are different verbs "carry" for different shapes of objects carried – and the rectangular suitcases which I had drawn fell smack in the middle between compact objects, for which there is one verb, and elongated objects, for which there is another. Thus, the speaker's apparent inability to describe the drawings stemmed from her difficulty in choosing the right verb "carry." Not being familiar with the phenomenon of verbal classification, I was unable to make sense of her confusion, until I was enlightened by the teacher. The results of my work on quantification in Maricopa eventually found their way in to my Ph.D. dissertation (Gil 1982), in which the awkwardly rectangular suitcases were duly replaced by unambiguously elongated sticks. At the time, though, I should have been able to do better by myself. But that was the point of the course – to teach us how to unearth, recognize, and then analyze those exciting and unexpected new linguistic objects, like verbal classification, that are out there among the world's 5,000 or 6,000 languages.

However, when confronted with a new language, it is sometimes easier to recognize the *presence* of exotic, unexpected, and hitherto-unknown items than to come to grips with the *absence* of familiar, commonplace, and presumed-to-be-universal entities. Our native language imposes a straitjacket from which it is often difficult to break free, in order to realize that certain grammatical categories, obligatory in our own language, may be absent in the language under investigation. Moreover, if our native language is European, then this straitjacket is likely to be reinforced by the weight of Eurocentric linguistic traditions, which either implicitly presuppose or else explicitly assert that certain grammatical categories are universal. Thus, fieldwork involves not only the *learning* of new items but also the *unlearning* of old and familiar ones.

The problem is mainly with the "zeroes." Within most linguistic theories, there are a variety of zero elements: null items, empty positions, or otherwise noumenal entities which, even though they cannot be seen or heard, are still believed to be there. To cite just one example in morphology, in a paradigm such as the Hebrew verbal past tense (using the verb 'act'), *paʕal-ti* (1:SG), *paʕal-ta* (2:SG:M), *paʕal-t* (2:SG:F), *paʕal* (3:SG:M), *paʕal-a* (3:SG:F), *paʕal-nu* (1:PL), *paʕal-tem* (2:PL:M), *paʕal-ten* (2:PL:F), *paʕal-u* (3:PL), the third person singular form *paʕal*, is commonly considered to contain a zero suffix, *paʕal-Ø*. This is because in all other forms in the paradigm there is an overt suffix marking person, number, and gender. Paradigmatic patterning is one good reason for positing zeroes, and there are other, equally good ones. But there are also some pretty bad reasons. All too often, we posit a zero element in a language just because our European languages, or our Eurocentric theories, lead us to believe that there should have been something there. Becker (1995: 291) notes that "each language, from the point of view of another, appears full of holes." But "appear" is crucial here: the hole, or zero element, has no existence other than in eye of the beholder.

This issue can be most keenly appreciated in the treatment of Southeast Asian languages, in which many of the staple categories of traditional grammatical theory are apparently lacking – see Ratliff (1991), Riddle and Stahlke (1992), Huang (1994), Bisang (1996), and Gil (in press). For example, theoretically-oriented syntactic descriptions of Southeast Asian languages often posit a category of verbal INFL(ection): see Ernst (1994) for Mandarin, Huang (1991) for Hokkien, Lehman (1998) for Thai, Ramli (1995) for Malay, and many others. Why so? Because English inflects its verbs; therefore this must be part of Universal Grammar; therefore Mandarin, Hokkien, Thai and Malay must do so, too. Even if they seem, on the surface, not to. Moreover, the problem is not limited to the practitioners of specific theoretical frameworks. Many would-be atheoretical fieldworkers – while deriding their theoretically-oriented colleagues for their excessive abstractness and lack of concern with linguistic diversity – fall into the same trap when characterizing the grammars of Southeast Asian languages in terms of categories whose justification stems, once again, from Standard Average European. Some of the many grammatical categories often imported uncritically from traditional grammatical theory are parts of speech such as noun, adjective, and verb; grammatical relations such as subject and direct object; and a host of more specific construction types, including relative clauses, conjunctions, reciprocals, and many more. As a result, descriptions of Southeast Asian languages often resemble Alice's grammar, with Eurocentric paradigms such as [mouse]$_{\text{NOUN}}$, [mouse]$_{\text{ADJECTIVE}}$, [mouse]$_{\text{VERB}}$, and so forth.

This chapter provides a personal account of my fieldwork experiences with several Southeast Asian languages, focusing on Hokkien, Tagalog, and Malay/Indonesian. It is the story of my ongoing struggles to unlearn the grammatical categories of my native languages (Hebrew and English), and liberate myself from a Eurocentric linguistic education (degrees from Tel Aviv University and UCLA). It is the tale of my efforts to come to grips with the patterns and structures of diverse languages and to describe them as they should be described, on their own terms. And finally, it is an attempt to share some of the excitement of viewing the world from a new perspective, that of a non-European language, which, through familiarity, ceases to be exotic.

2.   Macrofunctionality in Hokkien

Different languages carve up reality in different ways. Color terms are a celebrated case: for example, the three Hebrew words *txelet* 'light blue', *kahol* 'dark blue', and *yarok* 'green' cover the same domain as the two English words 'blue' and 'green', which in turn cover the same domain as the single Riau Indonesian word *hijau*. Kinship terms are another well-known case: for example, the two English words 'brother' and 'sister' span the same semantic field as the two Riau Indonesian words *kakak* 'elder sibling' and *adik* 'younger sibling', but each language slices up the pie differently – English by sex, Riau Indonesian by age. Similar cross-linguistic variation can be found in just about every semantic domain. Discovering such variation, and seeing the world through the perspective of a different language, is one of the greatest joys of language learning, and of linguistic fieldwork.

In some cases, a single form in English will correspond to two or more forms in the new language, for example English 'blue' and Hebrew *txelet* and *kahol*. In other cases, a single form in English will overlap with another form in the new language, for example English 'brother' and Riau Indonesian *kakak* . In yet other cases, two or more forms in English will correspond to a single form in the new language, for example English 'blue' and 'green' and Riau Indonesian *hijau*. In cases of the latter kind, the single form in the new language will appear to exhibit the property of *macrofunctionality*, being associated with a function which, from an English perspective, seems to be surprisingly large, encompassing the two or more functions associated with the corresponding English forms.

In cases of apparent macrofunctionality, a range of analytical strategies present themselves. At one end of the spectrum, one may characterize the macrofunctional form as having a single, unified meaning, and as vague with respect to the distinctions associated with the different English forms. At the other end, one may describe the form in question as being ambiguous, each of its meanings corresponding to that of one of the English forms. In between these two extremes, one may analyze it as being polysemous, that is to say, as associated with a set of distinct but related meanings: distinct in the sense that they bear different consequences with regard to grammatical structure, related in the sense that they share a single core meaning, or are related through a network of common meanings.

In general, the default hypothesis in all cases of macrofunctionality should be to posit a single, unified meaning. One of the dominant design features governing the structure of language is the principle of one-form-one-meaning, which says that each form in a language has a unique meaning different from that of each other form. An overwhelming body of empirical evidence can be cited in support of this principle – see, for example, Tobin (1990).

Nevertheless, the principle of one-form-one-meaning is far from exceptionless: ambiguity and polysemy are widespread throughout language. Thus, for each case of macrofunctionality that is encountered, it is necessary to invoke a set of objective criteria in order to choose between the various possibilities. One such criterion is the obvious one. If it is possible to define a single common and coherent meaning without recourse to an *ad hoc* listing of sub-meanings, then the form in question is vague or polysemous; if, on the other hand, no such common meaning exists, then it is ambiguous. A second criterion is cross-linguistic replicability. If a particular broad meaning is associated with a single form in a variety of geographically, genetically, and typologically diverse languages, then in each language the form in question is vague or polysemous; if, however, an apparent instance of macrofunctionality occurs in just one language, and does not recur cross-linguistically, then the form in question is ambiguous. (Some of the issues involved in distinguishing vagueness, polysemy, and ambiguity are discussed in Zwicky and Sadock 1975.)

Consider, for example, the Riau Indonesian form *hijau*, corresponding to English 'blue' and 'green'. Clearly, this form has a single unified meaning, which can be easily defined as a continuous area on the color space. Moreover, words with a similar meaning recur in a wide range of languages, for example Wari' (a Chapakuran language of western Brazil), Setswana (a Bantu language of southern Africa), Welsh, and Japanese. Therefore, the form can safely be characterized as vague or polysemous. In contrast, consider the Riau Indonesian form *tahu*, corresponding to English 'tofu' and 'know'. No amount of mental gymnastics will come up with a single unified meaning here; and in almost all languages these meanings are expressed by different forms. Hence, Riau Indonesian *tahu* can reasonably be characterized as ambiguous.

In practice, however, the treatment of macrofunctionality often suffers from a Eurocentric bias, whereby fieldworkers and other researchers tend to characterize a form as ambiguous simply because it corresponds to two or more forms in English, or is associated with two or more grammatical categories in the investigator's theoretical framework. (Indeed, this bias is even reflected in the prevalent terminology. Rather than *macrofunctionality*, many writers use the terms *polyfunctionality* or *multifunctionality*; however, these latter terms presuppose that the function is constituted from a plurality of more specific functions, thereby implying that the form in question is ambiguous or polysemous, as opposed to being simply vague – as per the default assumption.)

The following is an example of macrofunctionality from Hokkien, a language belonging to the Southern Min group of Sinitic. (The data presented below are from the dialect of Hokkien spoken in Singapore.) In Hokkien Chinese, nominal attribution is expressed via a construction of the form ATTRIBUTE e^{24} NOUN, with the marker e^{24} occurring between the attribute and the head noun. (There are additional ways of expressing nominal attribution, involving other markers, but we will not be concerned with these here.) Some examples of nominal attribution containing the marker e^{24} are given in (1) – (6) below:[1]

(1) $a^{44(>44)}\text{-}beŋ^{24}$ $e^{24>22}$ $p^he ŋ^{24>22}\text{-}ko^{53}$
     Ah Beng   ASSOC   apple
     Ah Beng's apples

(2) $si^{21>53}$ $e^{24>22}$ $p^he ŋ^{24>22}\text{-}ko^{53}$
     four   ASSOC   apple
     four apples

(3) cit^4 $e^{24>22}$ $p^he ŋ^{24>22}\text{-}ko^{53}$
     DEM:PROX   ASSOC   apple
     these apples

(4) $aŋ^{24}$ $e^{24>22}$ $p^he ŋ^{24>22}\text{-}ko^{53}$
     red   ASSOC   apple
     red apples

(5) $tou\Reverse^{21>53}$ $tieŋ^{53}$ $e^{24>22}$ $p^he ŋ^{24>22}\text{-}ko^{53}$
     table   top   ASSOC   apple
     apples on the table

(6) $a^{44(>44)}\text{-}beŋ^{24}$ bue^{53} $e^{24>22}$ $p^he ŋ^{24>22}\text{-}ko^{53}$
     Ah Beng   buy   ASSOC   apple
     apples that Ah Beng bought

As shown above, the attributive e^{24} construction in Hokkien corresponds to (at least) six formally distinct attributive constructions in English: the genitive -'s construction in (1); the numeral construction in (2); the demonstrative construction in (3); the adjectival construction in (4); the prepositional-phrase construction in (5); and the relative clause construction in (6). So to a Eurocentric eye, it looks as though there are several different e^{24}s in Hokkien, or at least a number of different usages of a single e^{24} form (Bodman 1955). But is this indeed really the case?

Invoking the above two criteria, it is clear that Hokkien e^{24} is not multiply ambiguous. The unified meaning of e^{24} can easily be characterized; in fact it already has been above, namely as a marker of nominal attribution. More specifically, in a construction of the form ATTRIBUTE e^{24} NOUN, the attribute is interpreted as being associated, in some unspecified way, with the head noun. For example, in (1)–(6) above, the apples are understood as being associated in a contextually appropriate manner with, respectively, a person, a cardinality, an act of deixis, a color, a location, and an activity. Moreover, paradigms replicating (1)–(6) above, in part or in whole, recur cross-linguistically: for example, in many languages of sub-Saharan Africa (Welmers 1973) and in other parts of the world (Aristar 1991).

What this suggests, then, is that Hokkien does not have distinct attributive constructions corresponding to English genitive, numeral, demonstrative, adjectival, prepositional phrase, and relative clause constructions. Rather, it has a single attributive construction, involving the form e^{24}. (Analogous arguments for other East Asian languages have been proposed by Comrie 1996, 1998.)

For the fieldworker, the moral is quite clear: translational equivalence does not entail structural equivalence. Meaning is meaning, form is form – the two should not be confused. For example, just because the Hokkien $a^{44(>44)}$-ben^{24} bue^{53} $e^{24>22}$ $p^{h}en^{24>22}$-ko^{53} translates into an English relative clause construction 'apples that Ah Beng bought', this does not mean that the form in question is a relative clause construction in Hokkien. Thus, when encountering macrofunctionality, the fieldworker must unlearn the specific constructions of his or her native language, and of his or her theoretical framework, in order to be able to describe the constructions of the new language, as they really are.

Some additional, more specific lessons can also be drawn from the above example. Many speakers of Hokkien, when asked about constructions such as (1) – (6), will maintain that there are neither six different e^{24}s, nor a single one; rather, they will insist that there are two e^{24}s – one occurring in (2) and (3), the other occurring in (1), (4), (5) and (6). When asked why, they will offer two related explanations. The first is that the two different e^{24}s correspond to two distinct forms in Mandarin Chinese, *ge* and *de* respectively. Needless to say, this is irrelevant. For a Chinese person, Hokkien may be a "dialect," or debased form, of Mandarin, the so-called "proper" Chinese; but for the linguist, Hokkien and Mandarin are simply two different languages. To impose Mandarin grammar, with its two distinct attributive constructions, on Hokkien, is every bit as unjustified as is imposing English, with its six or more distinct constructions, on Hokkien. The second explanation that is offered is that the two different e^{24}s are written with two different characters. But linguistics is about spoken languages: writing is of a secondary, derivative nature, and should not be invoked in support of one linguistic analysis or another. Indeed, in the case at hand, the writing system is not specifically Hokkien; rather, it is a pan-Chinese system modelled largely after Mandarin. (For more detailed discussion of these and other methodological issues involved in the study of Sinitic languages, see Ansaldo 1999 and Matthews in press.) Cases such as this underscore the need for the field linguist to be on constant guard against admitting the speakers' own extra-linguistic biases as evidence for particular hypotheses. Speakers are just that, speakers; it is the fieldworker's job to engage in linguistic analysis.

A second lesson to be drawn from the above example relates to the relevance of phonology to syntactic and semantic argumentation. The reader will have noted the detailed notation of lexical tone in the above examples, and may have puzzled over the frequent use of the symbol >, as, for example, in $e^{24>22}$. This symbol marks the occurrence of *tone sandhi*, a phonological process whereby the tone associated with a syllable changes to another one: for example, in the form $e^{24>22}$, the basic, or citation tone 24 changes to the derived, or sandhi tone 22. (For discussion and analysis of tone sandhi in various dialects of Hokkien, see Cheng 1968, 1973, Chen 1987, and Peng 1994, 1997.) The tone changes that take place in Hokkien are given in (7) below:

(7)   basic tone   sandhi tone
   (a) 24   >   22
   (b) 22   >   21
   (c) 21   >   53
   (d) 53   >   44
   (e) 44   >   44
   (f) 32   >   4 (before p, t, k) / 53 (before $\textipa{P}$)
   (g) 4   >   21

As suggested above, Hokkien has an inventory of seven lexical tones, listed in the first column of (7). When sandhi occurs, each tone changes to another one of the same seven tones, as indicated in the second column of (7). (The dialect of Hokkien described here differs from that described by Chen 1987 in the following two respects: (a) the 22 and 21 tones in (7b) and (7c) are phonetically indistinguishable but differ with respect to their sandhi tones, whereas in Chen's dialect they are phonetically distinguishable; and (b) the 44 tone in (7e) remains unchanged, whereas in Chen's dialect its sandhi tone is 22.)

What is interesting from a syntactic point of view is *when* tone sandhi occurs. The distribution of tone sandhi in a given construction can be described in the following way:

(8) (a) ... [$ $ $] [$ $] [$] [$ $ $ $ $] ...
    (b) ... [S S B] [S B] [B] [S S S S B] ...

A sequence of syllables, denoted '$,' is parsed into constituents, or *tone groups*, as for example in (8a). Within each tone group, the last syllable retains its basic tone, denoted 'B,' while all non-final tones in the tone group change to their sandhi tones, denoted 'S,' as shown in (8b). Thus, the occurrence of tone sandhi effects a parsing of each and every construction in Hokkien, which correlates in part with the syntactic constituency of the construction.

With this in mind, let us examine the paradigm in (1)–(6). In every one of the examples, the marker e^{24} surfaces in its sandhi form, $e^{24>22}$, showing that it belongs to the same tone group as the following noun: ... $e^{24>22}$ $p^h e\eta^{24>22}$-ko^{53}]. Of interest to us here is the syllable preceding the attributive marker $e^{24>22}$, namely, the last syllable of the attributive expression. In example (2), the numeral $si^{21>53}$ 'four' occurs in its sandhi form, showing that the whole construction constitutes a single tone group, $[si^{21>53}\ e^{24>22}\ p^h e\eta^{24>22}$-$ko^{53}]$. In contrast, in the remaining five examples, the last syllable of the attributive expression occurs in its basic tone. This shows that $[e^{24>22}\ p^h e\eta^{24>22}$-$ko^{53}]$ constitutes a complete tone group, while the attributive expressions preceding it constitute another, separate tone group: $[a^{44(>44)}$-$be\eta^{24}]$ in (1), $[cit^4]$ in (3), $[a\eta^{24}]$ in (4), $[tou?^{21>53}\ tie\eta^{53}]$ in (5), and $[a^{44(>44)}$-$be\eta^{24}\ bue^{53}]$ in (6). Thus, the tone sandhi facts suggest that the syntactic bond between the attributive marker e^{24} and a preceding numeral, as in (2), is stronger than that between the attributive marker and other kinds of attributive expressions. (Interestingly, in the dialect described by Chen, the last syllable of the attributive expression undergoes sandhi if it is a numeral or a demonstrative; in his dialect, then, sandhi would occur also in (3).) This in turn suggests that e^{24} may exhibit a certain degree of polysemy, entering into two distinct attributive constructions, one with numerals (and for Chen also demonstratives), the other with all other kinds of attributive expressions.

While some fieldworkers like phonology, others are more interested in syntax and semantics, which is only fair. Some syntacticians and semanticists, though, are uncomfortable with phonology; indeed, many seem to feel particularly intimidated by lexical tone. At least in part, this is due to a Eurocentric perspective, and the absence of lexical tone from most or all of the languages of Europe. As a result, data from tonal languages are all too often cited with the tonal information omitted. For example, in volume 7 (1998) of the *Journal of East Asian Linguistics*, six of the ten articles are concerned with tonal languages; however, only one of these six articles cites data with lexical tones marked. The remaining five articles, containing data from several Chinese languages as well as two tonal African languages, Yoruba and Ewe, fail to mark the tones. But this is just as though a Hokkien linguist chose to cite English data without final consonant clusters simply because he or she could not hear or pronounce them. However, as the above example shows, phonological, and in particular tonological information can be relevant to syntactic and semantic analysis. What is more, when working on a new language, there is no way of knowing in advance which aspects of the phonology will turn out to be relevant to a syntactic/semantic analysis, and to what extent. The conclusion to be drawn is clear: the field-worker cannot study the syntax and semantics of a language without also giving due consideration to its phonology.

The Hokkien attributive marker e^{24} is but one of a lengthy list of cases which I have encountered in the course of my work, in which a form whose range of usages appeared, at first, extraordinarily broad, turned out upon closer reflection to be related, either through polysemy, or as instantiations of a single construction with a unified function. When I began working on my Ph.D. dissertation, it emerged that a distributive numeral, such as Japanese *sankozutu*, could mean either 'three each', or 'in threes'; the result-ing dissertation (Gil 1982) accounts for this range of meanings in terms of a single unified semantic relation of distributivity applying over a variety of syntactic domains. Some years later, working on Malayalam, it turned out that one and the same suffix, *-um*, could mean 'and', 'also', 'even' and 'every'; in a series of articles (Gil 1994a, 1994b, 1995a), these meanings are assigned a unified semantic representation in terms of the notion of con-junctive operator. At present I am studying the range of usages of the Riau Indonesian form *sama*, which, in different contexts, appears to be endowed with a wide range of functions, including 'and', 'with', 'same', reciprocal, agentive, oblique, and object of comparison; in work in progress, I am attempting to come up with a common core meaning underlying all of these usages, something along the lines of 'together'. Each of these cases, and many other similar ones, brought with it the satisfaction of suddenly realizing that what seems, from a Eurocentric point of view, to be an array of disparate entities is, from the perspective of the language itself, simply one and the same macrofunctional item.

3.   Syntactic categories in Tagalog

Tagalog, the major language of the Philippines, is a relatively well known language, with several good reference grammars, such as Blake (1925) and Schachter and Otanes (1972), and lots of discussion in the linguistic literature, for example Schachter (1976, 1977), Carrier-Duncan (1985), and Kroeger (1993). As a graduate student, I was fascinated by what I had read and heard about the language, and set off to the Philippines to check it out for myself. For a period of several years I elicited data from native speakers while at the same time learning to speak the language simply in order to be able to communicate with people. It took me too long, but finally I realized that the language that I was obtaining through elicitation and then writing articles about was not the language I was learning to speak.

Ask a speaker of Tagalog how to say 'The chicken is eating', and you might get a sentence such as the following:

(9) *Ang   manok   ay   kumakain.*
    TOP   chicken   INV   PROG-ACT.TOP:REAL-eat
    The chicken is eating.

As suggested by the above gloss, the structure of the Tagalog sentence bears a superficial resemblance to its English counterpart. The word for 'chicken', *manok*, is preceded by a grammatical formative *ang* which, among other things, marks it as definite; and the word for 'eat', with stem *kain*, is marked for voice, tense, and aspect by reduplication, *kakain*, and subsequent infixation of *-um-*, *kumakain*. Finally, *ang manok* is linked to *kumakain* with the grammatical marker *ay*, which occurs in a position reminiscent of the English 'is.' Indeed, sentences such as (9) above are still cited in some Tagalog pedagogical grammars as evidence for the claim that basic sentence structure in Tagalog is the same as in English, namely *subject – copula – verb*.

Nevertheless, most modern descriptions of Tagalog recognize the fact that sentences such as (9) occur relatively infrequently, and only in formal registers. When asked to translate the same English sentence, a speaker of Tagalog is actually more likely to provide the following:

(10) *Kumakain*   *ang   manok.*
     PROG-ACT.TOP:REAL-eat   TOP   chicken
     The chicken is eating.

In (10), *kumakain* 'is eating' precedes *ang manok* 'the chicken', and the marker *ay* is absent. In fact, most linguistic descriptions of Tagalog consider the construction illustrated in (10) to be the simple or unmarked one, and accordingly characterize Tagalog as exhibiting *predicate–topic*, or *verb–subject*, basic word order. As for the construction exemplified in (9), it is usually taken to be more complex or highly marked, the additional form *ay* being characterized as an explicit marker of *inversion*.

That is what the grammar books say, and that is what I was getting from elicitation from native speakers. But the language I was learning to speak, through simple immersion and the usual processes of second language acquisition, was turning out to be quite different. Just as frequently as the construction in (10), I was encountering, both in speech and in writing, constructions such as that of the following:

(11) *Manok   ang   kumakain.*
     chicken   TOP   PROG-ACT.TOP:REAL-eat
     The chicken is eating.

The above example differs from its predecessor in that the two main words, *manok* 'chicken' and *kumakain* 'is eating' are interchanged. However, the grammatical marker *ang* remains in the same position, and thus, in (11), is marking *kumakain* rather than *manok*.

Turning to the reference grammars, I soon found mention of "predicate nominal constructions," in which words such as *manok* 'chicken' occur in sentence-initial predicate position. But it was harder to find any discussion of constructions such as *ang kumakain*. To the extent that their existence was at all acknowledged, they were characterized as "nominalized predicate" constructions, having undergone a process of "zero-conversion" from VP to NP. A typical analysis of the constructions in (10) and (11) might look as follows:

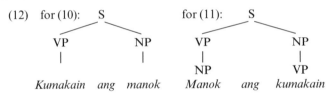

Occasionally, in line with the above, translations of constructions such as in (11) were offered involving English cleft constructions, for example, 'The one that is eating is the chicken'.

This, however, struck me as unsatisfactory for several reasons. First, I could find no explicit arguments in support of any such rules of conversion, changing a nominal *manok* 'chicken' into a predicate, and transforming a verbal *kumakain* 'is eating' into an NP. Structurally, (11) appears to be completely parallel to (10). And pragmatically, sentences such as (11) can be used in situations where an English cleft construction such as 'The one that is eating is the chicken' seems inappropriate. But secondly, what my ears and eyes were telling me was that constructions such as (11) occur quite naturally and commonly, with perhaps the same frequency as their counterparts in (10). Why, then, I wondered, should they be characterized as more highly marked, involving seemingly unmotivated grammatical processes of *zero-conversion*?

I troubled over these matters for years, but then, finally, the Eureka moment arrived. Here was Alice and the mouse all over again! If *manok* and *kumakain* can occur in all of the same positions, then what justification is there for assigning them to two different parts of speech, NP and VP? Of course, their translational equivalents in English, 'chicken' and 'is eating', belong to two different categories, NP and VP, but that is a fact about English, which cannot and should not be carried over to Tagalog. Trying to analyze a Tagalog sentence in terms of English parts of speech is like trying to describe English nominal morphology in terms of the six cases of Latin. In fact, the supposed zero-conversion of *kumakain* from VP to NP in sentence (11) makes no more sense than a would-be zero ablative suffix on an English noun.

Instead, I realized that Tagalog simply does without the traditional parts of speech: it has no distinction between nouns, verbs, and adjectives, nor between lexical categories and their phrasal projections. After some reflection, I came to the conclusion that what it has instead is a single open syntactic category, S, corresponding more or less to the traditional category of sentence. In particular, pairs of sentences such as (10) and (11) share a common syntactic structure, such as that indicated below:

(13) for (10) and (11):

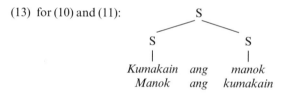

As soon as I had figured this out, the whole language fell into place, metamorphosing almost instantaneously from a strange, exotic, and somewhat bewildering labyrinth into a simple, elegant, and crystal-clear edifice. The absence of parts-of-speech distinctions accounted straightforwardly for a wide range of seemingly unrelated facts, first and foremost among which being the observation that almost all expressions enjoy the same distributional privileges: with but a limited number of exceptions, anything can go anywhere. But this insight only came when I was able to shed the blinkers of Eurocentric grammatical theories, and stop looking everywhere for nouns and verbs, or NPs and VPs; in other words, once I had unlearned the parts of speech of my native language, and of the syntactic theories I had been brought up on.

The possibility that Tagalog may be lacking many parts-of-speech distinctions, foreshadowed by Bloomfield (1917), has recently been raised by Himmelmann (1991) and Shkarban (1992, 1995); however, the above claims remain controversial. But the point here is not to convince the reader that this particular analysis of Tagalog is the best one – the relevant arguments have already been presented elsewhere, see Gil (1993a, 1993b, 1995b) for discussion of Tagalog, and Gil (2000) for more general theoretical considerations. Like any analysis, it may turn out to be quite wrong. Rather, the goal herein is simply to show how the Eurocentric bias in linguistics tends to lead researchers away from proposing certain hypotheses which, regardless of whether they are ultimately right or wrong, are at least plausible, and worth formulating.

But there is a further methodological moral to the story: eliciting data from native speakers is a valuable way of obtaining data, but it can never provide the whole picture of a language. Native speakers can translate sentences, and they can provide judgments of well-formedness, meaning, and appropriateness in context; but they can never produce an exhaustive list of all the interesting constructions in the language. When eliciting data from native speakers, you tend to get what you ask for. As a result, it is very easy to miss out on a whole lot that is there because it never occurs to you to look for it. In the case at hand, if I had stuck to eliciting data from native speakers, I would have encountered many sentences such as (9) and (10), but might never have come across sentences such as (11). It was only my exposure to the language, in speech and in writing, that brought to my attention the existence of constructions such as those in (11), and then convinced me of their prevalence and importance.

It is worth asking why speakers tend to offer certain sentences rather than other, equally grammatical ones. One reason for this is what I like to refer to as the *good informant paradox*: the better s/he is, the worse s/he is. When offering an English sentence to a native speaker, the more skilled informant will provide a translational equivalent that is as close as possible to the English source sentence, not just in meaning but also in structure. Accordingly, the more talented one's informants, the more likely one is to end up with a corpus of sentences which, although grammatical, are actually too much like their English source sentences, thereby providing a distorted picture of the language under investigation, and downplaying the degree to which it differs form English. In the case at hand, Tagalog speakers apparently felt that the English source sentence 'The chicken is eating' corresponds more closely to Tagalog sentences (9) and (10) than it does to sentence (11), and therefore didn't offer sentence (11), even though it is grammatical and an appropriate translation of the original English sentence.

This shows that in general, the elicitation of data from native speakers cannot provide an adequate empirical basis for the description of a language. But neither can any other single method, such as the collection of texts. There is no privileged field method in the study of language: linguists are like the proverbial blind men groping at the elephant, each from his or her own particular angle.

4.   Basic sentence structure in Riau Indonesian

Malay/Indonesian is one of the world's major languages, with up to 200 million native speakers. Actually, though, it is not one language, or even two, but a family of languages with about as much internal diversity as the Slavic or Romance language families. In the early 1990s, I got a job in Singapore and began learning the variety of Indonesian spoken on the islands right across from Singapore, in the Indonesian province of Riau. After a short while, it became clear to me that the language that I was learning, Riau Indonesian, was very different from the well-known standardized varieties of Malay/Indonesian, and had not been previously described.

Ask a speaker of Riau Indonesian to translate the English sentence 'The chicken is eating', and the answer might be as follows:

(14) *Ayam   makan*
chicken   eat
The chicken is eating.

As suggested by the above example, Riau Indonesian is an isolating language with very little morphology: in the above example, each word consists of a single morpheme.

As already pointed out, Southeast Asian languages typically exhibit a large degree of semantic vagueness, with various categories, obligatorily grammaticalized in most European languages, left underspecified. In Riau Indonesian, the characteristic Southeast Asian grammatical indeterminacy is perhaps at its most extreme. In the above example, *ayam* 'chicken' is unmarked for number, allowing either singular or plural interpretations; and in addition it is unmarked for (in)definiteness, permitting either definite or indefinite readings. Similarly, *makan* 'eat' is unmarked for tense and aspect, allowing a variety of interpretations, such as 'is eating', 'ate', 'will eat', and others.

So far, not too surprising, but this is only the tip of the iceberg. Arbitrarily keeping constant the singular definite interpretation of *ayam* and the present progressive interpretation of *makan*, the above construction can still be interpreted in many different ways, some of which are indicated below:

(15) *Ayam   makan*
chicken   eat
(a) The chicken is being eaten.
(b) The chicken is making somebody eat.
(c) Somebody is eating for the chicken.
(d) Somebody is eating where the chicken is.
(e) the chicken that is eating
(f) where the chicken is eating

(g) when the chicken is eating
(h) how the chicken is eating

Comparing the gloss in (14) with those in (15a)–(15d), we see that in the above construction, *makan* does not assign a particular thematic role to *ayam*: the chicken could be the agent, as in (14); the patient, as in (15a); or any other imaginable role, such as the cause in (15b); the benefactive in (15c); the locative in (15d); and so forth. And comparing the gloss in (14) with those in (15e)–(15h), we find that the construction as a whole may be associated with an interpretation belonging to any ontological category: an activity, as in (14); a thing, as in (15e); a place, as in (15f); a time, as in (15g); a manner, as in (15h); and others.

When learning Riau Indonesian, it took me some time to become aware of the extent to which underspecification is permitted. Again, it was only through exposure to naturally occurring speech that I was able to appreciate the widespread nature of the phenomenon. However, even after I had realized how pervasive this indeterminacy actually was, it still took me a long time to figure out how to deal with it.

My initial reaction was to attempt to provide a different analysis for each interpretation – or, as I would now say, for each of what seemed to me, mistakenly, at the time, to be distinct interpretations. For example, interpreted as (15a), *Ayam makan* might be analyzed as a "zero-marked passive." Or, interpreted as (15e), *Ayam makan* might be assigned the structure of a "zero-marked relative clause." But something was clearly wrong with this proliferation of zero markings. To begin with, it made the language look more abstract and complex, when my gut feeling was telling me that if anything it was more concrete and simple. A more specific objection was that each and every sentence in the language was turning out to be multiply ambiguous. But were these really ambiguities, or was this an artefact of imposing Eurocentric categories on a language that didn't really have them? It was time to listen more closely to the speakers themselves, and how they use the language.

Poets, diplomats, and a few other people construct ambiguous sentences deliberately, for their own specific purposes; but most ordinary people do not. Take a garden-variety ambiguous sentence such as *The chicken is ready to eat*. This sentence can be understood as either 'The chicken is ready to eat the food' or 'The chicken is ready to be eaten'. However, in any given utterance of the sentence, the speaker will have only one of these two interpretations in mind: it is virtually impossible to imagine a situation in which a speaker would utter the above sentence without caring which of the two interpretations it is assigned. This is a good reason to characterize the sentence as ambiguous with respect to the thematic role of *chicken*. Now consider the fact that, under the latter interpretation, the chicken could be fried, boiled, stewed, fricasseed, and so on. Although in many situations the speaker might know how the chicken is prepared, in many other situations he or she may not. But in those situations, the speaker simply would not care, and the sentence could still be appropriately uttered. Clearly, in such cases, we would not want to characterize *chicken* as ambiguous with respect to the mode of preparation. Rather, in such instances, as in many other similar ones, the expression may be characterized as vague with respect to the feature in question.

Now let us examine some specimens of spontaneous speech in Riau Indonesian. (In the following examples, the context associated with each utterance is indicated in square brackets.)

(16) *Kalau   ada   penjahat   mau   dia   dikejar.*
    TOP   exist   PERS-bad   want   3   PAT-chase
    [a monkey's owner, about his monkey]
    (a) If there's a bad guy, he'll chase him.   *singular*
    (b) If there are bad guys, he'll chase them.   *plural*

(17) *Aku   Cina   tak   makan   la.*
    1:SG   China   NEG   eat   CONTR
    [going out to eat, approaching a Chinese looking place]
    (a) I'm not eating Chinese food.   *patient*
    (b) I'm not going to eat in a Chinese place.   *locative*

(18) *Ini   bisa   juga.*
    DEM:PROX   can   CONJ.OP
    [playing laptop game, speaker discovers that another key also works]
    (a) This one can too.   *theme*
    (b) With this one you can too.   *instrument*
    (c) This one makes you able to do it too.   *cause*

(19) *Cantik   gol.*
    beautiful   goal
    [watching replay of football goal on TV]
    (a) That goal was beautiful.   *property*
    (b) That was a beautiful goal.   *activity*

(20) *Ini   bagus   bajunya.*
    DEM:PROX   good   shirt-ASSOC
    [putting on a newly bought shirt, admiring it in mirror]
    (a) This shirt is good.   *property*
    (b) This is a good shirt.   *thing*

Sentence (16) provides a relatively straightforward example of vagueness with respect to number: in the given context, the speaker has no reason to distinguish between singular and plural interpretations of the expression *penjahat* 'bad guy'. However, the remaining sentences provide more far-reaching and surprising instances of vagueness.

Sentences (17) and (18) illustrate vagueness with respect to thematic roles. In (17), *Cina* 'China' may be construed as referring either to the food, as in (17a), in which case it would be the patient of *makan* 'eat'; or to the restaurant, as in (17b), in which case it would be the locative. And in (18), *Ini* 'this one' may be understood as the theme of *bisa* 'can', as in (18a); the instrument, as in (18b); or the cause, as in (18c). However, in the given contexts, the various construals end up meaning the same thing, and it is hard to imagine that the speaker could have been intending to convey one interpretation to the exclusion of the other or others. Rather, in the contexts at hand, it is a safe bet that the speakers had in mind a single undifferentiated reading encompassing the given glosses.

Sentences (19) and (20) exemplify vagueness with respect to ontological categories. In (19), *Cantik gol* may be interpreted either as in (19a), denoting a property, being beautiful, predicated of an activity, the goal; or as in (19b), denoting an activity, the goal, with an attributed property, being beautiful. Similarly, in (20), *bagus bajunya* may be understood either as in (20a), denoting a property, being good, predicated of a thing, the shirt; or as in (20b), denoting a thing, the shirt, with an attributed property, being good. Once again, in the contexts at hand, the different readings end up meaning the same thing, and it is clear that the speakers were intending a single underspecified interpretation unmarked with respect to ontological categories and whether the property is predicated or attributed.

Thus, the above examples show that thematic roles and ontological categories are not obligatorily marked in the grammar of Riau Indonesian. This suggests that basic sentences such as (14)/(15) should be considered not as multiply ambiguous, but rather as vague with respect to thematic roles and ontological categories. More specifically, a sentence such as (14)/(15) may be associated with a single undifferentiated meaning, indicated in the gloss below:

(21) *Ayam   makan*
     chicken   eat
     Entity associated with chicken and with eating

The above gloss may sound awkward in English, but the idea behind it is straightforward. Combine any two expressions in Riau Indonesian, and the meaning of the resulting collocation is, quite simply, anything that is associated, in some way or another, with the meaning of the two constituent expressions. Each of the glosses in (14) and (15) can be construed as a particular case of the gloss in (21) above, obtained by the imposition of further semantic constraints.

Syntactically, too, basic sentences such as (14)/(15) instantiate a single general construction type, rather than a variety of distinct, zero-marked constructions such as zero passive, zero relative clause, and so forth. The simple structure of such sentences is indicated below:

(22) for (14)/(15):

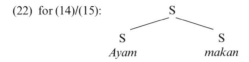

As suggested in (22) above, Riau Indonesian, like Tagalog, would appear to have just a single major syntactic category S: this reflects the fact that in Riau Indonesian, as in Tagalog, almost all expressions enjoy identical distributional privileges – just about anything can go anywhere.

Again, as with Tagalog in the previous section, the specifics of the above analysis may turn out to be controversial. (So far, there has been little discussion of Riau Indonesian in the linguistic literature: a preliminary analysis along the above lines, in Gil 1994c, is treated favorably in Kibrik 1997.) But the details of the analysis are not what this is about. Whatever the optimal treatment of Riau Indonesian may turn out to be, it can only be arrived at by unlearning Eurocentric grammatical traditions, and coming to grips with the structure of Riau Indonesian on its own terms.

At graduate school we are taught that, although languages often seem, at first blush, to be very different from each other, closer scrutiny will reveal these differences to be a superficial veneer just barely cloaking those deeper and more fundamental similarities. The goal of linguistic analysis, so we are told, is to demystify the apparently exotic features of different languages, and to seek out the commonalities which will form the basis for a general theory of language. The exciting and rewarding moments in linguistic analysis, so it is suggested, are those in which a strange and bewildering phenomenon in an exotic language is suddenly revealed, with the correct analytical tools, to be just like a well-known phenomenon in a well-studied language. Indeed, some of my fieldwork experiences have been of the above kind. However, my encounters with Riau Indonesian have led me in the exact opposite direction.

Before I started working on Malay/Indonesian, I had a preconceived notion of the language as being rather boring, with few of the interesting morphological and syntactic features characteristic of, say, related Philippine languages such as Tagalog. In fact, Malay/Indonesian seemed to me to bear a superficial resemblance to many of the well-known languages of Europe. The word order appeared similar, the amount of morphology was just right, and there didn't seem to be any of the complex morphological and syntactic patterns associated with Tagalog. However, it did not take long for me to realize that Malay/Indonesian was a wolf in sheep's clothing.

The more I worked on Riau Indonesian, the more exotic it became, the more different from Standard Average European. Time after time I found myself puzzling over a construction, only to realize that the best analysis entailed dispensing with the traditional categories of Eurocentric grammar. Again and again I would ask "is such-and-such a this or a that?," only to apprehend, sometimes after months or years, that I had been asking the wrong question, because the distinction between this supposed category and that simply wasn't relevant to the grammar of Riau Indonesian. After a certain amount of time working on Riau Indonesian, I came to the conclusion that it does not have the familiar grammatical relations of subject and object. Considerably later, I realized that Riau Indonesian, like Tagalog, does not distinguish between major syntactic categories. It is only recently that I have begun to accept that even the basic notions of reference and predication may be foreign to the grammar of Riau Indonesian. At every stage, I found myself casting off the notions of traditional Eurocentric grammar, in order to gain a more perspicuous insight into the language.

As was the case previously, with Tagalog, many of my insights into Riau Indonesian derived from the use of naturalistic data, such as that in (16) – (20) above. But in addition, much of my understanding of the language came from being able, after a time, to speak it – not natively, of course, but well enough to pass as a native for a brief period of time, in a dark spot, or over the telephone. It is a common layman's misconception that in order to be able to do research on a language, a linguist has to be able to speak it. But there is a grain of truth to the claim after all. Although most adults cannot acquire native competence in a new language, they can, with effort, achieve various degrees of near-native proficiency. After spending several years among speakers of Riau Indonesian, I found that I was able to introspect and come up with surprisingly subtle judgments with respect to grammaticality, semantic interpretation, and pragmatic appropriateness. Of course, it would be totally illegitimate to use such non-native intuitions as primary linguistic data. Nevertheless, such non-native intuitions may still serve a valuable function. Specifically, they may suggest various hypotheses which the linguist may then test against reliable sources of data. And in addition, they may provide the linguist with a kind of intuitive backdrop, or reality check, for hypotheses already formulated; in other words, a better "feel" for the language.

On a recent trip, I found myself on a boat, engaged in small talk with a fellow passenger, who, like many Indonesians, wanted to improve his English. Speaking to me in Indonesian, he asked how I would translate various sentences into English. I don't remember what the exact sentences were, but one of them could easily have been 'The chicken is eating'. My interlocutor was an inquisitive guy, and he soon noticed that the English sentences I was giving him contained more words than the Indonesian sentences he was starting with. So what is the meaning of 'the'?, he asked. But this was not the time and place for a lecture on definiteness. And what is the meaning of 'is'?, he went on. Then I began to wonder: what *is* the meaning of 'is'? Or rather, why on earth does English have a 'the', and an 'is', and all those other little words that Indonesian does so well without? As a linguist, I could provide all kinds of technical answers, but for an ordinary speaker of Indonesian, such answers would not be very satisfactory. Suddenly I realized that, after so many years of immersion in Indonesian, I had managed to unlearn my native language, and was now able to look at English through Indonesian eyes – non-native, admittedly, but still Indonesian. And seen through Indonesian eyes, English was a very exotic language indeed.

That was the moment when I really believed, deep down inside me, that my view of Riau Indonesian as sketched above might actually be right. And that was when I knew that I had finally turned the tables on Eurocentrism, and was able to deal with Riau Indonesian on its own terms.

5.   Eurocentrism and language engineering

The preceding sections of this chapter were about Eurocentrism, its effects on the field of linguistics, and what the worker in the field can do to transcend it. But the effects are not limited just to linguistics: in some cases, Eurocentrism also has a profound influence on the actual languages that are the objects of the fieldworker's attention.

No language exists in isolation. All languages are in constant contact with other languages, and over time, languages in contact begin to resemble one another, lexically and structurally. Most of these changes take place *naturally*, that is to say without any conscious efforts on the part of speakers to borrow from one language to another. Occasionally, however, linguistic changes occur *unnaturally*, through deliberate acts of language planning, engineering, and prescriptivism. And such situations often involve the imposition of European structures and categories on non-European languages.

A vivid example of this is provided by the history of Malay/Indonesian. When the Portuguese and the Dutch came to Southeast Asia, in the sixteenth and seventeenth centuries, they found varieties of Malay being used as a lingua franca over wide areas of the Indonesian archipelago. Recognizing the great value of such a common language, they set about to standardize it, to serve their own goals of proselytizing, trade, and colonial administration. As the colonial era drew to an end in the mid-twentieth century, the two major newly-independent countries, Malaysia and

Indonesia, resumed the process of standardization with renewed vigor, through the establishment of official language academies, the *Dewan Bahasa dan Pustaka* (Institute of Language and Literature) in Malaysia, and the *Pusat Pembinaan dan Pengembangan Bahasa* (Center for Language Development and Cultivation) in Indonesia. (A lively account of the history of Malay is provided in Collins 1996. Discussion of some of the issues involved in language planning in Southeast Asia can be found in Abdullah 1994 and Heryanto 1995.)

During the colonial era, Portuguese, Dutch, and then British prescriptivists often distorted the language in order to force it into a more familiar European mould. After Malaysia and Indonesia became independent, one might have expected this particular motivation for linguistic change to have become defunct; indeed, one of the goals of the language academies is the introduction of indigenous lexical items to replace foreign loan words. However, such linguistic purism is more or less limited to the lexicon – in the domain of grammar, the academies are busy making their language look more and more like English. In both Malaysia and Indonesia, there is a misguided belief that in order for a language to be able to fulfill the functions of a national language, it must have a well-developed system of grammar. Unfortunately, the only type of grammar that the language planners are usually familiar with is the Eurocentric grammar of European languages. Thus, Standard Malay/Indonesian has had a variety of linguistic features artificially grafted onto it that are reminiscent of European languages, including nominal number marking, verbal active and passive prefixes, and others.

In general, language engineering has more of an effect on the acrolectal, or formal registers, than it does on the basilectal, or colloquial varieties. Politicians, newscasters, schoolteachers, and other professional people are obliged to speak *properly* when engaged in their official capacities, but ordinary people in everyday circumstances couldn't care less what the prescriptivists think. In Malaysia and Indonesia, the situation is even more extreme than it is in many other countries: the standardized language and the colloquial varieties have drifted so far apart that they are of very low mutual intelligibility. Whereas Standard Malay and Indonesian are not much more different from each other than Standard British and American English, the colloquial varieties of Malay/Indonesian are as diverse as the different varieties of English, Dutch, and German. In Malaysia and Indonesia, educated people are basically diglossic, while uneducated people may understand very little of the standardized language, even if they are monolingual native speakers of some colloquial variety of Malay/Indonesian.

For a couple of years, I taught linguistics at the Universiti Kebangsaan Malaysia in Kuala Lumpur. My goal was to get the students to work on their own basilectal varieties of Malay. Whenever I had a new group of students, I would begin the class by asking them to translate a sentence from English to Malay. Imagine you're just coming out of a sports stadium, I would say. You turn to your friend and exclaim: 'That match was great!' How would you say that in Malay? Invariably, the first answer the students would offer would be something like the following:

(23) *Permainan   itu   sangat   menarik.*
NOM-play   DEM:DIST   very   interesting
That match was great.

All in all, the above sentence looks pretty much like its English source. The first word, *permainan* 'match', is a nominalized form of *main* 'play'; together, *permainan* and the following demonstrative *itu* form what appears to be a topic NP, which in turn seems to be followed by the comment *sangat menarik* 'very interesting'. So far so good; but after a little more discussion, I would then ask my students: So what would happen if you really said that coming out of a football match? People would think there is something wrong with you, is the answer I would get. The above sentence is in Standard Malay, and nobody really speaks like that. So how do people really speak, I would ask. Inevitably, the revised answer that I would then get would look something like this:

(24) *Best   la   dia   main   tadi.*
good   CONTR   3   play   PST:PROX
That match was great.

And everybody would laugh, because it sounds so inappropriate to hear colloquial Malay spoken in a formal, university setting.

A brief inspection of (24) will reveal that it is totally different from (23) not just in choice of words but also in syntactic structure. To begin, whereas in (23) the comment *sangat menarik* follows the topic *permainan itu*, in (24) the comment *best la* precedes the topic *dia main tadi*. This alternative word order is one of the expressive devices available in the spoken language, in this case to add vividness to the utterance. Of greater interest, however, is the internal structure of the topic expression, *dia main tadi*. In Standard Malay, like in English, activities are prototypically expressed with VPs, while things are prototypically expressed with NPs. However, if you want to talk about an activity, such as 'play', and then, for example, to predicate something of it, such as being 'great', you have to convert the VP into an NP. This can be done in two ways, either by choice of a different lexical item, such as the English 'match', or by use of a special nominalized form, such as the English 'playing', or the Standard Malay *permainan*. In such cases, then, the prototypical association of semantic and syntactic categories is disrupted, with an activity being expressed, non-prototypically, by

means of an NP, 'that match' or *permainan itu*. It is precisely because of
constructions such as these that descriptions of English and Standard
Malay require recourse not only to semantic categories such as activity and
thing, but also to syntactic categories such as VP and NP. But now let us
look at the topic expression *dia main tadi* in (24). Although functioning as a
topic, it shows no signs of having undergone any process of syntactic conversion, or nominalization; in fact, if it stood by itself, *Dia main tadi* would
constitute a complete and well-formed sentence, meaning 'They played'. In
Kuala Lumpur Malay, as in Tagalog and Riau Indonesian, there seems to
be no reason to distinguish between NPs and VPs, or for that matter
between any other major syntactic categories. Almost any word, or larger
expression, can go anywhere; in particular, a complete clause denoting an
activity, such as *dia main tadi*, can find itself, unchanged, functioning as the
topic of a bigger sentence, as is the case in (24).

The contrast between (23) and (24) thus highlights the effects of
Eurocentrism on the standardized varieties of Malay/Indonesian.
Although Kuala Lumpur Malay (24) contains an English loan word *best*
(with a somewhat modified meaning 'good'), the structure of the sentence is
radically different from that of its English source. In contrast, the structure
of Standard Malay (23) is actually quite similar to that of its English
counterpart. This is no coincidence. Rather, it is a product of prescriptivism, and the conscious attempt to force Malay into the grammatical mold
provided by European languages, and the theories constructed in order to
account for them. Regrettably, the effect of such language engineering is to
suppress the spirit of the language, and, by making it look more like
English, to diminish the overall amount of linguistic diversity in the languages of the world. Fortunately, however, such prescriptivism generally
fails to make significant inroads into the more basilectal varieties, which
therefore remain the harborers of the language's true genius.

6.   No description without theory, no theory without description

For me personally, fieldwork is an endeavor of ongoing joy. I love working
with people, and I revel in the data that they provide: the tone sandhi, the
voice affixes, the sociolinguistic variation, and so forth. Yet at the same
time, I delight in the search for the more highly abstract patterns and structures which lead towards a deeper understanding of the nature of human
language.

For many linguists, however, these represent two distinct activities in
irreconcilable opposition. Two buzzwords, *theory* and *description*, dominate the debate, as rallying points around which the combatants gather to
cry out their slogans. In one camp are the self-professed theoreticians, who

declare that the only worthy activity is that of theory construction: for many of them, *description* is a condescending word hurled at those poor, uninteresting souls who have failed to see the true light. In the other camp are the self-styled descriptivists, who accuse the theoreticians of engaging in fruitless, frivolous activities, wasting time and taxpayers' money in armchair speculation while languages are dying all around us undescribed. In reality, however, both sides are equally misguided.

While the need to document endangered languages is undoubtedly the most urgent task facing linguistics today, it is an illusion to believe that one can conveniently separate description from theory, and – in the context of the documentation of endangered languages, at least – engage in the former without having to bother with the latter. Since the bare facts about any language are infinite in number, a finite description of the facts has no choice but to posit categories and formulate generalizations governing these categories, which *is* theory. Conversely, any theory that is empirically grounded accounts for a certain range of facts, while leaving others unaccounted for. Which facts get to be dealt with is at least in part a matter of taste and inclination, with respect to which practitioners may legitimately differ. However, for those facts that fall within the scope of the theory, the account in question *is* description. The truth of the matter is that there can be no description without theory, just as there can be no theory without description. (This point is argued forcefully in Dixon 1997.)

For example, many a linguistic description contains a statement to the effect that the language in question has subject-verb word order; typically such a claim is backed up by examples of basic sentences such as 'chicken eat', 'boy run', and so on. However, as suggested in the preceding sections, even such commonplace categories as subject and verb are theoretical constructs, which may or may not be the ones most appropriate for the data under consideration. Indeed, the word order of basic intransitive sentences is potentially amenable to a variety of alternative accounts, making reference to different kinds of categories: for example, NP precedes VP, actor precedes verb, topic precedes verb, participant precedes monovalent activity, less complex constituent precedes more complex constituent, shorter constituent precedes longer constituent, and so forth. And this is anything but terminological hair-splitting. Rather, such alternative accounts bear empirical consequences: each one makes different predictions with regard to the word order of various other sentences. And if the language under consideration is endangered, one can only hope that these predications will be tested before the language is extinct.

The choice that faces the fieldworker is not between description and theory, but rather between two different modes of descriptive/theoretical activity. At one extreme is an approach which may be characterized as top-

down, or *templatic*. This is a method that has been productively institutionalized by the annual field expeditions organized by Moscow State
University, as described in Kibrik (1988). Well-known exemplars include
the grammatical descriptions produced in the UK and the US by the
Croom Helm Descriptive Grammars and Routledge Descriptive
Grammars, and in the former USSR by the many publications of
Izdatel'stvo Nauka, such as those in the series titled *Jazyki Narodov SSSR*
and *Jazyki Narodov Azii i Afriki*. In this system, the author produces a linguistic description in accordance with a pre-prepared and standardized
checklist, which spells out the topics to be covered and the order in which
they are to be dealt with. This way of doing things is intended to guarantee
a relatively complete coverage of the major features of the target language,
and to ensure that descriptions of different languages by different scholars
be readily comparable. Such descriptions are generally extremely user-
friendly. For example, when I was working on my Ph.D. dissertation, a
typological study of distributive numerals (Gil 1982), I knew that I could
pick up any grammar book by Nauk, zip through the table of contents to a
sub-sub-section titled *čislitel'nye* ('numerals'), and home straight in on a
brief, usually one-paragraph description of *razdelitel'nye čislitel'nye* ('distributive numerals') in the language in question. However, such conven-
ience comes at a price. Although guaranteed to be free of arcane theoretical
terminology, a description of this kind is anything but atheoretical. On the
contrary, by its very nature, a templatic description involves the imposition
of a universal scheme upon a particular language – and such a scheme necessarily invokes a host of theoretical assumptions concerning the relevant
units of linguistic description. And of course, such a universal template is
inevitably rooted in Eurocentric grammatical traditions, and may thus be
ill-equipped to handle the diversity exhibited by languages spoken in other
parts of the world.

Escaping Eurocentrism leads towards an approach that is diametrically
opposed to the templatic – one which might appropriately be characterized
as bottom-up, or *free-wheeling*. In accordance with this system, the data
themselves are taken as the starting point, and the description of the data is
what then provides the motivation for the postulation of appropriate categories and structures. Doing linguistics this way involves turning an atten-
tive ear to the language under investigation and listening to what it is trying
to say, even if this entails unlearning various aspects of one's native language, and of one's linguistic education. The bottom-up approach frees the
fieldworker from having to handle a particular theoretical framework, and
squeeze-fit the language into a set of predetermined and possibly irrelevant
grammatical categories. However, it presents a greater challenge: that of
organizing the data from scratch, identifying the interesting regularities,

and accounting for these regularities by means of various theoretical constructs. Perhaps the most well-known proponents of such an approach were the American Structuralists, as represented by Bloomfield (1917, 1933).

Ultimately, however, the construction of a true bottom-up linguistic description is a chimera. The fieldworker can switch a tape recorder on and point it at a speaker, but in order to do anything with the data, even to transcribe it, there is no alternative but to invoke at least some a priori categories: segments, syllables, words, utterances. Subsequent more detailed analysis may reveal such categories to be inappropriate, but you have to start with something. In practice, then, working with languages involves progressing simultaneously in both directions, top-down and bottom-up, with each of these approaches informing the other at all times. In this chapter, I have attempted to swing the pendulum, as it were, away from what seems to me to be an excessive top-down orientation with its concomitant Eurocentrism, and towards a more bottom-up mode of analysis. However, in any given situation, it is up to the fieldworker to find the right balance between these two idealized approaches to the study of language.

Fieldwork is thus an ongoing dialogue of opposites: the deductive and the inductive; the abstract and the concrete; the general and the particular. Like, for example, when some ideas about ontological categories are confronted with an exclamation uttered by a television football spectator on an Indonesian island, as in (19). For me, perhaps the greatest satisfaction in fieldwork comes from tying all of these opposites together to form a single holistic activity.

ACKNOWLEDGMENTS

Since this chapter reflects two decades of academic activity, it is impossible to acknowledge the many people who have contributed, in one way or another, to its coming into being: I can only mention a few who come to mind now. Ed Keenan was the one who introduced me to the study of linguistic diversity. Sharon Armon-Lotem was a sounding board for my ideas about syntactic categories. Peter Cole, Gabriella Hermon and Uri Tadmor have been around for the last few years, for ongoing discussions about doing Malay/Indonesian linguistics. Michael Israel helped me to a better understanding of the issues relating to polysemy and ambiguity. Andrew Carstairs-McCarthy stepped in at the right moment with some insightful e-mail messages about the non-indispensability of reference and predication. The Hokkien judgments cited in section 2 were provided by Clara Lee Pei San and Peh Cheng Hwee. The Riau Indonesian data cited in section 4 were spontaneously uttered by Ahmadsayuti and Arip. Finally, it was Kairil who introduced me to Riau Indonesian, and gave me the Indonesian eyes with which to view English. My years of fieldwork described in this chapter were made possible by the institutional support of Tel Aviv University, Haifa University, National University of Singapore, Universiti Kebangsaan Malaysia, and the Max Planck Institute for Evolutionary Anthropology. In addition, the work on Malay/Indonesian described herein was supported, in part by National Science Foundation, Grant numbers SBR-9121167, SBR-9729519, and INT-9423291.

NOTE ON TRANSCRIPTION

1 In the Hokkien examples, the superscript numerals, as in e^{24}, mark tones, using a scale from 1 to 5 where 1 is the lowest tone and 5 is the highest. In the interlinear glosses, the following abbreviations are used: ACT 'actor'; ASSOC 'associative'; CONJ.OP 'conjunctive operator'; CONTR 'contrastive'; DEM 'demonstrative'; DIST 'distal'; INV 'inversion'; NEG 'negative'; NOM 'nominalizer'; PAT 'patient'; PERS 'personal'; PROG 'progressive'; PROX 'proximal'; PST 'past'; REAL 'realis'; SG 'singular'; TOP 'topic'; 1 'first person'; 3 'third person'.

REFERENCES

Abdullah Hasan (ed.). 1994. *Language Planning in Southeast Asia*. Kuala Lumpur: Dewan Bahasa dan Pustaka.

Ansaldo, Umberto. 1999. Comparative Constructions in Sinitic, Areal Typology and Patterns of Grammaticalization. Ph.D. dissertation, Universitet Stockholms.

Aristar, Anthony R. 1991. On diachronic sources and synchronic pattern: an investigation into the origin of linguistic universals. *Language* 67:1–33.

Becker, Alton L. 1995. *Beyond Translation: Essays Towards a Modern Philology*. Ann Arbor: University of Michigan Press.

Bisang, Walter. 1996. Areal typology and grammaticalization: processes of grammaticalization based on nouns and verbs in east and mainland Southeast Asian languages. *Studies in Language* 20:519–97.

Blake, Frank R. 1925. *A Grammar of the Tagalog Language*. New Haven: American Oriental Society.

Bloomfield, Leonard. 1917. *Tagalog Texts with Grammatical Analysis*. (University of Illinois Studies in Language and Literature, vol. 3, no. 24) Chicago: University of Illinois.

1933. *Language*. New York: Holt, Rinehart and Winston.

Bodman, Nicholas C. 1955. *Spoken Amoy Hokkien*. Kuala Lumpur: Government Federation of Malaya.

Carrier-Duncan, Jill. 1985. Linking of thematic roles in derivational word formation. *Linguistic Inquiry* 16:1–34.

Chen, Matthew Y. 1987. The syntax of Xiamen tone sandhi. *Phonology Yearbook* 4:109–49.

Cheng, Robert. 1968. Tone sandhi in Taiwanese. *Linguistics* 41:19–42.

1973. Some notes on tone sandhi in Taiwanese. *Linguistics* 100:5–25.

Collins, James T. 1996. *Malay: World Language of the Ages*. Kuala Lumpur: Dewan Bahasa dan Pustaka.

Comrie, Bernard. 1996. The unity of noun-modifying clauses in Asian languages. In *Pan-Asiatic Linguistics: Proceedings of the Fourth International Symposium on Language and Linguistics*, vol. 4, pp. 1077–88. Salaya, Thailand: Mahidol University, Institute of Language and Culture for Rural Development.

1998. Rethinking the typology of relative clauses. *Language Design* 1:59–86.

Dixon, R. M. W. 1997. *The Rise and Fall of Languages*. Cambridge: Cambridge University Press.

Ernst, Thomas. 1994. Functional categories and the Chinese INFL. *Linguistics* 32:191–212.

Gil, David. 1982. Distributive Numerals. Ph.D. dissertation, University of California at Los Angeles.

1993a. Syntactic categories in Tagalog. In *Pan-Asiatic Linguistics: Proceedings of the Third International Symposium on Language and Linguistics (1992)*, ed. S. Luksaneeyanawin, vol. 3, pp. 1136–50. Bangkok: Chulalongkorn University.

1993b. Tagalog semantics. *Proceedings of the Annual Meeting of the Berkeley Linguistics Society* 19:390–403.

1994a. Conjunctive operators in South-Asian languages. In *Papers from the Fifteenth South Asian Language Analysis Roundtable Conference*, ed. Alice Davison and F. M. Smith, pp. 82–105. Iowa City: South Asian Studies Program, University of Iowa.

1994b. Conjunctive operators: a unified semantic analysis. In *Focus and Natural Language Processing*. vol. 2: *Semantics. Proceedings of a Conference in Celebration of the 10th Anniversary of the Journal of Semantics*, ed. P. Bosch and R. van der Sandt, pp. 311–22. (Working Papers of the Institute for Logic and Linguistics, 7)

1994c. The structure of Riau Indonesian. *Nordic Journal of Linguistics* 17:179–200.

1995a. Conjunctive operators: a cross-linguistic study. In *IATL: Proceedings of the Tenth Annual Conference of The Israel Association for Theoretical Linguistics*, ed. Alice Davison and F. M. Smith, pp. 72–90.

1995b. Parts of speech in Tagalog. In *Papers from the Third Annual Meeting of the Southeast Asian Linguistics Society*, ed. Mark Alves, pp. 67–90. Tempe: Arizona State University.

1998. Patterns of macrofunctionality in Singlish noun phrases: a questionnaire survey. In *Papers from the Fifth Annual Meeting of the Southeast Asian Linguistics Society*, ed. Shobhana L. Chelliah and Willem J. de Reuse, pp. 147–82. Tempe: Arizona State University.

1999. Riau Indonesian as a pivotless language. In *Tipologija i Teorija Jazyka, Ot Opisanija k Objasneniju, K 60-Letiju Aleksandra Evgen'evicha Kibrika (Typology and Linguistic Theory, From Description to Explanation, For the 60th Birthday of Aleksandr E. Kibrik)*, ed. E. V. Raxilina and J. G. Testelec, pp. 187–211. Moscow: Jazyki Russkoj Kul'tury.

2000. Syntactic categories, cross-linguistic variation and universal grammar. In *Anthology of Word Classes: Empirical Approaches to Language Typology*, ed. Bernard Comrie and Petra Vogel, pp. 173–216. Berlin: Mouton de Gruyter.

In press. English goes Asian: number and (in)definiteness in the Singlish noun-phrase. In *Noun-Phrases in European Languages: Empirical Approaches to Language Typology*, ed. F. Plank. Berlin: Mouton de Gruyter.

Gordon, Lynn. 1986. *Maricopa Morphology and Syntax*. (University of California Publications in Linguistics, 108) Berkeley and Los Angeles: University of California Press.

Heryanto, Ariel. 1995. *Language of Development and Development of Language: The Case of Indonesia*. (Pacific Linguistics, Series D-86) Canberra: Australian National University.

Himmelmann, Nikolaus. 1991. *The Philippine Challenge to Universal Grammar*. (Arbeitspapier 15, Neue Folge) Cologne: Institut für Sprachwissenschaft, Universität zu Köln.

Huang, James C.-T. 1991. Modularity and Chinese A-not-A questions. In *Interdisciplinary Approaches to Language: Essays in Honor of S.-Y. Kuroda*, ed. C. Georgopolous and R. Ishihara, pp. 305–32. Dordrecht: Kluwer.

Huang, Yan. 1994. *The Syntax and Pragmatics of Anaphora: A Study with Special Reference to Chinese*. Cambridge: Cambridge University Press.

Kibrik, Aleksandr E. 1988. Čto takoe 'lingvističeskie ekspedicii'? *Vestnik* 12:94–102.

1997. Beyond subject and object: toward a comprehensive relational typology. *Linguistic Typology* 1:279–346.

Kroeger, Paul. 1993. *Phrase Structure and Grammatical Relations in Tagalog*. Stanford: CSLI Publications.

Lehman, F. K. 1998. On the use of dah in Lai Chin questions and the operator syntax of functors. In *Papers from the Fifth Annual Meeting of the Southeast Asian Linguistics Society*, ed. Shobhana L. Chelliah and Willem J. de Reuse, pp. 211–31. Tempe: Arizona State University.

Matthews, Stephen J. In press. Y. R. Chao and universal Chinese grammar. In *History of Linguistics 1966*, ed. D. Cram, A. Linn, and E. Nowak. Amsterdam: John Benjamins.

Peng, Shu-hui. 1994. Effects of prosodic position and tonal context on Taiwanese tones. In *Ohio State University Working Papers in Linguistics, 44*, pp. 166–90.

1997. Production and perception of Taiwanese tones in different tonal and prosodic contexts. *Journal of Phonetics* 25:371–400.

Ramli Haji Salleh. 1995. *Sintaksis Bahasa Melayu, Penerapan Teori Kuasaan dan Tambatan*. Kuala Lumpur: Dewan Bahasa dan Pustaka.

Ratliff, Martha. 1991. Cov: the underspecified noun, and syntactic flexibility in Hmong. *Journal of the American Oriental Society* 111:694–703.

Riddle, Elizabeth, and Herbert Stahlke. 1992. Linguistic typology and Sinospheric languages. In *Papers from the First Annual Meeting of the Southeast Asian Linguistics Society*, ed. Martha Ratliff and Eric Schiller, pp. 351–66. Tempe: Arizona State University.

1995. Parts of Speech in Tagalog. In *Papers from the Third Annual Meeting of the Southeast Asian Linguistics Society*, ed. Mark Alves, pp. 67–90. Tempe: Arizona State University.

Schachter, Paul. 1976. The subject in Philippine languages: topic, actor, actor-topic, or none of the above? In *Subject and Topic*, ed. Charles N. Li, pp. 491–518. New York: Academic Press.

1977. Reference-related and role-related properties of subjects. In *Syntax and Semantics 8: Grammatical Relations*, ed. Peter Cole and Jerrold M. Sadock, pp. 279–306. New York: Academic Press.

Schachter, Paul, and Fe T. Otanes. 1972. *Tagalog Reference Grammar*. Berkeley and Los Angeles: University of California Press.

Shkarban, Lina I. 1992. Syntactic aspect of part-of-speech typology. In *Pan-Asiatic Linguistics: Proceedings of the Third International Symposium on Language and Linguistics (1992)*, ed. S. Luksaneeyanawin, vol. 1, pp. 261–75. Bangkok: Chulalongkorn University.

——— 1995. Grammatičeski Stroj Tagal'skogo Jazyka. Moscow: Vostočnaja Literatura.

Tobin, Yishai. 1990. *Semiotics and Linguistics.* London: Longman.

Welmers, William E. 1973. *African Language Structures.* Berkeley and Los Angeles: University of California Press.

Zwicky, Arnold, and Jerrold M. Sadock. 1975. Ambiguity tests and how to fail them. In *Syntax and Semantics 4*, ed. John. P. Kimball, pp. 1–36. New York: Academic Press.

6 Surprises in Sutherland: linguistic variability amidst social uniformity

Nancy C. Dorian

The last thing I would have expected to find in populations of exceptional social uniformity is marked individual linguistic variability, but that's exactly what I did find in long-term fieldwork with Scottish Gaelic in Sutherland, in the far north of mainland Scotland. I didn't originally set out to go to Sutherland, and I wasn't in search of linguistic variability when I arrived there. En route to explaining how Sutherland became my research site and what I found in it, I propose to look at some general issues in field research: What entices a student linguist into the field? How usefully can a research project be focused before the researcher is personally familiar with the field site? When is a fieldwork project "finished"? And finally, how do the professional and the personal experiences of fieldwork conflict or balance?

1. The library or the field?

A student making routine progress through an academic program volunteers for some discomfort in leaving the familiar academic environment for a fieldwork setting. Entering an unfamiliar social world is guaranteed to plunge the novice researcher into something like a second adolescence: a constant succession of uncomfortable situations in which he or she has no clear idea how to behave and is very likely to behave inappropriately. There must be some substantial inducements to coax the student forth, as of course there are: the excitements of novelty and discovery, and the satisfactions of making a first real trial of professional skills.

I don't recall any explicit discussions during my graduate years, either among students or between graduate students and faculty, about the importance or advisability of undertaking fieldwork as opposed to library research for a dissertation project. Students decided for themselves whether their interests and values made fieldwork attractive, and if so, whether their personal circumstances allowed them to go off to a field site for a year or more. Although the Department of Linguistics at the University of Michigan, where I was studying, didn't deliberately cultivate a sense of professional mission about undertaking fieldwork, several factors kept the possibility always before us. A linguistic field methods course was offered during the summer sessions, and a number of faculty members were themselves either experienced fieldworkers or well-trained Middle English lexicographers who also needed to exercise careful patience in amassing and accounting for primary data. Among the senior faculty, Kenneth Pike was a major presence, and his prowess as a fieldworker was legendary. His occasional "monolingual demonstrations" made a vivid impression on all of us. A speaker of some language unknown to Pike was produced, sworn to speaking his or her mother tongue exclusively, while Pike, armed with a few props such as two sticks and a leaf, asked questions using only Mixteco (a Mexican Indian language he spoke fluently) and miming. Pike wrote everything the speaker of language X said on a blackboard and after half an hour performed an instant grammatical analysis on the material. This was awe-inspiring to watch and no doubt created a certain fieldwork mystique among linguistics graduate students.

During my graduate studies Old English had been a delight to me. Here was English as I thought it ought to be, a fully Germanic tongue without the overlay of Romance and Latinate vocabulary that seemed chiefly to serve the causes of euphemism and hypocrisy ("prevaricate" indeed, if the lady had lied!). But somehow a dissertation on Old English struck me as an improper use of my training. I'd been given to understand that a linguist could use the field method techniques we had been taught anywhere, with any language. And since the techniques could be applied anywhere at all, why not go where my interest was highest and try them out on a language I'd wanted to learn more about since childhood, namely Scottish Gaelic?

2.   Somewhere ho!

Good advice is a boon when you're contemplating fieldwork and the problem of funding it. Mine came from Eric Hamp, famed Celtic scholar at the University of Chicago, who suggested that I link my fieldwork to the needs of the Gaelic Division of the Linguistic Survey of Scotland by offering to write a dissertation on whatever dialect the Survey director considered most in need of study. Hamp predicted that funding sources would see a study linked to an established project as well-focused and worthy of support, as one soon did. I was content to go wherever the Survey directed me and work on whatever project they proposed, since I was off to the country of my choice to work on my top-choice language.

In correspondence the Survey director had indicated that a phonological study of the Gaelic spoken in any one of three different Highland locations would be highly suitable from the Survey's point of view. He seemed at the

6.1 A three-woman Embo gutting-and-packing crew at a herring-fishing station. The picture dates from about the 1940s with Barbara Ross at right.

time to be leaving the final choice to me, but soon after my arrival in Edinburgh he handed me a list of names and wished me well for my work in eastern Sutherland – not the location I had mentally picked for myself among the three, and a daunting distance away on the map, almost as far to the north as one could go without dropping off the mainland altogether.

At the time I wasn't familiar enough with Gaelic dialectology to understand the motivation for the director's choice. He, however, knew that the Gaelic spoken by the fisherfolk of eastern Sutherland was a dialect of the extreme periphery, and that in classical fashion it differed notably from more central dialects. Furthermore, it was certainly under studied. The speakers whose names appeared on the director's list had provided answers to a vast questionnaire made up almost entirely of isolated lexical items used by the Survey to track historical phonological development across the whole of Gaelic-speaking Scotland. The questionnaire was well designed for its limited purpose, and the fieldworkers were skilled at their jobs, but most of Scotland's local Gaelic dialects were otherwise poorly known, especially those of the northern and eastern mainland. The director's final words to me reflected the extreme scarcity of solid information about the Gaelic of East Sutherland in the early 1960s. He warned me that I might find no speakers left in the three coastal fishing communities he was sending

me to, in which case I was to come back and he would give me another
assignment; and he urged me to find out, if I did locate speakers, whether it
was really true that the Gaelic of eastern Sutherland lacked preaspiration
of voiceless stops and affricates (preaspiration being a striking phonological feature of most Scottish Gaelic dialects). Far from finding no one to
work with, I soon had an informal census of local Gaelic speakers running
to more than 200 people, and the absence of preaspiration, so difficult for
the director to credit, proved to be one of the most obvious general features
of the whole dialect area, with implications for other parts of the phonological system.

The 200 or so local Gaelic speakers still available in East Sutherland did
not include many of the people whose names were on the Survey's list.
Survey fieldworkers had moved through eastern Sutherland in 1953 and
1957, and most of the elderly speakers who had served as their sources, or
had been mentioned to them as possible additional sources, had died before
I reached the area in 1963. After one man who *had* survived turned out to be
lively enough at 86 to make it advisable to keep a table between us at all
times, I abandoned the Survey list and searched out my own sources.

Whether I was relying on Survey sources or not, my work was still necessarily tied to the Survey's interests. My funding had been granted on the
understanding that I would target my research to their needs, and beyond
that they had given me the use of a Survey van for the year. Sutherland has
been thinly populated since early in the nineteenth century, when most of
the tenantry of the great Highland estates were summarily evicted, often
with conspicuous brutality, in order to "clear" the land for sheep farms.
There was some distance between villages, and because of the low population public transport was much scantier than is typical of most of Britain.
It was impossible to get from one village to another and back again on the
same day without private transport, and since the Survey wanted me to
cover three villages, the van was quite simply a necessity.

Probably the three-village assignment should have alerted me to complexities lying in wait for me in Sutherland, but I only supposed that the
Survey director thought I might have to comb through three villages to find
enough people to work with. Once I was on location the inconvenient truth
of the matter broke over me very quickly: my work was not the relatively
simple job of describing a uniform fisherfolk variety of eastern
Sutherlandshire Gaelic, but the very much more complicated job of
describing each of three slightly different local varieties of fisherfolk
Gaelic, one for each village. In the standard field methods fashion that I
had been taught, I began my work by eliciting commonplace vocabulary
that was likely to be monosyllabic, or at least short. "What do you say for
'garden'?," I asked. "*yɛs*," said an elderly lady in Brora, the northernmost

village. "*l'ɛs*," said her counterpart in Golspie, seven road-miles to the south. "*l'es*," said a woman in Embo, ten road-miles south of Golspie. These were small enough differences, but there was worse to come. 'Bone' proved to be *kʰrē:ū* in Brora and Golspie, with plural *kʰrā:vən*; in Embo it was *kʰrãĩ:* with plural *kʰrā:n*. Even when it came to a word as central to the lives of all these fisherfolk descendants as 'sea', they didn't agree: the word was *mur* in Brora and Embo, but *mwir* in Golspie. Things were no better when I moved from single words to connected material. My original Brora and Golspie sources gave 'if you don't plant oats' as *mər kʰur u kʰɔrkʰ*, but the equivalent in Embo was *mə kʰur u kʰɔrkʰ* or *mə gur u kʰɔrkʰ*, using a different form of the conjunction 'if . . . not' (the first word in each example) and one with variable effects on the initial consonant of the following word.

The fact that the Gaelic of these three fishing communities – so similar in their historical origins, so close to one another (especially by sea, once the chief communicative link), and so nearly identical in all economic and social aspects – differed in each locality had immediate consequences for my work. Every word or sentence I gathered had to be checked across all three villages, lest there prove to be local differences. And since there often *were* such differences, which then had to be checked for possible individual idiosyncrasies, it wasn't good enough to have a single excellent source in each village. Three converging sources struck me as the minimum needed to confirm a form in any one village, meaning that I needed to consult nine people regularly. If any disagreement turned up, I would have to check with still more speakers. This was a formidable prospect. I had the usual year, more or less, for my field research, conceivably adequate for detailing the phonology of one local dialect, but I now found myself faced with three speech forms, clearly related (the Brora and Golspie forms particularly) but still distinct. And the phonologies, my special assignment, were indeed slightly different, not just in terms of the about 300 lexical items which took a different phonological form in at least one of the three villages, but also in terms of phonological inventory and distribution of phones.

In Brora and Embo, I enlarged my speaker sample by drawing in relatives of the sources I'd first located (with start-up help from speakers of non-local Gaelic dialects in Golspie and Embo, and from an English monolingual supportive of Gaelic causes in Brora). In Golspie, it was the non-local Gaelic speakers again who suggested potential additions to my speaker sample, and the new people happened not to be closely connected to my original pair of speakers. The difference in the way my Golspie speaker sample was enlarged, compared with the Brora and Embo samples, proved instructive. The value to community language studies of following out the natural lines of social networks is well recognized, thanks to the Belfast work of James and Lesley Milroy (Milroy 1980), but in Golspie I found that there were sometimes insights to be gained by working across the grain of social networks as well. My interconnected speaker-networks in Brora and Embo that first year were friendly enough to be largely uncritical of one another, whereas certain tensions within the cobbled-together Golspie sample were more revealing of local language attitudes. It was in Golspie, for example, that I first heard one Gaelic speaker criticize another for being "too proud" to speak Gaelic. The notion that "pride" could keep someone from speaking Gaelic suggested that Gaelic was a social liability in the local context, and so it was. "Gaelic-speaking" and "fisherfolk" had become synonymous, as the rest of the coastal population went over to English, and since fisherfolk origins implied poverty and bottom-rung social standing, some people of fisherfolk descent signaled a wish to distance themselves from their origins by declining to speak Gaelic.

During my original fieldwork year, I occasionally encountered people said to be of fisherfolk descent and Gaelic-speaking who turned out not to be fully proficient speakers after all. Regretfully I crossed these interesting people off my list of potential sources. The Survey, like all dialect-geography undertakings, was particular about its information sources. Speakers had to be strictly local, preferably elderly, and not too geographically or socially mobile, since people of that description were the ones least likely to have been influenced by any non-local usages they might have been exposed to. Luckily for my future work, it proved difficult in East Sutherland to isolate the speakers who best met the Survey's criteria from their usual well-peopled social contexts. I was working with them in their own homes, and in several households there were Gaelic-speaking spouses or siblings who were younger than the speaker I had specifically come to work with, plus occasionally a grown son or daughter who spoke some Gaelic. Answers of their own popped out eagerly from some of these others when I put questions to the older speaker. Being young, polite, and deeply grateful to all the families who let me into their homes and tolerated my interminable questions, I considered it proper to write down whatever was offered. So I recorded these extraneous responses, too, and found myself confronted yet again by uncomfortably diverse data. I wasn't getting reliably identical responses, even though my sources in these cases were not just from the same village but from the same household.

The material from younger family members didn't find much place in my dissertation, since that document was also in effect my report to the Survey, and Survey standards excluded material from such sources. But it was in my notebooks, as was a small amount of material from the very few elderly Gaelic-speaking crofters (sub-subsistence agriculturalists) whom I unearthed in the rural districts round about the three villages when the Survey director handed me another assignment: gathering Gaelic place names for the place-name specialists of the School of Scottish Studies in Edinburgh. Supplied with bundles of oversized map segments, I quickly covered the areas that were well known to my fisherfolk friends, after which I dutifully headed off into the countryside to follow up on uncertain reports of occasional elderly crofters who still spoke Gaelic. I found three, each one the lone surviving Gaelic speaker of his district, and with their help dotted the highly detailed maps with Gaelic names for cleft, knoll, hillside, rivulet, and so forth: ancient indigenous place names certain to be lost all too soon. I worked on a bit with one crofter after the place-name task was complete, enjoying the visits to his particularly pleasant family and intrigued by the obvious small differences between his Gaelic and that of the nearest fisherfolk. I was interested, for example, in a number of initial consonant clusters with a prominent bilabial second element (as in the Golspie word *mwir* 'sea') that were typical of the Gaelic of the fisherfolk communities. I knew these to be unusual in terms of western Gaelic dialects, and now I found that they were absent even in the crofter Gaelic once spoken very near at hand.

Tying my fieldwork to the Linguistic Survey of Scotland's interests had a good many consequences. Fieldwork funding and the loan of a car were obvious advantages, as was the access I was given to spectrographic equipment at the University of Edinburgh between academic semesters. For a long while, however, I considered having been set to work on the Gaelic of three different villages a disadvantage, leading me to devote too much time to cross-checking material and not enough to exploring any one variety in real depth. Seemingly unrelated extra assignments, like the highly detailed place-name work, coming my way because I was an available fieldworker in a little known region, had also taken time and attention away from my work with fisherfolk Gaelic, however interesting my brushes with crofter Gaelic had been.

3.   The dissertation is done, but am I?

It doesn't seem to be necessary to like the people one is studying very much in order to do productive fieldwork. When Malinowski's diaries were published posthumously (1967), it appeared that he had not had a great liking or respect for the Trobriand Islanders (Van Maanen 1988: 36), and Erving Goffman told me, when I had a chance once to ask him directly, that he had not particularly liked the Shetland Islanders about whom he wrote so illuminatingly in *The Presentation of Self in Everyday Life* (1959). But liking the people you work with, as I did, certainly makes the fieldwork experience more enjoyable, and for some personalities and casts of mind it may be an important factor in determining the course of future research, since it

6.2 Barbara Ross at her home in Embo on her ninetieth birthday, June 1, 1996.

enhances the appeal of returning to work in depth in a particular fieldwork site.

Like many another sojourner in the Highlands, I was astonished by the generosity of people in whose midst I appeared as an unannounced stranger. People were often slow to believe that I could be interested in their local Gaelic, since they had heard nothing but negative comments about it all their lives, both from English monolinguals and from speakers of more conservative westerly Gaelic dialects. But once convinced of my interest, most people showed an almost unlimited willingness in helping me learn about it. Payment was out of the question, since the very mention of it proved offensive, and the small hostess gifts that I learned were acceptable at each of my visits seemed completely inadequate thanks to people who were giving up whole afternoons or evenings to answering my questions and were regularly pressing great quantities of tea and baked goods on me besides. Even after I left that first year, five of my sources carried on answering my questions, putting long lists of phonologically relevant lexical items and short sentences onto tape for me so that I could consult this material during the ten months that I had spectrographic equipment at my disposal while working on my dissertation. All of the tapes that arrived proved to be the spoken equivalents of letters as well, with added messages giving me news and good wishes in Gaelic, and sometimes including general Gaelic chats among my friends. These were not people easily forgotten.

Furthermore, I genuinely liked the East Sutherland variety of Gaelic from an aesthetic point of view, especially the Scandinavian-sounding tonality of its longest vowels and the unusual sonority of its many uninterrupted multivowel sequences. I was also acutely aware that my year's fieldwork had been barely adequate even to the single task of describing the phonology of this distinctive and little-known Gaelic variety. I lived frugally while I worked on my dissertation, saved money from my fellowship, and left for Scotland again five days after defending the dissertation.

Hard pressed though I'd occasionally felt, as I made my perpetual swings from village to village and fanned out into the countryside with the place-name survey maps, my limited connections with the Linguistic Survey and the School of Scottish Studies taught me very quickly how precious and how fragile the store of human knowledge and experience among the dwindling Gaelic speakers of East Sutherland was. The material most coveted by the place-name experts, for example, was not the Gaelic place names of East Sutherland itself, but the far rarer Gaelic place names the fisherfolk knew for ports farther down the east coast of Scotland, where Gaelic had not been spoken for centuries. The uniqueness of such knowledge, and the finality of this chance to capture it while some Gaelic-speaking fisherfolk still remained on the east coast, was impressed on me, and it stirred the incipient cultural conservator in me.

Phonologically I had certainly encountered phenomena that were curiosities for a Scottish Gaelic dialect, from those initial consonant clusters with /w/ as second member to word-final geminate consonants in unstressed syllables (these last difficult to hear until I met a few of them before vowel-initial words within the same noun phrase). That is to say, I already had evidence, by the end of one year's work, that East Sutherland Gaelic (ESG) was unusual in more respects than the absence of preaspiration, and I suspected that more surprises might come my way if I spent more time with the dialect. Another reason for my return trips to East Sutherland, in 1965 and after, was that I'd begun to feel a responsibility to document this unusual variety of Gaelic that clearly had a short life-expectancy; family transmission had ceased in this area, and there were no longer any young speakers. It didn't hurt, either, that the place was beautiful (even if one could hardly say the same for the climate) and that most of the people I worked with personified a fieldworker's dreams.

Originally I worked mostly by elicitation, which by good fortune my sources found congenial and easy (not by any means always the case in fieldwork). My field methods training had stressed elicitation, but the conversational limitations of my Gaelic were a more important reason for relying on it. Asking people to produce stories addressed to a tape recorder felt uncomfortable in purely social terms. The tape recorder provided no social reinforcement, such as smiles at humorous bits or nods in response to rhetorical questions, and until I was comfortable enough in the language to supply these ordinary human responses while the story was in progress, I was reluctant to put a microphone in front of people and ask them to tell stories into it. Knowing I should gather texts to exemplify the Gaelic of the three villages, I had done a few taping sessions at the end of my first year, but with my halting Gaelic I found them extremely awkward. It wasn't until 1967–68, when I was finally comfortable enough in the local Gaelic to make a reasonable conversational partner, that I did a more significant amount of taping; but by then I was working hard on grammar, which again made elicitation (translation tests) the technique of choice. I needed to cover a lot of grammatical territory, and since my sources had proved to handle elicitation with extraordinary ease and even with pleasure – several said it made them feel like the brainy, rapid-fire responders on a popular TV quiz show – elicitation was an efficient way to go about it.

As it turned out, elicitation had an unanticipated benefit. The social context in East Sutherland, and especially in Embo, where there was a larger pool of speakers, continued to favor fluid work sessions with more than one family member present. I tended to ask for a good many examples of any structure I was exploring, and during the course of a session a variety of individuals might give their versions of a particular structure. Over time it became apparent that people closely connected with one another were far from unanimous about how certain grammatical niceties were to be expressed. Because I spent a fair amount of purely social time in some of these households, I also heard spontaneous usages that strengthened an impression of ongoing grammatical change in certain constructions. Eventually it seemed important to check on this, and I embarked on batteries of translation tests designed to elicit key constructions from across the widest age-range of speakers available. It also seemed useful to go back, as I did with pleasure and interest, to some of the imperfect speakers whom I'd been sorry to drop from my speaker sample earlier on.

Most of the linguistic variation that was being investigated in the 1960s and 1970s was phonological, as in large part it still is today. In ESG, for whatever reason, there was relatively little phonological change in evidence, but a good deal of grammatical change was underway. I had been much impressed by Labovian studies demonstrating correlations between phonological change and social factors such as age, ethnicity, social class, and sex, so I looked long and hard at one clearly advancing phonological change, substitution of [ɚl] for the more traditional velarized lateral [ɫ]. But only age seemed to have any bearing on how general the use of [ɚl] for [ɫ] became (some younger speakers in Embo having begun to use [ɚl] even in word-initial position). When it came to grammatical change, the same was true: age played a clear role in the extent to which an observably advancing change appeared, but no other social correlates emerged.

The age differences led me to wonder whether, in excluding younger people as sources, descriptive linguists, who typically insisted on working only with the most traditional speakers, were missing an opportunity to find out just what sorts of changes might be likely to occur as a small and highly localized speech form went out of use. I made a point of enlarging my speaker sample again, this time in Embo, where Gaelic was still widely used and speakers ranged in age from the eighties to the low forties, or even to the upper thirties, if I included some individuals who spoke Gaelic imperfectly with certain older relatives. The results of translation tests presented to Embo's broad age-range of speakers showed, among other things, that case distinctions were progressively weakening and that one traditional form of the passive was being abandoned (though it was leaving its trace in changes introduced into the other traditional passive (Dorian 1973)). Certainly it was gratifying to find the sort of age-graded changes I'd anticipated when I started probing for these and other grammatical changes. But I was struck, at the same time, by the moderation of many of the changes I looked at. Gender signaling via pronoun reference, for example, was notably weakening, but Gaelic has a number of gender-signaling devices and one or two of the others weren't showing comparable weakening. It was true that a particularly conservative passive construction was fading out of use, but the passive itself was still fully expressible in ESG, even among the stronger of the imperfect speakers. The hyperabundance of plural and gerund allomorphs in ESG was diminishing, but it wasn't anywhere near the logical extreme of one universally applied suffix, either for plural or for gerund. It was very far from it in fact: even the imperfect speakers still showed plenty of variety in each case (Dorian 1978b). The limited nature of grammatical "decay" in ESG, even with the dialect's ultimate extinction in sight, seemed to me as significant a finding as the presence of age-related grammatical change, and I tried to give it equal attention.[1]

When I finally felt more or less prepared to write a descriptive monograph on ESG, the training I'd had at the hands of those meticulous Middle English lexicographers at the University of Michigan came into play. I had depended on an unusually large number of sources in my ESG work, originally because the three-village assignment made it unavoidable, then also because sad losses among my elderly early sources made me seek out new speakers as the work went on, and finally because exploring grammatical change called for comparison across as broad an age-range of speakers as possible. It had become obvious long since that no single entity existed that could be labeled "East Sutherland Gaelic" and described in uniform fashion.

Not only were there differences from village to village, and from older speakers to younger, but much more awkwardly there were also differences within a single age-group in a single village, as there were among Embo speakers about whether the initial consonant of a following verb would or would not be voiced after *mə* 'if . . . not', as in 'if you don't plant oats' (*mə kʰur u kʰɔrkʰ* or *mə gur u kʰɔrkʰ*). Trained as I was to acknowledge differences, the descriptive monograph I eventually wrote, already laden with details about diverse usages because of geographically distinct variants, sprouted another layer of detail that recorded the dialect's stubborn resistance to uniformity even within the bounds of any one village (Dorian 1978a). Given what I knew of the dialect by then, it would probably have been more difficult to ignore the untidiness and portray ESG in terms of some sort of ideal normalization, than to do as I did and describe the rampant lack of agreement.

In the present half-century, the conventions of writing descriptive grammars have permitted reliance on a very small group of sources, or even, as was true of the last Scottish Gaelic dialect grammar produced before my own (Oftedal 1956), on a single highly intelligent and highly cooperative source. This practice reduces the likelihood that linguists will encounter markedly variable usage, or feel obliged to come to grips with it if they do. Oftedal, my immediate predecessor in Gaelic dialect studies, noted that the Gaelic of his single source and that of the man's wife differed in a number of respects, despite the fact that the two had grown up as next-door neighbors; but after noting the existence of such differences in an early footnote, he never referred to the wife's Gaelic again. Theoretical preoccupation with detecting the commonalities of universal grammar has meanwhile made it less likely than ever that descriptivists would be interested in pursuing evidence of individually differentiated usage, even if the differences should be of the rather striking sort that Oftedal encountered in the Hebridean dialect he was describing. In both traditional dialect geography and more recent correlational sociolinguistics, researchers have worked chiefly by multi-person single-interview survey, so that persistent differences in the usage of a single individual who is interacting with familiar interlocutors have little or no opportunity to emerge. The level of individual variability I was describing for speakers in socially homogeneous villages such as Brora, Golspie, and Embo seemed unusual, consequently, and by my own account this variability was turning up in small-village speech varieties on their way to foreseeable extinction. Under these circumstances, then, it wasn't surprising that even a highly knowledgable Gaelic dialect researcher, when reviewing my monograph, took the myriad details of variable usage noted for ESG as an indication of the dialect's obsolescence (Ó Dochartaigh 1983).

Reasonable though his conclusion seemed, I realized on reading it that obsolescence did not in fact provide an adequate explanation for what I had encountered and that the full range of ESG variability was still unaccounted for. Other large-scale projects intervened, and so unfortunately did severe health problems, but with what I trusted was the sort of dogged insistence on respecting the data that my lexicographer mentors would have smiled on, I turned back eventually to the unresolved issue of excessive variability in ESG. Gaelic was dying above all by transmission failure in East Sutherland, not by disuse among those who had grown up with it. When I began my work, Gaelic was still both the first language and the stronger language among a good many older people, and their ESG could reasonably represent the conservative norm for a number of instances of change in progress. But there was a large amount of variability in the dialect that didn't seem to correlate particularly with age or proficiency differences, and was found in the Gaelic of older and younger speakers alike.

For an investigation of the sort of inter-speaker and intra-speaker variability that I had become interested in, the former fishing communities of East Sutherland had some major advantages. Each bilingual group formed an unusually clearly demarcated population, for example. Despite some cross-village marriages, the Gaelic speakers in each village had recognizably local ways of speaking and could be identified as producing Brora, Golspie, or Embo Gaelic. Living in small clusters of separate streets, as the fisherfolk had, and speaking in each case their own distinctive Gaelic (plus a somewhat distinctive English), the Gaelic speakers of each village formed as clear and unambiguous a speech community as one could hope to find. Their way of life had been locally unique and highly distinctive. Although the fishing industry had died away, all of the fluent bilinguals in my study (and even a number of the imperfect Gaelic speakers) had been deeply involved as children in the shore work that long-line fishing entails, such as gathering and preparing bait, baiting the hundreds of hooks, gathering fir cones for the fish-smoking process, and in the case of the girls, also doing some door-to-door fish selling. This meant that in the childhood years during which Gaelic emerged as the mother tongue, the speakers I worked with had experienced virtually identical social and economic conditions: all lived in a few densely populated streets, in houses of the same general structure and in households sharing identical labor patterns; all were poor and burdened by the same social stigma; all spoke Gaelic in the home; all came from a highly conservative Protestant religious background. Almost no one lived in the fisherfolk streets who did not fish for a living, and after the school years, finished by age 14 in nearly every case, contacts with non-fisherfolk were limited and almost entirely commercial. Even religious life was socially segregated, since there were separate services in Gaelic and in English, with the former attended chiefly by the fisherfolk.

Variationist studies have long since demonstrated that the social features of large urban populations in particular, and even the generally smaller number of social distinctions within rural populations, find expression in significant patterns of similarity and difference in the use of phonological and grammatical features. I had gone to the Highlands expecting to find the same sort of phenomena there as well, yet years had passed and I had had nothing of this sort to report on. The very socioeconomic uniformity just described might play some role, of course, and if asked about my lack of findings that's certainly what I would have pointed to. Yet there wasn't any shortage of variability. Just the opposite, in fact – there was rampant variability.

Faced with this problem, I realized that at last I stood to reap the rewards of the three-village assignment set me by the Survey. Because I had always worked in all three villages and had regularly documented their distinct usages, I knew the purely geographical dimension of ESG variability intimately. I could therefore subtract that form of variation, as well as the strongly age-related variation I had already looked at, and focus on the intra-village and intra-speaker variation that remained. I had recognized this sort of variation early, because it turned up among my sources in puzzling ways. Among my early sources, an Embo brother and sister were unusual in having no other siblings, and in both having married within the home village and lived there lifelong. They also happened to live in adjoining houses as adults and to have a good deal of daily contact. Yet although they claimed they had never noticed it, their speech habits were mysteriously different: the sister, the elder by four years, used *stɛ* by preference for adverbial 'in', the brother *sčax*; the sister favored *tə(nə)* for conjunctional 'when', the brother *nə(rə)*; the sister used *mwĩç* for the locational form of the adverb 'out', the brother *mwĩ*; the sister used monosyllabic *hã:n* more often than *hã:nig* for 'came' and *hũn* as well as *hũnig* for 'saw', while the brother used only the disyllabic forms of each. Since they were close in age but of opposite sex, the most obvious hypothesis was that these were sex-differentiated usages in Embo. But that simply wasn't the case, as even the most minimal checking quickly showed. The problem, in fact, was that there were *no* apparent social explanations for this very prevalent kind of variation: socioeconomic background was uniform; age didn't play the obvious role here that it did in the identifiable changes in progress (although decreasing age could be shown to correlate with a trend toward the favoring of certain variables in several instances); sex could usually be eliminated as a factor; and there was no clustering of favored variants among people who had lived in the same street. I had variation in plenty; what I didn't have was an explanation for it in terms that variationist studies would have predicted.

This is a fascinating conundrum the full dimensions of which I'm still tracking, in fact, especially since learning how to tape-record from the phone (with the permission of those on the other end, needless to say). The still growing database so far supports certain conclusions to which I was inclined in 1994, when on the (mistaken) assumption that I wouldn't be able to expand my database much, I wrote about the matter (Dorian 1994). The most fundamental of these was that social homogeneity need not imply linguistic homogeneity. Where the two do not correlate, it seems by the East Sutherland evidence that three conditions may play an important part. First, some circumstance must lead to the emergence of an array of variants. The terrible upheaval of the nineteenth-century evictions, in the fisherfolk case, with some degree of population mixture occurring at that time, may account for some of the variation in East Sutherland, and processes of language change for a bit more (decay of former grammatical distinctions, for example). Second, some circumstance must prevent particular variants from acquiring a link with particular social features among groups within the population of speakers. In the fishing communities, small population size and density of interaction, plus a notably uniform socioeconomic background, presumably play this role. Third, some circumstance must impede local speakers' access to any standard-language norm that may exist for the language and keep them from developing normative judgments in connection with local variants. In the fishing communities the aberrance of the local dialect (which made importation of church-Gaelic norms or more mainstream-dialect norms unworkable) and Gaelic illiteracy (women) or very limited literacy (most men) have this effect.

One critical question that the high degree of intra-village and intra-speaker variability in the fisherfolk communities raises is this: if ESG currently represents the only clear-cut case of such prominent but socially unmarked variability, as it appears to, is that because these former fishing communities are genuinely unusual, or is it because the way fieldwork is normally practiced, and to what ends, has precluded recognition of similar cases? There is evidence in the literature to suggest that a considerable amount of socially unweighted linguistic variability exists in small communities that are buffered in one way or another from the development of normative judgments, but in-depth community-wide studies of other small and relatively isolated speech communities with unwritten vernaculars will be needed in order to find out whether it reaches ESG proportions elsewhere. The question can only be addressed if some linguists can be persuaded – even without a Linguistic Survey to give them a nudge – to depart from the usual practice of working with a talented principal informant, plus or minus a few backup sources, and to take up the challenge of whole-community fieldwork in small communities where people speak a local vernacular that is sharply different from any written languages in regional or national use. That might seem something of a luxury at a time when we're just coming to grips with a crisis of underdocumentation in the face of impending large-scale language loss. Yet it seems important to determine whether the expectation of a general consensus on phonological and grammatical norms, deeply inculcated in literate researchers whose professional training (and life experience as well, in most cases) took place in highly normed settings, creates a bias inappropriate to the accurate description of some languages in use in small, preliterate, and socially undifferentiated speech communities.

4.   The scholar and the sojourner

Fieldwork is simultaneously a professional and a personal experience, which of course is the source of much of the tension it engenders. To my thinking, fieldwork is inherently stressful. Work undertaken in a strange setting depends on the goodwill of people whose traditions you're not fully familiar with and whose values you'll probably never completely fathom; and sooner or later (or more likely both) you're bound to offend against local norms. I don't think I ever prepared to leave for Sutherland without being visited by a recurrent anxiety dream exquisitely well tuned to the East Sutherland social environment. In the dream I found to my horror that I had omitted calling on some one person during my extended round of obligatory fresh-arrival visits. The omitted person changed each time, but the sweaty anxiety provoked by my sudden awareness of an unforgivable oversight never did. Once in the field environment itself, a consistently difficult personal challenge for me was the fishbowl nature of life in a small-village setting. Much as I came to appreciate the vivid drama of village life, where every human folly or unlucky flick of fate's indifferent hand is soon common knowledge, I never got used to being so utterly conspicuous as I unavoidably was. Even so I was very lucky, since personal privacy is respected in Highland Scotland, and I enjoyed a great deal of it whenever my work didn't require me to be out and about.

The linguist arrives at a fieldwork site with a research agenda, looking for native speakers of a certain language and seeing the local people initially as sources of expert knowledge; she may or may not come to see them also as individual people. Local people see the newcomer as an individual (a pretty eccentric individual by local standards); they may or may not come to see her also as a researcher, depending on whether their culture provides any analogs to such a role or whether they've previously encountered people with similar preoccupations. Short-term fieldwork is likely to accentuate the researcher-and-sources aspect of fieldwork, since the scholar soon moves on to a new project in a new site. Long-term fieldwork can sometimes be managed on the same basis; the researcher might, for example, fit neatly into the role of employer, i.e., someone who returns at intervals and provides jobs for local people. But the tension between the scholar, whose priority is the gathering of information, and the sojourner, who moves among increasingly familiar people and increasingly connects with them *as* people, can be acute and painful, and never more so than when professional priorities call for subordination of the more human connection. Anthropologist Barbara Tedlock tells of being taught the Zuni cure for fright, an unexpected token of friendship and trust, after a near-accident *en route* to what was intended as a farewell visit to long-term Zuni consultants. Her immediate professional impulse was to ask a great many questions about this curing treatment she hadn't previously known of, but personal circumstances ruled that out (Tedlock 1992: 286–87):

> I kept quiet. Partly because I couldn't bring myself to objectify the situation so quickly, and partly because of Hapiya. . . . He had given us some of his sacred medicine knowledge, a bit of his own life, his own breath. . . .
> I also kept quiet because we had something difficult to tell Hapiya. We were starting up new fieldwork, and this time it was far from the Southwest, in Guatemala. It was hard to find the words to explain to him why we would study elsewhere.

People don't see themselves as objects of study. Finding that others do see them that way produces strong reactions. More often than not the reactions are negative, as some eloquent Native American responses to anthropologists' studies have demonstrated (Deloria 1969); but occasionally a sense of validation and self-worth is roused instead. Social bias against the people who became the East Sutherland fisherfolk arose shortly after 1800, at the time of their involuntary resettlement as destitute evictees from inland glens, and solidified in the following century, as severe poverty attended their painful transition from agriculture to fishing. The bias against the fisherfolk population was mirrored in a bias against their variety of Gaelic, so that a scholar who aspired to speak it herself, and who returned repeatedly to study it further and to write books about it, represented a vindication of sorts to some speakers. The scholar was indeed very deeply interested and even admiring, and in this particular setting a sincerely interested scholar made a welcome sojourner, too.

As low as fieldwork tensions were for me in the East Sutherland setting, they were always present as I blundered about in an environment and a language not my own. In retrospect I wouldn't wish the tensions or even the painful blunders away. They belong to the learning process of an immersion experience and are often the engine of discovery, casting linguistic and cultural differences into sharp relief. Some of the special insights of fieldwork may hinge on them. Because they're uncomfortable and unforgettable, they loom large in the consciousness of fieldworkers (and no doubt also in the memories of the people who live where the researcher worked). Occasionally they surface poignantly in their memoirs (e.g., Briggs 1970), to instruct us nearly as usefully as they did the memoirs' authors. In learning to do fieldwork, as in learning to drive, the learner knows that some mistakes are inevitable. The learner's hope in both cases is that the first few mistakes will be of a survivable magnitude so that the learning process can continue.

NOTE

1 In retrospect this seems even more important than it did at the time, since three linguists working with geographically and structurally very different languages have lately found striking evidence of grammatical elaboration among the final speakers of obsolescent languages: Rob Pensalfini (1999) in Jingulu, an Australian Aboriginal language; Alexandra Aikhenvald (in press) in Tariana, an Arawakan language of the Brazilian Amazon; and Silvia Dal Negro (1998) in Pomattertitsch, a Walser dialect of northern Italy. Obsolescence processes clearly needn't be an unremitting progression into collapse and decay.

REFERENCES

Aikhenvald, Alexandra Y. In press. Areal typology and grammaticalization: the emergence of new verbal morphology in an obsolescent language. In *The Interface between Comparative Linguistics and Grammaticalization: Languages of the Americas*, ed. Spike Gildea. Amsterdam: John Benjamins.
Briggs, Jean L. 1970. *Never in Anger: Portrait of an Eskimo Family*. Cambridge, MA: Harvard University Press.
Dal Negro, Silvia. 1998. Spracherhaltung in der Beiz – das Überleben von der Walsersprache zu Pomatt/Formazza. *Wir Walser* 36:13–16.
Deloria, Vine, Jr. 1969. *Custer Died for your Sins*. New York: Macmillan.
Dorian, Nancy C. 1973. Grammatical change in a dying dialect. *Language* 49:413–38.
    1978a. *East Sutherland Gaelic: The Dialect of the Brora, Golspie, and Embo Fishing Communities*. Dublin: Dublin Institute for Advanced Studies.
    1978b. The fate of morphological complexity in Scottish Gaelic language death: evidence from East Sutherland Gaelic. *Language* 54:590–609.
    1994. Varieties of variation in a very small place: social homogeneity, prestige norms, and linguistic variation. *Language* 70:631–96.
Goffman, Erving. 1959. *The Presentation of Self in Everyday Life*. Garden City, NY: Doubleday.
Malinowski, Bronislaw. 1967. *A Diary in the Strict Sense of the Term*. New York: Harcourt, Brace and World.
Milroy, Lesley. 1980. *Language and Social Networks*. Oxford: Basil Blackwell.
Ó Dochartaigh, Cathair. 1983. Review of Dorian 1978a. *Scottish Gaelic Studies* 14:120–28.
Oftedal, Magne. 1956. *The Gaelic of Leurbost, Isle of Lewis*. (A Linguistic Survey of the Gaelic Dialects of Scotland, 3: Norsk Tidsskrift for Sprogvidenskap, supplementary vol. 4) Oslo: Aschehoug.

Pensalfini, Rob. 1999. The rise of case-suffixes as discourse markers in Jingulu – a case of innovation in an obsolescent language. *Australian Journal of Linguistics* 19: 225–40.

Tedlock, Barbara. 1992. *The Beautiful and the Dangerous: Encounters with the Zuni Indians*. New York: Viking.

Van Maanen, John. 1988. *Tales of the Field: On Writing Ethnography*. Chicago: University of Chicago Press.

7   The role of text collection and elicitation in linguistic fieldwork

Shobhana L. Chelliah

I here advocate an approach to linguistic fieldwork in which text collection and elicitation are interwoven in a finely tuned, constantly modulated way. By text collection I am referring to the practice of compiling and analyzing naturally occurring speech and narratives in the language under study; by elicitation I mean either the use in language analysis of native-speaker intuitions or translations of decontextualized utterances from a contact language to the language being studied. Both practices are well motivated: text collections are reservoirs of cultural and linguistic information, and elicited forms provide crucial evidence necessary for the formulation of grammatical generalizations. In my own fieldwork experience with Meithei, a Tibeto-Burman language spoken in Northeast India in Manipur state, I have found that linguistic generalizations that result exclusively from elicitation tend to be unreliable. Likewise, language description based solely on textual data results in patchy and incomplete descriptions. I conclude that reliable and usable field data can only be collected when both text collection and elicitation are used.

1.   Using text collection in conjunction with elicitation

My investigation of Meithei began, predictably, with the elicitation of wordlists and minimal pairs. I used such elicitation to build a rudimentary understanding of the phonology of Meithei. I then attempted the elicitation of paradigms of verb conjugations and noun declensions in order to discover the basic inflectional morphology. I studied case marking and word order through the elicitation of simple sentences with verbs that could be expected to require one, two, or three arguments.

At this stage I found it helpful to attempt a thumbnail grammatical sketch of the language. This helped me discover what information I needed to refine my analyses. I then collected some simple texts on which to test my hypotheses. I considered any piece of running speech or conversation a valid "text." Although I documented variables such as speaker age and dialect, I did not limit myself to a particular demographic. Fortunately, as I was working on a language with almost two million speakers, I had no trouble finding willing participants. During a nine-month period, I collected thirty-five texts, including conversations, folktales, radio news broadcasts and plays. As far as content was concerned, the only restriction I placed on myself was to avoid potentially volatile topics such as local politics, drug trafficking in Manipur, or the policies of the Indian Central Government in Manipur.

I transcribed my first text, a folktale, with the help of a consultant. Since the text was on tape, it was fairly easy to play back the story, pause the tape at intervals determined by the consultant, ask the consultant to repeat the segment slowly, and transcribe the repeated portion phonetically. I was also lucky enough to be able to hire some linguistically sophisticated consultants, give them a tape recorder and have them transcribe the texts on their own in a practical phonemic alphabet. I then re-transcribed the texts and included phonetic details in the transcript. I had to check the content for accuracy because consultants sometimes "cleaned-up" texts by:

(a) removing scatological or sexual references, seemingly useless repetitions, and discourse markers or interjections because they seemed unsightly in written Meithei;
(b) replacing borrowed words, archaic words, or dialectal variants with indigenous, current, or prestigious variants, respectively; and
(c) rewriting or rearranging episodes in well-known narratives according to personal preference.

The next step was to get a free translation and a word-for-word translation of the text. Translation sessions from the language studied to the contact language, which was English, were invaluable. I learnt something new with almost every word my consultants helped me translate from the first texts I collected. In terms of phonology, I began the tough process of learning to differentiate tones, and I noted rules of assimilation and tested my hypotheses about phonemic distinctions. In terms of semantics and the lexicon, I learnt antonyms and synonyms of lexical items. These were rarely offered in list form; rather, they were presented in sentences which I dutifully recorded, along with all the pragmatic and cultural information my consultants offered me. My main consultant, Thounaojam Harimohon Singh, was particularly adept at providing Meithei paraphrases, explanations, or cultural notes to the text we were studying. This kind of opening up was encouraged by working on texts. Unlike the early elicitation sessions where my consultants fell in line with my agenda, during these translation sessions it was the consultant who was in control. All material incidental to the translation of the text was offered by him/her.

2.1   *Circumventing translation effects with data from texts*

Many of the seeming contradictions that came up during elicitation were
straightened out by supplementary information from texts. First, I found
the elicitation of paradigms for tense to be particularly useless since there
is no one-to-one correspondence between form and function for the indication of tense and modality in Meithei. For example, the past tense can
be indicated by the marker of mild assertion as in (1) or strong assertion as
in (2).

(1) *laʔĭ*
    lak-lə-ĭ
    come-perfect-nonhypothetical
    came

(2) laʔe
    lak-lə-e
    come-perfect-assertive
    came

Either of these could show up in elicitation of the past tense. Additionally,
consultants found it difficult to explain what the difference was between the
examples when they occurred out of context. To determine the difference
between (1) and (2), I found sentences with (1) in texts and asked consultants to oppose (2) in the same situation. From this I found that while (1)
means 'came', (2) means 'certainly came'. Similarly, when consultants were
unable to explain the meaning of the verbal suffix *-ləm*, except to say that it
occurred in past tense verbs, I presented them with examples (3) and (4) and
asked them to describe the situations in which they would be used. By using
the scenarios provided in texts as a starting point, I was able to elicit the
crucial information given in parentheses.

(3) *məhák   čárəmkhre*
    mə-hák   čá-ləm-khi-lə-e
    3rd psn-here   eat-evidential-still-perfect-assertive
    He (obviously) has eaten already.

(4) *məhák   čákhre*
    mə-hák   čá-khi-lə-e
    3rd psn-here   eat-still-perfect-assertive
    He (says he) has eaten already.

In this way, I was able to arrive at the hypothesis that *-ləm* was used with
propositions that were based on inferential evidence. In order to check on
my hypothesis, I then scanned other texts and repeated the process with
other sentences and situations.

    In order to vary activities during fieldwork sessions, I combined text-
derived questions on unknown morphology, phonological processes, fast

speech phenomena, and the refining of free translations with one or two of the following tasks:

(a) eliciting translations of English sentences to investigate specific topics such as the structure of questions, relative clauses, complements, adverbial clauses, or negation;

(b) transcribing/translating a new text;

(c) taping new texts with prompts such as pictures which my consultants would have to describe or comic strips from local magazines and newspapers that they would have to provide a script for (I found comic strips especially useful because the context was controlled enough that I could attempt translations on my own);

(d) recording conversations in Meithei on the days I had back-to-back meetings with native speakers (to ensure some amount of naturalness in the conversation, I usually left the room after I turned the tape recorder on); and

(e) asking consultants to fill in a verb morphology questionnaire that I devised by generating a list of all the possible suffix and prefix combinations in Meithei. I asked consultants to form sentences with verbs using these combinations.

2.1.1   Calques All of these activities were profitable. I soon learned, however, to be wary of data gained through (a) above. I noticed that the more complex my English sentences got, the more my consultants either provided calques, omitted categories, failed to provide non-prototypical constructions, or were influenced by the contact language. This tendency was especially pronounced when the translations required grammatical knowledge that my consultants did not possess. This is illustrated by (5). When I was investigating complementation, I first attempted eliciting subordinate clauses by asking for the translation of English sentences like 'Thoibi believes that Khamba is dead'. There were two deleterious effects to this method. First, in one of my early attempts to study this phenomenon, one consultant consistently translated the subordinator 'that' with the Meithei demonstrative pronoun 'that', which is actually never used as a subordinator. Second, notice also that my consultant did not provide me with an exact translation of the sentence I had requested.

(5) Calque with demonstrative pronoun *mǝdudǝ* 'that':
    Thoybi   khə́ŋləmmí   mǝdudǝ   Khǝmba   hátkhre
    Thoybi   knows   that   Khamba   killed
    Thoybi knows that someone killed Khǝmba.

My consultant, though an educated woman, fluent in English and Meithei, had not been exposed to syntactic studies of Meithei which discuss sentence structure in terms of main and subordinate clauses. Such studies simply did not exist at that time. Also, she had not taken a class in English grammar recently. Apparently, she could not see the structure of the sentences I gave her; rather, she saw only the surface string of words and so gave me a calque. Thus, it was imperative for me to supplement the translation of English sentences with the study of complementation in analyzed texts. There I discovered a rich system of subordination involving adverbials, nominalizations, and subordinators based on the quotative.

2.1.2   Categories missed in elicitation While it was possible to elicit prototypical constructions, it was much rarer for consultants to offer less common variants during translation work. For example, where elicitation uncovered one word-order possibility in sentences with subordinated clauses, several more were discovered through studying texts. Similarly, I discovered only two quotative complementizers through elicitation. By combing through texts of varied genres, however, I was able to find eleven others. Formed on the verb root *háy* 'say', each quotative occurs with unique nominalizing morphology: for example, *háyrə́gə* 'after that', where 'say' is suffixed by the adverbial participial *-lə́gə*, and *háybəgi* 'regarding that', where the root is suffixed by the nominalizer *-pə* and the genitive marker *-ki*. With elicitation it is common to miss a category or construction simply because the investigator is unaware of its existence.

An example of an easily missed category is evidentiality, perhaps because, to use Silverstein's terminology (1979: 234), it is a covert category, low on the "hierarchy of elicitability." Indeed, evidentiality is not discussed in many grammars of Meithei because these are based on either Sanskrit or Latin grammatical models (e.g., Pettigrew 1912, Shastri 1971, Grierson and Konow 1967), and such models rarely explicitly describe evidentiality as a category. Thus, descriptions of the category have not entered into Meithei textbooks, and the category is not high in the grammatical consciousness of either educated or uneducated speakers. However, evidentiality is robustly manifested in disparate formal systems in Meithei (Chelliah 1997: 295–312). It can be signaled through choice of complementizer as in (6), choice of nominalizer as in (7) and derivational verb morphology as in (8).

(6) Quotative complementizer *háybədu* is used with eyewitness accounts:
    əhə́ldunə   yén   huranbə   háybədu   úy
    that old man   chicken   stealing   that   saw
    I saw that stealing of the chicken by the old man.

(7) Nominalizer *-jat* 'kind of, sort of' signals indirect evidence:
    məsi   phúrəbəjatni
    this   is a type of having been beaten
    It looks like it might have been beaten.

(8) Derivational suffix -*həw* 'start' signals an event witnessed at its beginning:
turen   pahəwwí
river   began to overflow
I saw the river overflowing.

Now, even though I had suspected that complementizers did code evidentiality, I was unable to elicit evidential values for them through translation. Questions like "How do you say, 'I saw/know/heard that he fell'?" resulted in calques with the verbs 'see', 'know', and 'hear' rather than through a change of the complementizer. Thus eliciting translations from English or Hindi was certainly an ineffective way to uncover the Meithei system of evidentials. What was effective was the elicitation of native-speaker reactions to paradigmatic substitutions of morphology that apparently had evidential value. The texts provided the context that made the exercise feasible. I discovered, for example, that the quotative complementizer *háybəsi*, which is composed of the verb 'say' followed by the nominalizer and the proximate determiner, is used for unsupported assertions, whereas *háybədu*, which is composed of the verb 'say' followed by the nominalizer and the distal determiner, indicates that there is eyewitness evidence for the subordinated complement.

Finally, clause chaining, which common in Tibeto-Burman languages (DeLancey 1989: 2), is hard to elicit, primarily because it is typical of narratives but not of everyday conversation. Additionally, consultants have a tendency to simplify during elicitation sessions to accommodate to the language fluency of the investigator, and to practical restrictions such as speed of transcription.

2.1.3   Influences of the metalanguage on translation For translation to be effective the consultant should be a fluent bilingual, that is, "reflective and creative . . . [and able to] transform the sentence according to the spirit of the [studied] language" (Bouquiaux and Thomas 1992: 41). However, whenever possible, fieldworkers select consultants that are authentic speakers of the language to be studied. I looked for consultants who were functionally bilingual but preferably were only marginally touched by the non-native culture and language. Thus, more often than not, my consultants did not have the knowledge of English necessary for effective translation of the nuances of English into Meithei.

Also, if the metalanguage variety used by the consultant is different from that used by the elicitor, problems can arise. Harold Schiffman (p.c.) comments on this point regarding his fieldwork on Tamil:

Another problem with the whole business of elicitation of individual sentences/examples is that if it's done through English etc. you get two different varieties of English being used, e.g., American and Indian English, and the latter is often not isomorphic with American/ British when it comes to things like aspect. I did my dissertation on Tamil aspect and couldn't even get proper examples of certain things because my English wasn't at all like the English of the people I was asking questions of; the only people who could really help me were American-trained linguists.

Since some of my consultants spoke a rather unstable Meithei-English interlanguage, I had to "translate" their translations into standard English. I soon learned to recheck my corrected translations with more fluent speakers of English, because there was no one-to-one equivalency between my consultants' idiolect of English and my own. This is illustrated in (9) where ME stands for Meithei English and SIE for Standard Indian English.

(9) ME   What do you intend to do?
    SIE: What are you going to do?
    ME   This is the last trip of rice.
    SIE   This is the last time the rice is going to come around.
    ME   . . . be in good soil and have abundant resources.
    SIE   . . . be in a place that will nurture one's research.
    ME   He is not being.
    SIE   He is dead.

Given the varying levels of proficiency with and cultural influences on different varieties of English, it is imperative to have reliable context in order to get equivalencies with Standard English.

2.2   Circumventing the unreliability of grammaticality judgments with data from texts

One of my methods of checking on language data was to take sentences from texts, create minimal pairs or sets by substituting words or morphemes, and then ask consultants what the sentence meant once the change had been carried out. Some investigators use a similar tactic where they create sentences out of whole cloth in the studied language and then query the consultant about the grammaticality of the sentences. Georgia Green states that this method is justified because

once you go beyond the easy (The farmer killed the duckling) parts of a description, distinguishing among competing hypotheses just about necessarily involves you in getting judgments about unusual, often marginal sorts of sentences. It should not be surprising that people have difficulty judging these, and vary widely, and may be inconsistent. (cited in Li 1994)

In a review of the literature on using grammaticality judgments as linguistic evidence, Sorace (1996: 377–78) points out four main reasons for intra-speaker and inter-speaker inconsistencies, which can be summarized as follows:

(a) Parsing strategies: sentences which are grammatical but are tough to parse are often deemed ungrammatical even when they are not. For example, the following sentence seems ungrammatical, unless it is read with the appropriate intonation: "The horse raced past the barn fell."

(b) Context and mode of presentation: when consultants are faced with a sentence that is not clearly grammatical after a list of unequivocally grammatical sentences, they tend to label the fuzzy example ungrammatical.

(c) Pragmatic considerations: decontextualized sentences can be judged inconsistently depending on the context built for those sentences by the consultant.

(d) Linguistic training: linguists are more varied in their judgments than naïve speakers.

Additional observations about asking for introspective judgments are reported by Ross (1979: 136), who points out that speakers of a language typically share very clear intuitions about certain sentences, either accepting them without hesitation as grammatical – he calls these the "core" sentences – or rejecting them outright as ungrammatical – he calls these the "fringe" sentences. There is also the set of sentences about which speakers cannot unequivocally give a judgment on grammaticality or ungrammaticality – the sentences in the "bog." When native speakers are repeatedly questioned about these indeterminate sentences, they reach a point of "satiation" and become befuddled about their own intuitions. Summaries of further studies on judgment fatigue can be found in Luka (1995) and Hudson (1994). Additionally, Haj Ross (p.c.) has pointed out to me that there are constructions in English which sound fine initially, but on closer inspection defy interpretation. Consider, for example, "More smokers smoke more Camels than any other brand."

What do we learn about the language under consideration, or language in general, when judgments are variable and our theories are based on these judgments? It is true that theories of grammar are based on idiolectal performance data from which we try to extrapolate a description of competence (the *grammar*) (Shütze 1996). However, when performance is widely inconsistent, with crucial examples sometimes being partially or outright rejected and others partially or outright accepted, resultant theories cannot be reliable, because in these cases it is the fieldworker who decides which judgment is going to take precedence in his/her presentation of the data. As a result theoretical ends guide the description. Even if the sole aim of descriptive work is to establish an adequate theoretical explanation for a specific grammar which fits in with a universal grammatical model, letting "the grammar itself decide" (Chomsky 1957: 14) which sentences are legitimately part of this language and which are not comes dangerously close to letting the linguist create structures that really are not part of the grammar or omit structures that really are. This is especially problematic for endangered languages, where much responsibility for documentation and language revitalization is put in the hands of the linguist.

Grammaticality judgments, then, are not the most reliable way of getting to grammatical competence. In fact, anyone who has done fieldwork has had sessions where a consultant has simply given up trying to be honest about grammaticality judgments. The more candid consultants might tell you to stop your method of elicitation, which is what happened to Jacques Guy:

> That was around 1970–71 when I was doing fieldwork in Espiritu Santo. . . . I was quizzing Hilaire Chalet, who despite his French-sounding name, was a full-blooded native of Malekula [Vanuatu, Melanesia], on these two native languages, when, suddenly, he said to me: "Listen, Jacques, I am going to tell you: you must not quiz me as you do because you confuse me. I no longer know. You must listen to what I say the first time. If you ask me again, I no longer know." (cited in Li 1994)

I had a similar experience trying to understand the interplay between semantic role and contrastive focus markers in Meithei. To understand this system of argument marking better, I made lists of simple sentences and a list of the suffixes that occurred on non-oblique arguments in paradigmatic opposition. I then generated a list of sentences with all possible combinations of argument-suffix combinations, as in (10–13) where *-nə* is the contrastive marker, *-pu* is the patient marker, and *pammí* means 'likes'. The question to my consultant was: "If (10) means 'Ram likes Sita', are (11–13) grammatical and what do they mean?"

(10) *ramnə   sitapu   pammí*

(11) *sitapu   ramnə   pammí*

(12) *ram   sitapu   pammí*

(13) *ramnə   sita   pammí*

My main consultant, a highly imaginative and patient worker, was thoroughly exasperated after no more than ten minutes of this exercise. For one thing, building context for some of the sentences was time consuming and, because of the mental gymnastics involved, exhausting. Also, sentences which sounded ungrammatical at first began to sound quite acceptable after a few minutes.

There are also problems on the phonological level with creating constructions for consultants to comment on. Minor but important modulations in vowel length, tone, stress, or intonation can cause grammatical utterances to sound ungrammatical. Indeed, ungrammaticality judgments may be based simply on mispronunciations by the fieldworker.

Finally, because consultants may be influenced by prescriptive knowledge about language rules (Birdsong 1989) and because consultants may not understand the terms "grammatical" and "ungrammatical" (Dixon 1992: 88), the fieldworker is forced into using misleading metalinguistic terms. For instance, the consultant may be asked if a sentence is "good" or if one "can say" a sentence. Not only may a sentence be judged bad because of the lack of context, it may also be judged bad for cultural reasons, such as tabooed communication between addressee and addresser. Most fieldworkers have encountered the consultant who will agree that one can say a sentence and then, at some later rechecking stage will add, "You might, as a language learner, say this sentence, but I never would."

The use of texts in guiding elicitation allows for the controlled use of native speaker intuitions. In my study of case marking and contrastive focus (Chelliah 1997: 93–129), I was able to effectively tackle questions about argument marking by sorting through texts and basing further elicitation on occurrences of argument marking in sentences in context. Thus consultant judgment fatigue was much less of a problem.

Another advantage of organizing elicitation sessions using texts as a starting point is that texts provided pragmatic context that my consultants and I could share. Some researchers claim that no sentence is truly "out of context" because, as Georgia Green puts it,

[W]hen speakers "judge sentences" they are not judging abstractions on purely formal criteria; they are judging the reasonableness of someone uttering that sentence with some communicative intention. Even when speakers think they are making that judgment in a "normal," "neutral" or "null" context, they will differ on how they define that term. The rest of the time they will vary even more widely, because they will vary, as individuals, in how imaginative they are in constructing POSSIBLE context in which uttering that sentence might make sense [emphasis in original]. (cited in Li 1994)

However, one of the dangers of relying solely on context created at the moment of elicitation is that consultants may assume they share presuppositions and knowledge about the context with the investigator, and therefore, while providing accurate statements, will not supply information that to them seems obvious (Hopkins and Furbee 1991: 69). It may be deemed impolite or a waste of time to do so. In order to avoid such miscommunication, it would seem preferable for the consultant and investigator to be "on the same page" with regard to context. It makes sense to put the onus of context building, not on the speaker or the investigating linguist, who probably does not know enough about the culture to do so effectively, but on a narrative or other naturally-occurring discourse. An added bonus, of course, is that the type and number of responses that one gets will not be limited by differing degrees of imaginativeness on the part of the consultant.

2.3   *Circumventing consultant and fieldworker biases*

Many researchers feel that grammatical descriptions based on a single idiolect can result in a valid picture of the structure of a language. Theoretically, this may be an acceptable tenet, but in practice, restricting the consultant pool to a single speaker is fraught with danger. Individual consultants are often affected by the enthusiasm of the investigator when results apparently simplify linguistic analysis. Once the native speaker has "caught on" to the theoretical point the investigator wants to make, it is difficult to tease out dressage effects from accurate language data. Some fieldworkers believe in "training" a consultant not only to understand simple directions, methods of translation, and metalinguistic tools, but also in analysis and theoretical issues. Take, for example, this hypothetical address to a consultant: "I was wondering if you could move this noun out of this conjoined noun phrase because that would be really wild. You can't do that in most languages." Might not this method of questioning influence the consultant? If this type of elicitation and training must be carried out in order to further language analysis, then it is imperative, wherever possible, to widen the pool of speakers with whom formerly culled data can be rechecked for possible dressage effects.

If the language being studied has a grammatical tradition, this tradition may limit and guide the introspective statements of the consultant, thereby causing misrepresentation or omission of data. I have a striking example of this from my study of case and semantic role marking in Meithei. Most linguistically sophisticated speakers of Meithei are familiar with the analysis of Meithei case marking based on Sanskrit or Bengali grammatical models: subjects are marked with nominative case regardless of their semantic role in the sentence. In elicitation, educated speakers consistently provided sentences where subjects were marked. In texts, however, only subjects of causative verbs are consistently marked, whereas subjects of other verbs can occur with contrastive focus or other pragmatic marking. Now, it just so happens that the agentive marker which marks the subject of causative verbs, as illustrated in (14), is homophonous with the contrastive focus marker which can occur on any argument, as illustrated in (15).

(14) *məhákn̥ə*   *ənáŋbu*   *kə́phəllí*
      mə-hák-nə   *ənáŋ-pu*   *kə́p-hən-lə-í*
      third person-here-agentive   child-patient   cry-causative-perfect-
                                                          nonhypothetical
      He made the child cry.

(15) *əybunə*   *Ramnə*   *nuŋširəbədi* *phə́gədəwni*
      əy-pu-nə   *Ram-nə*   *nuŋši-rəbədi* *phə́-gədəwni*
      I-patient-contrastive   Ram-contrastive   love-if   good-would be
      If Ram (not Chaoba) loved me (not Sita), it would be good.

It appears that speakers who had studied prescriptive grammar felt that "correct" Meithei sentences should have subjects that are case marked, and because the contrastive and agentive markers happen to be homonyms, they were able to implement this prescriptive rule. Speakers attributed the lack of marking on subjects in everyday conversation to the "carelessness" or "laziness" of speakers. I would never have discovered the fact that consistent subject marking was an artifact of prescriptive grammar had I not supplemented elicitation with the study of narratives and other naturally-occurring data.

The many Sanskrit-based grammars of Meithei which have encouraged the enforcement of this prescriptive rule are testaments to the fact that grammarians can also be influenced by personal theoretical and grammatical training. Similarly, we don't expect the fieldwork that leads to grammatical description to be theoretically uninformed, since one's theoretical training determines which aspects of language are to be studied and how the data should be presented. This is as it should be, since theoretical training provides necessary focus for language investigation. However, since there is circularity in linguistic inquiry – linguistic data forms the basis for linguistic theories and linguistic theories guide the gathering of linguistic data – fieldworkers should be constantly vigilant for theories that constrain or misshape their understanding of the data. To this end, the fieldworker should be familiar with more than one theory or grammatical tradition and develop an awareness of the limitations of each.

A consultant's knowledge of prescriptive rules can also influence the recording of phonological and phonetic data. Fast speech phenomena rarely show up in elicitation, not only because there is no running discourse which provides the environment for fast speech phenomena, but also because speakers carefully monitor pronunciation, often backing up and correcting themselves when such phenomena occur. Speakers sometimes dismiss forms produced in fast speech as "errors." For example, I was unable to get a translation for the form *háyšutətəw* in isolation; however, after getting my consultant to listen to the conversation it occurred in, I was told that it was a "mispronunciation" of *háyribə əsidə təw* 'do in the manner instructed'. A similar problem occurs with eliciting data for diglossic languages like Tamil. In these cases, consultants will tend to style shift from the colloquial to the formal pronunciation since the formal is perceived as being "correct" and the colloquial as "lazy" or "dialectal." The Observer's Paradox is certainly as relevant in descriptive fieldwork as it is in sociolinguistic fieldwork: a speaker's sensitivity to prescriptive rules can lead them to, as Sorace (1996: 379) puts it, "formulate adaptive rules that . . . modify their mentally represented grammars, often in order to avoid the production of stigmatized forms."

When one consultant provides the text, another helps with the transcription and translation, and yet another works with the investigator on additional questions raised through the text, the important step of rechecking material with more than one speaker can be accomplished. One could argue that rechecking with other speakers can also be done with elicited data. However, this raises a diplomatic problem in the interpersonal relationships between the fieldworker and consultants. If a high amount of respect is accorded the provider of the data to be checked, another consultant might be tempted to view mistakes as variation, or just forms that he or she is not familiar with. On the other hand, if the second consultant does not respect the original consultant, he or she may be overly critical of the data. These subjective influences are attenuated through work with texts, because then the second speaker is only being asked to offer an opinion about a sentence in context, and is not being put in the position of questioning the competency of either the original speaker or the elicitation process.

3.   Conclusion

I have outlined above a practical method of interweaving text collection and analysis with elicitation. This method helps guard against the collection of aberrant data that can result from translation effects and the unreliability of grammaticality judgments. Grammatically obscure categories are less likely to be missed when text collection is an integral part of the investigation process. Finally, the use of textual data challenges both the consultant and the linguist to look beyond the prescriptive rules of the grammatical traditions and theoretical models that influence their respective understandings of language. Although text collection, transcription, and analysis are time-consuming and initially daunting tasks, the development of our theories would be well served with accurate language descriptions which, I believe, cannot be accomplished without text-based elicitation.

REFERENCES

Birdsong, David. 1989. *Metalinguistic Performance and Interlinguistic Competence.* New York: Springer-Verlag.
Bouquiaux, Luc, and Jacqueline M. C. Thomas, trans. by James Roberts. 1992. *Studying and Describing Unwritten Languages.* Dallas: Summer Institute of Linguistics.
Chelliah, Shobhana. 1997. *A Grammar of Meithei.* Berlin: Mouton de Gruyter.
Chomsky, Noam. 1957. *Syntactic Structures.* The Hague: Mouton.
DeLancey, Scott. 1989. Case marking patterns in Tibeto-Burman languages. Unpublished ms., University of Oregon, Eugene.

Dixon, R. M. W. 1992. Naïve linguistic explanation. *Language in Society* 21: 83–91.

Grierson, Sir G. A. and Konow, S. (eds.) 1967 [1903–28]. *Linguistic Survey of India*, vol. 3, parts 1–3: *Tibeto-Burman Family*. Delhi: Motilal Banarsidass.

Hopkins, Jill D. and Louanna Furbee. 1991. Indirectness in the interview. *Journal of Linguistic Anthropology* 1:63–77.

Hudson, Richard. 1994. Summary: linguists versus normals. *The Linguist List*, vol. 5–855 (July 29, 1994). http://www.linguistlist.org

Li, Wen-Chao. 1994. Summary: native speaker judgments. *The Linguist List*, vol. 5–745 (June 27, 1994). http://www.linguistlist.org

Luka, Barbara. 1995. Judgment fatigue, summary part II: Stromswold, Ross, Tang, Boyland, Beasley *The Linguist List*, vol. 6–1045 (August 3, 1995). http://www.linguistlist.org

Pettigrew, W. 1912. *Manipuri (Mitei) Grammar*. Allahabad: Pioneer Press.

Ross, John Robert. 1979. Where's English? In *Individual Differences in Language Ability and Language Behavior*, ed. Charles Fillmore, Daniel Kempler, and William S.-Y. Wang, pp. 127–63. New York: Academic Press.

Shastri, Kalachand. 1971. *Manipuri Vyakaran Kaumudi* [Manipuri Grammar]. Imphal: T. Abir Singh, O.K. Store.

Shütze, Carson. T. 1996. *The Empirical Base of Linguistics: Grammaticality Judgments and Linguistic Methodology*. Chicago: University of Chicago Press.

Silverstein, Michael. 1979. Language structure and linguistic ideology. In *The Elements: A Parasession in Linguistic Units and Levels*, ed. Paul R. Clyne, William F. Hanks, and Carol L. Hofbauer, pp. 193–247. Chicago: Chicago Linguistic Society.

Sorace, Antonella. 1996. The use of acceptability judgments in second language acquisition research. In *Handbook of Second Language Acquisition*, ed. William C. Ritchie and Tej K. Bhatia, pp. 375–409. San Diego: Academic Press.

8   Monolingual field research

Daniel L. Everett

> I have no idea whether I am doing the right thing or not, or how valuable
> my results will be. It all weighs rather heavily on my mind.
>
> *Margaret Mead to Franz Boas, January 16, 1926* (cited in Freeman 1999: 115)

The purpose of this paper is to present the methodology, axiology, and
teleology of monolingual fieldwork – how to do it, the values and ethics of
engaging in it, and its ultimate aims. The paper also argues that monolingual fieldwork should not be restricted to only those environments in which
other methods are not available, but that it should be the method of choice,
wherever the linguist is able. In connection with this, I argue that language
learning, so crucial to the monolingual approach, is a vital part of all fieldwork.

A good case can be made for the claim that the most important tasks
facing linguistics today are the preparation (or discovery or theorization or
invention – choose your predicate) of grammars of little-studied or unstud-
ied languages and the construction of theories of the nature of human language. Neither of these vital tasks should be postponed. Neither should
they be compartmentalized or isolated from each other. Ideally, the terms
fieldworker and *theoretician* ought to designate the same set of individuals.

The reason I believe that fieldwork is vital to our understanding of the
nature of human language is that I also believe that what we have yet to learn
about languages and Language greatly exceeds what we already know. Using
a simple image, Figure 8.1 represents what I bet we will discover about our
current state of knowledge and its relation to our current state of ignorance.

What are the linguist's objectives in fieldwork? I will assume that they will
include at least: (i) discovery of new facts about human language; (ii)
testing theoretical claims (even if these are nothing more than discovering
and documenting what Boas and his students called the "patterns" of language); and (iii) learning more about people. Crucial to all of these objectives is the skill of knowing how to learn in the field. The linguist must have
some ideas about how to get the right data. Language learning is vital for
getting the "right" data. Let me give a personal example.

166

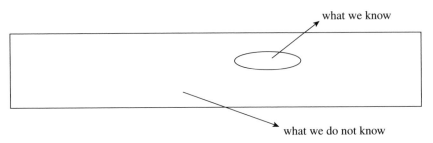

what we know

what we do not know

Fig 8.1

In 1982, I had nearly finished my Ph.D. dissertation on Pirahã, an Amazonian language isolate; I had spent nearly fourteen months working with native speakers and had concluded, among other things, that the Pirahã grammar had no relative clauses. All my attempts to elicit them had been met with examples of parataxis. So, trying to elicit something like 'The man (who(m)) you saw yesterday left today', I would get from my speakers examples like 'You saw a man yesterday. He is leaving today.' I therefore concluded that there were no relative clauses in Pirahã.

Then one afternoon a young boy, Paitá, the son of my main language teacher, Kohoibííhiai, came to my house just as his father had decided to sharpen a nail for the tip of a fishing arrow. Kohoibííhiai said to Paitá, "Go get the nails, the nails which Dan gave me yesterday." *Voila!* A relative clause. (Actually, it was a correlative clause, but it still works for this story.) One question that arises in relation to this anecdote is how a field researcher could have missed "seeing" such clauses for fourteen months. I have no answer to this. Nevertheless, the more interesting and useful question is how I finally discovered the relative clause in Pirahã. I could only do this because I had learned to speak the language and was able to follow and understand (at least the gist of) a Pirahã conversation not directly involving me. In fact, I require of anyone wanting to work with me on a Ph.D.-level description or analysis based on fieldwork that they learn to speak the language first. This ought not to strike a theoretical linguist as strange. Language learning is arguably a natural expectation for linguists working within a Chomsky-inspired research program. And this idea is hardly original with me. Chomsky has long argued that introspection can be an important source of data for any grammar. It struck me upon my first reading of descriptive methodologies such as Longacre's *Grammar Discovery Procedures* (1964), that Paul Postal (1966) was right in his review of Longacre's book when he claimed that Longacre and others regularly omitted the two most important steps in the analysis of any language in a field situation: (i) learn the language; and (ii) generate, test, and regenerate hypotheses on a daily basis.

Each essay in this volume is based on its own particular set of assumptions about what fieldwork is. These assumptions reflect the personal experiences of the authors. My background has, not surprisingly, informed my own assumptions. Therefore, to avoid misunderstanding deriving from a potentially solipsistic view, let me make explicit what I understand fieldwork to be:

Fieldwork describes the activity of a researcher systematically analyzing parts of a language other than one's native language (usually one the researcher did not speak prior to beginning fieldwork), within a community of speakers of that language, prototypically in their native land, living out their existence in the milieu and mental currency of their native culture.

So one cannot do fieldwork on one's native language. Nor can one do fieldwork with a single, dislocated speaker (or non-community of such dislocatees). This does not deny the obvious fact that one can study one's own language or that one can study with a dislocated speaker or two. But it is intended to reunite fieldwork with its rightful definition, an extant alienation produced by the co-opting of the term *fieldwork* by many linguists (including candidates for assistant professor positions desiring to impress search committees) suffering from postmodernist insecurity. Fieldwork in this narrow sense is among the two most important tasks facing linguistics. It is the most urgent. Once again, the principal tasks perennially facing linguistics are (i) development of a theory of language, and (ii) establishment of an adequate empirical basis for the best effort at (i).

If we accept the thesis that writing grammars is one of the most important tasks of the field, we are obligated to say what we mean by a "grammar of a language." Ideally, this would be an encyclopedic study in several volumes, detailing the history and classification of the language, its semantics, pragmatics, textual structures, phonology, phonetics, morphology, sentential syntax, and lexicon, supplemented by many well-chosen texts (e.g., texts describing or preserving significant cultural knowledge). But more realistically, good, comprehensive grammars can come in a single volume, of which Keren Rice's *A Grammar of Slave* is one of the best examples that comes to mind (Rice 1989). These kinds of language studies, "thick descriptions," to borrow and extend anthropologist Clifford Geertz's (1973) term, enable us to see how the parts of the grammar fit together. As linguists of all theoretical persuasions have come to realize, data from various parts of the grammar, often apparently unrelated, are necessary in order to build convincing argumentation for one or another portion of a grammar. A comprehensive grammar, supplemented by natural texts and a lexicon, is a necessary condition for theoretical exploration of any significance on a given language.

But fieldwork, the basis for comprehensive grammars, is either not taught at all or not taught comprehensively in the majority of linguistics departments. As far as I can tell, those few departments that do teach field methods never offer courses in monolingual fieldwork, even though such training is necessary for research on many endangered languages. Thus linguists who do risk a fieldwork experience are often and understandably insecure, as Mead was, especially since their advisors may have had relatively little fieldwork background themselves, or if they in fact are experienced, may have offered only minimal field training. One goal of this chapter is to let linguists know that they do not need to experience the self-doubts Mead expressed. There are sound methods for doing research which guarantee at least some valuable scientific returns if all conditions are met.

Most linguistics field methods classes begin with the assumption that the fieldworker and the language consultant speak a language in common. This is true for many parts of the world, of course. But there are many places where the linguist cannot expect to gain access to the language under study via a larger national or trade language. More importantly, though, I want to make the point that in all cases, there are significant advantages to working monolingually which can outweigh the advantage of working through a second, more accessible language. Moreover, for many endangered languages of the Amazon and elsewhere, high quality linguistic documentation and description will require that linguists be trained in issues and techniques important to success in such situations.

So writing grammars is complicated by the fact that many of the world's languages are spoken exclusively, or practically so, by people who either speak no other language or whose repertoire of languages does not include one available for study or spoken by the field researcher prior to fieldwork. Such field research settings are called "monolingual situations." Field research on these languages cannot be done via a trade language, as much fieldwork is. Rather, to study the linguistic properties of such languages the field linguist will ultimately have to learn to speak the language under study (or teach the language consultants another language to facilitate research, an option I will ignore here). But it does not follow that linguistic analyses must be delayed until after language learning. Before the language is learned or, better, while it is being learned, it is possible to acquire a good deal of information about its lexicon, syntax, morphology, and phonology. And the information gathered in these initial days and weeks of field research in a monolingual situation can be used by the linguist to "bootstrap" to greater speaking and analytic knowledge of the language in question.

To rephrase slightly, a monolingual field situation is, roughly, a situation in which fieldwork cannot proceed unless the linguist learns to speak the language under study. Linguists usually bridle at the suggestion that being a linguist means being a polyglot. Some of the best work in the field, so the story goes, is done by linguists who speak only their native language. History will have to judge this. I certainly agree that it does not seem that speaking the language under study is a sufficient condition for producing good work on it. Nor is speaking a language a necessary condition for producing some useful insights about that language, especially if one's objectives are narrow (narrower, for example, than producing a grammar of the language). But be this as it may, if one does not speak a language, one is working with a self-imposed handicap. Why should anyone want to turn down the clues, insights, intuitions, and constant grammar-learning and practice inherent in language learning if one is genuinely concerned with a deep professional understanding of (aspects of) the language in question? Time is likely to be the main reason most linguists avoid language learning. But time constraints ought not to be so highly valued that they are knowingly allowed to seriously impede the quality of the research. Speaking knowledge of a language is the development of tacit, intuitive, cognitive familiarity with the language as a cultural, communicative vehicle. Analytic knowledge is the development of an explicit, objective theory of the grammar of the language. These are very different things, yet support one another. Each is poorer without the other.

Yet, even factoring in the time constraints, monolingual fieldwork enjoys advantages over other methods (as well as some disadvantages as we see in section 1.5). For example, working monolingually prepares and requires researchers to come to grips with the fact that fieldwork is holistic. Although we may tell novices to follow this or that order of research (e.g., articulatory phonetics, phonology, morphology, syntax), experienced fieldworkers know that we must in fact do everything at once. One needs information from just about every part of the language to figure out every other part of the language. Language learning is a natural, enjoyable, and maximally productive way to gain familiarity and understanding of the interactions between different components of the grammar simultaneously.

The axiological motivation for this approach is partially felt in the apparent truism that indigenous peoples are not library books. They do not exist merely to be consulted for data and then placed back on the shelf while the researchers return to their careers. When one makes a decision to do fieldwork, it is imperative that one also recognize that this decision entails a responsibility to aid the community in which the research is being conducted. And aid implies relationship – one cannot provide meaningful, community-internal help (in non-emergency cases) without being to some degree integrated into the community. Such integration is not easy. It requires the building of bonds of trust, respect, and friendship. And these bonds are dependent on language-mediated communication (i.e., not just pointing and friendly expressions, as I have heard some claim to be equally effective). The monolingual method better integrates the linguist into the community. By learning the language, the linguist places himself in a subordinate role within the community. Instead of being the "teacher," the linguist enters as a student. This demonstrates respect for the speakers of the language under study and can establish a non-threatening, minimally disruptive social role for the linguist. More directly, this strategy benefits the research.

The monolingual fieldworker will soon be forced to realize that he or she is a student of the community – ignorant, clumsy, and useless in many ways by local standards. A necessary condition of integration and trust is lacking initially – respect. The researcher must earn the community's respect. But how is this to be done? There are several ways. But, relative to our discussion, respect is most often gained as native speakers can see some point to all the linguist's strange activities. And in my experience, the point they most want to see and most easily recognize is progress in language learning. The fieldworker who is not progressing in language learning will be enigmatic and harder to respect (although there are ways of earning respect without language learning in some cases). This reinforces the claim that monolingual work requires an ambitious level of commitment.

But why should the fieldworker set such an ambitious goal as gaining respect and integration into the local community? At the very least, one might ask whether all fieldworkers need such global fieldwork goals. For example, what about the fieldworker who is not concerned with the entire language or grammar? Should a worker concerned only with a narrow slice of the grammar feel obligated to work monolingually? There are two answers to this. First, narrow interests are best served outside of fieldwork. If one is exclusively concerned with, say, the interaction of quantification and WH-movement, then one ought to study a well-documented language and not attempt research in a field setting. Second, if a person does wish to pursue fieldwork in a monolingual setting with a narrow goal, this can be done but will require no less dedication to a holistic approach before the narrow question can be asked rightly. The expression of self-doubt from Margaret Mead cited at the beginning of this chapter is hardly unique among fieldworkers. Every field linguist will struggle with it. The ethics of fieldwork require the often unsettling exercise of constant self-appraisal in the field. The field researcher is away from his or her advisor and peers, settling into a situation of uncertain duration and even more uncertain results. All around, people are talking in unintelligible syllables. If there is a Universal Grammar, it is of little immediate help in the first days of fieldwork, to put it mildly. What is of immediate importance to the field researcher is a well thought-out methodology. (This is not to say, however, that Universal Grammar is useless. The fact that there is an upper bound on possible variation between languages, set by a universal set of constraints on what a possible human grammar can be, is what makes field methodology and linguistics possible. If languages could vary in unlimited ways, neither a science of grammar nor a methodology for "grammar discovery" would be possible.)

1.   The monolingual method

1.1   Preliminaries

It is important to recognize that monolingual fieldwork is much more than an alternative methodology. It entails a higher level of commitment than any other form of research in linguistics. This is so because when one begins monolingual research, one can only be certain of this: more than eighteen months of one's life will be spent at a single task with no guarantee of any results of relevancy to current theoretical issues in one's field. Given the present structure of the field, this makes monolingual field research a high-risk enterprise which in the worst case could result in lack of job competitiveness, denial of tenure, or lowering of one's post-tenure professional trajectory. Why is this? Because one cannot be sure what will be found or whether success will be achieved in getting a data sample with the features necessary to tell a comprehensive story about theoretically interesting issues. And finding out whether or not one's efforts have been successful in this sense can take a long time. (Of course, from an empirical/descriptive perspective, there will always be valuable results.)

So how does this high-risk commitment begin? First, prior to beginning fieldwork, the researcher must familiarize himself with all that has been written about the language in question, its history, classification, and related languages, as well as with extant literature on the surrounding languages and areal characteristics of the relevant part of the world. Whenever possible, the future field linguist will also learn to speak as much of the language as is possible before entering the local linguistic situation. On the other hand, for many monolingual situations there will be little useful information on the language available. This is, after all, why such situations will generally attract the attention of the field researcher – they are places where work has yet to be done. In such cases, the linguist will literally have to begin the research by pointing. But how does this come about? That is, how does one start? I will address this initially with some anecdotes.

1.2   Day one

Let's begin with what I will call "Day One" stories. By "Day One" I refer to that period of time from the initial *National Geographic* strangeness of the first contact to the point where the researcher is somewhat comfortable in the environment and is developing relations of trust with the people, prior to beginning elicitation and formal study in earnest.

1.2.1   Anecdote one

In the early afternoon of December 7, 1977, a single-engine Cessna 206 aircraft flew me to the Pirahã village known in Portuguese as "Posto Novo." As I stepped out of the plane, airsick, hot, and woozy, I saw the Pirahã for the first time. The first man I saw was singeing the hair off a large rodent; in the bright, hot sunlight, the smell and smoke of the dead animal almost overwhelmed me in my nauseated condition. The Pirahã had already surrounded me, at the same time that the pilot was preparing to leave me. (A missionary who spoke none of the language but who had visited the village previously, had agreed to spend ten days with me, as I tried to acclimate, so I was not alone. It only felt that way.) Yet in spite of the apparent difficulties, and although the Pirahã were talking in what sounded to me like unintelligible gibberish, within the hour I was gathering data and had hypotheses on basic constituent order and the number of (surface) tones in the language. This in spite of the fact that I was unable to ask anything of the Pirahã in any language I knew. My ability to begin the research was only possible because of rudimentary training in monolingual methodology.

In general, any strongly motivated person of average intelligence can learn as I have in such situations. For example, there have been many priests, explorers, anthropologists, and naturalists over the past five centuries in Brazil who have been able to glean varying amounts of information from various languages, without ability to speak to the people (and, in many cases, without any linguistic training). Therefore, the first and most important condition for monolingual field research is motivation. As an example of motivation, consider another "Day One" story.

1.2.2   Anecdote two

Arlo Heinrichs, the first linguist to work with the Pirahã (eighteen years prior to my own contact), had confronted a much more difficult situation than I. In 1959, after days of paddling his canoe up the Madeira, Marmelos, and Maici rivers, Heinrichs established himself near a small Pirahã village along the Marmelos river. But no Pirahã would talk to him, because the Pirahã disdain foreigners who speak no Pirahã (i.e., all foreigners prior to Heinrichs). However, Heinrichs was determined to learn the language. So he left two pots of strong, very sweet coffee on the fire. Pirahã love coffee. They began to appear in pairs, individually, and in family groups to sample the coffee. Although no one would speak to Heinrichs directly, they did converse among themselves. Heinrichs wrote down what he heard with likely translations and tried to use the bits of the language he was learning with the native speakers. Eventually, he learned enough to greet people and make some conversation. He then succeeded to get a couple of men to sit with him and teach him phrases in the language. From this start, Heinrichs developed an impressive fluency in the language and a very useful database (which is currently part of my own Pirahã database).

1.2.3   Anecdote three   Finally, consider the case of Aretta Loving, a linguist among the Awas of New Guinea. She reports:

> We were especially on the lookout to learn to say "What is this?" After two weeks we were tired of pointing and we wondered if the Awas were not equally tired of seeing us point. Evidently they were not, for they continued to be gracious enough to give us new words as we continued to point. One day, we were cooking some greens around an open fire. I pointed to the food, directing my "question" to an elderly man standing looking into the pot. He turned to the man next to him and said *"anepomo."* I repeated this thinking this was the name of the greens. He and several others smiled and then leaning towards me, he said *"tura. . . ."* (Loving 1975: 268)

What Loving had learned here was not what she had asked, but something much better – the precious phrase, "What is this?" This accomplishment was only possible due to her persistence and her cultivation of a non-hurried, long-range perspective on her fieldwork.

1.3   Consultants

We are now through Day One. A certain amount of pointing and elicitation has been done. People know the linguist and trust is building. As fluency and relationships develop, the linguist will be able to enlist more dedicated, specialized help. This may be in the form of the traditional *language consultant* relationship, where an individual is hired to work several hours per day with the linguist. But I recommend against this for several reasons:

1. First, working with a language consultant in this way, although useful in some respects, can have a negative effect on the society and the language-teacher himself. Employing a particular person will undoubtedly affect their role and relative economic status in their community. The social consequences of such change are likely to be negative in many cases. They are usually unpredictable, potentially compromising the integrity of both the researcher and the language teacher.

2. Working with a single consultant entails that most data gathered will

come from a single source. Consider the following (possibly apocryphal) story, told to me a few years ago. A linguist working in Mexico discovered one day, after five years of fieldwork, that his language consultant was not a native resident of the village where he was working, nor a native speaker of the language he was studying. He spoke a related language which had already been studied extensively. All the work was a waste. Even if this type of horror story is purely fictional, it underscores the need to vary language teachers in order to increase the likelihood that the data gathered is representative of the speech community.

3. Working with a single language consultant also has the effect of limiting the linguist's personal relations within the speech community to the single language consultant and his or her relatives and friends. But the linguist needs instead to be strongly linked within the community. In monolingual situations there is often more distrust and uncertainty about the outside world than in bilingual communities, where language ability is evidence of greater awareness and contact with outsiders.

4. Concentration on a single consultant makes it much more difficult to evaluate different speakers' talents for language teaching. There may be better teachers in the community than the current language teacher. But this cannot be known without experimentation and work with a range of people. Ultimately, the quality and quantity of the data gathered depends on the quantity and quality of the language teachers used.

So how is one to work with a larger number of speakers, if it is agreed that working with a single language consultant is undesirable? Let's consider two possibilities, which I will label "serial teaching groups" and "serial teachers."

By "serial teaching groups," I mean having several groups of two or three individuals each (these groups should be gender-uniform, if possible, at first) which work in succession. So, for example, one group of two or three could work for an hour in the early morning, another at noon or mid-morning, and still another in mid-afternoon or so, depending on the time constraints of the consultants or the linguist. Working with small groups in this fashion has several advantages over the typical, single language consultant mode. Let me mention just a few here.

This method allows the linguist to put the language to use right away. In monolingual situations the linguist needs to use and learn the target language. Without it research cannot be done. Therefore, the likelihood of learning it and learning it well is tremendously increased as the need for using the language ensures that the language is put to use daily, immediately. This in turn helps to make the linguist's relation to the language more personal, more immediate, more real, and more understandable in the eyes of the people.

It also provides the linguist with alternate phrasings and pronunciations. When linguists works with a small group, they are able to record multiple answers to the same question. This will usually provide moderately different phrasings, prosodic structure, and segmental pronunciations. This type of variation is quite important as one attempts to discover the grammatically relevant "mean" for pronunciations and prosody, as well as to learn about possible permutations of syntax and morphology allowed for a given context. This is vital in monolingual elicitation, where the linguist cannot simply ask the language consultant for a translation for this or that utterance but must instead piece together a meaning from the context.

By working in a group session, the linguist increases the opportunities for discussions and consensus on answers to questions. The group format allows the different native speakers to discuss their answers and reach consensus. This itself can also bring disadvantages (reaching the wrong consensus, for example), but the advantage is tremendous in the monolingual setting because the linguist's ability to communicate, especially early on, will be more limited than in a bilingual setting, and language consultants working together can help one another figure out more accurately what it is that the linguist is after.

This method also puts immediate peer-pressure on individual language consultants for thoughtful answers. A single language consultant is often tempted to give the easiest answer possible, especially when what the linguist really wants might require some thought and reflection. In many monolingual settings, speakers simply are not used to desk-work and find it extremely boring and tedious (as many of us still do!). With a pair of friends watching, however, the individual speaker is less likely to give unresponsive answers to questions, because he or she will assume that the others in the group are watching. In my experience, speakers of all languages delight in telling other speakers that they answered this or that question incorrectly. A human frailty, no doubt; but it is a frailty which can be put to good use by the linguist in group language consultant sessions. Still, because it can occasionally produce tension, the linguist must be vigilant not to allow correction of one speaker by another become humiliating or more than a little bit uncomfortable.

Another advantage of the group method is that it is more fun for language consultants. Indeed, group sessions are usually more fun for all involved, including the linguist. And it is vital that the linguist have fun, especially in monolingual situations where successes in elicitation and analysis are fewer and farther between in the initial stages than in bilingual situations.

Working in groups also provides for better and quicker relationship development for the linguist. Once again, the linguist is out to build relationships. Language-learning sessions in a group provide an excellent basis for developing ties of trust and friendship with the local language community. They are much better in this respect than individual language consultant sessions.

Finally, language consultants grow less weary in a group context. In the course of an hour or so, many language teachers get tired. The quality of responses drops off significantly as speakers tire, especially in more demanding monolingual situations where the linguist is groping for words and often being very unclear regarding what is being sought. But the group method keeps each informant fresh and increases the quality and reliability of the data.

On the other hand, a useful alternative (or complement) to the serial group method is the serial individual teachers method. I have used this research method in most of my fieldwork with success and enjoyment. It involves working with four to nine language consultants per day (or so), for fifteen to twenty minutes each. This short time period keeps the language teacher fresh, builds relationships quickly, and is less likely to single out a particular individual for attention. I strongly suggest using both of the serial approaches discussed here for fieldwork.

Fieldwork also involves relating to consultants by developing a work routine that overlaps with theirs in various ways. The linguist must also give time to developing relationships, eliciting data, and improving language-speaking ability. I would recommend the following in the typical monolingual setting:

First, attend to daily living tasks – hauling water for drinking and bathing, collecting and cutting firewood, and housecleaning. Usually one can then begin work with speakers early in the morning, around 6 a.m. After each of the serial language consultant sessions, the linguist should take a break from the desk and circulate among the speakers, practicing what he or she has learned. Different kinds of vocabulary are learned best in the environments in which their related activities are conducted. The linguist should, therefore, work with the people, hunt with the people, fish with the people, and farm with the people. A little bit of everything should be attempted in the first few months to expand vocabulary and usage.

The linguist should avoid (with a few exceptions) working more than three hours per day on new data collection. More than this leads to accumulation of data faster than it can be processed. And data not processed in the field is almost completely useless when the linguist gets back "home." To avoid the temptation of gathering too much too fast, much of the linguist's time should be spent in what I call "perambulatory elicitation" – walking around the village or community asking questions, and trying to use the information recently learned. Once again, we should remember that a great deal of the linguist's success depends on the goodwill of the people. Few situations demand the resources of the entire person more than monolingual fieldwork. One must learn to incorporate linguistic learning into activities that develop warm personal relations.

Fieldwork requires an additional physical attribute: Richard Nixon said somewhere that one of the most important qualifications of a good lawyer is "an iron butt." Fieldworkers need tough derrières as well. A field linguist needs to spend at least six hours per day at the desk analyzing and processing data.

1.4   Conduct and substance of the work session

1.4.1   Conduct of the work session Now let's turn to some suggestions which I have found useful for working in a monolingual setting. The first step is to create the proper context. Consider the following ideas.

1. The consultant should be made to feel at ease. Do not start the session by eliciting data. Ask about the consultant's family (if appropriate). Offer a drink of water, coffee, or appropriate refreshment. (According to Paul Newman (personal communication) the correct behavior in West Africa is not to *offer* a drink, but rather just to bring it. If one offers something, the culturally polite response is for guests to refuse it, no matter how thirsty they might be.)

2. It should be made clear that when errors occur, they are the fault of the linguist. The language helper has plenty of other things to do besides answer the linguist's questions. The researcher created this situation. It is up to him or her to make it successful, and an enjoyable experience for the language consultant. One ought never to show displeasure with the language consultant. In fact, the consultant often knows better than the linguist what is needed. I have listened to some of my early sessions with Pirahã teachers and realized, to my chagrin, that they were giving me exactly what I needed but that I was acting impatiently, thinking that they were missing the point altogether.

3. One should be liberal with smiles. This is important and not as trite as it might sound.

4. The work session should be carefully planned. One ought to develop a Plan B, Plan C, and Plan D, in case the initial plan does not work out. Otherwise, uncomfortable silences will result while the linguist tries to wriggle out of the situation. Such silences often make consultants uncomfortable and can make them feel that they have done something wrong. Body language and facial expressions are important and most people read them well; but one must be on guard to avoid communicating negative information inadvertently. Linguists ought not to forget that their research and career goals depend on the language teacher's willingness to help.

5. But if Plan A is not working initially, one should persist. A little discomfort on the part of the linguist or the consultant should not be feared. On the other hand, one must know when to give up, regroup, or reattack the problem another day or with another consultant.

6. Consultants should always be made to feel that they have helped, even if the linguist thinks otherwise. Generally all information received in a consultant session is invaluable, but commonly the value of the consultant's apparent deviations from the linguist's goals is only seen later, after the linguist has learned more about the language and better understood what the speaker was doing in that session.

1.4.2   Substance of the work session Let's turn now to another question related to the organization of the consultant session, namely, what one ought to begin working on in the first sessions. Remember that language learning is coming along well, so some awareness of various aspects of the grammar will already be emerging. I recommend following the traditional, time-tested sequence below:

> lexicon → simple phrases → phonetics → phonology → morphology →
> syntax → semantics → phonetics (begin sequence again)

Phonetics is repeated in this sequence because some articulatory phonetic analysis is crucial for phonological analysis, while other aspects of phonetic analysis depend on a deeper understanding of the grammar as a whole.

But where does one begin and what course does one follow? Nouns are the best place to begin because, in general, the context necessary to communicate the linguist's intention and language consultant's answer is conceptually less complex. Following some initial work on nouns, the linguist might turn to elicitation of pronouns, working through the different persons and numbers, such as first, second, third, fourth, dual, trial, and paucal. Body parts are useful ways of eliciting possessive forms of pronouns, in phrases such as 'my arm', 'his arm', 'our arms', and 'their arms'. Following the elicitation of individual nouns and pronouns, noun phrases can be built up. For example, modifiers of different types can be used. So one could elicit 'green leaf' and contrast this with 'yellow leaf', then 'two green leaves', then 'two big green leaves', and so forth. In carrying out this research monolingually, especially as sketched below, props are very useful. Initial analysis and elicitation should include natural objects, e.g., water in containers of different levels of relative volume, leaves grouped by size and color, sticks by size and thickness, rocks by size, color, and shape; and cultural objects, e.g., bow and arrows, nails, boards, boxes, hammers, and cans. Some of the latter objects, for example, are useful in eliciting aspectual differences, e.g., 'I hammered the can' versus 'I hammered the can flat'. A closed box with something loose in it can be shaken with a puzzled look in an attempt to elicit the phrase 'What is it?'

From nouns one can move to verbs. Verbs are trickier since their contexts are harder to grasp. I have found that acting out different events is a useful way of eliciting different verbs, e.g., 'jump', 'fall', 'throw', 'hit', and others. As with nouns, simple individual verbs should be elicited and then expansions of these can be collected, such as verb phrases or, perhaps more easily and more usefully, verb paradigms. Verb types can then be worked on, looking for differences in valency, ranging from avalent to trivalent, and aktionsart or aspect.

Let's turn now to consider in more detail the areas to be covered by most fieldwork using the simple lexical and phrasal data that the fieldworker has begun to collect. First, the fieldworker should figure out the sound system. In this effort, one should look for corpus-external evidence as well as the data found in elicitation and texts. This additional information can provide extremely useful evidence for argumentation and analysis. To give a few examples: try to determine if there are nicknames or hypocoristic forms in the language. In Everett (1998) I offer evidence for my analysis of Banawá syllabification based on hypocoristic formation. One can also use the computer, with a program, e.g., Sound Edit, for checking intuitions. I have played back words which I have computationally altered for speakers, asking them whether they find these altered forms 'pretty' or 'ugly' (which, for the Pirahã at least, indicate (very roughly) whether they think the word is grammatical or ungrammatical). Altering the pitch, amplitude, or duration of words can provide insights into the prosodic intuitions of the native speakers which the linguist could not otherwise collect. Using the computer in the field (with the relevant software) is very important to analysis and better fieldwork. One can also check the native speaker's intuitions by training speakers (if it is possible in a particular culture!) to tap out the rhythm of individual words, then words in phrases. As Peter Ladefoged and I have shown, this can be very useful to discovering and supporting analyses of stress systems (Ladefoged, Ladefoged, and Everett 1997). Language games are also useful, although they are generally a fortuitous discovery of linguists well-integrated into the community. Many studies over the years have shown the usefulness of language games to linguistic analysis, revealing phonetic, phonological, and morphological structures of words, at a minimum.

Morphological analysis can proceed more easily once some of this initial investigation of the phonology has been carried out. This analysis is arguably the core of the grammar and is much more difficult than is often realized. In most journals and books, the presentation of (at least) non-Indo-European examples will include a morpheme-by-morpheme gloss. But articles and books almost never contain any information that would inform the reader as to how the researcher determined these glosses. In most cases, the source of the glosses is a previous study by yet another linguist. But fieldworkers know that the hardest part of analyzing most languages (this is particularly true of so-called polysynthetic languages) is figuring out what individual morphemes mean. These can only be translated by understanding how they are used. And this itself can only be determined by a careful study of their occurrence in speech, including the contexts in which the relevant speech was uttered and recorded. For example, in an extremely interesting and enlightening study, Ivan Lowe (1990) discusses the evolution of his understanding of different affixes related to the general notion of causality in the Amazonian language Nambiquara. He illustrates in this study how the analysis of morphemes is subtle, difficult, and heavily dependent on a full understanding of the discourse and sentence-level functions of each of the morphemes involved. It is difficult to imagine an analysis of this quality coming from someone who does not speak the language.

In my data on Pirahã (about 1.5 gigabytes, archived on the Summer Institute of Linguistics' (SIL) LinguaLinks program), I have recorded (I think) every instance of every morpheme I have ever encountered in more than twenty years of fieldwork. Using the LinguaLinks program, I am able to call up any morpheme in the corpus and immediately see the context in which the morpheme occurs. However, while this allows me to develop reasonable hypotheses about the meaning of individual morphemes, each hypothesis must be tested by discussing the morpheme in question (quite indirectly as a rule) with various native speakers.

Finally, for morphological analysis it is vital to verify and study every context in which a morpheme occurs in elicited and natural, connected speech. The translation and analysis of the morphemes of a language are the foundation for nearly all other linguistic analysis. Much of the culture is embedded in the semantic categories of the morphology. And this is also nearly always the hardest part. But in spite of the difficulty, the meaning of morphemes can be checked in a monolingual field situation. There are at least four sources of clues that can be used: paraphrase, repetition, discourse, and developing intuition. Get other speakers to paraphrase and comment on texts and the data of other language helpers. This practice necessitates having three or four analog recorders (plus perhaps one digital recorder for phonetic studies) in the field: two for a session in which a speaker, on one machine, records translations or makes comments on material played on a second machine, as well as one analog recorder for backup. The paraphrasing and comments can often lead to accurate determination of a specific morpheme's meaning. Getting different speakers to repeat morphemes will also lead to paraphrases. Repetitions are often hard to get. But play a tape of the word or phrase to be repeated and ask "What did he say? Could you say it again for me?" This is an extremely useful, albeit simple, tool. Study the appearance of morphemes in natural texts. Do their usages in texts fit with your hypotheses? Do you see new uses? Finally, one learns the meaning of morphemes as one develops fluency in the language. Without this, I am very skeptical of any linguist's ability to accurately or comprehensively account for the meaning of many difficult morphemes.

Finally, syntax is a vital part of the study of any language. I would suggest both elicitation of individual sentences (especially in the "serial group setting") and texts. From texts one can cull interesting sentences and test these further, even forming paradigms with them, to check with native speakers. Remember, though, that syntactic analysis must follow morphological comprehension. This is especially true in most modern theories of syntax in which the lexicon drives the grammar. How can one understand the grammar without understanding the lexicon? The answer is, one cannot.

Ideally, the linguist will already have an outline of material and will follow a set of questions prepared in advance. Remember, though, that it is impossible not to "blow it." It is also impossible to avoid failing to hear things that were said and hearing things which were not. But persistence is crucial. What one does after a mistake, how one reacts to tension and error, will deeply affect one's relationships in the community and, eventually, the success of the research program. Therefore, I offer the following slogan: the most important step in fieldwork is not what you do first, but what you do next.

1.5   Disadvantages

Before closing this section, however, honesty compels me to discuss some of the real disadvantages to the monolingual method.

Monolingual field research will add at least six months to any field program. This is about the length of time necessary for the average linguist, in good health and strongly motivated, to learn to speak the language in question at a level of 2+ to 3, on a scale from 0 (no knowledge) to 5 (native speaker). This is the minimal level of ability necessary to guide the collection of linguistic data in the target language. It is also the minimal level necessary for reasonable conversational ability (necessary in order to "try out" what one is learning in natural conversations) and somewhat reliable intuitions about phonetics and semantics. The length of time involved in such situations needs to be made clear, because it is an important factor in anyone's decision to work with most endangered languages. On the other

hand, there is probably no more urgent task facing linguistics than the documentation and description of endangered languages, so that the field as a
whole has to develop an incentive system for younger scholars interested in
such work. (Senior scholars generally have more liberty to pursue such
research because they have tenure.) But time is not the only disadvantage to
working monolingually. Another important one is frustration.

It will be extremely exasperating in the early stages of monolingual fieldwork for the linguist to know so little of what is being said and going on
around him. This is a serious disadvantage. I have known some fieldworkers
to give in to the temptation to take the easy way out and simply start writing
up "interesting" theoretical papers on the data that appears to be understood, before the language is learned to at least a moderate level of fluency.
This is a hard temptation to avoid since it entails pushing back the theoretical payoff – exactly what most linguists expect to win them their job or
tenure. It is risky to stay the course in monolingual fieldwork. But for the
sake of science and, one would hope, for one's career, it is important not to
give in and to press on to fluency in the target language.

There are serious, nonlinguistic frustrations as well to working monolingually, which should not be overlooked. George Cowan of SIL faced some
such frustrations in working with the Amuzgos:

> [T]he monolingual approach is a serious barrier to maintaining the good-will of the
> people, until such time as the language is mastered sufficiently to enable the investi-
> gator to make himself adequately understood on questions of morals, principle,
> and the like. (Cowan 1975: 272)

I have faced related problems in my work in Amazonia. It can be extremely
frustrating, and sometimes downright dangerous, not to know how to
express oneself or how to understand discussions and behavior of the type
alluded to by Cowan. There are two kinds of potential problems in this
regard. The first is inadvertent conflicts with the values of the host culture,
by using inappropriate words or expressions. For example, using the word
for 'vagina' in place of the word for 'land', as I did once among the
Paumaris when trying to say "I really like the Paumaris' land" to a group of
women who had come to visit. This was a rather embarrassing error which
caused some discomfort for all present for a few minutes (but is funny to
think back on). The second is miscommunication in exchanges explicitly
concerned with morality. For example, many peoples I have worked with
consider it extremely useful and relevant to discuss the religious basis of
morality with an outsider (it helps them know, among other things, what
kind of person they are allowing to stay among them). One's inability to
explain the moral basis of one's behavior can place one under suspicion. I
spanked one of my children once while among the Pirahã, only to discover

that overt anger towards anyone is the major "sin" in Pirahã society. Inability to explain why I had done this strange thing caused some people to wonder about my moral character (and mental stability, no doubt).

Let's turn now, though, before we allow ourselves to be convinced that this is not the way to do research, to what I consider to be very important epistemological advantages of learning the native language in fieldwork.

2.   Epistemologically respectable fieldwork

2.1   *Quality control over data collection process*

We want our research results to be as reliable as we can make them. The monolingual method is important in this regard for several reasons. I focus here on three, since I believe that these three correlates of the monolingual method are vital to the usefulness (in the sense of the epistemology of pragmatism) and falsifiability (Popperian epistemology) of field research results. These are: (i) quality control over the process of data collection; (ii) purity of data collected; and (iii) replicability of the results. Let's begin with a consideration of (i).

The field cannot and must not tolerate hasty research. But in many cases it has, knowingly or unknowingly. Grammars are cited without carefully evaluating their plausibility. All grammars ever done need to be rechecked and expanded. Why compound the empirical problems of the field by working too quickly or accepting second- or third-hand information? The field is the most important laboratory of linguistics. But average linguists are willing to accept most of what they are told from the field, because they have not had any first-hand experience and so do not know what kinds of questions to ask to find out about the reliability of the data collected. There should not be any special dispensation of credulity awarded for doing fieldwork – just because one has chosen an admirable task does not mean that one is doing it admirably. All of us who engage in fieldwork need to be challenged regularly. But I suspect that there are fewer challenges to the results reported in grammars and other research reports from the field than there ought to be because of a general unfamiliarity or discomfort with the doing of fieldwork. This strikes me as a recipe for narrowness and empirical flaccidity throughout the field.

So how does monolingual research improve quality control over the data collection process? It does this by forcing the linguist to discuss with native speakers and reflect deeply on the meaning of each grammatical construction collected, in the context of a slow process of language learning. This is not to say that bilingual field research does not involve discussion or reflection. But learning monolingually requires it; there is no way around it. One cannot simply gloss an example in a trade language, and consider the matter closed. One must rather struggle to figure out the meaning of each example in such a way that the gloss emerges as an intellectual victory, not merely an approximation to some word or phrase in a language that the language teacher does not speak as well as the language they are teaching.

2.2   Purity of data collected

The linguist also wants to be sure that the data collected is natural, and as unfiltered through intermediate cognitive structures as possible. These cognitive barriers are abundant when working through a third language, i.e., one that is neither the native language of the linguist nor the teacher, and simply serve to lower one more veil between the data and its collection and interpretation. For example, I have asked questions in Portuguese of Amazonian Indians who were fluent in Portuguese. The responses have occasionally, however, produced native responses in SVO constituent order, even when I know that the language being investigated is not usually SVO. So, I am forced to ask myself, is the SVO order I am getting merely a valid (pragmatically influenced?) alternative which I had not noticed previously, or is it influenced by the Portuguese order of my elicitation examples? It is hard to tell (even looking at texts cannot indisputably answer this question). If I learn to ask questions in the target language, although this will not of itself totally eliminate ambiguity, I remove a potentially devastating source of false leads. It is impossible to estimate the possible misanalyses that the linguistic community has absorbed over the years due to the bilingual method.

2.3   Replicability of results

The final epistemological advantage of the monolingual method I would like to consider is replicability, perhaps the single most important prophylactic for empirical flaccidity, and a necessary condition for most scientific research. Linguistic research is no exception. Although exact duplication of all analytic results in linguistic research is difficult, it is nonetheless important that fieldwork be verifiable. Learning to speak the target language is a tremendous help in subjecting one's analyses to verification by other linguists. My own research results were subjected to this type of verification in 1995, when Peter Ladefoged came to work with me on the documentation of the phonetics of four Amazonian languages – Banawá, Pirahã, Oro Win, and Wari'. As my wife and I drove to the small airport in Porto Velho, Brazil, to meet Ladefoged's plane, I commented that I felt like I was about to be audited by the IRS. After nearly eighteen years of research and publishing on Amazonian phonologies, data that I had collected and reported on in a series of publications were about to be verified instrumentally by an eminent linguist. At the same time that I worried about being exposed as a fraud (lingering sixties paranoia), I was excited about the implications of having my claims about Amazonian languages, controversial as many of them were, verified.

Ladefoged was able to complete his verification of previously reported data and analyses only because we were able to discuss our plans and examples with native speakers. For example, getting an individual with little experience of the "outside world" to allow a stranger to insert tubes up their nostrils (for measuring nasalization) is nontrivial. Only because of previously established relations of trust and communication was this type of experimentation possible among the Pirahã. This illustrates one way in which replicability, and more detailed verification of previous research on Pirahã, depended directly on my ability to explain my plans and goals to the speakers.

3.   Conclusion

Let's conclude by summing up the most important advantages of working monolingually. First, working monolingually deprives the linguist of "crutches." You cannot get out of hard situations by switching to a trade language in a monolingual situation. You must instead find a way to communicate in the target language. Dependency on the target language is perhaps the greatest aid to language learning. If you don't need it, you won't learn it.

Second, the fieldworker is required to learn more about the culture and context of the grammatical constructions under study by this method. The monolingual field researcher is forced to annotate exactly how, when, and where the data were collected. This is important for cultural and linguistic analysis in general. But it is crucially important to the monolingual worker since without this type of information, the analysis and language learning simply cannot proceed. Learning a language monolingually requires copious recordings of cultural information, as much of the context of a particular utterance as is possible or feasible. The annotation of cultural/contextual information is vital to reconstructing, within the linguist's grammar, the sinew and fiber of the speaker's grammar. Another linguist's ability to falsify (or test) a grammar is dependent upon the ability to enter the language, find the grammar segment that needs to evaluated, and check it against its background. No one works independently of context. No one evaluates independently of context. By keeping careful notes, the monolingual researcher is forced to leave a more complete record and "trail" of the research than the bilingual researcher, and a far better record than researchers who merely give isolated sentences and their translations.

Third, the linguist develops intuitions more quickly and acutely. The monolingual method draws the linguist naturally to texts, even more than the average text-oriented linguist. The reason is that the monolingual researcher necessarily bases many initial conclusions on the only kind of data available, conversational data, as well as monologues. By bringing dialogue into the data-collection process from the beginning, the linguist is better able to "feel" the naturalness and usefulness of specific constructions. Such intuitive relations to the data are, to be sure, no substitutes for quantitative evaluations or theory-based analytic judgments. Nevertheless, they are an excellent source of hunches, doubts, and beginning ideas.

Fourth, the linguist is aided in the development of relationships by trying to speak the language under study. An additional component of field research, one often overlooked by linguistic training, is what I will call the "power-differential." The linguist generally enters a particular culture as someone with more power and prestige than (at least) the average member of the local community of the research. The linguist using a trade language further underscores his or her foreignness and an association with the community most closely identified with the trade language used. The resultant cultural distance between the linguist and the speakers of the target language is rarely positive, and its effects can be subtle. For example, linguists may think of themselves as fitting in well, only to realize later that the results were partially contaminated by the consultants' desire not to offend or displease persons of greater social standing.

Methodology is a vital component of science. The linguist, like any other scientist, must be explicit about the methodology employed. In this paper I have argued that, in spite of some nontrivial disadvantages, working exclusively in the target language, what I have called "the monolingual method," is the preferred method of fieldwork, bringing with it scientific and personal advantages which cannot be otherwise obtained when working through another language.

ACKNOWLEDGMENTS

I would like to dedicate this chapter to Kenneth Pike, Kenneth Hale, and Terrence Kaufman, the fieldworkers whom I admire most. It is Pike who first introduced me to the concepts and philosophy of monolingual fieldwork. I am grateful for comments from the various audiences who have seen my own "monolingual demonstrations," especially those attending my colloquium at the 1998 Annual Meeting of the LSA, Swarthmore College, Presidency College of Madras, India, and the University of Pittsburgh – I regularly use such demonstrations in introductory linguistics classes. I am also grateful to Tony Woodbury and Kenneth Pike for detailed, valuable suggestions for the preparation of this chapter. I especially want to thank Martha Ratliff for her patient help in extricating me from the briarpatch of my own prose and for asking many probing and extremely useful questions. The research and experiences which underlie all of the concepts I attempt to develop in this chapter have been made possible by the generous support of several funding agencies. In particular, I want to express my gratitude to the National Science Foundation for supporting all of my Amazonian research from 1993–1999, under grants SBR-9631322 and SBR93-10221. Finally and most importantly, I want to acknowledge my indebtedness to the dozens of patient and generous speakers of languages of the Americas who have helped me over the past twenty-three years personally, professionally, and spiritually.

REFERENCES

Cowan, George. 1975. The monolingual approach to studying Amuzgo. In *Language Learner's Field Guide*, ed. Alan Healey, pp. 272–76. Ukarumpa, Papua New Guinea: SIL.

Everett, Daniel L. 1997. Syllable Integrity. In *Proceedings of the Sixteenth West Coast Conference on Formal Linguistics (WCCFL 16)*, ed. Emily Curtis, James Lyle, and Gabriel Webster, pp. 177–90. Stanford: CSLI for the Stanford Linguistics Association.

Freeman, Derek. 1999. *The Fateful Hoaxing of Margaret Mead: A Historical Analysis of Her Samoan Research*. Boulder, CO: Westview Press.

Geertz, Clifford. 1973. *The Interpretation of Cultures: Selected Essays*. New York: Basic Books.

Ladefoged, Peter, Jenny Ladefoged, and Daniel Everett. 1997. Phonetic structures of Banawá, an endangered language. *Phonetica* 54:94–111.

Longacre, Robert E. 1964. *Grammar Discovery Procedures*. The Hague: Mouton.

Loving, Aretta. 1975. On learning monolingually. In *Language Learner's Field Guide*, ed. Alan Healey, pp. 267–71. Ukarumpa, Papua New Guinea: SIL.

Lowe, Ivan. 1990. Cause and reason in Nambiquara. In *Amazonian Linguistics: Studies in Lowland South American Languages*, ed. Doris L. Payne, pp. 543–73. Austin: University of Texas Press.

Postal, Paul. 1966. Review of *Grammar Discovery Procedures* by Robert E. Longacre. *International Journal of American Linguistics* 32:93–98.

Rice, Keren. 1989. *A Grammar of Slave*. Berlin: Mouton de Gruyter.

9   The give and take of fieldwork: noun classes and other concerns in Fatick, Senegal

Fiona Mc Laughlin and Thierno Seydou Sall

> The world is like a Mask, dancing. If you want to see it well you do not stand in one place.   Chinua Achebe, *Arrow of God*

The narratives that follow are an attempt to convey two perspectives, that of the linguist (Mc Laughlin) and that of the "informant" (Sall), on a particular moment of linguistic fieldwork carried out in Fatick, Senegal in 1989. The text has come together from conversations both tape recorded and remembered, written drafts and translations of drafts, and individual readings and critiques by each of the authors. During the process of discussing and writing these dual narratives we have had to confront the issues and problems of ethnographic representation in a very direct manner since we have, in a sense, entered into a dialogue about the representation of ourselves and each other. On several occasions we thought that we were undertaking an impossible task because the challenges of such representation seemed to be overwhelming. We have not solved them, we are merely more aware of them than ever. Perhaps the ambivalence of our perspective can best be conveyed through a conversation we had in Dakar in July, 1998.

SALL: Somehow one has the impression that we are always the object and never the subject. We are the "material" that toubabs[1] come to study.

MC LAUGHLIN: But this time, by presenting your own narrative, don't you think that you have an opportunity to be the subject instead of the object?

SALL: (Laughter). I'll talk about myself, but only at your initiative. So where does that put us?

Part I: Fiona Mc Laughlin

1.1   *Fatick 1989*

In January, 1989, as a Ph.D. candidate in linguistics at the University of Texas at Austin, I arrived in the small provincial capital of Fatick, Senegal, to conduct fieldwork for my doctoral dissertation (Mc Laughlin 1992). I arrived in Fatick after a change of field site, language, and topic from those

in my original grant proposal, accompanied by my husband, Leonardo
Villalón, who was doing fieldwork for his own dissertation in political
science. Due to what in retrospect was probably unfounded sensitivity to
potential political unrest in Casamance in southern Senegal, we had
allowed ourselves to be persuaded by American authorities in Dakar to
change our field site from the comparatively lush and tropical region south
of the Gambia to an area further north, somewhere in the savanna belt of
the West African Sahel, a sandy arid region south of the Sahara desert.
After researching several possibilities, we settled on Fatick, a rather unre-
markable town in the interior, but a good site for my revised fieldwork
project in terms of linguistic makeup.

Although I have conducted linguistic fieldwork on many occasions both
in Fatick and in other places since 1989, I have chosen in this essay to focus
on and describe that first intense period of fieldwork for a variety of
reasons. The first is to situate the experience in time and place. No matter
how much time linguists devote every day to eliciting or otherwise collecting data, going over recordings and field logs, organizing notes into the
description of a language, and matching details of the raw material with
our theoretical concerns, we are at the same time living in a society of which
we in some sense become a part, through our relative degrees of integration
or alienation; thus, the experience of fieldwork is inextricably intertwined
with the experience of the field site and sense of place. During the year I
spent in Fatick, our lives were disrupted by what are still referred to euphe-
mistically in Senegal as *les évènements*. While the news that the Berlin Wall
had been opened, crackling across on the six a.m. BBC broadcast, seemed
remote and of little immediate relevance in Fatick, a wave of unprece-
dented violence against the Moorish[2] population that spread throughout
Senegal during Ramadan in 1989 had real effects on our life. Mawluud Fall,
our Moorish shopkeeper neighbor, was "repatriated" to Mauritania, a
country he had never even visited, and Leonardo, who had so often been
mistaken for a Moor, had to lie low for several days in a friend's house in
Dakar. Situated historically and geographically, each field experience is
unique, and as such contributes a case study to the corpus of accounts of
linguistic fieldwork, from which we can in turn start to extrapolate generalizations about the nature of such work. A second reason to focus on this
initial experience of fieldwork is that for many linguists, or indeed for many
who conduct fieldwork in other disciplines, dissertation fieldwork is frequently the only period during which it is possible to spend so much time in
the field, since professional and personal obligations later on make it much
more difficult to absent oneself for extended periods of time. Finally, a narrative of the first period of fieldwork is also, perhaps, more useful to potential fieldworkers in the sense that it recounts the process of learning to be a

fieldworker, with all the mistakes and successes involved in such an apprenticeship with oneself.

Fatick is a Sahelian town. It is hot, dusty, and by any standards materially poor. At the time that I lived there, many of its inhabitants made a tenuous living from cultivating peanuts and millet in the sandy fields surrounding the town. The success of their crops depended almost entirely on the caprices of the rainy season since there was no alternative to rain as a system of irrigation. The day after we arrived in Fatick, in January 1989, the town was ravaged by pilgrim crickets. Writhing clouds of red insects swooped down on the town, and for several hours we were subjected to the demonical sound of tiny gnashing jaws destroying mango and guava trees, stripping palm fronds, and leaving Fatick almost without foliage or shade. With a certain resignation about the harshness of life in the Sahel, Maal, the chief of police, shrugged his shoulders as we surveyed the damage after the crickets left and said *"Kenn mënuci dara"* ('No-one can do anything about it.'). Fatick's residents provide a wry but accurate commentary on life in their town when they joke, *"Fatick, c'est fatigant."*

Sufi Islam is the predominant religion of both Fatick and Senegal as a whole. Most Senegalese Muslims follow the religious guidance of marabouts (Sufi leaders) who occupy a place of great influence in Senegalese society and whose popularity is reflected in the cultural and material aspects of everyday life. The main constraint that living in a Muslim society entailed for us was a minor and self-imposed one. Leonardo's research focused on the role of the Sufi brotherhoods in local and national politics, and both out of consideration for many people – including the several local marabouts he was working with – and also to prevent tainting our reputation and thus endangering our fieldwork, we neither bought alcohol locally nor consumed it publicly. Our frequent association with religious leaders, attendance at (usually all-night long) religious events, and general interest in Sufism led to some apocryphal stories about us in the town – namely, that we were Muslims and that we fasted during Ramadan and prayed five times a day. We had to dispel this misconception delicately, since we wanted neither to misrepresent ourselves nor to offend anyone.

In the first weeks that we were in Fatick, we spent our time and energy on the important banalities of setting up a healthy and basic but comfortable place to live. We rented an old and somewhat decrepit colonial house that had four large square rooms and an outside kitchen. The Lebanese landlady, who had moved to Dakar, had left some rudimentary furniture which we supplemented with beds and chairs made locally out of ronier palm fronds. The house had high ceilings and a generous overhang on the roof which kept it cool much of the time and at least bearable in the hottest months. Our bedroom was made more comfortable by the addition of a table fan and a mosquito net. In the yard we found a concave stone that had once served as part of a water-filtering system. With the help of Djibi Ndiaye, an elderly man who had worked for the Lebanese family and who still lived in a small room at the back of our house, we scrubbed it out and reconstructed the whole system. The water filtered through the stone, dripping through a piece of cheesecloth into a large terra cotta jar from which we filled our bottles for drinking water. Because of recent changes in the water level, the tap water in Fatick is slightly salty, so we had unsalted deep well water delivered to the house on donkey carts. The mosquito nets and water-filtering system helped protect us from two of the most common health threats, malaria and water-borne illnesses; and the house we had chosen provided a refuge from the scorching heat. During the year that we lived in Fatick we were rarely sick and were able to work well in our relatively comfortable study.

The equipment that I took with me to the field was minimal, in part because I was unsure how reliable my electrical supply would be. Computers had not quite become *de rigueur* (or affordable) for graduate students at the time, and I did not buy one until I came back to Austin from doing fieldwork. I did not have a big equipment budget in my grant from the Wenner-Gren Foundation, so I took with me two good microphones, a year's supply of blank cassettes, and a bag full of 3×5 blank note pads and boxes for slip files. In Dakar I bought notebooks for field logs and a multipurpose dual deck cassette player/radio that I used for all my field recordings, as well as for playing music and listening to the radio.

The focus of my research was noun classification. The revised goal that I had set for myself in Fatick was to research the morphophonology of noun classification in three northern Atlantic (Niger-Congo) languages, Wolof, Pulaar (Fula), and Seereer-Siin. These languages have some of the most extensive and elaborate noun class systems found in natural language. Pulaar has twenty-one classes, Seereer sixteen, and Wolof ten, and the nominal systems of all three are characterized to some extent by stem-initial consonant mutation conditioned by noun class. From a theoretical perspective I was interested in what these languages could tell us about the nature of morphological agreement, how derivational and inflectional morphology intersected in the class systems, and how consonant mutation could best be accounted for within an autosegmental framework. I had already had some experience with two of the languages by the time I arrived in Fatick. In my field methods class at the University of Texas we had worked with a native speaker of the Guinean dialect of Fula. This, in addition to the fact that Fula was a key language in the literature on autosegmental phonology, sharpened my interest in looking at Fula for myself, and also at related languages. I already spoke Wolof fairly well, since I had taken an intensive course in Dakar in the summer of 1986, and I had continued studying and speaking Wolof during the six months I spent in Dakar in 1988, just before moving to Fatick. I had also written a qualifying paper on Wolof noun classification as part of the requirement to be admitted to Ph.D. candidacy, so I was familiar with the problems of noun classification in that language, although I was not altogether prepared for doing fieldwork on a topic that involved so much variation. Apart from the few written accounts of it that I had been able to find, Seereer was the unknown language in the picture.

1.2   Work in the field

The core of the linguistic fieldwork experience lies in the intense work one does with native-speaker assistants, thus the choice of assistants is one of the most important aspects of fieldwork, but also one over which the linguist, in many cases, does not have complete control. It is difficult to know at first who will make a good assistant and who will not, so before engaging anyone as a more or less permanent assistant, I worked with several people on a trial basis. My very first attempts to find an assistant for Seereer were close to home. I tried to work with RN, the young woman we had hired to cook and do laundry for us. I was baffled at first when I asked her for the word for the cardinal number two and she replied, "I say *haɗak* but everyone else says *ɗik*." I questioned her about the alleged discrepancy but got nowhere. After a few elicitation sessions followed by checking the data informally with other Seereer speakers who stopped by the house, I realized that several of the lexical items that RN had given me were not typical of the Fatick Seereer speech community at large. Eventually she told me that she spoke like her mother, who was from one of the islands in the Saloum Delta, thus she spoke the Nyominka dialect rather than that of Fatick. As I got to know her over the course of the year, I realized that RN's speech was much more like that of other Seereer speakers in Fatick than she had led me to believe, but that she had supplied me with the Nyominka forms because she considered Nyominka to be a "deeper" or more authentic form of Seereer. This was not the last time that I would run up against the problem of "deep" forms of language. It recurred like a leitmotiv in my elicitation sessions and in the numerous conversations I had with people about language. In fact, it eventually became such a problem with Wolof that I abandoned formal elicitation altogether and switched to gathering data on noun classes from natural discourse.

In order to meet people and start establishing social networks, Leonardo and I volunteered to give English classes two evenings a week in a local school. Here I met two of my future assistants – SN, with whom I worked

9.1 Fiona Mc Laughlin (linguist) and Thierno Seydou Sall (Pulaar teacher).

on Seereer, and Thierno Sall, with whom I worked on Pulaar. The two turned out to be radically different in their understanding of what my goals were. SN, who was from the old Seereer neighborhood of Ndiaye-Ndiaye and who spoke French well, was convinced that my interest in his language was a first step towards finding out the "secrets" of Seereer culture, and never missed an opportunity to tell me that my undertaking was futile because the old people who knew those secrets would never impart them to me. Perhaps because he thought of my attempts to find out about Seereer as a tool for something else, he had an enthusiastically pragmatic approach to things. I had some trouble at first distinguishing between voiced and voiceless glottalized stops in Seereer, but each time I asked SN for clarification he said that the way in which it was pronounced was unimportant, and people would still understand what I meant to say. No amount of explaining what I was doing made any impression on him, and I quickly had to abandon working with him. He was quite disappointed about his dismissal and anytime I saw him afterwards I felt very guilty about it, until finally I was able to secure him a job as an interpreter for a team of American medical anthropologists.

Thierno, on the other hand, proved to be an excellent assistant. Although his formal education was limited to religious and Arabic language training with a marabout, he had won a scholarship to a teacher's training college in Sudan, and was now employed as an elementary school Arabic teacher in Fatick. He understood from the outset what my goals were, and as we started to work together he was frequently two steps ahead of me, supplying me with the forms I wanted before I had to ask for them. Moreover, Thierno started to become very interested in how I was analyzing his language, and after each elicitation session he asked for explanations about his language, and started picking up the technical linguistic terms to describe Pulaar. After working with him for an extended period, I had complete confidence in his ability to record forms accurately, and after I left the field I even asked him to send me some forms by mail. The exchange of expertise between Thierno and myself was rewarding, and moved the level of the fieldwork dynamic from the extraction of raw material to a real intellectual exchange. Rather than being a solitary activity, my linguistic data collection had become the shared work of two people. Despite his lack of formal education, Thierno turned out to be a natural linguist, and several years later, after his uncle commented on my lack of fluency in Pulaar after I had spent so much time working on the language, he was able to explain to him successfully in Pulaar what linguistics was.

As I amassed more and more data on the languages I was working on, I started spending longer hours in the evening organizing my slip files and cataloguing data. For every hour I spent eliciting linguistic forms, I spent roughly four hours going over them. Although it was not without its rewards, there was a certain tedium involved in this solitary work of double-checking and cataloguing, so when I got tired of it I switched over to the more exciting work of sketching out preliminary analyses, which eventually brought me back to more questions about the data I was working with.

1.3   Giving and taking

Meanwhile, I started working with MD, a student who was in his last year of high school. He had come by to introduce himself as president of the high school English club and I found out that he was a native Seereer speaker. Partly because he was so eager for contact with Americans, I decided to try working with him and proposed a short trial period. Although he did not seem particularly interested in what we were doing, MD was not difficult to work with and we continued to work together over the course of a few months, but not without some problems. Our problems were not of a linguistic nature, however. MD had at first told me that under no circumstances did he want to be paid for working with me. I, on the other hand, wanted to establish a professional working relationship which, in retrospect, I wanted to use for my own protection, so I insisted on paying him and told him that there was a budget in my grant destined for that purpose alone. I paid MD the equivalent of four or five dollars an hour for approximately ten hours a week, a sum that added up to a civil servant's salary and which, for a high school student, was enormous. One day, however, MD came on a formal visit to see me. After exchanging greetings he started into the purpose of his visit: "The human voice is a gift of God," he said. I suspected instantly that he wanted to be paid more and inappropriately suggested that this was the case. He vehemently denied it, so I retrenched and we started a very polite and formulaic back and forth about the value of the human voice. Finally, after half an hour of conversation, MD told me that a German linguist, who had been in the area several years earlier and had recorded some Wolof speakers, was now selling the cassettes in Germany and making lots of money from them. I doubted the veracity of the story, but saw where the conversation was heading. I then went on to talk about the field recordings we were making, to let him know that they really had no market value. I told him that if he wanted, I would give him copies of all of them (adding that I thought they would be very boring for him to listen to), and I even offered to write up a contract saying that I would not sell them, if that made him feel better. At this point we went back to the theme of the human voice being a gift of God. I told MD I agreed with him, but pointed out that just about everyone was in possession of this gift. We talked in circles for a while longer, but then I went straight to the point again and said that if he wanted to be paid more I was afraid that it was not possible. I added that it was his choice whether he wanted to continue working or not, and that if he did not, I would find someone else, and, I added, very easily. He left and said he would come back for our regular session the next day.

I was upset by MD's veiled request for many reasons. I knew that I was paying him a very fair price, in fact more than any high school student could possibly think of earning, but at the same time his request had made me very uneasy. It was in a sense both a legitimate and an illegitimate request. As the extent of Fatick's material poverty continued to reveal itself to me, I became increasingly ill at ease with both my surroundings and myself. My unease stemmed primarily from my own pessimism about whether I would ever be able to integrate myself into life in Fatick, given the fact that the economic disparity between myself and the people around me was so overwhelming. Leonardo and I were, by virtue of the fact that we were toubabs, prime targets for continual requests for money. It seemed that not a day went by without someone catching up with me on the street or coming to the house to ask me for money for a naming ceremony, a medical prescription, bush taxi fare to visit a relative, new clothes for a religious holiday, or even a guitar! My response was emotional and frequently manifested itself as anger. The anger had to do with my desire to be treated as an individual and not just as a source of money. It reached its peak one day when a woman whom we did not know came to the door to ask Djibi Ndiaye bluntly "Where is the toubab? I need money." I was furious. While I wanted to believe that my economic status was incidental to my personality in terms of how people evaluated me, it was clear from that woman's comment that my personality was not even incidental to her, it was merely irrelevant. The only important thing about me was that I had money.

There was a darker side of this anger which took the form of a moral crisis. To say that I was not a wealthy person, merely a graduate student with a $7,000 grant, was a lie, because in the context of Fatick I was one of the wealthiest people in town. My moral crisis stemmed from the fact that I could occasionally go to Dakar for a weekend, have dinner in a good French restaurant, and maybe buy a Baule mask at one of the many art dealers' shops on Rue Mohammed V for a sum of money that could make a significant difference in the life of numerous Fatickois. It might provide someone with medicine or malaria prophylaxis for the family; it might mean the difference between being able to send the children to school that year or not; it might allow Arame Gueye, the woman who sold peanuts on the corner near our house, to replace the leaky thatched roof on her hut. "Money," Thierno told me at some point during that year in Fatick, "is for solving problems." So was it immoral of me to go to Dakar and spend money on unnecessary things? Was it immoral of me not to give substantial sums of money to the people I knew in Fatick in order to help them? Now that the initial excitement of moving to my field site, settling in and starting work had faded, I had started to become obsessed with these questions and how I was to come to terms with the poverty around me.

My moral crisis began to have deleterious effects on my fieldwork. The clear sense of purpose in the field that I had at the outset became obscured by these other pressing issues so much so that fieldwork now seemed almost to be a futile undertaking, an insignificant activity. Several events, all of which were linked to material poverty, conspired to contribute to my troubled state of mind. A newborn girl, the sister of Cheikh Thiam, a young boy who ran errands for Djibi Ndiaye and who had become part of our household, had been named after me. In her father's compound someone had died, and there was a suspicion of cholera. The health officials came to inspect the compound and said that the dead man's clothes should be burned; however, later on that day I learned that the clothes had not been burned, but simply washed and redistributed to other members of the household. Then, arriving back in Fatick from a weekend trip to Dakar, we found out that a young woman we knew well had just given birth prematurely to a baby the night before and it was doubtful whether the baby would survive. We went to the hospital to find her but were told that she had already left and was trying to take the baby to a hospital in Dakar. After half an hour of walking in the noon sun, we found the woman and her mother standing with the baby in the bush taxi park, waiting for a van to fill up with passengers so they could leave for Dakar. We found out later that there was an ambulance in Fatick for that purpose, but no one had the money to pay for gasoline. The prospects of the van filling up before four o'clock, when people were up and about again, were slim. Even though we had just arrived from Dakar, we had little choice but to pay for all the remaining seats in the van and head back to the capital with the baby. The ride was nightmarish, and by the time we got to Dakar the baby was dead, or as people said, it had "returned," never fully having been in this world. As I thought about it, I realized I had known more people in Fatick who had died in the short time I had been there than in the rest of my life.

I cannot say just how I worked my way out of the paralysis that had affected me and back into a renewed enthusiasm for the work I was doing. Certainly, the moral crisis was not resolved, and nine years later working in Dakar I have still not resolved it, although I have managed to find my own way through it. Getting away from Fatick for a trip to Mauritania shortly before Ramadan no doubt helped, since upon my return I felt that I was coming back to a place I knew and where, in an awkward way, I fit in. A few days after I returned, I walked in town with Abal Diallo, my neighbor and director of the Fatick Chamber of Commerce. Abal Diallo, dressed that day in a deep purple damask boubou with gold embroidery, was by Senegalese standards a prosperous man. As we walked, numerous people came up to greet him and make requests of him. He deflected some of the requests graciously with jokes and laughter, but to some he gave money. I commented to Abal that he got as many requests for help as I did, to which he replied, "All the time." A few days later Ndaan Diouf came into town from Dakar. Ndaan was an entrepreneur who owned the cloth shop next to our house, and he had plans to start a peanut butter processing factory in Fatick. As we were standing talking to him outside the shop, an elderly woman dressed in shabby clothing came up and prostrated herself before him, touching his feet and the hem of his boubou and repeating his last name: "Diouf, Diouf, Diouf." Ndaan was visibly embarrassed by the woman's display of submission in our presence and hastily exchanged some words with her, opened his wallet, handed her some money, and sent her on her way. She clutched the bills in her hand and muttered something about how good Ndaan Diouf was as she walked away. Because of his embarrassment I did not ask Ndaan who the woman was, but afterwards I asked Arame Gueye, the peanut vendor who had witnessed the unusual scene. "She's his slave," Arame told me. When I asked what that meant, she told me that it meant that Ndaan had to give her money. I questioned others about the event and found out that the behavior I had seen was an artifact of a social structure that had once been three-tiered in nature, the lowest tier being occupied by *jaam* or slaves. By this time I decided that there was more to the exchange of money than met the eye, and that there were certain rules, unknown to me, that were governing the exchanges. The muezzin from the local mosque who used to visit us with some frequency had stopped coming by, and told Djibi Ndiaye that it was because we never gave him any money. "Griots,[3] all they do is ask for money," Djibi volunteered. I talked to Thierno one day about the great number of requests that I got from people. Too discreet to say anything directly, he simply said, "Yes, there are some people who ask for things all the time." He then added that people asked him for money all the time, too. By this point I was coming closer to understanding the hierarchical social structure shared by most of the ethnic groups that made up Senegalese society, where people are divided into endogamous groups, known in Wolof as *géer*, *ñeeño*, and *jaam*. *Jaam* are slaves, but in Wolof and Seereer society the category has all but disappeared; *ñeeño*, usually translated as 'casted groups', are artisans such as blacksmiths, leather workers, and griots or verbal artists, all of whom work with dangerous materials, including language; and *géer* are non-casted people, generally referred to in French or English by what is somewhat of a misnomer: 'nobles'.[4] This social structure makes for an elaborate patron-client network, in which *géer* give money and other gifts to *ñeeño* in return for securing their reputation. And even above and beyond these social considerations, the act of giving places one in a superior social position to a dependent. Seen in this light, those who asked me for money were giving me the opportunity to establish my reputation! And so it was. In the town, I was frequently embarrassed by people stopping me with their friends to say in front of me how good I was because I had given someone money to buy school books for her children. I felt almost more awkward in these situation than in those where I was asked directly for money, and quickly learned the formulaic response: "*Ñoo ko bokk*" ('We share it.')

I had occasion to reflect on all the work that had gone into establishing myself in Fatick when twice I felt threatened by association with American visitors whose behavior was untoward or inappropriate in the context of Fatick society, and I realized how proprietary I had become about my field site. After living in Fatick for several months I had learned how to conduct myself in a socially appropriate manner, had established a network of acquaintances, friends, and, as it turned out, dependents, and was thus a member, albeit a somewhat awkward one, of Fatick society.

1.4   The elusive noun class

In looking at the noun class data I had elicited from MD, Souleymane Faye, a Seereer linguist at the University of Dakar, commented that MD must be a young speaker since the data contained numerous Wolof loan words. I decided to collect a corpus of noun class data in Seereer from an older, less urbanized speaker, and began working with ED, a peanut farmer who lived in Ndiaye-Ndiaye. Up until that point I had done all my elicitation through the medium of French, Senegal's official language, but because ED did not know French we had to work through the medium of Wolof. Although I spoke Wolof well, I would still have felt more comfortable working through French. After overcoming my initial trepidation, however, I found that there were some advantages to working on Seereer through Wolof. Since the two languages are structurally similar, it was easier to find exact equivalents between Seereer and Wolof, such as an iterative verbal extension, or an imperfective aspectual marker, or an inchoative verb, than between Seereer and French. In fact, in working through the medium of French on both Pulaar and Seereer, assistants frequently gave me a Wolof translation in addition to a French one, since the Wolof mirrored more directly the forms in those languages. In comparing ED's noun class forms with MD's, I saw that Souleymane Faye had been right. The variation between the two speakers' forms clearly showed the effects of Wolofization, the spread of

Wolof as Senegal's lingua franca, at the expense of other languages. Although ED had grown up speaking both Seereer and Wolof, he had always lived in the Ndiaye-Ndiaye neighborhood, spoke only Seereer at home, and used Seereer when speaking with his siblings. MD, on the other hand, had been to school, where Wolof dominates as the language used outside the classroom, and at home he had used both Seereer and Wolof – Seereer with the older people in his family, and Wolof with his brothers and sisters.

Variation in Seereer noun classes was something I could live with: at least it was consistent for individual speakers. Wolof noun classes, on the other hand, exhibited not only variation between speakers, but within the repertoire of a single individual. I had noticed this already as a language learner: my Wolof teachers in Dakar would tell me one day that a noun was in a certain noun class, and the next day they would put it in a different class. The same was true in eliciting data on noun classes in Wolof. People with whom I worked would frequently tell me that they said one thing, but that the "real" noun class was something else, and then later they would assign the same noun to yet a third class. I tried to find some patterns in the data I was getting, but found it difficult. One trend that I noticed was that in eliciting data, if my assistant assigned a noun to one of the rarer classes, then the next few nouns that I elicited were also assigned to that class, almost as if the order in which I was eliciting them was determining the class. As I reflected on what was going on, I realized that I had been working with speakers of urban Wolof, all of whom were in some sense aware that their language differed from rural dialects of Wolof spoken in the Wolof heartland. The two most noticeable characteristics of urban Wolof are, first, extensive lexical borrowing from French, and second, the tendency of nouns to be assigned to the default class. The people with whom I worked on eliciting Wolof were constantly holding their own speech up to be compared with a "deep" dialect of Wolof (*olof bu xóot*) of which they had only an imperfect knowledge.[5]

While discussing the Wolof problem with Thierno one day, he told me that he had spent several years living in a Wolof village as a teacher, and that he had a good command of the rural noun class forms. If I was interested, he suggested, we could go through my noun list and he would give me the classes for all of them. I rejected his offer on the grounds that he was not a native speaker of Wolof, an issue that I later had reason to reconsider. It did not matter to me what dialect of Wolof I recorded, but I could not seem to get beyond the interference of prescriptive notions in any of my elicitations. At this point I decided that I was getting an interesting metalinguistic commentary from elicitation sessions on Wolof noun classes, but not what I was after. I decided to abandon formal elicitation and rely entirely on natural speech for noun classes and see what the results were, a strategy that met with success. There were one or two individuals with whom I was in contact on a daily basis for extended periods of time, and I focused on their speech. I found much more consistency in their speech than I had found in elicitation, and even the discrepancies tended to fall into patterns. There was heavy use of the default class, and in cases where they used two classes for the same noun, one of the two was, without fail, the default class. I became so accustomed to listening for Wolof noun classes that I found myself doing it all the time, even while listening to Senegal's preeminent rock star, Youssou Ndour, singing in Wolof. In listening to people in town, in the market, or in bush taxis, I could not always tell if their first language was Wolof, but given my experience with native Pulaar and Seereer speakers who spoke fluent Wolof, and learning that many of them could not remember a time when they did not speak Wolof, the very notion of a "native speaker of Wolof" was thrown into question. I had rejected grammatical judgments on Wolof from Thierno because he was a native Pulaar speaker, but could not he, or others like him, also be native speakers of Wolof? In this context, could it not be possible to have more than one native language? Although at the time I did not hold these views, I now think that the urban–rural distinction in Wolof is a much more salient variable in distinguishing between varieties of the language than whether the Wolof speaker has another mother tongue, such as Seereer or Pulaar.

1.5   Speaking Wolof

Linguistics was, predictably, just as misunderstood in Fatick as anywhere else. People in the town thought that I was learning to speak Seereer and Pulaar and were astonished that after so much work I could say so little. I had, however, devoted considerable time to learning Wolof, and found that the rewards more than justified my efforts. Not only did speaking Wolof facilitate social integration, but, as I have already illustrated, it also proved invaluable in my linguistic investigations. Being able to listen to and understand most anything in Wolof said within earshot opened up my experience of the language in a way not yet possible with Pulaar or Seereer. Rather than having to elicit linguistic forms, they came rolling at me from all sides during my waking hours, so much so that I sometimes found it overwhelming. I carried a small notebook around with me and took notes on all kinds of topics, ranging from noun classes in natural discourse to Wolof and French code mixing, and eventually amassed a wealth of unorganized data.

Some of my discoveries about Wolof came from corrections to my own speech. For example, in recounting an event to Cheikh Thiam, the seven-year-old boy who spent much time at our house helping Djibi Ndiaye, I was dismayed when he told me that no one spoke the way I did. It seemed that each of my Wolof sentences was in itself grammatical, but when strung together in the context of a narrative they became quite ungrammatical. In this way I was introduced to the grammar of Wolof discourse above the clause level. A second experience alerted me to the differences in speech between male and female speakers. In bargaining for fish in the marketplace I called the fish vendor *sama jigéen* ('my woman'), a common phrase that I had heard people – but as it turned out, only men – use in just such a context. Much to my humiliation, everyone within earshot burst out laughing at my utterance, and soon word had spread all over the market that I had spoken like a man.

One of the topics that interested me the most, but to which I would have had limited access without my knowledge of Wolof, was the phenomenon of surrogate speech (Yankah 1995: 8). *Géer*, or other socially prominent people in Wolof society, refrain from speaking robustly in public, and have griots or verbal artists speak in their stead. A common situation in a public talk given by a socially prominent person is for that person to speak softly so that the audience cannot hear very well, and for the griot to report loudly what he or she said, often adding interesting embellishments. One night I attended a talk given by a Tijani marabout and was able to sit close enough to the front so that I could hear what the marabout said before the griot reported it. The marabout was quite eloquent but spoke softly. He used many French words in his Wolof, which in this case were intended to show his erudition. In reporting this discourse the griot expunged the French words and substituted somewhat arcane Wolof words, thus exhibiting to an appreciative audience his mastery of *olof bu xóot* or "deep Wolof" and, especially interesting to me, its requisite noun classes. But when the marabout stopped using French terms conspicuously, the griot sprinkled the reported discourse abundantly with French to show his own expertise in that language. Because of the griot's linguistic prowess, an aura of erudition was reflected back onto the marabout. The implications of that speech event are too complex and far reaching to elaborate on here, but it is clear that without my knowledge of Wolof, the surrogate speech event would have been closed to me. While formal linguistic elicitation works in some instances it may not be sufficient, as my experience with Wolof noun classification clearly shows. In such cases the knowledge of a field language is invaluable in that it further enables the linguist to observe the language in its natural environment.

1.6   Conclusion

Although it is a perhaps a cliché to say so, the period of fieldwork that I spent in Fatick conducting research for my dissertation was in many senses an initiation. It was an initiation into working as a field linguist by learning to trust my own judgment without being able to confer with fellow students or the professor in a field methods class. After returning to Austin from Fatick I was thus anxious to write my dissertation, graduate, and move beyond my status as a student. It was also an initiation into the larger academic community of Africanists, most of whom share the experience of having done fieldwork on the continent, a common base that has played a great role in fostering interdisciplinary research among Africanists. And finally, the time I spent in Fatick was an initiation into the realities of living in the third world, with all the dilemmas and rewards involved in such an experience.

Part II: Thierno Seydou Sall[6]

2.1   *My home town, 1989*

It had already been several days since I first noticed the presence of a couple of toubabs in Fatick. (A toubab never passes unnoticed in a little Senegalese town like Fatick.) I crossed them in the streets of Fatick and sometimes I saw them pass near my house. I had no idea what they had come to look for in my home town.

One day, I learned that free English courses were being given by an American couple, and for someone like me, who had studied alone and who was preparing, as an independent candidate, to take secondary school exams, where English occupies a very important place, it was a golden opportunity. In fact, up to that point I had never studied at school at all. I had received only a religious education in Arabic at the *daara* (Koranic school), and through this education in Arabic I eventually won a scholarship to study at the African Islamic Centre in Sudan. This in turn had allowed me to become an Arabic teacher in the primary schools upon my return to Senegal, a profession that I exercised at that time. But through my own efforts I had learned to read and write in French, which is the official language of my country, and so through the medium of reading I had access to the different subjects taught in school programs, such as mathematics, natural science, English, history, and geography.

So I went to find out more about the English courses, and the Americans in question turned out to be none other than the toubabs that I had been seeing for some time in the town. My inquiries came rather late because the English courses were about to finish, but to console me the Americans invited me to come by their house so they could give me some English books that they had used in the program.

Through our discussions and conversations they discovered that I was an

Arabic teacher, a fact to which Leonardo was not indifferent, since he was there to do research on a subject that was related to Islam for his doctorate. But I think that it was especially the fact that I am Haalpulaar, a speaker of Pulaar, that captured their attention. In fact, Fiona, who was preparing a dissertation in linguistics, needed both a Haalpulaar assistant and a Seereer assistant, and it was I who would eventually become the Haalpulaar assistant. I think that the fact that I also spoke other languages like Wolof, which is spoken by the majority of Senegalese, Seereer, which is spoken by the majority of the inhabitants of the region of Fatick (Siin), Arabic and French, was a favorable factor in my becoming her assistant.

2.2   Being a linguist's assistant

Fiona, who was a linguistics student, had engaged me as her assistant for collaboration on a linguistic project on noun classes in Pulaar. This collaboration, which gave me great satisfaction both on the intellectual and material level, was carried out with only minor difficulties. What few difficulties there were revolved around three points. First, although I speak several languages, I did not have a clear notion of what the field of linguistics actually was, and so I had some trouble in the beginning understanding what my "student" expected from me. I call her my student because when I think in Pulaar or Wolof, I really cannot call her anything else. For me, a student is someone who wants to know, and she was the one who asked me questions to find out about my language, and I tried to answer them. When I started working on the project with Fiona, because we did not know each other well at the time, it was very hard for me to be natural in talking about my language. I had a tendency to focus on what was correct and what was incorrect in Pulaar because I thought that there were certain expectations about the way I should speak. I thought that if I knew something was incorrect, even if I normally said it that way, I should try and give her the correct form. For example, the word for the plural form of curdled milk is really *kocce*, but most people say *kosameeje*, so I told her *kocce* first, and *kosameeje* afterwards. I thought she could use this information to eventually speak good Pulaar, but after she explained it to me, I quickly understood that her goal at that point was not to speak Pulaar, but to study a part of the mechanism of the language. I should say that for many people it is not easy to understand that one can study a language in any way other than learning to speak it. I had a vivid example of this when I went home once with my student. My uncle spoke to her in Pulaar, but she could not reply. My uncle was astonished because he thought that she had studied enough Pulaar by now to be able to speak it. So I was obliged to make a great pedagogical effort to explain the reality of the situation to him, but he still seemed to find it bizarre. I was a bit bothered because I had the impression that my uncle thought that if my student still did not speak Pulaar, it was because my teaching was not good!

I also had some difficulties regarding my own language. Pulaar is my native language which I learned in a natural way rather than a structured way. I was thus unable to know the difficulties and the limits of my language. So I started work with absolute confidence, but as the work advanced I started to discover difficulties about things that I had taken for granted, and I ran into some insurmountable limits. For example, one day we were doing compounds composed of two nouns, and I had to give Fiona the noun class for those words. For some of the words, the noun class could be that of either the first noun or the second noun in the compound, but for others there was only one possibility. After a while I started to question my own judgment. I did not know what sounded right or wrong to me any more, and so we had to stop. Another example was that I at first thought that I could translate anything from French or Wolof into Pulaar, but then I realized that there were ideas that Pulaar could not manage very well because it was, above all, a question of culture before being a question of vocabulary.

The other difficulties that we had were tied to my level of French. Our working language was French, but my competence in French was nonetheless still lacking. (One could say the same of my student's competence in Wolof.) Added to that was interference from local languages, all of which together meant that I spoke a rather idiosyncratic type of French. It happened more than once that my student understood something other than what I had intended to say, or that I said something that I had not meant to say. But when things did not work in French, we repeated them in Wolof and that usually worked. I think that this was the first time that I had occasion to speak French for hours on end, so it was a good opportunity for me to practice what, up to that point, I had learned only through reading and listening. My French improved considerably through our discussions. Not only did I become used to speaking French, but I was also able to correct myself. This was an opportunity for me to examine the way I spoke French and to improve it. So I was learning.

I also learned a lot about my own language, Pulaar. I had never paid any attention before to the existence of noun classes in Pulaar, even though I evoked them every time I spoke. I also found that a few classes were associated with a category of meaning such as liquids or a certain shape. My student was puzzled one day when I told her that many words in the class that took the article, *ngoo*, were almost but not completely flat, like a hand. She did not understand what I meant, so I held my hand out as if to receive something, and showed her how it was almost flat, yet curved up at the edges, like the wooden spoon for stirring porridge (*holfo ngoo*), or the cover for a milk bowl (*ñorgo ngoo*), or a bird's beak (*hoggo ngoo*). I discovered grammatical phenomena of which I had not been conscious since I spoke Pulaar correctly without having to think about grammatical rules, and I also learned some linguistic terms. A few years later, when I was teaching in a school in Dakar, one of my superiors was talking about the way Wolof could make a noun out of a verb by changing the initial sound [f] to [p] or [s] to [c]. I was able to tell him that it was called consonant mutation, but I think that he was annoyed that I knew this, and held it against me for quite some time. Nonetheless, these advances on the intellectual front, and being able to discuss intellectual questions on a consistent basis, were for me a real source of satisfaction.

My student was interested in noun classes in Wolof as well as Pulaar, and although she wanted to get the forms from someone who was a Wolof, as opposed to a Haalpulaar like myself, we discussed the problems associated with that language. I grew up in a Seereer village in a Haalpulaar family, so when I was a small child I spoke Pulaar and Seereer better than Wolof, but even then, I cannot remember ever not having known Wolof. When I was fourteen I went to Dakar where my Wolof improved, and then I spent five years in Kayor, the heart of Wolof country, where pure Wolof is spoken. By pure Wolof I mean Wolof with very little French in it. Fiona thought that I could not give her the noun classes in Wolof, but for me, it would be the same thing as giving them to her in Pulaar. I speak Wolof very well. Maybe I am mistaken, but I think I even speak Wolof better than certain Wolofs who live in Dakar or Fatick, even though it is possible that I have an accent in Wolof. I correct other people's Wolof, and I correct their noun classes. Part of the reason that people in Dakar do not know the right noun class is that Wolofs there mix and live with non-Wolofs, so the Wolof of those who are not Wolof influences the Wolof of those who are, and it goes around that way. In fact, non-Wolofs make no distinction between classes when they start speaking Wolof, so they use the article *bi* indiscriminately for all the classes. I speak deep Wolof, which is different from urban Wolof in that there are rarely any French words in it, and there are often words that people in Dakar do not know, so they use French. All the same, I can understand that Fiona wanted to be prudent and not get the Wolof noun classes she needed from a Pulaar speaker like myself.

2.3   *The socio-cultural dimension*

In the beginning, when I first met my American friends, I was of course aware of the very great cultural and economic distances between us, and it took some time to overcome my fears and hesitations. My fears were "two-way" in nature. That is to say that I feared making my friends victims of my prejudices, just as I feared being a victim of their prejudices, too. At first, because I was worried about offending them, I could not behave naturally around them. I was afraid of becoming too familiar with them, and afraid of visiting them too often (which would be normal among Senegalese), even though I had the impression that they encouraged me to do so. And when I did visit them, I was afraid to stay for a long time because I thought I might overstay my welcome.

On the other hand, although very soon after I got to know my friends my fears were assuaged, there are certain prejudices we have about toubabs which means that we have no choice other than to be prudent, and thus a bit unnatural, around them at first. Of course these prejudices are sometimes silly, but sometimes they are well founded. We have seen toubabs who, once they are here in Senegal, consider everything that falls under their eyes to be a touristic object. They do not hesitate to take photographs of people in markets and other public places, without authorization, as if those people were animals. And one cannot help but wonder about what they will ultimately do with those photos. Every time I see postcards of young women with naked breasts bathing in the river, I wonder if they were ever asked their opinion or informed about the final destination of those photos. Today, ten years later, I realize that perhaps I had too general a vision of toubabs by putting researchers and tourists in the same category, but sometimes I also have to wonder what it is that is so interesting about us that so many researchers, it sometimes seems like thousands of them, come here to study us. We are always the object of the studies, and the object of tourists' photographs.

As I continued to work with Fiona I started to feel more at ease around her and her husband, but there was one barrier that I had a great deal of trouble overcoming. It was very difficult for me to invite them to my house and to meet my family because they would see the conditions in which I lived, in a household where the standard of living was of the very lowest. Poverty showed itself on every level. For example, a single room in my house served at the same time as a bedroom, living room, storage room, and sometimes even a kitchen! My family is a large traditional family in which no one of my generation had ever been sent to school, and there are practices that are unhygienic that we and many other Senegalese are in the habit of doing, such as keeping a communal drinking cup on top of the water jug for everyone – including people with colds or other illnesses – to drink out of. Bad hygienic conditions are the result of two factors: overcrowding, which is in itself a consequence of poverty, and lack of education. I have always been conscious of the inhumanity of these living conditions, despite being used to them, but I thought that inviting people whose standard of living was exactly the opposite (so as not to say "people who had almost everything") would be to expose myself and leave me open to humiliation. But despite that hesitation, I also thought that it was not rational to see things in that way, because there should not be any shame associated with being poor, since I was not to blame for it. I thought that I should be able to show myself to people as I am, naturally and without being ashamed, but it was a struggle for me. Although the situation has changed now, I regret that I did not invite them sooner and more often to my house that year when they lived in Fatick.

Once my relations with the American researchers were well established, I found myself in an ambiguous position. For many Senegalese, to have good relations with toubabs is synonymous with having material advantages, and they are not always wrong. And there was no shortage of people who wondered why I did not take advantage of my "privileged" position. Some even asked me to intervene with my friends on their behalf in order to solve financial problems or obtain visas for the United States, for example. Such a conception of relations with toubabs put me in a rather awkward position. Because of this conception of relations with toubabs, certain people would not hesitate to prostitute themselves, so to speak, in order to fulfill their material needs. Consequently, anyone who frequents toubabs could easily be suspected of such behavior. And for someone like me, having received an education at a *daara* and belonging to a traditional family where individuals are controlled by social pressure, that would be shocking. All these reasons, then, contributed to the fact that I sometimes felt the need for discretion in my relations with my American friends, although I eventually began to feel at ease with them in public.

When Fiona first proposed to me that I be her assistant, I immediately accepted without thinking of being paid. I was predisposed to do it, not only because I knew that I would derive intellectual advantages from it, but also because I thought it was my moral duty, all the more because Fiona had given free English courses to the inhabitants of Fatick. Then some time afterwards she proposed discussing the payment before beginning work. I let her know that I did not expect to be paid, especially since this did not cost me anything. I had the time and the work did not demand any preparation on my part. But she insisted. So I told her that I could not fix the payment and that she should just do as she pleased. In any case, I was prepared to do the work with or without payment. She proposed a sum, and I admit that I was very surprised. She proposed 1,500 CFA francs, the equivalent of five dollars. After all her insistence, I found the sum quite ridiculous, but I did not say anything because I would still have been willing to do the work for nothing. But my surprise was even greater when after just a few days of work she went to pay me. I had expected 1,500 CFA francs for a month of work, but she counted the hours that we had worked together and gave me a large sum of money. And since at the outset I had not expected payment, this sum was like a gift for me. I admit that I was very happy that year, and I was able to solve a lot of problems with that unexpected money!

ACKNOWLEDGMENTS

Fiona Mc Laughlin would like to thank Dan Lefkowitz, Sara Trechter, and Julia Watson for discussing and encouraging the idea of a collaborative fieldwork narrative. Both authors thank Leonardo Villalón for the role he played in the fieldwork process and in critiquing its recreation in this account. For critical commentary on the text, we also thank Ibrahima Athie, Mansour Bâ, Adama Kone, Moussa Sissoko, and Charlie Sugnet.

NOTES

1 *Toubab* is a term (derived from Arabic word for 'doctor') used in many parts of West Africa to refer to a Westerner or a white person.
2 The Moors are a Hassaniya-speaking Berbero-Arab ethnic group who constitute the majority ethnic group of Mauritania. Smaller communities of Moors are also found in Senegal, Mali, and other countries in West Africa.
3 A griot (Wolof *géwél*; Pulaar *gawlo* (sg.), *awluɓe* (pl.)) is a West African verbal artist or musician whose typical occupation is praise-singing and the recital of genealogy.
4 Caste in societies of the Western Sahel is a controversial topic. Various reconsiderations of the hierarchical nature of these societies are presented in the collection of essays in Conrad and Frank (1995).
5 The issue of variation in Wolof noun classes is discussed in Irvine (1978) and Mc Laughlin (1997).
6 This narrative was originally written in French by Sall and translated into English by Mc Laughlin.

REFERENCES

Conrad, David C. and Barbara E. Frank (eds.). 1995. *Status and Identity in West Africa: Nyamakalaw of Mande*. Bloomington: Indiana University Press.
Irvine, Judith T. 1978. Wolof noun classification: the social setting of divergent change. *Language in Society* 7:37–64
Mc Laughlin, Fiona. 1992. Noun Classification in Seereer-Siin. Ph.D. dissertation, University of Texas at Austin.
     1997. Noun classification in Wolof: when affixes are not renewed. *Studies in African Linguistics* 26:1–28.
Yankah, Kwesi. 1995. *Speaking for the Chief: Okyeame and the Politics of Akan Royal Oratory*. Bloomington: Indiana University Press.

10   Phonetic fieldwork

Ian Maddieson

Phoneticians typically distinguish three principal sub-disciplines within phonetics: these are concerned with how speech is produced, the nature of the sound itself, and how a human being reacts to speech stimuli. These first two areas are commonly referred to as articulatory (or physiological) phonetics and acoustic phonetics. The third encompasses auditory and perceptual phonetics; that is, it concerns both the way that the human auditory system works and the effects of various levels of further processing in the brain, in which a speaker's linguistic knowledge and experience play an important role. It is frequently difficult to separate auditory and perceptual effects since their investigation commonly relies on overt responses collected from listeners in which the sum of both kinds of processes is necessarily reflected.

A phonetic research project, whether in the field or in the laboratory, may be directed at investigating articulatory, acoustic, or auditory/perceptual facts alone. However, many studies consider the relationship between articulatory or auditory/perceptual facts and the acoustic layer which mediates between them. A naïve native speaker's sub-conscious phonetic knowledge about his or her language concerns only production and perception, and not acoustic properties, nor the strictly auditory processes which transform the acoustic signal. However, the articulatory organization of speech must succeed in encoding information in acoustic form, and the perceptual apparatus must succeed in extracting the information from the acoustic signal. Because a good deal is known about articulatory/acoustic relationships, an examination of acoustic patterns can provide indirect information on articulation. For example, looking at the acoustic pattern of vowels may permit inferences to be made about production mechanisms which are hard to observe directly. Much is also known about the auditory/acoustic relationship, and examining acoustic data in the light of this knowledge helps to clarify which aspects are likely to be of perceptual significance. Less is known about perceptual processes *per se* and so about the perception/acoustics relationship. It is clear, though, that any two utterances which differ functionally in their sound structure must contain some

211

perceptible difference. Looking at the acoustics therefore provides us with information on perception.

A quite different division of phonetics into subfields is provided by the linguistic perspective selected by the investigator. For example, the chosen objective may be to give an overall view of the sound system of a particular language, to analyze an individual speech act, to characterize general human phonetic abilities, or to find the best way to apply phonetic understanding in some practical way, such as in language teaching or speech synthesis. Some investigators are interested in characteristics of individual speakers or of groups, such as those established by class, age, or gender, or by a clinically-relevant distinction between "normal" and "abnormal" populations. Researchers in areas such as discourse analysis or the analysis of performance style usually focus on examining particular "texts." Descriptive linguists are concerned to understand how a speaker's phonetic knowledge is integrated with the rest of the grammar of the language. Many phoneticians are interested in language universals, processes of diachronic sound change, and other issues where integration of data on numerous languages is required.

In this chapter, it will be assumed that the main purpose in mind is field research on what has been called linguistic phonetics: that is, on the phonetic properties and parameters underlying linguistically-relevant contrasts at segmental, prosodic, or other levels of analysis. This is the kind of phonetics which is most closely related to phonology (indeed, some would say there is no boundary between these domains). The primary objectives of the chapter are twofold. One is to provide some guidance to descriptive linguists interested in adding greater depth to their phonetic analyses, or seeking answers to analytical problems touching on phonetics which they encounter in fieldwork. The other is to provide encouragement and advice to phoneticians who feel most at home in a laboratory setting but are considering field research. Different sections of the chapter will be tacitly addressed more to one or the other of these objectives, but it is hoped that it can be read as a coherent whole. It is, naturally, colored by my own experiences. Research issues and fieldwork settings vary enormously, and the resources available influence what is feasible for the individual researcher. With some imagination it should be possible to see how some of this advice might be applicable to different objectives and circumstances.

1.   Phonetic fieldwork and experimental phonetics

In its oldest incarnation phonetic fieldwork was conducted with nothing but eyes and ears, and a notebook and pencil. The education of a phonetician, most especially in the influential tradition represented by figures such as Henry Sweet and Daniel Jones in Britain, and Paul Passy in France, consisted mainly of performance and ear-training exercises designed to produce familiarity with exemplars of all the major categories of sounds recognized in a standard phonetic typology. The idea was to train the student to know what to do to produce each "type" (and numerous variants) and to pair that with a knowledge of a corresponding percept. A phonetician was a kind of "super-speaker" who could introspectively pair the production and perception data inculcated by this method. Once trained, the phonetician could, in principle, go out to any field setting and determine the phonetic patterns encountered there by looking, listening, and repeating, and usually writing down these impressions in a transcription representing the learned pairings of articulatory recipes and percepts. Today, many linguists-in-training receive only a very attenuated form of this kind of practice in listening to and imitating speech sounds. Consequently, many feel insecure in dealing with unfamiliar kinds of speech patterns, or may simply feel under-equipped to make a good phonetic transcription.

Although it can achieve impressive results, as in late nineteenth- and early twentieth-century dialect surveys of European languages, a weakness of the classic performance and ear-training school is that it provides no way to verify an observer's conclusions. An assertion that some segment in a language is produced with a particular articulatory posture, and is perceptually equivalent to a segment in another language, remains an assertion. It can be cross-checked by sending another observer. But if they disagree, there is no obvious way to resolve the disagreement. Nowadays, phonetics is a discipline in which simple observation and introspection are considered insufficient in many domains, and conclusions are expected to be supported by appropriate documentation and numbers. This means that although the methods of acquiring and processing the data may have become more complex, the need to rely on confidence in one's own subjective judgements is much reduced. The reward of greater complexity is greater certainty.

There is in fact a long tradition of instrumental and experimental work in phonetics, but it did not move to a central position in the field until the middle decades of this century. One factor in this development was the enormous growth in the understanding of the acoustics of speech at this time, driven both by developments in instrumentation and in theoretical models. By their nature, acoustic facts are not directly accessible to a native speaker or the phonetician super-speaker – only their perceptual consequences are. Here was a rich field of investigation newly opened up; moreover it provided tools to illuminate aspects of production and perception. Other new tools for investigating articulatory movements, muscular activation, brain responses, and so forth continue to become available. Ideas on hypothesis formation, experimental design, and statistical validation evolve. And everything is driven faster by the digital revolution in data-processing and the ability to put ever-growing computational power within easy economic grasp. These changes affect not only the way that phoneticians work but also the kinds of issues they investigate. For example, because the necessary information can be more easily acquired and examined, much greater attention is now given to temporal and dynamic parameters in speech.

Not all the current techniques of experimental phonetic investigation lend themselves to application in the field. For example, most methods of tracking the movements of the articulators over time, and ways of examining brain function, remain laboratory-bound at present. However, a number of techniques for investigating speech production are easily transportable to field situations. Recorded speech data can always be subjected to acoustic analysis to extract directly the acoustic information and make indirect inferences on articulatory and perceptual facts. And many types of perceptual experiments can be designed to be presented in the field.

Phonetic fieldwork will have rather different characteristics, according to whether obtaining phonetic data is the primary goal or is subsidiary to other purposes. A specialist phonetician might plan a field trip in search of particular data. Or a linguist who has principal interests in a different area of linguistics may want to cover some point of phonetic interest as part of a more general description, or perhaps comes across a problem where it seems that phonetic data may resolve a question of the interpretation of phonological, morphological, syntactic, or discourse patterns. Particularly in the first case, there are a number of things which set phonetic fieldwork apart from linguistic fieldwork on other aspects of a language. A phonetic study often involves a very large amount of subsequent work in the lab on relatively small quantities of data collected in the field, which requires careful forethought to ensure that the data collection is well planned. One may need to ask subjects to do things which might be perceived as invasive of personal privacy, and one may need to obtain specialized equipment and transport and operate it in the field. Moreover, the issues which arise over working on phonetics with speakers are in some ways unlike those which are raised in other linguistic investigations. The following sections will discuss a number of these topics, and offer some suggestions drawn from experience on how to plan and conduct at least some types of phonetic research in the field.

2.   Working with speakers

All linguists must deal with the lay person's difficulty in understanding a linguist's analytical approach to language. Judging from my experience, members of a community in which a linguist is conducting fieldwork most often initially make sense of what one is doing by interpreting it as an interest in learning to speak and understand the language. That is, being able to communicate in the language, to express and understand meaning – rather than understanding the mechanics of the linguistic system – is taken to be the goal. The problem this creates is twofold. The first is the ethical one of explaining what you are actually doing in an honest and comprehensible way. The second is that of explaining to a willing collaborator how they can help in meeting the research objectives, once these have been understood and agreed to.

Solving the first of these problems can be quite hard. In my particular circumstances I have found I can explain what I am doing fairly simply: I am a scientist who is interested in all the different kinds of sounds that are used in languages all over the world, and the language I have come to study has some special characteristics which make it important to include in this project. This is usually sufficient. Other linguistic projects may be much harder to explain, or may touch on issues that are more sensitive than an investigation of sounds is usually perceived to be. Nonetheless, in some cultures, recording a voice, or taking pictures of a speaker's face, may raise issues of privacy and ownership. Being as informed as possible before beginning fieldwork may help the researcher to avoid being surprised by such reactions. Younger, urbanized, or otherwise less traditional speakers may be less inhibited in these ways, but still fluent enough to serve as good subjects for data collection. Even in this case it is still good to ensure that their co-operation will not be viewed negatively by elders or other authority figures in the relevant community.

Establishing a good working relationship with willing subjects is also a difficult challenge. Focusing on sounds is very remote from the functional use of the language for daily communication. And lay language does not include a useful vocabulary for discussing the properties of speech sounds, or the movements of the speech apparatus which produce them. For phoneticians (and perhaps also phonologists) the difficulties resulting can be severe. For reasons that will be laid out below, most phonetic investigations involve *comparison* between items in controlled contexts. To carry these out requires finding examples with specific sound patterns (e.g., finding minimal sets of words illustrating phonemic contrasts).

Such a search involves asking for items sorted by sound. This is a very unnatural linguistic act, since the readiest access that speakers have to their knowledge of their language is semantically and functionally organized. It is usually extremely hard for a speaker to grasp that you really are interested just in the sounds and only marginally in the meaning, and it is necessary to guard against expending a lot of your working time listening to a speaker's efforts to clarify the semantics of words and phrases you have asked for or elicited. In my own work, which is largely focused on segmental and tonal contrasts, I usually start by eliciting through translation a longish list of "basic" words for items like body parts, household items, local foodstuffs, and features of the natural environment. A few basic verbs may also be included (e.g., eat, sleep, die), but verbal forms often raise greater problems of understanding their morphological complexity. A preliminary sorting of the words elicited will show if there are any minimal pairs or other sets of well-matched contrasts to use as a starting point and will guide subsequent, more targeted elicitation.

A simple illustration of this process is given by the data in table 10.1. I was interested in compiling a set of words which would give a good idea of the typical acoustic qualities of the five distinctive vowels of Bagwalal, a North-East Caucasian language spoken in and around Kwanada in Dagestan. Since truly laryngeal consonants create no coarticulatory displacement of adjoining vowels, they provide a very good context for examining "target" vowel quality. The preliminary wordlist which I had prepared, selected from a lexicon previously collected by Russian colleagues on the fieldwork team, contained three words with the vowels /e, a, o/ in the first syllable sandwiched between two /h/s. In two of these (see table 10.1) the second vowel was a copy of the first, so the first vowel would not be affected by any vowel-on-vowel influence. This seemed like a promising beginning for a good set of words for examining vowel quality. I was able to ask a speaker, "Can you think of a word that begins /hihi . . . /" and they retrieved the rather specialized word /hihil/. This refers to a small channel dug to prevent water collecting in a depression, or a small earthen ridge erected to guide water flow in the desired direction. All the speakers I recorded turned out to know this word at least passively. No words beginning /hoho . . . / or /huhu . . . / could be discovered, at least within the time available, so a compromise had to be made. The word /hoha/ met the consonant criterion, but no word beginning /huh . . . / could be found. The best word beginning /hu . . . / had a coronal consonant after the vowel, which may front a back vowel. A better option was therefore a word with an initial /b/, as shown in table 10.1.

Speakers generally can access information about word beginnings much more easily than about later parts of a word, so the search outlined above worked quite well. Looking for words that end in a particular way can be much harder. With sufficient practical phonetic skill, it may be possible for the investigator to pronounce a 'candidate' word with the desired characteristics, and jog a speaker's memory into recalling that such a word or something like it does exist. A broadly useful technique is to start with a familiar word and ask for words that "sound similar" to it. In those parts of

Table 10.1. *Bagwalal vowels in /h/ context*

i	*hihil*	drainage channel		
e	*heher*	behind		
a	*hahari*	laugh (v.)		
o	*hoha*	strand of hair		
u	*hur*	log, firewood	*buha*	collect

the world where the concept of rhyme is familiar, it may be possible to elicit lists of words which rhyme with another, which can be an excellent short cut to obtaining minimal sets of contrasting initial consonants. However, do not expect this to work unless rhyming is part of the local tradition of verbal skills. I tried to obtain rhyme sets from an Avatime speaker in Ghana who had been exposed to rhyming English poetry in school (Avatime is a Niger-Congo language also known as Siya). Although I showed examples of rhyming words in Avatime, his access to word similarities remained dominated by similarities between onsets.

Some familiarity with an alphabetic writing system on the part of the speakers can be an advantage, so that "possible" words can be suggested by writing them down. This may provide a way to avoid some of the blocks that can be created by an investigator's imperfect attempts to pronounce items. Moreover, something written down can be taken away and pondered over. Several of the Bagwalal speakers I worked with knew the adaptation of the Cyrillic alphabet used to write Avar, and could use this to write down word-shapes of words I thought or hoped might exist, and thus take them home in the evening and ask friends and family members a question like, "Is /tɬ'am/ a word in our language?" Mediating through a written form seems also to make it easier to access the variety of word-shapes which might be the result of inflectional or other processes, rather than just one standard lexical entry shape of any word. The longer one works with a given language, naturally the more it may be possible to construct appropriately controlled data sets from one's own knowledge. Typically, preparing a data set for the examination of prosodic patterns requires a deep knowledge of a language.

A few words should also be said about the selection of subjects. In many communities one will be pointed towards older speakers as those who speak "the real language." In fact, there are all too many language communities in which it is only the old people who have a fluent command of a language which is in the process of being discarded by younger generations. In such conditions obviously the older generation has the richest information on the language to offer. However, for phonetic research there can be some particular problems with collecting data from the oldest speakers. Older speakers are more likely to have problems with articulation, whether from simple physical reasons such as lack of teeth or use of artificial teeth or from the effects of some deterioration in motor control of the articulators. Also, the changes in tissue texture that come with aging affect the acoustic signal in ways that can make analysis harder. Vocal fold vibration tends to be more irregular and inefficient, so that analysis of vocal fold vibration patterns becomes more difficult. Furthermore, excitation of vocal tract resonances is less efficient, and so most kinds of spectral analysis are more problematic in such voices. Older speakers may also be less comfortable with some of the experimental techniques used by phoneticians. Thus, while an older speaker is often the best to work with in preparing and organizing one's data, middle-aged or younger voices are better to record, and younger speakers are usually easier to work with in experiments. Despite these observations, there may be good reasons for including older speakers in a group recording a wordlist, for example, as they may be the best speakers to serve as cue-givers to younger ones. Furthermore, their inclusion in the group can serve to convey a message about the seriousness of the research enterprise.

In this section, only a few issues related to elicitation of exemplary speech material have been touched on. Field phoneticians must also deal with explaining to speakers the experimental techniques and methods of data recording they plan to use. A little more will be said about the particular issues that come up with particular techniques as these are discussed in turn.

3.   Types of information

What kinds of information might one wish to collect in a field phonetic analysis? Phonetic studies are usually oriented along one of two axes – investigation of those issues that have to do with the properties that underlie a lexical (or morphological, etc.) *contrast*, or investigation of issues concerned with *variation* superimposed on these distinctions, such as markers of phrasal structure, gender identity, semantic focus, and so on. The study of variation also encompasses all the effects due to the fact that speech is produced by a continuous stream of movements which overlap in time and adapt to their neighbors. We extract a (largely) linear string of segments from this stream, but any given instance of a segment will be a particular coarticulatory variant proper to its context. Because this is so, contrast and variation are never entirely separated.

The analysis of contrast will obviously concern the segmental inventory of the language – its consonants and vowels – but may also involve distinctions of quantity, tone, and accent. Intonation and other aspects of phrasal phonology also involve contrast, but by their nature these will be superimposed on a stream of segments. In looking at speech production, the relative timing of events is often of great interest, as it is also for perception. However, it is important to be aware that timing is often investigated by measuring acoustically-delimited intervals. These do not directly align with the timing of articulatory movements, nor can they be directly equated with perceptual intervals. The most basic types of perceptual investigation concern identification and discrimination – that is, whether something can be recognized for what it is or can be differentiated from another speech signal. Perceptual judgements of interest can also be collected on comparative salience, matters of syllabification, and quite a few other matters.

4.   Organizing data for collection

Only a few phonetic questions have categorical answers; a much larger proportion require comparison. This is because many phonetic matters inherently concern relations, and almost any measured value is only interpretable in relation to other numbers. Hence the data collected must be designed to make the necessary comparisons possible. For example, in Archi, another North-East Caucasian language of Dagestan, it was hypothesized that both plain and pharyngealized uvulars occur. In the field, direct observations of articulations in the pharynx are not possible, so inferences must be drawn from acoustic analysis. Unfortunately, we also cannot say with much precision what effects pharyngealization has on the acoustic patterns of uvular stops. So we must draw conclusions essentially by showing that there is a difference between the two classes of uvulars, that the difference patterns in expected ways, and that it cannot be explained by other factors. That is, the comparison must be a *controlled* one in which all other aspects are held constant as far as possible. If the uvular consonants of the same type (e.g., voiceless stops), in the same position in a word, and in the same vowel context fall into two groups, then the hypothesized difference is supported. That is, we must look for pairs of words as closely matched as possible except for the hypothesized difference. Among the best candidates found were the pair /raq/ 'stream' and /daqˤ/ 'comb' as illustrated in figure 10.1. Comparing the right-hand side of the spectrograms, it can be easily seen that the spectral patterns of the final consonant releases in these two words are quite distinct. Moreover, this difference cannot be accounted for by influence of different preceding vowels or other factors independent of the consonants. This is not the place to discuss in detail how the conclusion that pharyngealization is involved can be justified in this case, but the example does show quite clearly that the contrast is located in the consonantal segments.

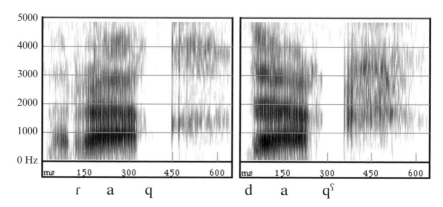

10.1 Spectrograms of the Archi words /raq/ 'stream' and /daqˤ/ 'comb' spoken by a female speaker, illustrating differences in stop release spectra and prevocalic transition (from Maddieson 1999a).

Most phonetic data collection needs to be done with careful attention to setting up for appropriate paradigmatic or syntagmatic comparisons. A lasting regret of mine is that when collecting data on linguo-labial consonants in Vanuatu in 1986 (Maddieson 1989), I carefully sought out and recorded controlled comparisons of these interesting consonants with their bilabial counterparts, but I did not think to include words with alveolar stops, nasals, and fricatives in matching positions. Thus, although I could later compare the linguo-labial sounds with (arguably) their nearest neighbors from the articulatory point of view, I could not compare them satisfactorily with their nearest neighbors from the auditory point of view.

It is also important to stress the essential nature of constructing data sets so that one factor can be singled out from others. In speech, any observation or measurement you make will be affected by many different factors. So, for example, the (acoustically-determined) closure duration of a stop will be affected by its place of articulation, its position in a syllable, its proximity to stress, its vocalic environment, the speech rate adopted by the speaker, the frequency of the word in which it is occurring, and many other factors. If you want to be able, say, to show that duration differences are part of what distinguishes the set of four coronal stops which occur in the Central Australian language Western Arrernte (which is true, see Anderson 1997), there are two alternatives: either you must collect an enormous body of data, which by its sheer quantity evens out all the influences; or you must collect a smaller data set in which factors are balanced. Practical considerations in fieldwork always weigh in favor of the second choice.

But the data collected – whether perceptual judgements, articulatory data, or simple recordings – should normally include repetitions so that the consistency of a pattern can be examined. For many kinds of studies, a number of subjects should be used. Using multiple subjects provides a control against individual idiosyncrasies, whether due to differences in the shape of the speech organs, different personal histories, differences of perceptual strategy, or other factors. The work is not finished until comparisons of interest have been subjected to an appropriate statistical test of their significance to confirm that any conclusion drawn is reliable.

5.   Techniques

A phonetic analysis will always begin by looking and listening. Newer techniques have supplemented but not supplanted straightforward observation of what a speaker is visibly doing and what the result sounds like to the ear. Any investigation starts with a preliminary idea of what is going on in order to decide what kinds of more specific data to collect using what kinds of techniques.

Most investigations will involve making audio recordings which may be analyzed alone or in relation to data of other types. Recordings should be made where there is minimal background noise and where there is little or no reverberation. A hard but valuable skill to acquire is to train yourself to listen to the ambient noise in any setting. In ordinary life we manage to filter out many sounds that are not important to the task at hand, and it actually takes an effort to pay attention to all the components in the background noise. Sit quietly and listen before making a recording, select the quietest spot you can find, and eliminate any noise sources you have control over, e.g., turn off the refrigerator, chase away the domestic animals, have the baby fed. If possible, avoid recording in sparsely-furnished rooms with flat walls, as the sound waves will reflect back off flat surfaces creating a slight echo effect. Such a reverberation gives the recording a quality sometimes described as "hollow." Away from urban areas a desirable recording environment can, surprisingly, often be found in an open-air setting. When recording speakers of the Australian language Tiwi on Bathurst Island, north of Darwin, walking a half mile away from the village got us away from engine noise and out of a reverberating classroom. The trade-off was some wind noise in the eucalyptus trees and the occasional loud cries of kookaburras. Since both were intermittent, I tried to monitor when wind gusts or bird calls coincided with a speaker's voice and asked for the word to be repeated an extra time. Recording more repetitions than you plan to analyze is one way to try to protect against the likelihood of being obliged to discard some tokens due to overlying sounds.

It is also necessary to monitor the recording while in progress to guard

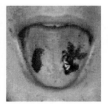

10.2 Samples of palatograms of Bagwalal /sim/ 'lip' (far left) and /s̄im/ 'bile' (center left), and linguograms of the same words from a different speaker (from Maddieson 1999b).

against overloading the signal. While occasionally overloaded signals generally do not interfere with transcription of texts, lexical lists, and other kinds of materials, overloads are a significant problem for acoustic analysis. It is good to start a recording session with an announcement containing sufficient information to document the recording – minimally language, speaker, and date. In this way, this information stays with a tape when it is copied and in the event the labels come off. In general, it is better to keep a recording going if an error is made by a speaker rather than stopping and restarting the machine. Simply ask for another repetition, clarify a semantic ambiguity, or do whatever needs to be done to obtain the desired utterance while the machine is running.

One of the simpler techniques for investigating some aspects of tongue articulation in consonants is palatography. There are a number of variants of the method but all involve covering the tongue or the roof of the mouth with a medium that is transferred to the other surface when something is said. One method (Ladefoged 1997) uses a mixture of about equal parts edible vegetable oil and pharmaceutical-grade charcoal powder, which is painted onto the speaker's tongue while it is poked out. The speaker must be instructed to avoid any premature contact between tongue and palate and then to say one carefully chosen word containing just one lingual consonant (since labial and glottal consonants do not involve the tongue these may be present without distorting the desired results). The pattern made by the transfer of the mixture onto the upper surface of the mouth can then be examined by placing a mirror in the mouth. The results can be preserved by photographing or videotaping the view in the mirror. Sample data are shown in figure 10.2, comparing the articulation of the initial fricatives in the Bagwalal words /sim/ 'lip' and /s̄im/ 'bile'. The /s̄/ in the word on the right is described in the literature as *strong* – the palatograms show that it is produced with a narrower central escape channel for the air at the front and more contact along the sides.

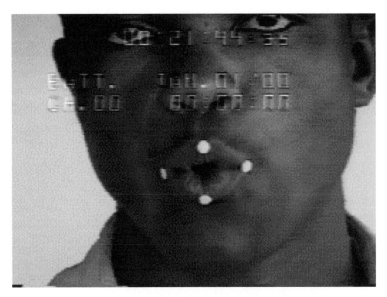

10.3 Lip position in Avatime /xʷ/ in the word /axʷa/ 'charcoal'.

Palatography can be complemented by linguography. This involves painting the same mixture onto the roof of the mouth, including the inside surfaces of the teeth, having the speaker say the word again, and then examining the pattern of contact shown on the tongue. Linguograms are also shown in figure 10.2.

The images in figure 10.2 were recorded with a video camera. This is also a very useful tool for recording externally visible articulatory movements, especially of the lips. Placing small adhesive paper dots on the speaker's skin while filming gives precise measurement points, which can be tracked from frame to frame. Figure 10.3 shows the maximum degree of lip rounding observed in a labialized velar fricative /xʷ/ of Avatime. Here the issue was precisely whether this segment had a secondary articulation of labialization or should be regarded as a doubly-articulated fricative. The video showed that the lip position was highly rounded and the aperture was too wide to cause frication at the lips (Maddieson 1998). The standard speed of video cameras is about 30 frames a second, that is, one picture about every 33 milliseconds. This means that rapid movements, such as stop releases or trills, cannot be studied very well, and even that the culminating points of slow movements might be missed. Filming multiple repetitions reduces the risk of misinterpretation, and some cameras offer a higher frame rate ("slow-motion") option.

Recording of air flow and pressure is another valuable field technique, as

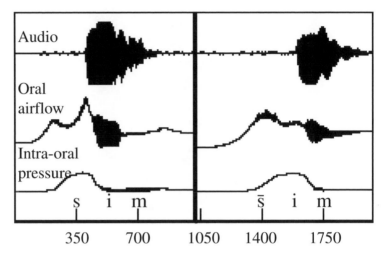

10.4 Air flow and pressure records of Bagwalal /sim/ 'lip' (left) and /s̄im/ 'bile' (right).

this can be done without bulky equipment. This technique provides direct information on questions of speech aerodynamics, such as the higher intra-oral pressure generated in ejective stops compared with pulmonic ones, or differences in oral airflow patterns such as those illustrated in figure 10.4. This shows the same pair of Bagwalal words as figure 10.2, spoken by yet another speaker. There is a high peak in airflow just before the vowel in the word with the "weak" initial fricative that is not present in the "strong" case, showing that another difference between these two segments is that the weak one is aspirated. We can thus use the aerodynamic data to infer something about the relative timing of laryngeal actions and oral articulations. Aerodynamic records often provide a good way to indirectly study the timing of articulatory movements. For example, measuring the airflow through the nose is often the best way to determine if some, all, or none of a vowel is nasalized.

Selected types of perceptual experiments are quite easy to present in the field. It is easy, for example, to obtain judgments on whether two speech samples are the same or different, or judgments of their degree of similarity, or opinions of the "goodness" of a single token. Most such field experiments will probably use edited natural speech. Anderson (1997) tested how much cues due to a preceding vowel affected the identification of the four coronal places of articulation of Western Arrernte by playing samples of words with the initial vowel edited out. Other field perceptual experiments have used synthesized speech, especially in obtaining judgments about vowel quality (Hombert 1984).

6.   Equipment

The most important part of a field phonetician's kit is almost always a satisfactory system for audio recording. It's useful to think of this as consisting
of three elements: a microphone, the recording device, and the recording
medium. The choices among different options will depend in various ways
on the purpose of the recording, where and how it is being done, and practical considerations such as cost and availability. A few of the major considerations are laid out below.

Using an appropriate microphone is crucial to any recording. If the
microphone cannot faithfully capture the signal you want, no analysis can
recover the information later. Equally, if the microphone simultaneously
captures too many other sounds, the desired information may be covered
up by background noise. Technically, there are two main factors to think
about in selecting a microphone: the frequency response range and the
directionality. For recording speech, a microphone with a relatively flat frequency response between about 50Hz and 20,000Hz (20kHz) is best. For
many purposes, the upper limit need not be above about 12,000Hz, and for
some specialized applications there must be no lower limit. Many recording
devices have built-in microphones, but these often have very poor frequency
response characteristics and their use is not recommended. Fortunately,
satisfactory stand-alone microphones are not expensive. Selecting a microphone with appropriate directionality can help limit background noise
problems. A unidirectional (sometimes simply "directional") microphone
is designed to pick up sound primarily coming from in front of its "head."
When the speaker being recorded is positioned in front of this kind of
microphone, the sound of his or her voice is automatically enhanced relative to any sounds coming from another direction. Having the speaker wear
a head-mount, which holds a directional mike close to the speaker's mouth,
is the best way to record a single speaker at a time. The most common type
of directional mike is often labeled "cardioid." (This term describes the
shape of the area from which sound is picked up.) Omnidirectional microphones pick up sound from any direction. They are useful for recording
group interaction, but will record any background noise as well.

Microphones also differ in the way that they actually convert the acoustic
signal into an electrical one. The two common types are called dynamic and
capacitor (or condenser) microphones. Dynamic microphones are more
robust, hence for all but certain specialized tasks they are generally preferable, but they do not have the very low-frequency sensitivity that a capacitor microphone has, and they lend themselves less easily to miniaturization.
Capacitor microphones require a power supply, often a small battery of the
type used in hearing aids, digital watches, and other small devices. Since

these batteries are hard to obtain in many parts of the world, be sure to take spares! Otherwise one mistake in forgetting to switch off the mike can drain the battery and render your microphone useless.

A few years ago audio recording meant using an analog tape, either reel-to-reel or cassette. There are more choices now to consider for recording device and the recording medium, and these options are likely to grow more and more varied in the near future. The three main options at the present time are cassette tape, digital audio tape (DAT), or digital recording directly to computer (with many options for subsequently saving the data). Before long, it is likely that field-usable devices that record directly to a CD or DVD (or similar medium) will be available, which may be superior to all of these. Meanwhile, the principal advantages and disadvantages of the three options mentioned can be summarized as in table 10.2 below. In brief, cassette recordings are the simplest and have the big advantage that, if needed, extra cassettes can be bought almost anywhere in the world. DAT recorders are also simple to deal with and faithfully record the full desired frequency range, but the tapes are more expensive, their robustness over time has not yet been tested, and it is not certain that this format will last. Recording directly to a computer has two big advantages: flexibility of control, and the fact that data are immediately available to be edited, analyzed acoustically, and otherwise processed with suitable software. The two main problems are that computers do not yet function as reliably as one may wish, and data storage formats are subject to rather frequent changes.

It is always best to have a complete backup system for recording, so that failure of one component does not bring work to a halt. I usually take different systems rather than exact duplicates; different microphones and recording devices are used for the somewhat different purposes for which they are best suited, but can be pressed into service for other functions in the event of a breakdown. Be sure to check that you have all the cables and adapters that you need to "mix and match" your equipment.

The built-in speakers found in most recording systems are of poor quality, and some recorders or computers have no loudspeaker to play back a recording. Hence, it is useful to have headphones and/or a small portable loudspeaker in the field. Small speakers that run on readily available batteries (AA, for example) are inexpensive, and these are easier to use than ones which require a transformer to connect to an electric power system, even assuming that such is available. Perceptual experimental stimuli are often best presented to listeners using headphones, as this limits distractions and allows the loudness of presentation to be more reliably standardized.

Video cameras, like audio recording equipment, are today available in analog or digital formats. There is little doubt that digital video has significant advantages, most especially in the ease and clarity with which single

Table 10.2 *Comparison of some recording options*

	Cassette	*DAT*	*Direct to Computer*
Equipment simplicity	Simple.	Simple.	More complex.
Operational simplicity	Simple.	Simple.	More complex.
Length of recording	Long. (Longest duration tapes are thinner, less durable.)	Long. (Fewer tape length choices than with cassettes.)	Generally quite limited, depending on set-up.
Availability of media	Cassette tapes can be bought almost anywhere in the world. Cheap.	DAT tapes not easily available. More expensive.	Standard diskettes relatively widely available. Other media not. Price varies.
Frequency response	Highest frequencies lost.	Response up to 20kHz.	Frequency response controllable by user.
Data vulnerability	Low. Long-term storage good.	Moderate. Long-term storage prospects unknown.	Can be multiply backed-up; otherwise high. Long-term storage highly vulnerable to changing formats.
Data transfer for editing or analysis	Must be digitized.	Can be digitally transferred.	Immediately available for editing and analysis.

frames can be viewed. Using a built-in or camera-mountable light source gives more reliable control over lighting conditions. Most cameras allow the pictures recorded to be reviewed through the eyepiece, but models with a larger separate screen are more useful.

The equipment needed for palatography and linguography is relatively simple. The essential components are the tools and ingredients to mix and apply the medium used, and mirrors. Individual-serving size glass jam jars are great to mix the medium in. Buying packages of small cheap paint-brushes sold as children's toys makes it cheap to use a clean one to mix and apply the medium for each speaker. I travel with a kit of three mirrors of different sizes to accommodate to different-sized mouths; special high-quality ones can be bought from dental supply houses, but small, easily available make-up mirrors will serve very well.

A convenient hardware/software system for field collection of air flow and pressure data, originally developed for the UCLA Phonetics Laboratory, is available from SCICON Research and Development. Both Macintosh (MacQuirer) and PC (PCQuirer) versions of the software are available. The hardware allows for recording up to four channels of data in addition to an audio signal. The intra-oral air pressure behind a labial or coronal constriction can be measured through a flexible plastic tube passed between the lips. To measure pressure behind a dorsal constriction, a tube must be passed through a nostril and into the pharyngeal cavity, which is considerably more tricky. Air flow through the mouth and the nose can be recorded using a special mask fitting over the nose and lips and divided into two chambers. Methods of calibrating aerodynamic measurements are described in Ladefoged (1997).

Laryngeal settings are most often studied indirectly, especially though acoustic analysis (Ní Chasaide and Gobl 1997), but electro-laryngography offers a more direct way of measuring contact patterns of the vocal folds. The Laryngograph company makes a very compact battery-operable device designed for field application of laryngography.

A final component of value in a field kit is software for signal editing and acoustic analysis. The editing functions are essential for preparing listening experiments, and a preliminary acoustic analysis in the field can often help to clarify what is happening. Most software designed primarily for music editing, such as SoundEdit or Sound Forge, has good tools for editing which can be used as well for speech. However, a number of packages designed especially for acoustic analysis of speech are also available. A good option, especially for analysis of fundamental frequency and amplitude, is the CECIL software which can be downloaded from the SIL web site. Winpitch is another excellent and economical system for fundamental frequency and amplitude analysis. The MacQuirer and PCQuirer software mentioned earlier includes powerful and flexible acoustical analysis tools. The Multispeech package from Kay Elemetrics is another very powerful system operating on PCs. Specialized systems for creating and presenting perceptual experiments are PSL, available from the University of California, Santa Cruz (UCSC) Perceptual Science Laboratory, and Psyscope, available from University of Pennsylvania. SynthWorks from SCICON provides a user-friendly synthesis package.

7.   Final remarks

The majority of field reports on languages give rather minimal details on their phonetic properties, sometimes nothing more than a list of symbols. Consequently, a major aspect of their grammar remains underdescribed, and the data on which cross-linguistic phonetic generalizations can be founded remain inadequate. It would be welcome if precise articulatory descriptions (particularly of consonants), analysis of major acoustic characteristics, descriptions of timing and suprasegmentals, and details of interactions between segments, suprasegmental properties, and position in a structure were all to become considered essential to any satisfactory language description. I hope that the practical suggestions in this chapter will encourage field linguists whose aim is to produce descriptive grammars to include more phonetic information, and that they will persuade phoneticians who feel more at home in the laboratory to consider undertaking fieldwork. I am certain that phoneticians and general field linguists could rewardingly cooperate to realize these goals.

REFERENCES

Anderson, Victoria. 1997. The perception of coronals in Western Arrernte. In *Proceedings of Eurospeech 97*, vol. 1. Paper T2B.5. Rhodes (Greece).

Hombert, Jean-Marie. 1984. Espace vocalique et structuration perceptuelle: application au Swahili. *Pholia* 1:199–208.

Ladefoged, Peter. 1997. Instrumental techniques for linguistic phonetic fieldwork. In *The Handbook of Phonetic Sciences*, ed. William J. Hardcastle and John Laver, pp. 137–66. Oxford: Blackwell.

Maddieson, Ian. 1989. Linguo-labials. In *VICAL (Papers from the Fifth International Conference on Austronesian Linguistics.* vol. 1: *Oceanic Languages)*, ed. Ray Harlow and R. Hooper, pp. 349–75. Auckland: Linguistic Society of New Zealand.

1998. Collapsing vowel harmony and doubly-articulated fricatives: two myths about the Avatime phonological system. In *Language History and Linguistic Description in Africa*, ed. Ian Maddieson and Thomas J. Hinnebusch, pp. 155–66. (Trends in African Linguistics, 2) Trenton, NJ: Africa World Press.

1999a. Archi phonemes. Paper presented at the annual meeting of the Linguistic Society of America (Los Angeles).

1999b. Strength matters? *Proceedings of the 14th International Congress of Phonetic Sciences,* vol. 3, ed. John J. Ohala, *et al.*, pp. 1965–68. Berkeley: Department of Linguistics, University of California.

Ní Chasaide, Ailbhe, and Christer Gobl. 1997. Voice source variation. In *The Handbook of Phonetic Sciences*, ed. William J. Hardcastle and John Laver, pp. 427–61. Oxford: Blackwell.

11 Learning as one goes

Keren Rice

What does one need to know, ideally, when beginning to do fieldwork? As I think back to when I first did fieldwork, review my years of active and intensive fieldwork, and consider teaching a field methods course, many different things come to mind. In this article, I will concentrate on a few lessons about the linguistic aspects of fieldwork that I learned early on in doing this work, including the following items, which can perhaps be thought of as slogans to keep in mind when preparing to do fieldwork:

a) Pay careful attention to information about the language that the speaker you are working with wants you to hear.
b) Know the available literature and respect it, but keep in mind that there is always more to learn.
c) Avoid isolating areas of the language so that you lose track of the fact that language is a complex, dynamic system.
d) Bring as much knowledge as you can, from all domains – about language, about linguistics, about people.
e) Do not straightjacket the language into categories that you bring to it – let it live on its own.
f) Do not think that language is a monolithic entity within a community. There is variation within language, and this must be part of any analysis.
g) Not all speakers have the same strengths.
h) A good working relationship is an evolving thing. Both speakers and the linguist must get to know one another.
i) Be open to learn.

Each of the above lessons is highlighted for me by a particular situation or situations in which something came to consciousness for me. These various lessons are intermingled in the discussion below as they overlap and merge in various ways.

Before beginning, let me provide some setting. I have done fieldwork on Slave [slevi], an Athapaskan language spoken in parts of the Northwest Territories, Alberta, and British Columbia, Canada. Slave is spoken in a number of communities ranging in size from around 50 to around 1,000 people. In most communities, there is a fair degree of bilingualism amongst the middle generation, while there are older people who speak little or no English, and younger people who speak little or no Slave. Conditions vary from community to community. At the time that I was most involved in fieldwork, many middle-aged and older speakers had low levels of formal education, and next to no one had written literacy skills in Slave.

1.   On the mystery of tones in the Hare dialect of Slave

My first fieldwork was on the Hare [hær] dialect of Slave, spoken in a community of the Mackenzie River valley. Before I first went into the field, I had read everything available on this dialect, on Slave as a whole, and on Athapaskan languages in general. One of the points made in the rather sparse literature on Hare was that verb stem high tones were lost in this dialect. This point was made by Hoijer (1966), a very highly respected Athapaskanist, based on unpublished field notes from 1929 made by Fang-Kuei Li, an outstanding scholar who had worked on several Athapaskan languages and who was very interested in questions of tone. I thus approached this dialect, the first Slave dialect that I encountered, expecting to hear high tones on noun stems, on postpositions, and on prefixes, but not on verb stems; and, in fact, I did not hear or transcribe tones on verb stems, as they really weren't there under most conditions (see section 2 for more detail on "under most conditions").

Consider the examples in (1) that compare forms from the very closely related dialect of Bearlake with my early transcriptions of Hare.[1] When I was doing this work, I had access to a fair amount of material on nouns from other Slave dialects, but next to no material on verbs was available. The reader thus has the benefit of the Bearlake forms, forms that I did not know at the time. (The Hare forms show the transcription I used in my early days of fieldwork.)

(1)   Bearlake   Hare
    a. nɛ-ʔá   nɛ-ʔa   you sg. eat
       2sgS-stem
    b. whɛ-h-chú   wɛ-h-shu   cloth-like object is located
       SA-Cl-stem
    c. y-i-dá   y-i-da   I sat
       SA-1sgS/perf-stem

In the forms in (1), the Bearlake words have a high tone on the verb stem. The Hare forms do not have this tone, nor is there a tone elsewhere in the verb.

As I repeated words such as those in (1) back to the Hare speakers with whom I worked, they made me say the words over and over and over, and were not satisfied with my pronunciation. When I compared the Hare forms in (1) with words like those in (2), I slowly became aware that I was missing something.

(2)   Bearlake   Hare
   a.   *nɛ-dǫ*   *nɛ-dǫ*   you sg. drink
        2sgS-stem
   b.   *whɛ-ʔǫ*   *wɛ-ʔǫ*   it (default object) is located
        SA-stem
   c.   *wh-i-da*   *w-i-da*   I sit
        SA-1sgS/perf-stem

Finally, the day that I was to leave the field arrived. I had made progress with many aspects of the complex Slave verb, but the tones still had me baffled. I asked one of the people that I worked with frequently if there was anything else that she thought I should know before I left. She decided to try the tones one more time, and pronounced three words for me until I began to understand what was going on. I write these three words (3a) (3c) (3d) here in the transcription that I came to. (Example (3b) is included for completeness.)

(3)   Bearlake   Hare
   a.   *wh-i-da*   *w-i-da*   I sit
        SA-1sgS/perf-stem
   b.   *wh-i-ke*   *w-i-ke*   we two sit
        SA-1plS-stem (dual S)
   c.   *y-i-dá*   *y-i-da*   I sat
        SA-1sgS/perf-stem
   d.   *y-ɛ́-h-k'ɛ́*   *y-ɛ̂-h-k'ɛ* s/he shot it
        disjoint anaphor-SA-Cl-stem

In (3a) neither Bearlake nor Hare has a high tone in the word, and the words are identical in the two dialects (save regular segmental differences). In (3b), both dialects have a high tone on the pre-stem syllable (this represents the first person plural subject) and the forms are again identical. Notice that in (3c) the high tone that occurs on the verb stem in Bearlake is not simply lost in Hare; rather it is preserved, but not where one might expect it to be – it falls on the syllable before the verb stem rather than on the stem itself. There thus is a real difference between the Hare forms in (3a) and (3c), with the locus of difference being on the pre-stem syllable rather than on the verb stem. Finally consider the form in (3d). In Bearlake, both the pre-stem syllable and the stem bear a high tone. As expected, in Hare the stem is not marked by high tone. However, the syllable before the stem has an extra high tone (which I represent with the symbol ^). Here, the high tone of the prefix and the high tone of the stem combine with each other, creating a phonetic extra high tone. (See Rice 1989a, 1991b, for details.)

How did I figure this out? I had to learn two lessons in order to be able to do it. First, and most important, I had to learn to pay attention to the individuals I was working with and hear what they felt to be important. When I took a field methods course, it had been stressed that the linguistic fieldworker should not pay too much attention to the informant, as that individual had no training in linguistics and there was no particular reason to trust their intuitions. While this never really sat right with me when I took the course, I still had to learn for myself just how wrong it was. Without the help of the individuals with whom I worked, it would have taken me far longer to figure this out, and many other things as well. One should never discount the ability of native speakers to think about their own language and see generalizations, whether they have the formal vocabulary to express those generalizations or not. This lesson is reinforced time and time again through fieldwork; it is this lesson that for me led to more and more of the kind of cooperative fieldwork that I do now rather than the linguist-centered fieldwork that I was trained to do and did in my first years of working on my own.

The second lesson that I learned from this incident was that it is always necessary to respect work that has come before, but at the same time to maintain a healthy skepticism about it. Fang-Kuei Li, who had transcribed Hare verbs as if stem tones had simply disappeared, was an outstanding linguist and did excellent work on Athapaskan languages that has stood up over the decades. He was very interested in tone, and much of his work on Athapaskan languages was spent trying, with Sapir, to sort out the tonal system of the family (see Scollon and Scollon 1979). Yet the chances are better than not that Li's transcriptions of verbs were simply wrong. While he worked in the late 1920s and I began fieldwork in the mid-1970s, it seems unlikely that the verb stem tones could have been lost altogether and then regenerated themselves on the pre-stem syllable just in those cases where other Athapaskan languages have marked tone on the verb stem. Coming to this understanding of Hare verb stem tones thus made me realize that, no matter how outstanding the linguists were who worked on a language in the past, there is always more to learn about even the most fundamental of points.

2.   Tones again: tones and variation

Having sorted out that verb stems in the Hare dialect of Slave did indeed have underlying tones associated with them, many questions arose. One question concerned the effect of stem tones on prefixes. The examples given above all have prefixes from what is known as the conjunct domain in the Athapaskan literature. There is also a second type of prefix, called disjunct prefixes. The disjunct prefixes are less closely bound to each other and are in general lexically contentful; the conjunct prefixes are for the most part functional in nature. The phonology of these two prefix types is very different. When the stem tones fall on the pre-stem syllable, do they equally affect all pre-stem syllables? Another important question involved the effect of postverbal material on verb stem tones. Slave is a Subject–Object–Verb word-order language in which there are various tense/aspect/mode particles that can follow the verb stem. Is it always the case that the stem tone surfaces on the pre-stem syllable or can the presence of postverbal material affect the placement of the tone of the verb stem? These questions became pressing to me once I figured out that there actually were verb stem tones in the Hare dialect, tones that just surfaced on the pre-stem syllable rather than on the stem itself. Investigating these questions opened my eyes to another very important characteristic of language, its variability within a community.

Consider first what can happen with underlying high tones when a disjunct prefix rather than a conjunct prefix precedes a verb stem. Again, I contrast Bearlake and Hare material. (The segmental differences between the two Slave dialects shown in (4) represent regular sound correspondences.)

(4)   Bearlake   Hare

a. *na-dǫ*   *ra-dǫ*   s/he drinks again, drinks another
    iterative-stem

b. *na-ʔá*   *rá-ʔa, ra-ʔa*   s/he eats again, eats another
    iterative-stem

c. *ná-zé*   *rá-ze*   s/he hunts
    continuative-stem

Example (4a), where neither the prefix nor the stem has high tone, is identical in both dialects. Example (4b) is a form where the stem has high tone, but not the prefix, as the Bearlake form tells us. Given the patterning seen in (3), we would expect that in Hare the prefix would carry the high tone and the stem would be toneless. This is indeed possible; but there is a second possibility, namely, the prefix can remain without a high tone. The disjunct prefixes thus differ from the conjunct prefixes in that the retention of the stem tone is not mandatory. The form in (4c) tells us something else. In this case, both the prefix and the stem bear high tones in Bearlake. In Hare, the stem tone, as expected, is not present. However, given the patterning in (3d), we might expect to get an extra high tone on the prefix. This does not happen.

Such patterning is of course very exciting for the linguist, as it provides additional evidence of the need for phonological domains. However, the data are also confusing, as the variation in (4b) is allowed. I spent quite a while sorting out that this variation was real. It is easy to seek out factors that might suggest that only one of the forms is really correct – one comes from fluent speakers, the other from non-fluent speakers; the speaker made a mistake; etc. – however, the fact is that both forms exist, and are found under similar conditions. The dialect is not monolithic, and the variability is something that the linguist must account for in addition to the uniformity.

The forms with postverbal material show similar kinds of variability. Here I found two patterns.

(5)   Bearlake   Hare
   a. *ná-wo-h-shá*   *rá-wó-h-sha*   I will go
      continuative-optative-1sgS-stem
   b. *ná-wo-h-shá nị*   *rá-wó-h-shá nị*   that I will go
      continuative-optative-1sgS-stem comp
   b′.   *rá-wó-h-sha nị*   that I will go

The form in (5a) shows the now expected difference between the dialects – when the verb stem has a high tone in Bearlake, this tone falls on the pre-stem syllable (the optative here) in Hare. The forms in (5b) and (5b′) show the variation that can exist when postverbal material, in this case a complementizer, follows the stem. In the form in (5b), the stem tone in Hare occurs both on the pre-stem syllable and on the stem itself – in this dialect the stem tone is retained on the stem in the presence of postverbal material. In the form in (5b′), on the other hand, the stem tone occurs on the pre-stem syllable only – in this dialect, the stem tone is never placed on the verb stem no matter what environment the stem is in (Rice 1989a: 124).

When I was doing this fieldwork in the 1970s, language was considered to be rule-governed behavior. However, a naive notion of rule-governed behavior can lead one very much astray. Rule-governed does not mean the absence of variation, something that is well-understood now, I think, but was not so well understood at that time. A speech community can tolerate a large amount of variation that is not, for most speakers, something they are necessarily consciously aware of. It is important that the linguist not try to make judgments of what is right and what is wrong, but take all of the language, and figure out what it is, including all of its internal diversity and variability. Diversity can be as systematic and rule-governed as uniformity, and such diversity is not to be dismissed as mistakes, poor speech, and the like, something that is often tempting to do in the presence of overwhelming amounts of material to sort through. It is rather to be embraced, and an understanding of diversity in addition to uniformity leads to a deeper understanding of both the language in question and language in general.

3.   The challenges of *dll* classifier, *s*- conjugation verbs

The challenges of Athapaskan verbal morphology are notably complex, and the verb has a wide reputation for being indomitable. In particular, the morphology and phonology involving aspectual, subject, and classifier material is highly intricate. One task that someone working on the phonology and morphology of the Athapaskan verb must undertake is to find paradigms that illustrate all combinations of aspect, subject, and classifier. This sounds like a straightforward task, but in fact it turned out to be a rather difficult one, for a reason that took me a long time to understand.

In Slave and many other Athapaskan languages, the morphology and phonology of the aspect–subject complex differ depending upon which classifier the verb has. Four so-called classifiers are normally identified in Slave: Ø, *h* (< *ł*), *d*, and voicing (< *l*); I will refer to this last classifier as *l*). Each verbal entry includes a classifier, and they can be used productively as well to mark voice and valence. In the perfective aspect, the form of the aspect–subject complex depends on two factors. The first is the classifier associated with the verb, with Ø and *h* patterning together and *d* and *l* patterning together. The second is the type of morpheme that precedes the aspect. The data in (6) illustrate some of the complexities of the so-called *s*-conjugation perfective. (The *s*- conjugation is a morpheme that marks accomplishment situation aspect, see Rice 2000b for discussion.) The verb illustrated here has the *h* classifier. The abbreviation 'O' indicates that the verb is transitive, taking a direct object. The situation aspect–subject portion of the verb is in boldface. These data are presented to illustrate the complexity of the *s*- conjugation (glossed here as SA, or situation aspect).

(6) a. *s*- conjugation, word-initial position, *h* classifier
  i. O *w-í-h-k'ε*   I shot O
    SA-1sgS/perf-Cl-stem
  ii. O *wɛ́-h-k'ε*   s/he shot O
    SA/perf-Cl-stem
  b. *s*- conjugation, following a lexical item (disjunct prefix), *h* classifier
  i. O *ra-w-í-h-k'ε*   I shot O again
    iterative-**SA-1sgS/perf**-Cl-stem
  ii. O *ra-wɛ́-h-k'ε*   s/he shot O again
    iterative-**SA/perf**-Cl-stem
  c. *s*- conjugation, following an object prefix, *h* classifier
  i. *nɛ́-w-í-h-k'ε*   I shot you (singular)
    2sgO-**SA-1sgS/perf**-Cl-stem
  ii. *y-ɛ̂-h-k'ε*   s/he shot it
    disjoint anaphor-**SA/perf**-Cl-stem
  d. *s*- conjugation, following inceptive, *h* classifier
  i. O *dɛ́-h-k'ε*   I started to shoot O
    inceptive/**SA/perf**/1sgS-Cl-stem

ii. O *dê-h-k'ε*   s/he started to shoot O
    inceptive/**SA/perf**-Cl-stem

Notice that the conjugation marker, which I have labeled situation aspect (SA), differs in form depending on the person of the subject and the type of morpheme it follows. Sometimes it has the segmental form [w] (a, b, c(i)); sometimes this segmental form is absent (c(ii), d); sometimes a tone is present (c(i), c(ii), d); sometimes it is not (a, b). (The high tone on the pre-stem syllable in this verb is lexically part of the verb stem; see section 1). While complex in form, these paradigms were not hard to obtain. Developing a nice account of the morphophonemics of this paradigm was not easy, but it was not terribly difficult to describe the environments in which the segmental form occurred alone, in which the tonal form occurred alone, and in which the two co-occurred.

The verb illustrated in (6) has the *h* classifier, and the patterning of Ø classifier verbs is similar. However, *d/l* classifier verbs pattern differently. While it was easy to obtain paradigms for *d/l* classifier verbs with the *s*-conjugation marker in word-initial position (parallel to (6a)), following an object (parallel to (6c)), and following the inceptive and other similarly pat-terning morphemes (parallel to (6d)), it was extremely difficult to find good examples of this morpheme following a lexical item (disjunct prefix; par-allel to (6b)). I recall vividly one occasion in which I finally found a verb in which everything was right: the verb required a *d/l* classifier and a disjunct prefix was present. I started on the paradigm. In the case of first person sin-gular and second person singular, everything was fine and as I had pre-dicted it would be. Third person was the form that had bewildered me and for which I had no predictions. I waited expectantly. To my surprise, and to my extreme disappointment, the person I was working with gave me a verb form that involved a different verb stem with an *h* classifier! I asked if the original verb stem, with the wanted classifier, could be said, and got no response. I had no model from which to create a form to find out if it was a possible form, and I had no idea why the verb stem suddenly changed. I was at an impasse, and had to leave this topic aside. I did later on find the forms that I needed; it was partly a matter of time.

What was the problem in getting the forms at the time that I wanted? Partly it may have been because the morphophonology was complex, but this seems like an explanation from the outsider's perspective. Overall, I believe that it was something else, something that I did not understand at all at the time. In Slave, many verbal concepts have a pair of verb stems rather than a single verb stem. For instance, there are two verb stems that translate basically as 'handle', two that translate as 'drink', two as 'tear', and so on. At the time that I was doing the work on paradigms, I knew that two stems existed for many verbs, but I did not have any understanding about what constituted the differences between them. It turns out that the stems, while conveying largely the same information, have a very different sense about them. In one case, the verb embodies a way of carrying out the event that is highly valued culturally – it is humble, polite, and so on (see Rushforth and Chisholm 1991, Rice 1989a: 784). The other verb stem does not embody this; it is not negative in force, but rather ordinary. Once I understood the difference between the two types of verb stems, I was able to find English translations that would help me get the stem that I wanted, and it was at this point that I was able to fill in the paradigms. I think now that my frustration in eliciting the *d/l* classifier *s*- conjugation perfectives arose because the shift in subject person changed the situation in such a way that the verb stem that I wanted was less appropriate than the one that the speakers shifted to. Since I did not know how to sort out the meanings of the very similar, but different, verb stems, I was unable to give translations that would allow me to elicit the material that I wanted, and instead experienced great frustration.

What did I learn from this? By trying to work on verb paradigms alone, I lost sight of the fact that the paradigms are but one piece of the whole language system. It was impossible to isolate the prefixes that I was interested in from the larger verb system. In this case, an understanding of the lexical semantics of verb stems was required to take the next step.

This lesson repeats itself time and time again in doing fieldwork, and I will give one more example of it here, again involving tones. In fieldwork that I did in the 1980s on the Slave dialect spoken in Fort Nelson, British Columbia, I again had trouble coming to grips with tones, as there had been considerable shifts in tone patterns. In this Slave dialect, the final syllable of a word in isolation always has low tone. In context, however, a lexically high-tone morpheme may retain its high tone even when it is in word-final position, depending upon its syntactic environment (Rice 1987, 1989b). This is, of course, a very common situation in languages; however, it highlights the problem at hand. Any description that focused simply on isolated words would take the low tones on final syllables to be a characteristic of the word. The phrasal properties would be ignored, leading in this case to a mistaken analysis.

4.   Tones yet again, and the joys of pronominals

Just as a wide range of types of information is necessary to come to an understanding of a language, so it is also important to obtain data from a broad range of sources. Even in the phonological problem involving tone in Fort Nelson Slave discussed in section 3, it was important to figure out what the syntactic structure was, as the exact details of how the tones appeared are sensitive to syntactic environment. It is necessary to have an understanding of this not just at the clause level, but at the discourse level as well, since tones can vary depending upon where the word containing them falls in a discourse. Thus, to truly understand the tones of Fort Nelson Slave, elicitation had to be coupled with connected speech (Rice 1987, 1989b).

The need for a wide range of data is particularly evident in work on systems that function beyond the sentence. The most obvious of these are pronominals and tense/aspect. I will focus on an example involving pronominals. In Slave, as in many Athapaskan languages, a distinction is often made between pronouns that refer to humans and those that refer to nonhumans. The Slave subject pronoun *kɛ/gɛ* (the form depends on dialect) and the object pronoun *go* refer to humans although they can also be used for dogs. From elicitation alone, I thought that these were the only possible referents for these pronouns. However, textual work showed me that in addition, they refer to beings that are considered to be intelligent, or capable of control. This can include animals when they are capable of speaking and controlling in human-like fashion. The following sentences, cited from Rice (1989a: 1019–20), are from a story about a cultural hero breaking the necks of ducks.

(7) **gots'ę́** gondeh t'áh   ʔɛyi gots'ę́ **toɡɛh**ʔe   łahcho
    3pl to 3S calls because there area to 3plS swam to shore together
    gogha ehjị
    3pl to 1sgS sing
    gok'o   k'ɛaɛhdlá
    3plPoss neck   3S breaks
    Because he called to them [ducks], they swam ashore to him. I sing for them. He breaks their necks.

In these sentences, the ducks are alive, and the pronoun *go* is used. However, once the ducks are no longer alive, this pronoun cannot be used, and instead one of the pronouns *mɛ* or *yɛ* is found instead, where the form depends largely on the syntactic context (Rice 1989a, 2000a).

(8) **y**ɛyíɛ   káịdhah
    3 inside   3S took out
    mɛké   zǫ   łee   yíɛ kátheʔa   ʔayílá
    3Poss foot   only ash   in   3S stick out   3S made 3O
    yidedzéh
    3S ate up 3O
    yɛké   k'ɛt'á   łee   k'ɛh   dɛaʔɛdįhgé
    3Poss foot   back   ashes on   3S put
    He took out their insides. He made only their feet extend out of the ashes. He ate them up. He put their feet back in the ashes.

In this set of sentences, the ducks are still important to the discourse; however, they are no longer alive and thus the pronouns used in the sentences in (7) are no longer possible. In elicitation, I never encountered examples like those in (7) where the pronouns called human could refer to non-humans, although once I found these pronouns in discourse I was able to elicit them. The discourse context taught me that the feature of the "human" pronouns in question probably has to do with the ability to control or possible agentivity. When a non-human is vested with controlling or agentive powers by being given the ability to speak, it too is treated as human. Thus, while the pronouns in question are often referred to as third person humans, it turns out that [human] is not in fact the most appropriate feature to be using.

Some linguists shy away from elicitation to as great a degree as possible. However, I believe that neither elicitation alone nor text material alone is adequate to come to a full description of a language. To plumb the depths of a language, all sources are of value – elicitation, texts, casual speech, stories, and conversations. All of these fed into my fieldwork and helped me to achieve a better understanding of Slave; I do not think that I could have done without any one of them. Texts, conversations, and the like provide invaluable information about language in use. They allow one to answer important questions involving, for instance, topic and focus. They do not flesh out other things, however. For instance, there are many important aspects of language that people know but that may not come up very frequently, or at all, in texts and conversations. A full understanding of the distribution of pronouns in the complement of what are called direct discourse verbs in Slave (see Rice 1986, 1989a) would very likely have been impossible based on texts alone. In addition, texts on their own cannot lead one to understand what is not possible in a given language; they only provide a subset of what can actually be said. Elicitation can provide us with this information. It is necessary to use diversity in techniques to achieve as full a picture of a language as possible.

5. On intransitive verbs and other areas: the importance of theoretically-driven research

What kind of knowledge should one bring to the field situation? It is important to bring as much as possible, but, at the same time, it is necessary to use that knowledge carefully and not indiscriminately.

Let me begin with bringing as much as possible to the field situation. The more you know about the language and the language family, the more depth you bring with you. The more you know about language in general, the more ideas you have about what you might find in any particular language. The more you know about linguistic theory, the more areas you have to investigate, even if the goal is descriptive linguistic work. Knowledge in each of these areas leads the researcher to a different set of questions, questions which should, in the end, help the researcher come to the fullest possible picture of the language.

I'll now turn to the cautionary note. It is important to bring a high degree of knowledge to the field, but it is also necessary to be careful not to let that knowledge force the language into categories which are not those of the language itself. I will now discuss an example which shows, I think, both the value of bringing theoretical knowledge to empirical work and, at the same time, the need for caution in interpreting data that appears to be consistent with a particular theoretical position.

It has long been recognized that intransitive verbs can have two types of subjects. Stated in terms of thematic relations, the subject may be either an agent or actor or it may be a patient with respect to the verb. In Slave, verbs in each class exhibit a number of distinct characteristics. For instance, some intransitives can occur with incorporated nouns as subjects while others cannot; some can be causativized, but others cannot. In Rice 1991a I proposed that two classes of intransitives exist in Slave, and argued that the distinction between these two classes was a structural one: the difference between unergative (external subject) and unaccusative (internal subject) (see Perlmutter 1978, for example, on this distinction, which is called the "Unaccusative Hypothesis"). In writing my paper, I was influenced by various articles that I had been reading around that time. These articles led me to consider a variety of tests that one might use to determine whether an intransitive verb was unaccusative or unergative, and I looked in some depth at incorporated nouns, possible bases for causativization, and the patterning of third person oblique objects. For instance, I found that certain types of intransitive verbs could occur with incorporated nouns (9a), while other types of intransitive verbs could not (9b). The incorporated noun is in boldface.

(9) a. incorporate possible
   te-*wé-h-shu*   blanket is spread out
   mat, blanket-SA- Cl-stem
   b. incorporate not possible
   *ꞁi̜-*y-i̜-se*   the dog cried
   dog-SA-perf-stem

This structural classification of verbs like (9a) as unaccusative and those like (9b) as unergative led, I believe, to a good basic distinction between the two types of intransitives. Internal subjects could be incorporated while external subjects could not be. The treatment had strong theoretical precedent (see for instance Baker 1988), and fit well with the tests being used for distinguishing intransitive types at the time. It is unlikely that I would have looked at the range of different tests without having had the theoretical lead of the Unaccusative Hypothesis.

The theory was good in this way. However, at the same time, the theory blinded me to the treatment of some counterexamples which I was aware of but initially disregarded, because the theory couldn't accommodate them. These were of two types. First, one and the same verb could sometimes take an incorporated subject and sometimes not, depending on properties of the subject. For instance, (10a), with the noun 'drifted snow' incorporated, is fine, while (10b), with the same verb and 'dog' incorporated, is ungrammatical. Incorporated nouns are in boldface.

(10) a. *k'ɛ-**tsi**-i-tɬah*   the snow drifted
         incorporate: *tsih* 'drifted snow'; verb: *k'ɛ-tɬah* 'singular/dual go around by land'
     b. **k'ɛ-**tɬ̣i**-i-tɬah*   the dog went around
         incorporate: *tɬ̣i* 'dog'; verb: *k'ɛ-tɬah* 'singular/dual go around by land'

The Unaccusative Hypothesis had nothing in particular to say about such examples where certain types of nouns could be incorporated and others could not be with a single verb. Second, it had nothing to say about similar types of ambiguity with other tests. For instance, unergative verbs with third person subjects generally take one pronoun as a third person oblique object, and unaccusative verbs with third person subjects generally take a different one. However, unaccusative verbs can, under some circumstances, occur with the oblique object pronoun generally associated with unergative verbs.

I wasn't aware of how relevant the counterexamples were until much later (Rice 2000a). I realized that there are two different structural positions in which subjects can appear in Slave – this is a direct result of the careful definitions coming from the theory – but these have to do with characteristics of the subject and the verb rather than with characteristics of the verb alone: agentive human subjects of intransitives are normally external, while other human subjects may be external or internal; non-agentive, non-human, non-controlling subjects are generally internal. These facts are accounted for far better under a hypothesis in which subject properties determine the placement of the noun than they are under a hypothesis in which lexically listed structural properties of the verb determine its patterning. While the structural hypothesis accounted for the bulk of the data, there were forms about which it did not have anything to say. This incident taught me the following lesson: it is necessary to take into account the data that you know of, even those pesky forms that just don't seem to make any sense. This is often difficult to do as a hypothesis not only directs you to examine a particular question, but may lead you away from considering those properties that do not meet that hypothesis. Thus, the theoretical background that I brought with me was both a help – I saw as a constellation a set of properties that I would have otherwise viewed as independent – but also a hindrance – the theory blinded me to the significance of certain types of forms that I was aware of.

Despite such problems, awareness of theoretical issues has been immensely valuable to me. Because the verb in Athapaskan languages is highly complex, most of the research on these languages has focused on the verb. However, there are interesting questions that arise from a study of nouns, questions that I was led to investigate through theoretical issues. In many Athapaskan languages, stem-initial fricatives in nouns participate in voicing alternations in certain environments, with the voiceless fricative appearing in absolute-initial position and the voiced fricative in most other positions. This can be seen in possessive forms, where the fricative is voiceless when word initial and voiced when a prefix precedes. The relevant segments are in boldface.

(11) *sa*   month, sun   *bɛ-zá*   his/her months
     shę   song   *bɛ-yéné* his/her song

In compound forms as well, an initial fricative of a second noun is voiced.

(12) *tɛh-zá*   polar bear
     tɛh 'water' + *sa* 'bear'

However, under certain conditions, an initial fricative of a second noun fails to voice.

(13) *fe-shíh*   stone mountain
     fe 'stone' + *shíh* 'mountain'
     cf. *bɛ-yí*   his/her mountain

The environments in which voicing took place and failed were interesting to me for theoretical reasons. It was through the study of phonological issues concerning feature specification and prosodic domains that I was led to investigate this question more carefully, learning that both structural and phonological factors played a role in determining when an initial fricative took on the voiced form. Through this investigation, I came to the generalization that the compounds exhibited in (12) and (13) differ in meaning, with the (13) type forms occurring when the noun has the meaning N_2 made of N_1 and the (12) type appearing otherwise (Rice 1985, 1989a). This led me to read about other languages with similar types of distinctions between compounds and so made me aware of additional characteristics that distinguish the compound types from each other. Without the theoretical perspective that I brought to this work, I would have had a far shallower understanding of compounds than I ended up with.

Let me add one more example of how theory has helped me in coming to a deeper understanding of a particular language. One way of forming a perfective stem in Athapaskan languages is through the addition of a nasal suffix. This suffix can be seen most clearly in Slave in vowel-final verb roots, where it surfaces as nasalization on the vowel, indicated by the hook under the vowel. (Nasalized /a/ is regularly realized as [ǫ].)

(14) a. *ʔa*   handle default object, imperfective
     b. *ʔǫ*   handle default object, perfective

With consonant-final stems, the effect is different; here one finds an alternation between an [h]-final form and a vowel-final form.

(15) a. *deh*   plural go, imperfective
     b. *de*   plural go, perfective

What happened to the [h]? What happened to the nasal? It is through coming to an understanding of a phonological feature which I have called [sonorant voicing] that I began to understand just how these forms were related to one another. This feature has a dual effect: it nasalizes a vowel, and it voices an obstruent that can be voiced. Voiced obstruents in syllable-final position have no phonetic realization in Slave, while voiceless obstruents in this position neutralize to [h]. The particular theoretical analysis that I brought to this question allowed me to propose a unified treatment of all syllable-final consonants, not just stem-final consonants. A more traditional theory of distinctive features would not have lead me to this unified analysis (see Rice 1993, 1994, 1995).

What, then, can linguistic theory do for the fieldworker? To begin with, linguistic theory provides an explicitness that is extremely important in language description. It forces the linguist to be careful in the use of terms and to define exactly what we mean when we use a particular word. It is all too easy to use a traditional term and then allow it to compel an analysis that does not really fit. By carefully defining what a term means, it is easier to see when it is in fact inappropriate. In addition to forcing explicitness, linguistic theory demands that one make testable hypotheses. Given a particular theoretical claim, one should expect to find that certain things are grammatical and other things are ungrammatical. Both these pieces of information are important in understanding a language, as the set of things that are not grammatical helps one delimit just what it is that a language consists of.

Work in linguistic theory guided my fieldwork in many ways. In areas where there was not already a basic descriptive framework for looking at the languages, the theory led me to questions that I had to be sure I understood in order to provide as full a description of the language as possible. It forced me to look more deeply at the topics discussed above, and at areas such as anaphora and topicalization than I might otherwise not have examined in detail. As time went by, and the theoretical issues that were important changed and new theoretical issues arose, theory opened new doors for me, doors that I do not think would have been opened otherwise. For instance, my understanding of intransitives was definitely furthered by recent theoretical work in this area (Rice 2000a). My understanding of wh-questions was guided by theoretical developments and by discussion with linguists working in this area (Rice 1989a). The recent work that I have done on quantification is guided by work on quantifiers and their scope; my recent work on situation aspect is clearly guided by theoretical work in this area that sets out what systems are found (Rice 2000b). The Slave situation aspect system is far from identical to those described in the theoretical literature, and in this sense I can make a contribution to the theoretical literature on situation aspect. (For instance, situation aspect is covert in most languages, but is overtly marked in Slave.) These are issues that I may well never have chosen to investigate if it were not for the theoretical literature.

For me, good theoretical work is work that allows me to examine properties of a language that I would not otherwise have looked at or to see a language in a different way than I did before. It may help me unify aspects that I had until that time seen as distinct, and it may help to separate aspects that I had until that time seen as unified. The best theoretical work is very exciting as it aids in seeing a language in a new light. By contrast, taking a tiny piece of a language and showing that it can be accounted for under the latest theoretical advance is not, to me, an exciting activity.

6.   On paradigms, complementizers, and distributives: speaker strengths

Another lesson that I learned from fieldwork concerns the strengths of different speakers. Sometimes you will find a speaker who is wonderful at paradigms and just spits them out, one after another. Other speakers do not enjoy doing paradigms at all. I worked with one speaker like this: I was interested in paradigms and he was interested in meanings, especially idiomatic extension. It was only when I realized that working on paradigms with him was not a good use of our time that we were able to establish a strong working relationship. My knowledge of the lexical semantics of verb stems and prefixes greatly improved through our work together.

In Hare, two complementizers are in regular use, *nį* and *gú*. I was concerned with learning their distribution and trying to figure out if there was any difference in meaning. A dissertation on Navajo (Schauber 1975) made me think that there might well be differences between them, both in the structure that they required and in their meanings. Several speakers were quite happy to give me numerous examples with the complementizers, showing that they could both appear in the same sentence frames. People suggested that there were some meaning differences between the sentences, but could not be more explicit than that. One day I was working with someone whom I did not work with very often, as she did not particularly enjoy the verb paradigms that I was focused on at that time. I decided to ask her about these complementizers. She was able to give me a clear explanation of the differences between them by providing the settings in which the different sentences would be used. An example of a minimal pair for complementizers is shown in (16), from Rice (1989a: 1249).

(16) a. *sú* [*hɛjǫ súhga rírítǫ   nį*]   *kodinɛhshǫ*
       Q   here   sugar   1plS brought   comp   2sgS know
       Do you know if we brought the sugar?
       (possible answers: yes, I know; no, I don't know)
    b. *sú* [*hɛjǫ súhga rírítǫ   gú*]   *kodinɛhshǫ*
       Q   here   sugar   1plS brought   comp   2sgS know
       Do you know if we brought the sugar?
       (possible answers: yes, we brought it; no, we did not bring it)

The meanings of the two questions differ; in (16a) it is the main verb that is questioned, while in (16b) it is the complement and the main verb together. After coming to this understanding, I was able to work productively with a number of speakers on the functions of the complementizers – the one speaker who helped me figure out the difference between sentences such as those in (16) provided me with the insights to know what direction to go next.

Although I worked with many speakers trying to elicit distributive forms of the verb, I found myself having tremendous difficulty. I could recognize a distributive when I came across one by the presence of the distributive morpheme, but I was unable to create the forms, as there were major changes in verb morphology when one switched from a non-distributive to a distributive form (Rice 1989a). I was close to the point of deciding that the distributive was losing ground in the language when a speaker with whom I was working said, "Oh, you mean . . ." and provided me with an English gloss for a distributive form. Armed with this gloss, I returned to the problem of distributives and worked with many different people, all of whom easily formed distributives. It was only because of stumbling across the appropriate gloss with one speaker that I was able to learn that distributivity is indeed an extremely important category in Slave and to deal with it in the way that it deserved. Without this speaker, it would have been easy to dismiss it as basically unproductive.

Just as speakers vary in their strengths, so do linguists. Each linguist brings to fieldwork his or her own set of inherent talents, interests, and abilities. One linguist might be most interested in phonology, and another in syntax. One might be excellent at fine details; another might be stronger at building a conceptual framework. Often cooperation between linguists can lead to the best work. Much of the work that I did on syntax would have been impossible without numerous discussions with other linguists who work in this area. Talks with linguists working on other Athapaskan languages helped me sort out the rather opaque voice/valence system of Slave. It is important to bring in others and take advantage of each other's strengths.

In discussing strengths, it is necessary to take circumstances into account. Sometimes situations may dictate what kind of work one may do. For instance, in one community that I worked in, the older generation had grown up speaking only Slave, but when their children went to school, they all learned English to communicate with their children. The consequence was that the language was little used in the community. In this community, I found that there were very few speakers who, for instance, wanted to work on verb paradigms or stories. Many people, however, were interested in nouns. Thus, in doing fieldwork on this dialect, I worked intensively on nouns of all types – plain nouns, possessed nouns, deverbal nouns, diminutives, augmentatives – and discovered that the dialect differed in fascinating and surprising ways from other dialects. What looked at first like negative circumstances in fact turned out to yield something very exciting.

Before closing this section, I want to focus on one additional lesson. It is easy to start fieldwork having read everything available on a language and having a particular area in mind to investigate. This could be anything from an unexplained gap in a segmental inventory to the meaning of a particular morpheme to the possibilities of noun incorporation to the functioning of pronominals as agreement or as arguments. You might have mapped out an elicitation session designed to allow you to check out exactly what you need to confirm (or disconfirm) your hypothesis. You enter the first meeting with a speaker excited about what you will learn. What usually arises out of this situation? In one word, unless you are working with a speaker who is familiar with how linguists work, disappointment. It is easy to see why. First, you are asking someone to give you details of their language when, as far as they can tell, you have no knowledge of the fundamentals of the language. Consultants often consider themselves to be language teachers, and know well that you can't run before you can walk. Second, you do not know the speaker. Will they understand the glosses that you give? Are you working in an area that is a strength for them? Such a situation is likely to produce poor quality work – something is learned, but it may have little to do with the language.

7.   Conclusion

In this article, I have focused on several aspects of methodology that I believe to be important to fieldwork. As a fieldworker, it is necessary to embrace all sources of material and learn from them, but at the same time to treat them with necessary skepticism. It is also important to remember that language is a complex system, that there is variation within uniformity, and that it is very difficult to isolate one component of a language completely from another, since the pieces interact in intricate ways. Finally, the relationship with speakers is of the utmost importance: interpersonal interactions can be the greatest reward, or the greatest downfall, of fieldwork. Altogether, these add up to a single overriding lesson; namely, diversity is found in language, in speakers, and in techniques. Diversity must be allowed to suffuse fieldwork, and trying to impose sameness more often than not leads to frustration and confusion, and to incomplete analyses. Through a focus on diversity, systematicity and uniformity ultimately shine through. Of course no one person can be expected to do everything, and each individual must decide which aspects of language and linguistics excite them. Different individuals will make different choices. Properly done, all of it takes us to a deeper understanding of our goal, an explicit knowledge of what language can be.

ACKNOWLEDGMENTS

Many thanks to Leslie Saxon for her help with this article.

NOTE ON TRANSCRIPTION

1 I use orthography with two small exceptions: the orthography uses *e* where I use /ɛ/, and ə where I use /e/. The symbols that I use generally have the normal phonetic interpretations, although the exact details of the transcription are not relevant here. An acute accent represents high tone; a circumflex accent represents extra high tone; vowels without any marking are phonetically low tone or have otherwise predictable tones. The small hook under a vowel indicates nasalization. The following abbreviations should be noted:

sg	singular
S	subject
O	object
Poss	possessor
SA	situation aspect (conjugation)
Cl	classifier (a standard Athapaskan term)
perf	perfective
comp	complementizer

I have given morpheme-by-morpheme glosses of the Bearlake forms; these glosses hold for the Hare forms as well.

Several regular segmental correspondences between Hare and Bearlake are shown in these data; for instance, Bearlake [wh] (voiceless labiovelar glide) corresponds with Hare [w]; Bearlake [ch] (voiceless aspirated alveopalatal affricate) corresponds with Hare [sh] (voiceless alveopalatal fricative); Hare [r] corresponds with Bearlake [n]. These are not relevant to the discussion here.

REFERENCES

Baker, Mark. 1988. *Incorporation: A Theory of Grammatical Function Changing.* Chicago: University of Chicago Press.
Hoijer, Harry. 1966. Hare phonology: an historical study. *Language* 32:499–507.
Perlmutter, David. 1978. Impersonal passives and the Unaccusative Hypothesis. *Proceedings of the Berkeley Linguistics Society* 4:157–89.
Rice, Keren. 1985. Noun compounds in Dene. *Journal of the Atlantic Provinces Linguistic Association* 6/7:55–72.
——— 1986. Some remarks on direct and indirect discourse in Slave (Northern Athapaskan). In *Reported Speech Across Languages*, ed. Florian Coulmas, pp. 47–76. Berlin: Walter de Gruyter.
——— 1987. On defining the intonational phrase: evidence from Slave. *Phonology Yearbook* 4:37–57.
——— 1989a. *A Grammar of Slave.* (Mouton Grammar Library, 5) Berlin: Mouton de Gruyter.
——— 1989b. The phonology of Fort Nelson Slave stem tone: syntactic implications. In *Athapaskan Linguistics: Current Perspectives on a Language Family*, ed. Eung-Do Cook and Keren Rice, pp. 229–64. Berlin: Mouton de Gruyter.
——— 1991. Intransitives in Slave (Northern Athapaskan): arguments for unaccusatives. *International Journal of American Linguistics* 57:51–69.
——— 1991. Prosodic constituency in Hare (Athapaskan): evidence for the foot. *Lingua* 82:201–45.
——— 1993. A reexamination of the feature [sonorant]: the status of "sonorant obstruents." *Language* 69:308–44.
——— 1994. Laryngeal features in Athapaskan languages. *Phonology* 12:107–47.
——— 1995. The representation of the perfective suffix in the Athapaskan language family. *International Journal of American Linguistics* 61:1–37.
——— 2000a. Monadic verbs and argument structure in Ahtna, Slave, and Navajo. In *The Athabaskan Languages: Perspectives on a Native American Language Family*, ed. Theodore Fernald and Paul Platero. Oxford: Oxford University Press.
——— 2000b. *Morpheme Order and Semantic Scope: Word Formation in the Athapaskan Verb.* Cambridge: Cambridge University Press.
Rushforth, Scott, and James S. Chisholm. 1995. *Cultural Persistence: Continuity in Meaning and Moral Responsibility among the Bearlake Athapaskans.* Albuquerque: University of New Mexico Press.
Schauber, Ellen. 1975. Theoretical Responses to Navajo Questions. Ph.D. dissertation, MIT.
Scollon, Ron, and Suzanne B.K. Scollon. 1979. *Linguistic Convergence: An Ethnography of Speaking at Fort Chipewyan, Alberta.* New York: Academic Press.

12   The last speaker is dead – long live the last speaker!

Nicholas Evans

It is increasingly common for primary linguistic fieldwork to be conducted with "last speakers," as swingeing language extinction brings a belated attention to the need to document endangered languages. Data from "last speakers" must, however, be treated with caution, given that the variety they speak may have been simplified through various processes of language death (see Schmidt 1985: 41) – though this is by no means always the case – and/or heavily influenced by interference from whatever other language(s) they use in day-to-day communication. Nonetheless, many detailed and subtle grammars of Australian languages, for example, have been written on the basis of data from a single last speaker; recent examples are Dench's (1995) grammar of Martuthunira, and Harvey's (1992) grammar of Gaagudju.

Such works clearly validate the possibility of carrying out linguistic field-work with last speakers, but it is imperative that researchers be aware that the definition and identification of "last speakers" is highly problematic, and prone to constant redefinition from both the speech community's and the researcher's point of view. There are of course rather obvious cases, where the death of one "last speaker" is followed by the fortuitous discovery of another speaker, equally or more fluent, in some other location, or where the community's definition of total linguistic competence adjusts to the erosion of stylistic, grammatical, or lexical complexity, so that in a succession of what the community considers "last speakers" each knows less, in some objective sense (see section 1). However, my main focus in this chapter is rather on the way in which the broader social system determines individuals' perceived right to be a speaker, as well as their actual linguistic performance.

Much of the material in this paper is based on work I have carried out in northern Australia (particularly north-west Queensland and Arnhem Land) over the last two decades; this is augmented by comments and quotes from a number of colleagues. The importance of last-speaker issues to my own research can be gauged from the fact that, of the dozen languages I have been involved in documenting over this period, only two

(Mayali/ Kunwinjku and Iwaidja) are still being learned by children, seven were already down to one or two speakers by the time I began work on them, and the remainder, though boasting over a dozen speakers, have sometimes required concerted efforts to bring speakers together, either to establish a conversational quorum or to bring together people whose skills are complementary (e.g., a Kayardild monolingual with his/her English-monolingual child who nonetheless understands the language well enough to help with translation). My own experience is by no means atypical here, and for accounts of similar situations the reader is referred to Dixon (1984) on his own fieldwork experiences in north Queensland, White (1990), which discusses Luise Hercus' fieldwork, mainly in south-eastern Australia, and Sutton (1992) on his experiences of salvage fieldwork in Cape York.

Obviously, doing fieldwork in such situations is a race against time, and tracking down good speakers before it is too late involves a great deal of detective work. It is common to be told about particular individuals that they are "somewhere over the border in Queensland," "might be they went to Palm Island," or "probably living down Daly River way." Partly owing to these difficulties, many "salvage linguists" have stories of arriving a year too late to work with the last fluent speaker (e.g., Hercus 1969: 190).

Sometimes, of course, one is given detailed suggestions about how much various people know. On one occasion in 1990, I sat in an old shed during a thunderstorm with Big Bill Neidjie, a senior man of the Bunidj clan – who himself speaks Amurdak and some Gaagudju as well as the regional lingua francas Kunwinjku and Iwaidja – while he spelled out a program for what work needed to be done on the languages of the Cobourg peninsula. For each of Marrgu, Garig, Amurdak and Wurrugu he named the one or two remaining speakers. Over the following years, as these suggestions could be followed up by a series of researchers, this information was proved broadly correct, although with a pronounced male bias, an overestimation of the knowledge of some speakers, and an omission of the names of other speakers for reasons I will return to below.

But equally often one's inquiries are held up by the fact that some members of the descendant community either do not know where key people are, or are unaware that they speak the language. Just as important, lack of awareness of the distinction between "language-owners" and "language-speakers" can lead fieldworkers to narrow their search in the wrong direction, since the question "who speaks X?" will often be construed as meaning "who is an 'owner' of language X, and also speaks it?" Mark Harvey, for example, worked for many years on Warray with Doris White of Humpty Doo, a woman who he, and the other Warray descendants known to him, assumed to be one of the last surviving cohort of speakers (see Harvey 1993 for an interesting account of the field situation). Subsequently he discovered another speaker, Elsie O'Brien, living in Darwin:

Finding out about her was a matter of chance. I was checking genealogies with some people at Humpty Doo, and discovered her as the spouse of an uncle. I assumed that she must be dead, but was assured to the contrary and then informed that she spoke Warray. It took quite a while to find her, and she was quite mistrustful at our first meeting. However she was reassured by family connections and then things just zoomed off. Finding her made a huge difference to what I could say about Warray, as she was pretty much independent from Doris and the others.

The thing was of course that if I had been looking for Kamu people I would have found her easily. That is one point that I think you should make clearly for Australia. Fieldworkers should not necessarily look among language-owners for good language-speakers. In my experience around Darwin there is frequently a mismatch. I wish I had known this when I started work – I have since discovered that a number of now-deceased Wagiman and Kamu people were probably good speakers of Warray, but I never worked with them. (Harvey, e-mail, May 11, 1998)

The difficulties do not stop once one is in the happy position of sitting on the verandah, or on a couple of upturned flour tins, with someone one believes to be a "speaker."

Some of these problems are already familiar in the literature on fieldwork in language-death situations (see Dorian 1986): the decay and (sometimes) restoration of memory in a long-neglected language, the difficulty of knowing whether a given paradigmatic gap or syntactic construction is due to interference from the dominant language or is part of the original system, the difficulties that can arise in establishing rapport as an outsider to the community, and the artificiality of obtaining a fluent and punchy text in a language the audience does not understand. I will mention some of these in more detail below. But a further focus will be on other issues of a more sociolinguistic nature that arise in northern Australia from the particular constellation of multilingualism, small speech communities, assumptions about speakerhood and the social function of language competence and ownership, and restrictions on the social distribution of knowledge. I will also refer to certain types of language competence that I have observed in these communities, which lie outside the conventional taxonomy of speaking versus hearing competences, and which may be harnessed to use in salvage fieldwork.

By surveying such issues, and the way they influence language learning and use in these multilingual but traditionally non-literate speech communities, I hope to help linguistic fieldworkers gathering data on endangered languages to cast their net more widely, slowly and subtly than they might otherwise have done.

1.   Knowing a language versus owning a language

Most of the "last speakers" I will be discussing are members of speech communities in northern Australia which are traditionally characterized by extensive personal multilingualism and a societal emphasis on both language knowledge and language "ownership" as a means of demonstrating clan membership and affiliation to land and sea territory.[1] For example, it is believed that many resources, such as freshwater springs, turtles, and safe passage to particular sites, can only be accessed through correct use of the appropriate language variety (Brandl and Walsh 1982; Trigger 1987); clearly this provides a strong motivation to learn many linguistic varieties.

In areas like northern Australia where the ethic of multilingualism, and striking linguistic diversity, exists alongside widespread shift away from some languages, it is common to encounter "last speakers" who are highly multilingual – and perhaps therefore are the last speaker of a number of languages.[2] Because special talent as a language learner is what enabled such individuals to learn varieties offering limited exposure, they are often excellent informants, but there is also a risk that the variety taught to the linguist has been influenced by other languages they know. This issue will be taken up below.

A second problem arises from the fact that affiliation to language is primarily a matter of social group membership rather than actual competence. As a number of anthropological linguists have argued (e.g., Sutton 1978, Sutton and Palmer 1981, Merlan 1981, Merlan and Rumsey 1982, Rumsey 1989, 1993), the reigning social model over much of Australia posits a direct relationship between land and language, as well as between language and particular social groupings (typically but not always patrilineal clans). Individuals then derive the right to be recognized as speakers of particular languages indirectly, through their membership in clan or comparable groups (Rumsey 1989: 75):

> The mediated link is not between language and country (which are directly linked), but between language and people: Jawoyn people are Jawoyn not because they speak Jawoyn, but because they are otherwise linked (by patrifiliation, matrifiliation, or both) to places to which the Jawoyn language is also linked. . . . [N]ot everyone who speaks Jawoyn, even fluently, feels entitled to say "I am Jawoyn" or "Jawoyn is my language" (Merlan and Rumsey 1982: 37). The relevant relationship to language is not one of speakership, but one which is better glossed as language ownership (Sutton 1978, Sutton and Palmer 1981).

In Cape York Creole, this distinction is conveyed in the following way (Rigsby 1997): one is said to "speak" one's own clan language but to *mak* (i.e., 'mock' or 'imitate') the languages of other clans.

CLAN OR
INDIVIDUAL   ⇔   OTHER SOCIAL   ⇔   LAND   ⇔   LANGUAGE
GROUP

Figure 12.1. The indirect relationship between individuals and "their" languages.

The social model outlined above is illustrated schematically in figure 12.1. In many areas there is also an ideology that each distinct social group, down to clan level, should have some distinct linguistic features, and there are known cases where the fission of one clan into two leads to the emergence of two distinct "clan lects" or "patrilects" (Sutton 1978), even though the difference between them is confined to a few key vocabulary items (see Smith and Johnson 1986). In many parts of Australia, such as Western Cape York and North-Eastern Arnhem Land, such varieties each have their own name, and a problem facing salvage linguists in such regions, who are trying to get information on a particular language X about which nothing is known, is to find out whether they are dealing with a clan lect very similar to known varieties, a quite distinct language, or such other possibilities as an alternative name for a known variety (see Walsh 1997 for a good discussion of this problem).

Although neighboring groups will sometimes make statements like "that's just like our language – only they take it a bit light" or "we can hear that language – same like ours," there are so many confounding factors (e.g., the effects of multilingualism in promoting passive understanding of distinct languages) that such statements can only be really evaluated when data from self-identifying speakers is obtained. For example, Tryon's (1974) classification of Matngele and Kamu (which he spells Kamor) as sister dialects is based on work with Matngele people who had some knowledge of Kamu as a second-language variety. But later fieldwork by Mark Harvey with Elsie O'Brien, a first-language speaker of Kamu, has shown that they are fully distinct languages.

A corollary of the system outlined above is that people's actual language knowledge, which reflects the accidents of their life history, is a separate matter to the "ownership" of languages conferred on them by descent-based membership of particular social groups, such as clans. Many grammatical descriptions of Australian languages mention the fact that key informants were actually affiliated with groups speaking other languages. Several of Austin's (1981:13–14) key Diyari informants, for example, came from non-Diyari groups: Rosa Warren "whose mother was Aranda and father Arabana was born in 1917 and learned Diyari as a child living among people who had been at Killalpinna" and Frieda Merrick "was of Wangkanguru descent and learned Diyari as a young woman at Muloorina and Killalpaninna. Her knowledge of vocabulary was probably the most extensive of any speaker with whom intensive language work was undertaken." Recall, as well, the case of Elsie O'Brien discussed above, who though of Kamu descent (and speaking Kamu) turned out to also have a full knowledge of Warray.

This means that many informants will, in terms of social affiliation, come from other language backgrounds. But identifying and working with such people may be problematic, owing to a widespread belief that it is owning a language, rather than speaking it, which is the primary social determinant of one's right to make decisions about who to pass on knowledge about that language to; actual competence need in no way confer social recognition as a speaker. Particularly in the initial phases of investigation, it is often to the person who is regarded as "owning" the language that a linguist is referred, upon inquiring "who speaks X?"

This needs to be borne in mind when doing fieldwork on threatened languages, since the linguist can be faced with a situation in which the person with a right to speak for the language in fact knows very little, while someone else not recognized as having a right to speak for the language may know much more. Consider the following case, from Ian Green's fieldwork in the Daly River area (e-mail, May 12, 1999):

In the early 90s I worked on a Daly language called Warrgat (a.k.a. Merranunggu, Marranunggu, Maranungku). Of the two identified remaining speakers only one, Peter Melyin, known around the place by the nickname "Daffy," was available and willing to teach it to me. Peter was effectively a native speaker of Warrgat – it may not have been his first language, but he had spoken it from an early age – and he was its rightful custodian, with the authority to teach it to others as he wished. However, over the preceding few decades the closely related Marrithiyel language had pushed aside Warrgat as his primary "traditional" language, and as a result he had difficulty recalling its lexicon and constructions clearly. In addition he was having increasing difficulties with his hearing (hence the "Daffy" (< Eng. *deaf*) nickname). So language teaching sessions were slow and frustrating for everyone.

We were lucky to be assisted by Jack Yenmung (a.k.a. Jackie Skewes). Jack was a native Marrithiyel speaker, but had learnt Warrgat as a child and had used it off and on over a period of forty years or more. Jack had previously proven to be a brilliant Marrithiyel teacher, and he sat patiently with Peter and me, gently explaining things to the old man, prompting his recollections and quite often, with great deference, suggesting that there were proper Warrgat alternatives to the Marrithiyel or Marrithiyel-influenced forms that he was coming up with. Nevertheless, the work proceeded extremely slowly.

At this stage, Jack on his own, in the absence of Peter, was very uncomfortable answering questions about Warrgat. However, when Peter was subsequently called away on business, he gave Jack permission to take over the main teaching role with me. And, without wishing to detract at all from Peter's vast array of knowledge of country and culture, I have to say that the sessions began to fly. Once formally given the authority to talk about the language, Jack proved to be as insightful a teacher in Warrgat as he had been with Marrithiyel.

Shortly after this time both men became too sick to work on teaching language, and both subsequently passed away. Without the happy coincidence of having Jack around, linguists and Warrgat descendants would know a lot less about the language than we do now. It's odd how we as linguists on the one hand observe the fabulously multilingual nature of Aboriginal society but on the other can become very purist in our fieldwork endeavours and feel compromised at the thought of working with second or subsequent language speakers of the particular variety we're interested in. On reflection, I think that I unduly narrowed the scope of my data on the then moribund Marrithiyel dialect by failing to appreciate what fluent but non-native speakers might be able to offer.

The situation may be further muddied by the many political factors associated with both "owning" and "speaking" a language, which work against maintaining this distinction in as clear a form as was outlined above.

On the one hand, people with a peripheral claim to group membership (perhaps through a cross-grandparent, such as a father's mother or mother's father, or through long residence in the absence of a clear custodian, or through earlier adoption or bequest), often seek to strengthen their claim by regular fluent public use of the language associated with the group's country.

On the other hand, in at least some speech communities it may be regarded as a "shame job" for a clan elder to be unable to speak the language associated with their clan, and politically ambitious individuals may often have developed effective strategies for prominent public display of their language skills in a way that can disguise their limited repertoire. The fewer people that know the language, the more effective such a strategy becomes.

For example, one man I knew made a regular practice of short but voluble monologues in his language as he visited the camps of other people in the community, who were speakers of different Aboriginal languages or Aboriginal English. He usually began and ended with the grandiose announcement *ngada burrthangiju!* His performances gained him a reputation as someone who could "speak Q right through."[3] It was only when I became reasonably fluent in a related language that I realized that his oft-repeated flourish simply meant "I will fart!"

As a second example, I was once asked to translate a tape made of a community meeting in which representatives of a number of local clan groups, each with their own language, welcomed and addressed some visiting government representatives. Included in the set of languages were two languages, R and S, each known by at most two people. The speaker of R, who is reasonably fluent, made a cogent and varied address. On the other hand, the speaker of S, who tended to overstate his knowledge of his language, exploited the free word order that characterizes most Australian languages to eke out his limited knowledge into a speech long enough to give the impression of having a reasonable mastery of the language. His drawn-out delivery of the lines *irtya ngardab wurrad, wurrad irtya ngardab! ngardab wurrad irtya!*, which sounded impressively fluent to listeners knowing no S, actually boiled down to three permutations of a verbless clause: 'this (is) my country, country this (is) mine! My country (is) this!'

In addition to such cases, where the motivation for maintaining a facade as a fluent speaker is to bolster one's identity as a leader of one's clan or tribal group, it may happen that the use of traditional language, in circumstances predisposed to mystify or exclude understanding by a younger generation, is part of a trajectory from language as the shared vehicle of everyday communication to language as restricted ritual knowledge, comparable to ceremonial sacra not to be divulged to the uninitiated. Tamsin Donaldson (1985) describes something like this as occurring between the oldest remembered generation (the *ngurrampaa*) of Ngiyampaa speakers and their children:

> But in not speaking Ngiyampaa in front of younger people its remaining speakers are also drawing on traditional values within their own culture. Earlier generations died in possession of untransmitted ceremonially-derived knowledge because there were no younger people appropriately prepared through other, prerequisite, ceremonial experience to receive it. Someone now in her sixties described to me how in her youth she had overheard members of the *ngurrampaa* generation talking Ngiyampaa together "like music." They would drop their heads in sudden silence . . . at the approach of children. . . . The language itself was becoming in some respects like ceremonial knowledge. . . . The old people were becoming elegiac custodians of what was now primarily a cultural property, a heritage rather than the unselfconscious vehicle of daily life. (Donaldson 1985: 135)

Once language knowledge becomes identified with ritual or ceremonial status in this way, as happens in many situations of language death,[4] certain individuals can have a stake in misrepresenting their own level of knowledge so as to gain status in the community.[5] In searching for last speakers one can easily follow false leads as a result of this. However, as we shall see in section 2, one cannot simply conclude, when you finally sit down with a "speaker" and find them unable to give much language data, that they do not know the language: there may be other reasons for their reticence.

It should be noted here that the politics of language ownership often survives the death of its last speakers. Although I do not normally find the testing of sentences for acceptability a very enlightening procedure in

Aboriginal speech communities,[6] I have often had to cross-check sentences that I recorded from other speakers or half-heard "on the fly" during conversations. The commonest response to such queries is "Who told you that?" And the nature of the response to cross-checked sentences, which may range from "yeah, that's right, you've got it" to "never heard anyone talk like that" or "bit twisted, that one," often depends on how the original author of the utterance is regarded in the community, or more specifically by the evaluator, as much as on any structural characteristics of the sentence itself. What is more, this effect can shift over time, since certain dominant individuals whom no one dares criticize as long as they are alive may be negatively re-evaluated once they die.[7] To avoid being too misled by such currents, I regularly include a couple of test sentences, of whose status I am sure, in order to check out the sympathies of particular informants before passing to items of which I am genuinely unsure. However, the problem cannot be entirely avoided, and any grammar, dictionary or text collection in which speakers are identified as the source for words or sentences can expect to draw some criticism as to why a particular "wrong" form was included. Maintaining one's intellectual integrity while defending these inclusions to community representatives is one of the many tricky communicative challenges that a linguist faces in such communities.

The status attached to arcane language knowledge means that community definitions of who speaks their language will often change through time: speaking a language gets redefined from having a full command of all registers, to having a good command of the language but some gaps in grammar and lexicon and a compressed stylistic range, to knowing a certain number of fixed phrases and words, to knowing a few score vocabulary items, down to remembering a couple of words with an anglicized pronunciation. This is very much a continuum, and such linguist's labels as "full speaker," "semi-speaker," and "rememberer" at best label clear bench-marks along it. While working on Kungarakany in the decade between 1985 and 1995, I heard the label "the last Kungarakany speaker" applied three times by members of the speech community to different individuals: firstly, to a woman who was close to being a fully fluent speaker; secondly (after her death) to a man whose grammatical knowledge was less complete; and thirdly (after his death) to a woman who had a good knowledge of the lexicon but whose grammar and pronunciation were limited. The Kungarakany group were marked by strong interest on the part of many younger members in recording, writing, and practicing their language, and at any point there was always someone regarded as the most senior and knowledgable custodian. This trend continues today with other, even younger speakers.

Three important reservations need to be borne in mind by the field linguist as they decide where potential language speakers fit on this spectrum.

First, it is not possible to give an objective, language-independent definition of the transition from "full speaker" to "semi-speaker," since this depends on how far the structural changes and simplifications that accompany contact with a dominant language like English result in a common code used by a substantial body of speakers.

The results of such simplifications may of course be of lessened interest for syntacticians or typologists: young people's Warlpiri (Bavin and Shopen 1985) may lack the famous flexible word order of traditional Warlpiri; Neo-Tiwi (Lee 1987) may lack the striking polysynthesis of traditional Tiwi; New Lardil (Hale 1997) may have lost the tense-sensitive object-marking of traditional Lardil; and Young People's Dyirbal (Schmidt 1985) may no longer be syntactically ergative, and may have simplified the complex semantics assigning nouns to classes.

But viewed from other subdisciplines of linguistics they still have much of interest to offer, in terms of language contact, the emergence of new linguistic codes, the sociolinguistics of variation, and structure of semantic categories. Unless one has extremely focused theoretical interests – and I personally believe that it is difficult to carry out successful linguistic fieldwork from such a narrow interest base – then there is still great value to recording data about such emergent varieties. And, as mentioned above, with data from a single speaker it is difficult to decide whether one is dealing with a semi-speaker or a speaker of an emergent new variety – indeed, it remains an interesting theoretical question how far and where such categories can be distinguished.

Second, imperfect language acquisition may have different effects according to a language's structural type. Consider the simple sentence "The dog bit him." In a language where each constituent is represented by a separate word, with subject and object marked by case, the first effect of language simplification is to destroy the case system, but speakers are still able to construct sentences by putting together uninflected words. For example, a typical attempt at translation by young semi-speakers of Kayardild would be to say *dathina yarbud – baaja – niya*, literally 'that dog – bit – he'; this is understandable, and differs from traditional Kayardild only in the lack of object marking on the pronoun, which should be *niwanji* instead of *niya*. In a language like Marrgu, on the other hand, where both subject and object pronominals are marked by prefixes to the verb, and there are in addition a large number of portmanteau forms as well as further suppletions depending on the verb chosen, the effect of imperfect acquisition is much greater. When I asked the late Mick Yarmirr how to express the above sentence in Marrgu, he simply balked and said "I can't get that one": failure to learn the correct pronominal prefix combination left him unable to use the verb at all in this context.[8] Yet his fluency in Marrgu was not bad, and for other subject/object combinations, with other verbs (e.g., 'I want money' or 'The old people used to eat that'), he could immediately give a translation. In this case, then, the head-marking structure of the language exaggerated the effects of imperfect acquisition. (He had been removed from his Marrgu-speaking family on Croker Island at the age of seven to attend a mission school on Goulburn Island, so that though he learned Iwaidja, Maung, and Kunwinjku, his knowledge of his "own" language was limited.)

Third, field linguists must always bear in mind that their own technical definitions of "language," "language death," "semi-speaker," and so on may not correspond to the categorizations made by the speech community or the wider society. As mentioned above, over time communities may revise their criteria for what counts as being a speaker. As well as having important ramifications for their own identity, such redefinitions will be relevant in such issues as whether the community can demonstrate "continuity of tradition" in a Native Title claim, how far it can claim resources for bilingual or language-revitalization programs, and whether community members have a right to interpreting assistance in court. Given our current lack of understanding of which processes and strategies are most successful in promoting language revitalization, the demonstrated advantages of "compromise" over "purity" in assuring language maintenance (Dorian 1994), and the broadening of academic interest within linguistics to encompass non-canonical varieties, field linguists had best not be dogmatic in applying such terms as "semi-speaker" and "last speaker" to the communities they work with.

Before leaving the topic of how to determine who is likely to be a good last speaker, a couple more observations are worth making.

It is often the case that last speakers have often had either special life-circumstances or display special talents for language-learning. This can mean that there is not always a simple relationship between age and language fluency – against expectations. Younger speakers sometimes know more than their elder relatives, if they were gifted language learners or simply more interested in traditional matters. In other cases, an age difference of just a year or two makes a vast difference to fluency. And speakers of about the same age can differ widely in their language competence because early missionaries decided one was young enough to benefit from going to the mission school (and was hence placed in a dormitory where they were cut off from exposure to their language), while the other was deemed too old and continued to lead a relatively traditional existence.

A maverick factor at work in many parts of Australia is the role of white parentage. Under Australian law until well after World War II, children with white fathers were often separated from their mothers and placed in special schools or with adoptive white families simply on the grounds that they were "part white." To minimize the risk of this happening, such children were often kept out bush by their mothers and other Aboriginal relatives, and ironically sometimes ended up having a more traditional life than their darker-skinned siblings and cousins. (See the biographical notes on Algy Patterson, the main informant for Alan Dench's grammar of Martuthunira, in Dench (1995), and also the notes on some of Bob Dixon's main informants for Dyirbal and Yidiny in Dixon (1972, 1977).)

2. "Now we can talk": competence and performance of last speakers in sociolinguistic perspective

We now pass from problems of social categorization to the dynamics of individual language capability. In working in salvage situations, linguists must pay attention to a range of factors that can condition significant alterations over time, both positive and negative, in speakers' apparent mastery of the language.

For a range of reasons, last speakers are rarely comparable in fluency and range to speakers in healthy speech communities, and this reduction in fluency and associated simplification constantly throws up analytic questions. Examples from work on Australian languages are the issue of whether the language had a rhotic contrast (/r/ versus /ɹ/) prior to simplification (see Donaldson 1980 and Austin 1986 for discussion with respect to Ngiyambaa and Kamilaraay, respectively), of whether defective verb paradigms reflect imperfect language learning (see Harvey (in press) on this problem in Kamu), or of whether there is no formal marking of subordinate clause status.

Especially where little or nothing is known about the language, large domains of one's description are potentially open to three types of interpretation: that the speaker has simply failed to master the full complexities of some grammatical, phonological, or semantic domain; that the variety they mastered had already undergone simplification through contact with the replacing language; or that the language was in fact like that all along, and the speaker has actually mastered it as perfectly as speakers one hundred years before. In some cases parallels from related or typologically similar languages described in more favorable circumstances, or earlier recordings of the same language, can be used to resolve these issues. But in other cases such data is not available and an assessment of the speaker's overall competence may be the only evidence one can bring to bear.

Even more important is the way in which how the research is done can actually improve or depress the quality of what the speaker produces. Clearly the best results will be obtained when the dynamics of competence and performance, as embedded in the speaker's own culture, are well understood. Patient long-term work by the fieldworker may even enable the speaker to regain fluency through the renewed practice afforded by interaction with the investigator.

As with any speaker in advanced adulthood, competence will be shaped by the playing out over time of processes of learning, use, and forgetting, and this is something that should never be assumed to be simply frozen at a given level. In addition – and this relates to our earlier discussion of the relationship between "owning" and "speaking" a language – changes in the micro-politics of a community, as deaths and absences alter community perceptions of who has the right to give information about a language, can lead to certain speakers stepping forward who had previously been silent, or reluctant to speak, about their abilities. Finally, one needs to take note of a specific type of language competence found in north Australian communities that has not been recognized in the literature – I shall call it "amplifier competence" – which will also be affected – negatively, in this case – by the loss of other members of the speech community.

2.1   *Extension of competence through renewed practice*

Numerous cases have been reported where an elderly person, who on first encounter thought they had almost forgotten a language through lack of use, gradually recovers their fluency once regular interaction with a linguist affords an occasion for practice. Luise Hercus gives the following example:

After many futile efforts it became possible to locate three people . . . who could recall one short song and a few words of Madimadi. Hopes of getting any further had been abandoned, when Dr. Ellis discovered that Jack Long, originally known as "John Edwards," a full-blood Madimadi living at Pt Pearce in South Australia, remembered some of his language. Over a series of visits by Dr. Ellis and the writer he recalled more and more, and showed no confusion with any South Australian language, although he was over ninety and had left the Balranald district long ago. He had been a fluent speaker of Madimadi as a young man, and had been able to understand the related languages, Wadiwadi, Narinari, Njerinjeri, Ledjiledji and Wegiwegi, as well as Yidayida-Dadidadi. He was a person of outstanding intelligence. Most of the work on Madimadi is based on his evidence, corroborated by the minor speakers. (Hercus 1986: 102)

Bob Dixon's account of his experience working with Mbabaram speaker Albert Bennett is similar:

In 1964 I searched extensively for speakers of Mbabaram. Mick Burns (aged at least 75) was living in Edmonton, near Cairns, and gave about 50 words. Albert Bennett (then aged about 60) was contacted at his home near Petford, in the heart of traditional Mbabaram country. A first visit on 23 February 1964 yielded just 20 words, in a language Bennett had not used or heard spoken since his mother died, a score or more years before. I visited him again on 4 July, 26 July and 1 August 1964, obtaining about 200 words in all, and just a little grammatical data. . . . I saw Bennett again on 26 March 1967, 3 December and 14 December 1970 and 10 December 1971; he died in 1972. As he grew older and thought back more to his youth, Bennett's competence in the language improved. (Dixon 1991: 353)

Interference from another language may specifically reduce the use of constructions particular to the disappearing language. Tamsin Donaldson (1980: 115) reports how the last speakers of Ngiyambaa had abandoned a special "caritative" construction, as in (1), in favor of a transitive construction involving the English loan word *wandid-ma-l* 'want', as in (2). Donaldson notes that the caritative construction "slowly revived, once it had been elicited."

(1) *ŋadhu*   *yuwan-ŋinda*   *ga-ṟa*
    I + NOM   bread-CARIT   be-PRES
    I want (some) bread.

(2) *ŋadhu*   *yuwan*   *wandid-ma-ṟa*
    I + NOM   bread + ABS   want it-VBLSR-PRES
    I want (some) bread.

There are three types of method that investigators should use to encourage the return of fluency and constructional range in such situations.

    First, it is clear that the more quickly field linguists themselves can gain some communicative competence in the language, the more opportunity the speakers will have to regain their fluency through conversation, and the more natural it will seem to them to tell stories that utilize the full resources of the language. (A salutary exercise that will help put you in the position of a last speaker working with a linguist investigator is to try telling your favorite anecdote, complete with colorful embroiderings and humorous flourishes, to someone whose English is limited to a few words, and see how far you get.) It is also a way of making sure that the linguist is not being given simplified "foreigner-talk" versions of the language, although this is more likely to be a problem in a fully-functioning speech community. The late Steve Johnson told me that on the last day of his first field trip working on Kugu Nganhcara he happened to overhear a verb form that did not correspond to those he had been given in elicitation. When he asked his language teachers about it, they replied "oh – you want the REAL language now?" At the level of fluency he had attained, they had only judged him ready for the simplified, foreigner-talk version of the language.

    Second, they should do their best to locate other speakers who can be brought together to converse. For example, the Dalabon speech community is particularly fragmented (the ten or so best speakers are scattered over at least eight locations), so that they rarely get the chance to tell stories to a maximally appreciative audience; bringing speakers from different communities together for sessions of talk and story-telling has been a very productive way of getting texts with flair and color. However, even where multiple speakers can be located, there are many practical obstacles to doing this with older people, including infirmity, cost, distance, and sometimes personal enmity or rivalry.

Third, the existence of multilingual conversational norms, plus a tolerance of asymmetrical language choice, means that certain speakers may be in the habit of talking their language to acquaintances who "hear" their language even thought they do not speak it.[9] It has sometimes been asserted that last speakers become dysfluent as a result of having no one else to talk to. With the above sociolinguistic norms, however, a last speaker may get daily practice in the use of their language, even if they lack the pleasure of being fully understood. Charlie Wardaga, for example, regularly talks Ilgar to his children, wife, and other younger relatives, some of whom listen with great interest.[10] Many of these younger people understand quite a lot of what he says, through a combination of lengthy exposure and knowledge of closely related languages (in this case Iwaidja, which is about as close to Ilgar as Czech is to Slovak). Likewise, I have recordings of Alice Bohm telling lively Dalabon stories to an audience who do not speak Dalabon, but who speak the closely-related language Kunwinjku (about as close as Italian to Spanish) and have varying degrees of passive knowledge of Dalabon.[11] In such cases, then, it pays the investigator to work out the ecology of language choice in conversation, and bring both younger members of the speech community and members of other speech communities in regular contact with the solitary speaker.

Involving younger members of the speech community has other rewards, too, since such people may have unsuspected abilities in offering translations. In my most recent work on Kayardild, for example, I discovered that Ben Gabori, who when I began work in the 1980s appeared to have little speaking ability (he was then around thirty) and not much passive knowledge either, knew far more than I initially thought and was able to help in the translation of obscure words that some older speakers could not explain properly. I do not know whether this is due to increases in his knowledge over the last seventeen years, a change in his confidence as he has acquired elder status, or some combination of the above. Likewise, some of Charlie Wardaga's sons, who had told me they "couldn't speak Ilgar," eventually turned out to understand a great deal when they were able to contribute this knowledge in a low-key situation, such as sitting at some distance away on the same verandah while Charlie was talking, and not being asked directly.

Indeed, such junior members of speech communities may share with their elders a belief that they will, one day, come to speak their language.

12.2 Charlie Wardaga at Minjilang, Croker Island, in 1995.

Here we need to suspend certain assumptions about "critical periods" in language acquisition that have become dogma in psycholinguistics without being tested in small, multilingual, non-literate speech communities – and which are at variance with the belief and practice in many north Australian communities, where people keep learning new languages right through life. When Charlie Wardaga was asked in Federal Court (in the context of a Native Title hearing) why his sons could not speak his language, he replied "they too young yet." His sons ranged in age from late teens to mid-thirties.

I do not believe that such a view is totally unrealistic. For example, I have witnessed a case of a young woman who, though she grew up around Mayali-speaking people (including her mother), did not speak the language until she was seventeen, though she had a good passive knowledge; when I asked her about why she did not speak, she attributed this to "being shame" – a mixture of shyness and embarrassment. At this time she decided it was important to start speaking, and she began to spend time with older women working on traditional handicrafts. Within six months she became a fluent speaker. Many commentators on traditional Aboriginal learning styles in a range of domains (e.g., learning traditional craft skills) point to the existence of a long dormant period between the onset of observation and the onset of action (see Harris 1984). Applied to language learning, this can mean a much longer lag between passive and active competence than we are used to, and this can often be exacerbated by a feeling of being too junior to speak in public.

For such reasons, it is worthwhile for field linguists to try and enlist the interest and participation of younger members of the speech community. Depending on the circumstances, this is sometimes best done in an oblique way, since shyness may lead such people to demur if asked directly, saying they don't know anything. It is often more effective to get them to come along to sessions on some other pretext, or to stage elicitation sessions in places where younger family members frequently pass or gather for various reasons, giving them a chance to unobtrusively drift up and listen.

2.2   Loss of constructions through simplification for the benefit of non-speakers

Ironically, it may happen that a "purer" form of language, uninfluenced by the displacing language, is encountered when there is no longer a living speech community serving as a reference point for speech norms. Where, on the other hand, a sizable number of speakers, all past a certain age, must accommodate to another language spoken by younger members of the community, certain constructions may disappear totally under the influence of the dominant language.

An example of this occurred with Kayardild between the early 1960s and 1982 (Evans 1995). When I began working on Kayardild in the early 1980s the language was in regular use by about forty people, all middle-aged or older. Some of these were Kayardild–English bilinguals, while the oldest ten or so spoke practically no English. Although the Kaiadilt[12] speech community made its first contacts with English speakers in the 1940s, people under forty spoke only Aboriginal English, and the only language used in interaction with non-Kaiadilt was English (in various forms, ranging from pidgin through Aboriginal English to standard Australian English). In conversations between old and young Kaiadilt, the elders would use a (modified and simplified) form of Kayardild, and the youth a (simplified) form of English. As a result, by the 1980s certain English-derived constructions had found their way even into the Kayardild of monolinguals, displacing the original Kayardild expressions.

In related languages, the negative imperative consists of a special verbal suffix (cf. Yukulta *warra-ja!* 'go!', *warra-na!* 'don't go!'; Lardil *were-ne wangal!* 'don't throw the boomerang!'). But when I tried to elicit this form, I was always given a construction that combined a particle *namu* (< English 'no more', Kriol *namu*) with the positive form of the imperative (cf. *warraj!* 'go!', *namu warraj!* 'don't go!'),[13] and even in conversation between Kayardild monolinguals the expected form *warrana* was never heard. Yet on tapes made by Stephen Wurm during fieldwork in the 1960s the negative imperative suffix *-n(a)* regularly occurs, e.g., *kurrkana wangalk!* 'don't take the boomerang!' Wurm's informant, a woman named Alison Dundaman, was still alive in the 1980s; then in her late forties, she was a fluent Kayardild–English bilin-

12.3 Kaiadilt men on Mornington Island, 1982. From left: Darwin
Moodoonuthi (deceased), Dugal Goongarra (deceased), Pluto Bentinck.

gual. When I asked her about the -*na* forms, and played back tapes to her, she
said they were correct and that she used them. Other older speakers con-
curred. But this did not lead to any revival of the -*na* form by anyone in the
speech community, and I never heard it used spontaneously.

This, then, is an example of a construction dropping out of the speech of a
particular individual, between the ages of (roughly) twenty-five and forty-
five, and at the same time disappearing from a whole speech community, even
the oldest monolingual speakers, as part of a process of radical language
shift. A crucial part of this process is likely to have been the fact that all
Kayardild speakers made a number of modifications to their grammars to
facilitate communication with younger, non-Kayardild-speaking members
of their community, and that the continued salience of Kayardild ↔ English
conversational dyads set new grammatical norms affecting even the monolinguals in the speech community. The hypothesis that at least some "last speakers," isolated from these effects by the fact that they do not use their language
at all, will in some cases be less influenced by grammatical interference from
the dominant language, is one that needs further examination.[14]

2.3   Temporary factors

Other, more temporary factors may give a misleading impression of the
level of competence. Gavan Breen (1990: 67–68) tells how, on his first
encounter with Yandruwandha speaker Bennie Kerwin, "he was on the

grog and not very useful," but some years later, having met him in different circumstances, he discovered that "Bennie Kerwin was the best informant I had in any language until I moved to the Northern Territory and became involved with still viable languages." Peter Sutton (e-mail, March 30, 1999) gives a further example:

I know of two people, brother and sister, who (according to their own adult offspring) lost their English when close to death, and spoke only in a language they had spoken when very young and regretted having "lost." This is unusual but perhaps reflects how deep language memory can be. I knew both of them over many years and was aware that the sister had retained some tiny bits of the language (Flinders Island) at a conscious level, and her brother had retained a little of at least another (Barrow Point), but he had not used it much for most of his life.

Treatable medical conditions, hunger, exhaustion, or temporary memory loss and disorientation after minor strokes may all take their toll. As far as possible salvage linguists need to be on the look-out for such problems, and contacts with local medical staff are often invaluable in addressing them. Sometimes special strategies need to be devised: Bill McGregor's grammar of Nyulnyul is based almost entirely on material elicited from Mary Carmel Charles, who is completely deaf, by using written English prompt sentences (McGregor 1996: 7).

It would be wrong to imply that such temporary factors are always physical. As mentioned earlier, there is also a strong ideology of local appropriateness in Aboriginal Australia – the belief that particular languages are intimately linked to, and suitable for use in, particular places. This can lead people to feel hesitant about using their language "in other people's country," which is of course where many old people end up living out their lives – this is especially true of old people's homes and hospitals. I have observed dramatic improvements in the fluency of younger Kaiadilt[15] when travelling back with them to their own islands in the South Wellesleys, away from the mission on Mornington Island which is in Lardil country. On stepping out of the boat onto the beach they made statements such as "I can talk language alright now – I'm in my own country." With older people it can also happen that the intense emotions associated with visiting certain places from their youth will revive memories of stories and conversations they heard there, which may not surface anywhere else.

2.4   *Coming forward after the funeral*

Another time-bound factor on fluency is the question of who else is around – either in the broader sense of who else is alive at all, or in the narrower sense of who is in earshot, or in an influential position in the community. This follows from our discussion of the importance of being established as an "owner" of a language before one is accepted by the community as having the right to pass on information about that language, and from a general ethos of being unwilling to put oneself forward as an authority on some matter if there are others around perceived as having more right to that knowledge. In some cases this can mean that an individual A, who knows more of some language L than another individual B, has less of a right to be an owner of L than B has, so that B is publicly viewed as "the last speaker of L" despite his or her imperfect knowledge of the language. Then, following the death of B, A may come forward as a speaker, since the political impediment to them openly professing their knowledge has been removed.

Consider another example from the community of Minjilang on Croker Island in the Cobourg Peninsula region. Charlie Wardaga, as mentioned above, is one of the last speakers of Ilgar, and I began work with him on the Ilgar language in 1994. At this time I asked him which other languages he knew and he listed a number of others: Iwaidja (the numerically dominant language at Minjilang and lingua franca of the Cobourg Region for the last few generations), Kunwinjku (the lingua franca of Western Arnhem Land more generally, with a sizable population of speakers at Minjilang, as well as being the language of his wife and one of his grandmothers), Garig (spoken on part of adjoining mainland and a sister dialect of Ilgar), Manangkarri (the almost extinct language of Goulburn Island, still undocumented but said to be very close to Maung), some Marrgu, the language of Croker Island itself, and some Indonesian as well as (rather idiosyncratic) English.

Since I had done some work on Marrgu before, but had not found anyone with a full knowledge of this language, I asked him a bit about Marrgu and recorded a few words, as well as a few sentences of Manangkarri. He was unhappy giving Marrgu information, however, said he didn't know it properly, and later that day it became clear why: a senior Marrgu man came to visit me and asked me what I had been working on with Charlie. When I told him, he said "You can work with him on Ilgar, he knows that alright, but Marrgu isn't his language. If you want to ask about Marrgu, you come to see me." In fact I had done a few days work with him before, which had been less than satisfactory, owing to his restricted knowledge of the language, and this was becoming even more difficult owing to his increasing deafness. But I agreed I would come and work with him some more; he had an excellent knowledge of Marrgu place names, for example. Next day Charlie, who had obviously heard about the conversation, began by saying to me that we had better leave Marrgu, that he only knew a few words anyway, and that we should concentrate on Ilgar.

A bit of background on the clans and languages of the region will be useful here. Ilgar is the language belonging to Charlie Wardaga's clan, the Mangalara; the Mangalara estate comprises a number of small islands and their associated waters to the east of Croker Island: Grant, Oxley, Lawson and McClure Islands. He and other members of the Mangalara clan are also in the last stages of succession to the estate formerly belonging to the Yangardi clan (Peterson and Devitt 1997), which is nearly defunct owing to the lack of male descendants. The Yangardi estate comprises Darch Island, just off the east coast of Croker Island, plus some of the south-eastern portions of Croker itself. The process of settling the succession to the Yangardi estate has not been entirely straightforward, however, since the Mandilarri-Ildugij clan claims rights over Darch Island, as well as over some parts of the Mangalara estate (namely Oxley and Lawson Islands). The Mandilarri-Ildugij clan estate covers most of Croker Island, and although most members of this clan now speak Iwaidja, its traditional language was Marrgu, which is usually said to be the real language associated with Croker Island itself. This territorial tussling naturally created a background where being a language-owner of Marrgu took on a special political significance.

Some time later the senior Marrgu man died. It seemed to me at the time that this was the death of the last speaker. There was still some work I could do with a couple of middle-aged people – one woman, for example, though unable to talk spontaneously, had sufficient knowledge of the language that I could at least check wordlists recorded in the 1960s, and this was useful in improving the phonetic accuracy of our recording of interdental stops, working out the status of certain phonetic approximants, and of the large class of liquids which includes (at least phonetically) a flapped versus non-flapped contrast for laterals at three points of articulation, and three rhotics. Fragments of a couple of tapes made in the 1960s could also be transcribed with the help of these people. And I had the impression that they had become more willing to assist with this sort of work, following the death mentioned above. Overall, however, it looked like it would now be impossible to get any further with working out the complex verbal morphology of the language.

Around this time, however, Charlie Wardaga, with whom I had been continuing to work on Ilgar, began to volunteer Marrgu equivalents of Ilgar phrases and words. Often this would happen when sons of the former Marrgu speaker had drifted up to listen to our sessions, and they showed interest, sometimes repeating bits of Marrgu. As time passes it is becoming increasingly clear that he probably knows more than the late "last speaker" had – he is capable, for example, of giving mini-texts and, although the research is still at an early stage, shows no sign of being anywhere near the limits of his knowledge.

There are some phonetic differences in how he pronounces Marrgu. For example, where the other speaker would use a lamino-interdental fricative in a word like [inǧat] 'turtle', Charlie uses an interdental stop, pronouncing it [inḍat]. At this stage of research it is not clear whether this is an "accent" reflecting a transfer of pronunciation from Ilgar or Iwaidja, which lack interdental fricatives (and have only a tiny number of interdental stop tokens); whether it is due to dialect differences in the type of Marrgu they learned; or whether it is the type of norm-difference often found among different last speakers as the decline in interaction reduces the convergence of norms that occurs in a full speech-community.[16] In the case of his Kunwinjku, the reasonable level of documentation of that language allows us to clearly identify his Iwaidja/Ilgar accent, manifesting itself through the neutralization of the mid- versus high-vowel and short versus long stop distinctions and the failure to pronounce glottal stops. But in the case of his Marrgu, it is much more difficult to decide whether we are dealing with a less-than-perfectly-learned third or fourth language, or an authentic rendition. The only real way this might be resolved is if our work on the phonology and grammar can progress far enough that it then becomes possible to go back and transcribe the old tapes made in the 1960s from people who were clearly fluent speakers. Meanwhile, certain relevant biographical details have emerged that make it seem quite natural that Charlie Wardaga should know Marrgu. He grew up on Croker Island, for some reason was not taken away by missionaries to Goulburn Island and therefore remained in regular contact with Marrgu speakers. It also appears that Marrgu speakers used to visit the smaller islands in Mangalara territory quite regularly. And the fact that his mother belonged to the Minaga clan, whose estate lies on the western side of Croker Island and which appears to have been associated with Marrgu as well as Iwaidja, also gives him secondary rights to the Marrgu language, which count for more now that key individuals with primary rights are deceased. These biographical details suggest that he may have been learning Marrgu regularly from childhood.

The above example illustrates the ways in which a speaker's apparent knowledge can vary over time according to changes in who else is regarded within their community as having primary rights to speak for a particular language.[17] To show that this situation is far from unique, I will briefly mention two rather similar cases recounted to me by colleagues.

The first case, reported by Gavan Breen, arose during his work on Kuk-Narr. Here the relevant fact appears to have been first- versus second-language status rather than official "language-ownership":[18]

Roth . . . collected a short vocabulary of what looks like Nar or Nhang around the turn of the century and published it under the name Kundara; the name, but not the vocabulary, seems to correspond to the modern Guandhar, recorded by Sommer

(1972) . . . Gog-Nar was (re-) discovered by Miss Sandra Newland (1968[b]) . . . and she recorded about 1 1/2 hours of tape from the last native speaker, Michael Richards, in Normanton (1968[a]). Sommer (1972) recorded Richards, and soon afterwards he was taken to the Eventide Home in Charters Towers. I recorded ten hours from him there in August, with Saltwater Jack, who speaks it as a second language, helping and prompting but refusing to act directly as an informant. In October, Michael Richards died, at the age of about 90. In 1973 I recorded five hours with Saltwater Jack, also about 90 years old and now, in the absence of his friend, a willing informant. . . . (Breen 1976: 243)

According to Breen (p. 243), "the informants proved willing, friendly, patient and helpful, but both had most of the deficiencies one would expect in men of their age." What is relevant here, though, is that "as far as I can remember (more than a quarter of a century ago now) Saltwater Jack was about equal to Michael Richards" (Breen p.c.).

The second case, reported by Roberto Zavala (e-mail, December 7, 1998) from his work in Mexico on Olutec is a little different. A father had singled out his son as the person to whom the language should be taught, and while the father was alive only the son would speak Olutec, which he did fluently. It therefore appeared that he was the only member of the family who still knew the language, and likely to end up as the last speaker since the approximately thirty other speakers of Olutec were all older than he was (barring some semispeakers and rememberers in their fifties).

However, when Zavala was working with the son after the father's death, his younger sister turned out to be a comparably good speaker:

Antonio Asistente (73) and Alfredina Asistente (65) were the two Olutec speakers I was telling you about. Seferino Asistente was the father who died in 1994 before I even meet them. The first time that I noticed that Alfredina was also a speaker was one evening when Antonio and me were working in one of the paradigms and I asked him for 1:2 combination and he replied with a 2:1. Then Alfredina, who was preparing us a meal, said the combination 1:2 from inside the house. Antonio was completely confused and later on he explained that *he* did not know that she could speak since she never did that when their father was still alive. That is, she was not supposed to speak the language. In many other circumstances Alfredina corrected Antonio and provided a lot of information to our dictionary. Even though she also said that she did not speak the language. However, in my last field trip she was always participating in conversations when I invited speakers from other households to their place. I realized that she was completely fluent.

The literature on the ethnography of communication discusses a phenomenon sometimes called "the competence of incompetence" (Saville-Troike 1989: 25–26). In some speech communities, communicatively appropriate behavior involves speaking incompetently, ungrammatically, or hesitantly, as a way of showing deference to one's interlocutors. The examples discussed in this section illustrate a similar principle: that a variety of ways of deferring to respected senior members of a community can lead others to hold back from showing their actual language competence. This may be because they do not have primary rights as a "language-owner" (as in the case of Charlie Wardaga's knowledge of Marrgu); because their "second-language-speaker" status makes them hesitant to step forward as a knowledgeable informant in the presence of "first-language speakers" (as in the case of Saltwater Jack); or because they are deferring to wishes expressed by a senior person such as a parent (as in the case of Alfredina Asistente). Such cases illustrate that it is rash to make pronouncements on who is a "last speaker," and that patience, and repeated visits to a community over time, can often reveal a higher level of knowledge in some individuals than one originally suspects.

2.5   Amplifiers

We now pass to what is, in some senses, the opposite phenomenon: when the fluency of certain types of partial speaker disappears completely following the death of someone who knows the language better.

Aboriginal people often say, of some language, that they can "hear it" but can't "speak" it. This appears to align with linguists' concepts of active and passive knowledge, or of speaking and hearing competence, but in fact the situation is more complex, and can encompass a further type of knowledge I will call "amplifying." To give an example: when working in 1987 with another "last speaker," this time the late Butcher Knight, who spoke Umbugarla, I found it very hard to make out his pronunciation, owing to his great age and frailty. A somewhat younger man, Talking Billy (now also deceased) came to my aid, sitting with us as we worked and repeating Butcher Knight's mumbled utterances with sufficient clarity that I could make a reasonable phonetic transcription. I therefore inferred that he was at least a partial speaker of Umbugarla, and a couple of years later, some time after the death of Butcher Knight, returned to do some more work with him on Umbugarla. Without having Butcher Knight there to make the initial utterance, however, he was totally unable to recall any Umbugarla.

This is not the only time I have witnessed this situation. I experienced a similar situation when working on Kungarakany with its last full speaker, Madeline England, in the presence of a Malak-Malak man, Jimmy Tapnguk. Again, Tapnguk could repeat Kungarakany sentences when Mrs. England was the prompt, so to speak, and even gave me the impression (at a point where I did not know the language well enough to judge accurately) that the two were engaged in a relatively even dialogue. However, when recontacted some years later, after the death of Mrs. England, he was unable to give any Kungarakany at all.

Such cases are the opposite of what was described in the last section: here the death of one speaker precipitates a decline, rather than an improvement, in the abilities of another (special type of) speaker.

3.   Conclusion

My main purpose in this paper has been to show how many complex factors come into play when doing linguistic fieldwork on an endangered language. This makes it hard to assess how many speakers remain, who the best speakers are, and where to find them, and patient and sensitive detective work over a wide area will often be rewarded. In fact one can never be sure who knows how much, and certainly the first statements one is given about who speaks what can prove quite unreliable, in both directions. In multilingual regions, various seemingly unlikely people may turn out to have learned a language that is thought to have died out, while other individuals may maintain an unjustified reputation for knowledge they do not have.

Throughout the paper I have stressed that field linguists will have more success documenting endangered languages if they are sensitive to the sociolinguistics of the situation, and bear in mind that all sorts of factors determine people's ability and willingness to employ their language. Experiment with the mix of people present, such as by bringing in younger people or even speakers of other languages with a "hearing knowledge" of the language under investigation. In this way you can form an audience that will stimulate a good performance or encourage others to come out of the woodwork who may help with translation or who will repeat utterances more clearly. Don't give up on people who may deny knowing the language because they are not regarded as having the right to be authorities, and be aware that such people may feel happier giving information if inquiries are not addressed directly to them but to an official language-owner who may actually know less.

Do not make snap judgments of how much people know, but try returning to them later, or gradually bringing back their knowledge of the language through repeated sessions. Remember that all sorts of temporary factors may interfere with the difficult task of remembering a language that may not have been used for years, that they may be downplaying their knowledge (consciously or unconsciously) out of concern for other individuals, and that changes in the social situation may remove barriers to them taking on a teaching role.

Wherever possible take people to the places which may be vividly linked in their memories to using the language.

And bear in mind that nothing encourages a teacher more than a good pupil. Speakers may have their own ideas about how to teach you, and in what order, and they are more likely to judge your progress – and be encouraged to move to the next level of difficulty – by how far you can hold a basic conversation with a reasonable accent, rather than by your skill in constructing complex sentences. Their ideas about what to teach you may even extend to decisions about what order in which to teach you languages:

> Finally at Marree we met a very old lady called Alice, the last full Kuyani. But our hopes were dashed again: she said that her Kuyani relatives had been dead so long that now she could only speak Arabana. She and Maudie Lennie, who was looking after her, would both be delighted to teach me Arabana.
>
> Nobody could teach me Kuyani at that time. As it turned out, one day more than ten years later when I had become fluent in Arabana, Alice suddenly said "And now I will teach you my language, Kuyani." (Hercus 1994: 1)[19]

While I certainly would not want to argue that field linguists should simply wait to be taught in whatever way the speakers want to teach them – in many cases this would leave huge paradigmatic gaps, for example – setting up a rhythm where each takes it in turn to decide on the shape of the session can be encouraging to both sides. Ultimately, after all, it depends on the speaker to determine when, and what, they will teach.

However urgent the linguist may regard the task of documenting an endangered language, it is almost certain to be counter-productive to dash around and force the pace of elicitation beyond what the speaker is happy with. Instead, an enduring friendship and apprenticeship, played out in a range of social and geographical settings over what can be quite far-flung regional networks of people from different clan or tribal affiliations, and with a broad interest that takes in ethnographic as well as linguistic questions, is the most likely method of teasing out the fragile language knowledge which can so easily pass from long unspoken to forever unheard.

ACKNOWLEDGMENTS

I would like to express my deep gratitude to the Aboriginal people who have taught me about their languages. Although there are too many to name them all individually here, I am particularly grateful to Goldie Blyth, Alice Bohm, †Jack Chadum, †Alison Dundaman, †Madeline England, Pat Gabori, †Toby Gangele, Eddie Hardy, †David Kalbuma, Jimmy Kalarriya, †Butcher Knight, Mick Kubarkku, Peter Marndeberru, Khaki Marrala, †Darwin Moodoonuthi, †Roland Moodoonuthi, Big Bill Neidjie, †Vai Stanton, Charlie Wardaga, Mary Yarmirr, and †Mick Yarmirr, as well as to their families, for tolerating my often clumsy attempts to understand how their languages work, and for showing me, with great tact and humor, other ways of learning.

I would also like to thank the many Australianist colleagues who have discussed problems of field linguistics and ethnography with me, particularly Peter Austin, Paul Black, Gavan Breen, George Chaloupka, Alan Dench, Jeannie Devitt, Bob Dixon, Murray Garde, Ian Green, Ken Hale, Robert Handelsmann, Mark Harvey, Luise Hercus, Penny Johnson, Patrick McConvell, Bill McGregor, David Nash, Annette Schmidt, Jane Simpson, Peter Sutton, and David Wilkins. Particular thanks to Gavan Breen, Ian Green, Mark Harvey, Peter Sutton, and Roberto Zavala for sending me the accounts of some of their field experiences that I have cited here, and to Gavan Breen, Ian Green, and Peter Sutton for editorial comments on the manuscript.

Finally, my thanks to the various institutions that have supported my field research since 1982: the Australian National University, School of Australian Linguistics, the Gaagudju Association, Australian National Parks and Wildlife Service, Australian Research Council (grants "Non-Pama-Nyungan languages of Northern Australia," "Polysemy and Semantic Change in Australian Languages," and "Analysing Australian Aboriginal languages"), the Northern Land Council, the Carpentaria Land Council and the University of Melbourne.

NOTES

1 An interesting exception is Kayardild (Evans 1995), where a long isolated existence on the South Wellesley Islands created a totally monolingual speech community. When forcefully moved to the (then) Presbyterian mission on Mornington Island, no one beyond puberty ever learned a significant amount of English or Lardil (the local language), while those born on Mornington Island learned English and at most a limited amount of Kayardild. Only a handful of people, all aged between three and fifteen at the time of the move, became Kayardild–English bilinguals.

   A second (partial) exception is exemplified by the Kunwinjku/Mayali speech community, which with over 1,000 L1 speakers and at least another 1,000 L2 speakers is by far the biggest Aboriginal language in Western Arnhem Land. In my experience, very few L1 speakers of this dialect chain speak another Aboriginal language fluently, reflecting a typical "large-language" belief that members of other groups will know one's own language. This belief is in fact self-perpetuating in the sense that the number of Mayali/Kunwinjku speakers is growing as children whose forebears speak other neighboring languages, such as Dalabon, Umbugarla and Rembarrnga, have switched to speaking Mayali/Kunwinjku.

2 The situation portrayed in Werner Herzog's film *Where the Green Ants Dream*, in which the monolingual last speaker of an Aboriginal language addresses a courtroom in the only language he knows, and which no one else understands, is thus highly atypical, although the famous case of Ishi working with Kroeber on Yana may approximate this.

3 I have concealed or disguised the identity of a number of the individuals and languages mentioned in this paper, out of consideration for the speakers or their family.

4 Cf. Dorian (1986: 562–63): "In some communities where a language is nearing extinction, familiarity with the ancestral tongue may have special value for the few remaining speakers since it qualifies them, and them alone, to perform certain special rites or services. This in turn entitles them to particular respect as a link with a more intact ethnic past. . . . In the absence of a speech community large enough and vital enough to permit the investigator either to become a skilled speaker him- or herself or to obtain convincing community consensus regarding relative abilities of the remaining speakers, the investigator can find it all but impossible to determine which of the few speakers available are the most reliable and most skillful."

5 It is likely that the effects of ceremonial status on judgments of language knowledge are not confined to language death situations. Ian Green (e-mail, May 9, 1999) points out that "[i]n the Daly, as elsewhere, ritual verbal learning is very important ceremonially, and, should an initiate be under the charge of a teacher from a different language background, this will often involve learning the rituals in a new language and acquiring some ability to engage in basic conversation with the teacher in the new language. Initiates in these circumstances can be attributed by other community members with an unwarranted mastery of the language."

6 Again this reflects the dominance of social considerations. Responses to made-up sentences that I have proffered have ranged from acceptance of absolutely anything (two old Kayardild men used to react this way) to rejection of anything known to have been made up by me (even if I knew from a cross-section of other speakers that it was correct), on the grounds that I was too junior and lacking in any rights to the language to be allowed to make up new sentences as opposed to repeating sentences my classificatory father or other teachers had taught me. Attempts to camouflage the fact that I had constructed such sentences myself, by saying things like "I heard that sometime last week – I can't remember who from" simply met with disbelief, and attempts to get around this problem by saying I might have heard them from particular named speakers then tapped in to the social judgments outlined in the rest of the paragraph.

7 An example of such a change in the Cayuga speech community in Brantford, Ontario, which has a dwindling number of speakers, all past middle age, was recounted to me by Hans-Jürgen Sasse (p.c.). As long as Reggie Henry, a prominent member of the community, was alive, saying (truthfully) that a particular sentence or word-form came from him would guarantee that other speakers would accept the sentence. Once he died, however, this no longer worked, since they no longer felt bound by his rather prescriptive stance on how the language should be spoken.

8 It is an interesting question why he did not simply use the verb root, or generalize a form prefixed for some other person combination (e.g., *I > him*) and then use it with the appropriate free pronouns. The unavailability of an extracted verb root probably results from the complex morphophonemics in the language, which make roots hard to segment. His failure to employ the second alternative suggests he knew there was a form, was purist enough not to want to use an incorrect form, and as a "last speaker" was not in a situation where he had to devise a way of solving this problem in order to communicate regularly.

9 This can be linked to the insightful analysis of Australian Aboriginal communicative norms by Walsh (1991), who derives many conversational practices in northern Australia from a "broadcast" model of conversation, that makes the decision and ability to tune in or not the prerogative of the hearer.

10 On the other hand, he never talks it to his two sisters, both of whom do speak Ilgar, because of a strict taboo on conversation between opposite-sex siblings. This leaves him in the odd position of talking his mother-tongue to people who don't speak it, and not talking it with the couple of people who do.

11 Ian Green (e-mail, May 9, 1999) gives a further example from the Daly River region: "Bill Parry for a while presided over a mixed Marrithiyel and Ngan'gityemerri camp. Conversations would regularly involve Bill and one of the older women speaking in Marrithiyel, with the other two older women making their contributions in Ngan'gityemerri. Similarly, at Woollianna, I witnessed quite a number of MalakMalak – Matngele exchanges between two of the senior men."

12 Here, as elsewhere, I use the established ethnographic spelling Kaiadilt for tribal group, and the spelling Kayardild (phonemic, in the practical orthography) for the language name.

13 See Evans (1995: 387–88) for other examples of English-derived particles used instead of verbal inflections, such as *baymbay* (< *bye and bye*) instead of the apprehensive inflection plus the modal oblique case, and *marrbi* (< *might be*) instead of the irrealis use of the verbal past plus the modal ablative case. In these cases, however, the two constructions coexist among older speakers, rather than the particle totally displacing the verbal inflection as happened with the negative imperative.

14 Gavan Breen (e-mail, April 1, 1999) offered the following comment on this point: "I think a last speaker could well speak the language better than a speaker of a living language because s/he speaks the language as s/he knew it thirty or forty years ago when it suddenly went out of use (because, for example, most of the speakers were carted off to Cherbourg or Woorabinda or Palm Island). For example, my Antekerrepenh informants at Dajarra hadn't been affected by the anglicisations that have affected Arrernte here [in the Alice Springs region – NE]: using possessive with body parts, using "come" versus "go" in the English way, replacing native vocabulary with loans like *mape* (mob)."

15 These speakers were between the ages of 20 and 45 at the time, i.e., below the age of the youngest fully fluent speakers.

16 Cf. Schmidt (1985: 42), who comments that "[t]he fragmentation of Dyirbal norms is directly associated with the breakdown in Dyirbal communication network," and proposes the more general schema: "reduced social function leads to lack of uniformity leads to fragmentation of grammatical norms."

17 Obviously a definitive assessment of this case would be premature since it will depend on how far we get with our work on Marrgu over the years to come.

18 It is difficult to determine, now, exactly what "second-language" status would have meant at the time.

19 Gavan Breen (e-mail, April 1, 1999) gives another example: "Barry Blake recorded Mabel Garghetty in Wakaya in 1966, and so I recorded her in the same language in 1967, '68 and '69. I recorded another person in Bularnu in the same three years. I didn't get the opportunity to work on Bularnu in '70 and '71, and

then in 1972 Mabel (who wasn't a very communicative person) got round to telling me that her own language was actually Bularnu."

REFERENCES

Austin, Peter. 1981. *A Grammar of Diyari, South Australia.* Cambridge: Cambridge University Press.
  1986. Structural change in language obsolescence. *Australian Journal of Linguistics* 6:201–30.
Bavin, Edith, and Tim Shopen. 1985. Warlpiri and English: languages in contact. In *Australia: Meeting Place of Languages,* ed. Michael Clyne, pp. 81–94. Canberra: Pacific Linguistics C-92.
Brandl, Maria A., and Michael Walsh. 1982. Speakers of many tongues: toward understanding multilingualism among Aboriginal Australians. *International Journal of the Sociology of Language* 36:71–81.
Breen, J. Gavan. 1976. An introduction to Gog-Nar. In *Languages of Cape York,* ed. Peter Sutton, pp. 243–59. Canberra: Australian Institute of Aboriginal Studies.
  1990. Stories from Bennie Kerwin. In *Language and History: Essays in Honour of Luise A. Hercus,* ed. Peter Austin, *et al.,* pp. 67–87. Canberra: Pacific Linguistics C-116.
Dench, Alan C. 1990. *Martuthunira. A Language of the Pilbara Region of Western Australia.* Canberra: Pacific Linguistics C-125.
Dixon, R. M. W. 1972. *The Dyirbal Language of North Queensland.* Cambridge: Cambridge University Press.
  1977. *A Grammar of Yidiñ.* Cambridge: Cambridge University Press.
  1984. *Searching for Aboriginal Languages: Memoirs of a Field Worker.* St. Lucia: University of Queensland Press; Chicago: University of Chicago Press.
  1991. Mbabaram. In *The Handbook of Australian Languages,* vol. 4, ed. R. M. W. Dixon and Barry J. Blake, pp. 348–402. Melbourne: Oxford University Press.
Donaldson, Tamsin. 1980. *Ngiyambaa: The Language of the Wangaaybuwan.* Cambridge: Cambridge University Press.
  1985. From speaking Ngiyampaa to speaking English. *Aboriginal History* 9(1–2):126–47.
Dorian, Nancy C. 1986. Gathering language data in terminal speech communities. In *The Fergusonian Impact. In Honor of Charles A. Ferguson.* Vol. 2: *Sociolinguistics and the Sociology of Language,* ed. Joshua. A. Fishman, *et al.,* pp. 555–75. Berlin: Mouton de Gruyter.
  1994. Purism versus compromise in language revitalization and language revival. *Language in Society* 23: 479–94.
Evans, Nicholas. 1995. *A Grammar of Kayardild. With Historical-Comparative Notes on Tangkic.* Berlin: Mouton de Gruyter.
Hale, Kenneth. 1997. Appendix: New Lardil. In *Lardil Dictionary,* Ngakulmungan Kangka Leman (compiler). Gununa, Queensland: Mornington Shire Council.
Harris, Steven. 1984. *Culture and Learning: Tradition and Education in North-East Arnhem Land.* Canberra: Australian Institute of Aboriginal Studies.
Harvey, Mark. 1992. The Gaagudju people and their language. Ph.D. dissertation, University of Sydney.

Harvey, Mark. 1993. A fictitious wife. In *Did You Meet any Malagas? A Homosexual History of Australia's Tropical Capital*, ed. Dino Hodge, pp. 153–64. Darwin: Little Gem Publications.

In press. Structural change in verbal complexes in the Eastern Daly language family. In *Studies in Comparative Non-Pama-Nyungan*, ed. Nicholas Evans. Canberra: Pacific Linguistics.

Hercus, Luise A. 1969. *The Languages of Victoria: A Late Survey*. Canberra: Australian Institute of Aboriginal Studies.

1986. *Victorian Languages: A Late Survey*. Canberra: Pacific Linguistics B-77. (Revised and expanded edition of Hercus 1969.)

1994. *A Grammar of the Arabana-Wangkangurru Language. Lake Eyre Basin, South Australia*. Canberra: Pacific Linguistics C-128.

Lee, Jennifer. 1987. Tiwi today: a study of language change in a contact situation. Ph.D. dissertation, Australian National University.

McGregor, William B. 1996. *Nyulnyul*. Munich: Lincom Europa.

Merlan, Francesca. 1981. Land, language and social identity in Aboriginal Australia. *Mankind* 13:133–48.

Merlan, Francesca, and Alan Rumsey. 1982. *The Jawoyn (Katherine Area) Land Claim*. Darwin: Northern Land Council.

Newland, Sandra. 1968a. Koknari: elicitation material. Unpublished ms.

1968b. *Report of Linguistic Survey of the Normanton-Burketown Area of Northwest Queensland*. AIAS Doc. 68/752.

Peterson, Nicolas, and Jeannie Devitt. 1997. *A Report in Support of an Application for Native Title to Areas of Sea by the Mangalara, Mandilarri-Ildugij, Murran, Gadura, Mayarram, Minaga and Ngaynjaharr of the Croker Island Region*. Darwin: Northern Land Council.

Rigsby, Bruce. 1997. Structural parallelism and convergence in the Princess Charlotte Bay languages. In *Archaeology and Linguistics: Aboriginal Australia in Global Perspective*, ed. Patrick McConvell and Nicholas Evans, pp. 169–78. Melbourne: Oxford University Press.

Rumsey, Alan. 1989. Language groups in Australian Aboriginal land claims. *Anthropological Forum* 6(1):69–79.

1993. Language and territoriality in Aboriginal Australia. In *Language and Culture in Aboriginal Australia*, ed. Michael Walsh and Colin Yallop, pp. 191–206. Canberra: Aboriginal Studies Press.

Saville-Troike, Muriel. 1989. *The Ethnography of Communication*, 2nd edn. Oxford: Blackwell.

Schmidt, Annette. 1985. *Young People's Dyirbal*. Cambridge: Cambridge University Press.

Smith, Ian, and Steve Johnson. 1986. Sociolinguistic patterns in an unstratified society: the patrilects of Kugu Nganhcara. *Journal of the Atlantic Provinces Linguistic Association* 8:29–43.

Sommer, Bruce. 1972. *Report on Field Trip to Cape York Peninsula, December 1971 to July 1972*. AIAS Doc. 73/1350.

Sutton, Peter. 1978. Wik: Aboriginal society, territory and language at Cape Keerweer, Cape York Peninsula, Australia. Ph.D. dissertation, University of Queensland.

1992. Last chance operations: "BIITL" research in far north Queensland in the

1970s. In *The Language Game: Papers in Memory of Donald C. Laycock*, ed. Tom Dutton, Malcolm Ross, and Darrell Tryon, pp. 451–58. Canberra: Pacific Linguistics C-110.

Sutton, Peter, and Arthur Beaufort Palmer. 1981. *Daly River (Malak Malak) Land Claim*. Darwin: Northern Land Council.

Trigger, David. 1987. Languages, linguistic groups and status relations at Doomadgee, an Aboriginal settlement in north-west Queensland, Australia. *Oceania* 57: 217–38.

Tryon, Darrell. 1974. *Daly Family Languages, Australia*. Canberra: Pacific Linguistics C-32.

Walsh, Michael. 1991. Conversational styles and intercultural communication: an example from northern Australia. *Australian Journal of Communication* 18: 1–12.

1997. How many Australian languages were there? In *Boundary Rider: Essays in Honour of Geoffrey O'Grady*, ed. Darrell Tryon and Michael Walsh, pp. 393–412. Canberra: Pacific Linguistics C-136.

White, Isobel. 1990. Introduction. In *Language and History: Essays in Honour of Luise A. Hercus*, ed. Peter Austin, *et al.*, pp. 1–11. Canberra: Pacific Linguistics C-116.

Index